TECHNOLOGY AND THE NEW DIPLOMACY

For my parents, who are a constant source of strength.

Every thought is like a bell with many echoes.
William Butler Yeats

Technology and the New Diplomacy

The creation and control of EC industrial policy for semiconductors

THOMAS C. LAWTON
School of Management
Royal Holloway
University of London

Avebury

Aldershot • Brookfield USA • Hong Kong • Singapore • Sydney

Published by
Avebury
Ashgate Publishing Ltd
Gower House
Croft Road
Aldershot
Hants GU11 3HR
England

Ashgate Publishing Company
Old Post Road
Brookfield
Vermont 05036
USA

British Library Cataloguing in Publication Data

Lawton, Thomas C.
  Technology and the new diplomacy : the creation and control
  of EC industrial policy for semiconductors
  1. Technology and state - European Union countries
  2. Semiconductor industry - Europe
  I. Title
  338.9'4'06

Library of Congress Catalog Card Number: 97-70638

ISBN 1 85972 523 6

Printed in Great Britain by Ipswich Book Company, Suffolk

Contents

List of figures

Acknowledgements

This book has been crafted over several years and at numerous institutions and I am subsequently beholden to many individuals and establishments. The work was first made possible through a graduate research scholarship from the Irish Government. Officials at the Department of Education in Dublin were both able and obliging - the perfect mix of attributes in a bureaucrat! The project could not have come to fruition without the support structure provided by the European University Institute. There are many among the EUI's academic and administrative staff who gave of their time and thought to assist me during my three years in Florence. This book is based on a doctoral thesis at the European University Institute. There are several philanthropic individuals who toiled over numerous versions of that thesis, and without whose constructive criticisms I could never have completed this work. Susan Strange supervised the research in a calm and inspiring manner. To her I owe the greatest academic debt. Her experience and expertise helped shape my ideas and approaches, and although we seldom lived in the same country, her advice was constant. Roger Morgan provided encouragement and many useful sources of information during my years in Florence. Douglas Webber was a source of constant support and frequently played a needed devil's advocate as I moulded the work's final arguments. Michael Borrus and Lynn Mytelka were both admirably forceful and forthright in their criticisms, encouraging a clearer conception of the main arguments.

My time spent as a European Union Human Capital and Mobility Fellow at the University of Essex provided me with the opportunity to reassess the manuscript and to convert it into publishable form. Jeremy Richardson, as HCM project director, encouraged this venture and provided every opportunity for me to complete it.

Yves Doz and Jonathan Story at INSEAD provided me with invaluable facilities and a quiet place in which to finish writing this work's original version. The solitude of the Fontainebleau forests, together with the welcome respite offered by the cafés and clubs of Paris, allowed me to labour arduously but not incessantly.

The six months which I spent at the Berkeley Roundtable on the International Economy (BRIE) during the course of this research were both interesting and fruitful. The staff and directors of BRIE and the University of California at Berkeley provided a vibrant and accessible working environment and the San Francisco bay area is a spectacular surroundings within which to live.

I spent a hot and humid summer in 1992 working at the Delegation of the Commission of the European Communities to the United States. The staff of the Press and Public Affairs Section, then lead by Peter Doyle, were warm and relaxed and my time spent with the Delegation in Washington DC was both educational and enjoyable.

I am deeply indebted to those representatives of the European Commission, and of the European and American electronics industry and associated organisations, who gave of their time to assist me in my research. The JESSI office in Munich, the Eureka Secretariat in Brussels, and the SEMATECH offices in Washington DC and Austin, all proved co-operative and informative. For reasons of confidentiality, individuals shall remain anonymous. However, their contributions were all sincerely appreciated.

I have profited from discussions with numerous knowledgeable friends. At the risk of omission Kevin Michaels, Gary Murphy, Mark Lehrer, Paul McAleavey, Wolf Sauter, and Günter Walzenbach provided significant comment and criticism at various stages in the work's progression. Earlier chapter drafts were commented on by Alan Cafruny, Dieter Ernst, John Krige, Giandomenico Majone, and Stephen Martin. Further helpful comments regarding the work's methodology and structure have come from Stephen S. Cohen, Christopher Hill, and John Zysman.

The Autumn evenings would have seemed much longer were it not for the support of Kirstin during the work's conclusive stage. Her editorial assistance proved invaluable and her love and encouragement ensured that I completed this book to the best of my ability.

Finally, there are many individuals from my childhood in County Cork who nurtured in me a regard for scholarship. I owe much to my late grandfather, Tom Lawton. A rural Irish farmer who received little formal education, he instilled in me a respect for knowledge and a love of the written word. My parents, Jim and Eileen, trusted in me when few others did and resolutely supported me in all of my undertakings. This book is dedicated to them, as a small token of my immense gratitude.

Although I have endeavoured to account for all criticisms received, I accept complete responsibility for all remaining errors of omission, content and style. *Go raibh míle maith agaibh go léir.*

Thomas Lawton
London, November 1996

Preface

In undertaking this work, I was conscious of the difficulty which might be experienced in categorising it clearly and concisely. This was a deliberate strategy on my part. I wished to escape classification so as to advance a more rounded and eclectic elucidation. The extent to which I have achieved this objective is open to debate but the intentions were purely honourable. Although framed by international relations theories and examples, this book is a sectoral study in European political economy and in EU policy analysis, exploring the changing nature of European Community policies for the semiconductor industry. Particular attention is devoted to the relationship between large corporations and the European Commission in the creation and control of EC semiconductor policy. Transnational semiconductor firms, through their control of technology, have considerable power to set public policy and to influence the structure and operations of markets. With the gradual Europeanisation of industrial policy, these companies have widened their policy bargaining sway and become established as EC policy partners. I proceed to investigate the power-play within EC policy making, and comment upon the linkage between EC industrial policy and the European integration process. I conclude by reflecting on whether the European Union can draw any useful policy lessons from United States and Japanese state-firm policy bargains in the spheres of semiconductor trade and research and development.

On a more technical note, acronyms such as JESSI and SEMATECH are not always written in block capitals, simply to make the text more readable. Some interviews were conducted on the understanding that the information would be non-attributable. European Community (EC) is referred to rather than European Union (EU) due to industrial policy's structural and legal basis being in the European Coal and Steel Community Treaty and the Treaty of Rome rather than the Treaty on European Union (TEU). The TEU did however amend the Treaty of Rome so as to establish the first explicit recognition of an EC industrial policy.

1 Introduction

Knowledge and human power are synonymous.

Francis Bacon

In international relations, diplomacy operates within the parameters set by knowledge. The technology which knowledge brings shapes the rules of competition, and demarcates those with power from those without. A state's power within the international system of states, is in large part dictated by its access to knowledge. A geographically small state such as Japan can wield power within the system far beyond its size, due to its access to knowledge creation. A state which lacks direct access to knowledge, has little influence over the terms of a diplomatic bargain which it strikes with a knowledge-rich state. International diplomacy and inter-state relations revolve around the creation and control of knowledge.

International economic strength and political influence have never been confined solely to governments. The Venetian traders had political power within pre-Renaissance Europe, through the silk and spices which they brought to the region as a result of trade with Asia. The Dutch East India Company functioned as a power player within international relations before many of today's states were formed. It may even be described as a precursor to the modern transnational corporation, having offices situated in different countries around the globe. Its representatives negotiated with government officials from a position of relative strength. However, the influence of these trading companies evolved from their commercial importance, and not from their technological strength. By-and-large, governments still controlled the pace of technological development and the terms of its diffusion. A government's ability to defend its territory or to wage war, never rested upon non-state actors. A few companies were indeed politically influential, both within and beyond the borders of their home countries but ultimately it was states alone that bargained with each other for structural power[1].

This book is concerned with the changing nature of European Community (EC)[2] policies towards semiconductor producing firms. It is an important tale to recount, as industrial affairs have, since the early 1980s, been at the forefront of Europe's search for common areas of action. The creation of a single Community-wide industrial policy may thus be viewed as another substantial step towards economic and political union. Whereas other works look at the European Monetary System

(EMS) for instance, and test its success or failure as a policy to enhance integration, I look at industrial policy and endeavour to place it in the context of the integration process. One of the hypotheses developed in this work is that EC policy for the semiconductor industry evolved as part of the Community's efforts to create a common area of action for industrial affairs. The shift in policy emphasis away from the national and towards the EC level for this industry, established semiconductors as the Community's vanguard high technology industry in the post-Single European Act drive towards economic integration. This hypothesis can only be tested through a critical study of EC industrial policy. In undertaking such a study, I am aware of the need to advance a definition of this much abused concept, and to identify its constituent policy mechanisms. Moreover, it is essential to look at how policy evolves and who (i.e. which actors) exerts the greatest degree of control over the policy-making process.

This work also has important implications for international political economy theories concerning the nature and exercise of power. I argue that the ability to influence structural change gives an actor structural power, which in turn translates into relational power. Note that the use of structural in this context differs from its over-narrow use by Waltz and others in much international relations literature as referring only to patterns of the balance of power between states. I argue that the basis of this relational power is control over knowledge, or technology. In fact if this work has a general, more abstract purpose, it is to determine the importance of technology as a variable in the creation and control of EC industrial and trade policy. The thesis here is that transnational semiconductor firms, through their control of technology, have considerable relational power to set EC policy and to influence the structure and operations of markets.

Thus, three questions are addressed in this book. The first is how to explain and evaluate EC policy for the semiconductor industry. The second concerns the role of large firms relative to governmental actors, in the creation and control of EC semiconductor policy. The third concerns the significance of technology in shaping state-firm relational power, thus influencing international policy bargains.

It is neither feasible nor advisable at this time to conduct a sweeping, cross-sectoral study of EC industrial policy. Therefore, I will concentrate my study on one industrial sector, that of semiconductor electronic components, and investigate the construction, control, and consequences of EC industrial policy for that industry. I do this in the knowledge that in social scientific analysis, no results should be applied generally. In pursuing this single industry survey, I am aware that the emergent findings should not provide generalisations regarding broader EC industrial policy. However, lessons may always be drawn from specific circumstances, which are relevant to a wider grouping. This is particularly true for industries which constitute part of a larger industrial chain, as semiconductor components do in the information technology sector. It is therefore legitimate to comment on the relevance of the lessons learned from the semiconductor sector, for other European Community industrial policy areas.

1 Why semiconductors?

> The semiconductor industry is a global oligopoly in which a relatively small number of firms, head-quartered primarily in the United States, Europe, Japan, and Korea, produce, invest, and sell throughout the world. It is also an industry in which trade outcomes are manipulated by government policies, and in which bilateral trade barriers and trade deals have proliferated during the last decade, with spill-over effects on other nations (D'Andrea Tyson, 1993, p.151).

Semiconductor production and development is an ideal industry with which to assess the importance of knowledge and technological change within state-firm relations, and to test the new diplomacy hypothesis, concerning the governmental-corporate power realignment within the European Community. Thus, the semiconductor sector has been taken as a case study for three reasons: first, due to its profound enabling affect on national economies; second, because of its rapid rate of technological change; and third, as it is a dual-use technology, having both commercial and military applications.

The semiconductor industry has experienced a phenomenal growth rate since its inception, almost five decades ago. It has grown at an average of 10 per cent per annum since the 1950s. In 1970, just prior to the market introduction of the microprocessor, world microchip sales totalled $1 billion. By 1980, this figure had reached $10 billion; and over a decade later, it topped the $100 billion mark, reaching total world sales of $110 billion in 1994. This figure had topped the $150 billion mark by 1996[3] and is projected to reach over $270 billion by the year 2000[4]. Such tremendous growth rates are directly attributable to the industry's rapidly evolving technology, together with its ever-increasing product applications. New generations of semiconductor chips emerge roughly every three to four years. The industry is very research and development (R&D) intensive, with about 15 per cent of firms total sales being spent on R&D and another 15 per cent on capital production.

Semiconductor technology is constantly changing. For instance, the capacity of memory chips increased from 1 million bits of data in 1985, to 16 million bits by 1993. This is expected to evolve further and reach a capacity of 4 billion bits by 2005[5]. In real terms, this may be conceptualised as moving from an ability to store 30 pages of typed text on one microchip, to 500 pages; with the possibility of advancing to a small library by the middle of the next decade (*Business Week*, 4 July 1994). In conjunction with these advances in chip capacity, the technology is also furthering component miniaturisation. Thus, from a width of 0.5 micron in the mid-1990s, memory chip circuits are predicted to shrink to 0.1 micron by around 2008. This would signify a size reduction to a situation whereby a string of 2,500 transistors would be required in order to circle a single human hair[6]. In terms of applications proliferation, semiconductor technology is the core of the information age. Not only is it a high revenue industry in and of itself but it forms the basis of a much wider industrial sphere. Dataquest figures show that in 1990 for instance, the semiconductor industry had a world-wide production of $58 billion. Moreover, it constituted the core technology for an industrial base worth $613 billion globally. These dependent electronic equipment sectors were in the areas of communications ($96 billion), military and aerospace ($88 billion), consumer ($136 billion), industrial ($93 billion), transportation ($15 billion), and data processing ($185 billion)[7].

There is a further point which requires justification at this stage. I argue throughout that large semiconductor firms have more structural power, and thus greater relational power relative to governmental actors, than do firms within any other sector of an economy. I must therefore substantiate this claim, and illustrate why semiconductors firms differ from other companies (be they in the coal or the biotechnology industry) in terms of the nature and extent of their political power.

It is the concept of critical or enabling technologies which is central to the political influence held by the semiconductor sector[8]. Without the industry's ability to affect a wide array of other industries, as well as the defence sector, its bargaining position vis-à-vis government would be significantly less. Within the EC, electronics, and particularly active semiconductor components, are clearly seen by the European Commission as special. The key to understanding this position is that semiconductors affect other industries. From a Commission perspective:

> it was not only the European firms that were at issue, but much about the European economy more generally, since Europe would be more dependent without a solid electronics sector (Ross, 1995, p.116).

The notion that semiconductors are a critical technology, also lies behind the political influence held by the industry in the US. As Yoffie points out, in the US, the actual design and manufacture of semiconductors is a small industry by most traditional standards. The numbers employed in the industry are low compared with industries such as automobile or steel making for instance. Also, the industry is geographically concentrated, and is located mainly in the states of California, Arizona, and Texas (1988, p.83). This means that the number of congressional districts and senate regions influenced by the industry are relatively few. This situation would normally translate as little political influence for an industry at a federal government level. However, as I will show in chapter six, the opposite has in fact occurred. For instance, the 1986 Semiconductor Trade Agreement signified the first significant agreement signed by a US administration for a high technology sector, and the first motivated by loss of competitiveness rationale; as well as being the first American trade agreement which sought to extend market access abroad (Tyson, 1993, p.109).

Further to this argument concerning why I emphasise the pre-eminent policy bargaining power of semiconductor firms, I would point out the distinction I make between sectoral business lobbies and oligopolistic bargaining partnerships. In this work, I am talking about a small, oligopolistic, pan-European grouping of large firms, jointly possessing policy bargaining power, often at the behest of governmental actors. I distinguish this scenario from that where the combined

4

lobbying resources of an entire business sector (firms, politicians, consumer interest groups, labour unions, farmers organisations, users, suppliers, and so forth), coalesce to influence policy decisions. Thus, in terms of the policy influence of one group of firms relative to another group of firms (rather than the combined interest groups of one business sector relative to another), I argue that semiconductor firms enjoy a bargaining advantage.

A final point, already touched upon but in need of further emphasis, is the dual-use nature of semiconductors. Apart from semiconductor chips multitude of commercial uses, they also constitute the technological base of modern defence systems[9]. As the 1991 Gulf War illustrated, the nature of warfare has changed. We have entered a new era of warfare, symbolised by 'the triumph of silicon over steel'[10] - the so-called smart weapons systems. As Inman and Burton argue, guaranteed access to dual-use technologies such as semiconductors is now an issue in US national security considerations (1990, pp.133-4). This important dual-use dimension increases the political significance of semiconductor firms relative to companies in other areas of economic activity, and further enhances their bargaining power with governmental actors.

2 Technology and technological change

Technology, and the rapid pace of innovation, is one of the most dynamic forces for change in the international system. Through its impact on the industrial base of the modern state, it has a pervasive effect on a nation's long-term economic performance. Technology is knowledge, or more correctly, it is applied and applicable knowledge. More specifically, technology may be defined as 'the body of knowledge - scientific, technical, and managerial - permitting the development and introduction of new products and processes' (Woods, 1987, p.16). Williams described technology as 'the fourth and most important factor of production', and he determines that the capacity to produce technology equals power (1984, p.70). Access to know-how, to technology, is a constantly increasing factor in the world economy, in a way that access to markets has been in the past.

Four somewhat contemporary usage's of the term have been identified (Woods, 1987, pp.16-17). New technology is simply technology that did not previously exist; whilst leading edge technology is the most advanced modern technology within a particular industry at a given time. The two other usage's of the term are of most relevance to this research and help to rationalise our selective industrial focus. High technology - as defined by the OECD - applies to knowledge-intensive industries, which have a rapid rate of technological innovation, production volume growing faster than other industries, a significant share of government outlays on R&D, the highest growth rates of exports, and significant cross-border co-operation and competition in R&D, production, and marketing. From this classification, semiconductor devices may be identified as one of only about seven or eight 'high technology' industries (the others being aerospace, computers, pharmaceuticals, telecommunications, precision instruments, and so forth).

5

The fourth and final manner in which technology is referred to, takes us further in comprehending the importance of semiconductors within the modern political economy. A core technology is a technology which is essential to the development of an industrial sector. It may be specific to a given sector, or it may have more general application throughout an economy. Van Tulder and Junne advance three criteria for identifying a core technology. First, it leads to a large number of new products and production processes; second, a core technology is applicable across a wide range of economic sectors; and third, it saves labour, is flexible in its applications, economises on energy and raw materials, and is a low-level pollutant (1988, p.253). The authors go further in naming three clusters of core technologies. These are biotechnology, new materials, and microelectronics. Hence, semiconductor components constitute a core technology within the international political economy.

Technological change may be conceptualised as a dynamic and multi-faceted process, encompassing the invention, innovation, transfer, and diffusion of technology (Parayil, 1993, p.105). Schumpeter saw innovation as the most important element of technological change, precipitating what he termed 'creative destruction' in economies. By this he meant that through business innovation, technological change evolved, which in turn caused economic change (1939, p.84). Freeman envisages different scales of technological change. At one level, there are incremental innovations, bringing about a slow but sure technological transformation. Frequently these are limited in their impact. From this level, Freeman describes three other stages of technological change, each one increasing in the speed of innovation and in the extent of its impact (1987, pp.110-11). He describes the final level as 'changes in the techno-economic paradigm'. According to Daniel Bell (1979), human society has experienced four distinct revolutions in the character of social interchange. These have been speech, followed by writing, then printing, and more recently, information technology[11]. Each of these revolutions heralded a change in the techno-economic paradigm of the industrialised world. Within Bell's sectoral breakdown of information technology, microcircuits is of fundamental importance, being in effect, the meta-technology of the contemporary information age. In brief, meta-technologies are technologies whose development affects not just their own industry but the entire world economy. A meta-technology encompasses a range of interrelated product, process, technical, organisational, and managerial innovations[12]. Meta-technologies create new industries and structures and help to destroy others. A meta-technology has such wide-ranging implications that it is accompanied by structural crises which may create tensions in the international system. It challenges the existing social and political structures, introducing an instability until these structures are brought into line with the new technology (Turner, 1973; Dicken, 1986). The concept fits with the Kondratiev notion of long waves of economic activity associated with significant technological changes. Other production and organisational innovations tended to group around these changes. Their impact was ultimately diffused throughout economies. Meta-technologies have included steam power, steel, electricity, and the internal combustion engine. The microelectronics

6

revolution may be seen as the advent of a more contemporary meta-technology, or a change in the dominant techno-economic paradigm.

The basis of the microelectronics industry is the integrated circuit unit - more commonly known as the microchip. This circuit is fabricated within a pinhead-sized area of a silicon semiconductor wafer. The revolutionary nature of microelectronics lies substantially in the information storage capacity of the integrated circuit and the processing power of the more advanced form of chip, the microprocessor; and in the resulting impact on the speed and quality of communications between units - both within and across national boundaries.

Technology constitutes a core variable in the competitiveness of firms. Corporate competitive advantage derives in large part from the sophistication of a given firm's technology base; together with the firm's ability to constantly introduce or adopt new technologies (Rosenthal, 1993, p.9). Semiconductor-based technologies have precipitated revolutionary changes in the organisation of business entities, in the nature of production processes (e.g. the introduction of flexible manufacturing), and in relative cost structures facing companies. Similarly, technology also has what Clyde Prestowitz (1988) calls, a ripple affect on the rest of the economy. For example, a national (or EC) production capacity in microchips, increases the chances of a country creating or maintaining a presence in downstream user industries such as computer hardware, telecommunication equipment, and so forth.

In discussing the semiconductor industry, I am aware of the dichotomy which generally applies to this industry. Two major business segments may be delineated. The first is composed of the chip manufacturers, who make the actual semiconductor components. These companies transform simple raw materials - sand, water, and aluminium - into silicon wafers, upon which they then etch the microchip components. The second group of manufacturers within the industry comprises those firms which produce both the raw materials and the equipment for chip manufacturing[13]. These companies produce raw materials such as the gases and metals needed to make chips. They also manufacture the precision tools and manufacturing equipment which are used to create integrated circuits. Unless otherwise stated, this work will employ the term 'semiconductor industry' to mean chip component manufacturers.

The terms 'information technology' and 'electronics' are used interchangeably in this work, when referring to the industrial sector. I adopt a relatively simple definition of the electronics industry. It constitutes:

a group of sectors which produce goods and systems based upon semiconductor and software technology (Hobday, 1992, p.274).

Five main systems sectors may be identified: consumer electronics, telecommunications, defence, electronically controlled industrial equipment, and computing. Two enabling sectors are also included in the electronics industry. The first is the design and development of electronic systems software. The second is the semiconductor sector, which provides the basic components for all other sectors of the wider industry (Hobday, 1991, p.274).

My point of departure for an understanding of the globalisation concept derives from the OECD (1991) definition, which sees it as:

> the set of processes which result in the increased inter-relatedness and economic interdependence of previously fairly separate national economies; and the conditions in which an increasing fraction of value and wealth are produced and distributed world-wide, within a system of interlinking private networks[14].

Globalisation is a much-used but often ill-defined concept. Eden identifies three of its main components (1991, p.213). The first is described as convergence, that is the trend for underlying production, financial, and technology structures to approach a common average standard. O'Doherty refers to this simply as 'the development of world markets, regulated by universal standards' (1995, p.15). The second component is synchronisation, i.e. the increasing tendency for the Triad economies to move in tandem, experiencing similar business cycle patterns. The final element delineated by Eden is interpenetration. This refers to the growing importance of trade, investment, and technology flows within each domestic economy.

In terms of practical manifestations, globalisation is evident through the rapid growth in international trade and international financial flows; as well as the way in which economic booms spread more readily from one country to another, as do recessions. Moreover, interest rates in one economy may now affect investment in others (*The Economist*, 7 Oct. 1995, p.15). Globalisation has undoubtedly enfeebled the state, significantly limiting the economic sovereignty of countries. As a former British Chancellor of the Exchequer put it:

> the plain fact is that the nation state as it has existed for nearly two centuries is being undermined...the ability of national governments to decide their exchange rate, interest rate, trade flows investment and output has been savagely crippled by market forces[15].

Most notably, the inter-firm world-wide information and communication networks which have resulted from advances in technology, have opened up vast new opportunities for transnational corporations to deploy their resources on a global basis.

3 The New Diplomacy: an introduction

Technology is now part of political discourse, as governments have realised the impact of technology on international relations. Governments vary in the way they influence and exploit technological changes. For example, traditional policy instruments for technology include regulation, procurement, trade protectionism, and support for research and development. A further approach has been adopted over the past two decades: that of government bargaining with the enterprises that control the development of technology. It is with this policy process that this work is most interested. Such an approach is forced upon governments due to their need to access the technology which firms control. No government freely chooses to negotiate for access to that which is essential to the welfare of its society. Bargaining per se constitutes a dilution of state autonomy; it symbolises an inability to wield sole authority over its territory and citizens, and a decline in a nation's authority within the international system. As Keller argues, information represents power, but that power is now shared (1990, p.128).

The state-centric view of international relations is obsolete in the era of the global economy. More importantly, it is an outdated approach to adopt for any analysis of systemic power in the information age. A minority of international relations and international business scholars have argued this point since the early 1970s (Kindleberger, 1969; Galbraith, 1973; Vernon, 1974; Hodges, 1974; Chandler, 1977; Williams, 1984; Strange, 1988; Sally, 1994). These authors expound the notion that transnational corporations (TNCs), through their international sales, investment, and production webs, have challenged the power of states as the pre-eminent actors in the international system. As Strange argues:

> It is only when you think of power in terms of the ability to create or destroy, not order but wealth, and to influence the elements of justice and freedom as part of the value-composition of the whole system, that it becomes obvious that big business plays a central, not a peripheral role [in the international system] (1993, p.102).

This reality developed as firms outgrew their national markets and national laws, and began to produce for a world market, using a global corporate strategy (Strange, 1993, p.102). This process escalated during the 1960s and through the 1970s. The underlying reasons for this dramatic increase in the numbers of TNCs stem from information technology. As information technologies - especially microchip technology - developed and diffused rapidly from the early 1960s on, the globalisation of sales and production was rendered more attractive and attainable (Strange, 1993, p.105). Williams supports this assertion that technology (information technology in particular) is central to the creation and operations of TNCs (1984, p.71). Therefore, it is rational to propose that, as is argued in this work, those TNCs that control core technologies facilitating globalisation (thus influencing structural power), pose an even greater threat to the power and autonomy of states.

In addition to their control over production, TNCs also have an impact upon the other three pillars of the international system. These are finance, security, and knowledge (Strange, 1988). I shall develop this argument further in chapters two and six. It is sufficient to argue here that the ability of TNCs to influence the nature and rate of modern capital flows, military defence systems, and cultural norms, gives them significant bargaining strength and relational power relative to governmental actors.

Building on this argument, I advance Alfred Chandler's proposal that TNCs have superseded market mechanisms in the co-ordination of national and global economic activities and in the allocation of resources (1977, pp.ix-xvi). In the words of John Kenneth Galbraith, the TNC 'transcends the market internationally as it does nationally' (1973, p.167). That is to say, market forces continue to generate demand, but TNCs direct the product flow and determine the resource emphasis for future production and distribution[16]. For example, 40 per cent of world trade is between subsidiaries of the same companies. Thus, as a countervailing force to governments in the international economy, TNCs provide a more tangible and more influential force than do market mechanisms.

Transnational semiconductor producers have an impact on policy because first, they control the technology and thus shape the knowledge structure which governments need access to if they are to exercise relational power vis-à-vis other governments in the system; and second, these firms are actors in their own right. They have their own policy agendas and power-related objectives. In effect, they want a role in policy-making, in order to further their own corporate interests.

Therefore, large, global firms have emerged to challenge not only market forces for pre-eminence in the international economy, but also to contest the authority of the very states from which they emerged. An uneasy truce now reigns: states have been forced to cede policy power in return for access to the technology which global firms control. The firms in turn defer to the states, as they remain the gatekeepers to the territory wherein lay the existent or potential markets. A 'new diplomacy' has emerged in international relations as global firms and national governments bargain over the terms of this technology-for-market access agreement. Within the parameters of this new diplomacy I contend that the bargaining power of firms relative to governmental actors is enhanced for enterprises which control a core, enabling technology.

Thus, this work aims to investigate the nature and (to a lesser extent) competitive effects of the new diplomacy, and to establish the role which technology plays in determining the power balance therein. In doing this, I develop an elaboration of the triangular model of bargaining (state-state, state-firm, and firm-firm) set out by Stopford and Strange (1991)[17]. I add in two more dimensions to what they termed the New Diplomacy; to wit, bargaining between the European Commission and firms, and between the European Commission and the governments of states. With this model, and using empirical data from both published and unpublished sources, as well as interviews, I explain the change in EC industrial policies in the sector since the early 1980s, and comment on the effect these policies have had on corporate competitiveness. Central to this will be a critique of a core dimension of the wider policy set - the Joint European Submicron Silicon (JESSI) programme. Due to the financial outlay involved in JESSI, its large number of participants, and its governmental-corporate nature, it is a valid subject upon which to centre the work's empirical study. The basic argument is further supported by a shadow comparative analysis of US and Japanese policies for the efficient production and marketing of semiconductors.

4 Survey of the argument

This book's core chapters - four, five, and six - are each a level of analysis for the work's dependent variable (EC policy for semiconductors). Consequently, these sections analyse the variable from a firm, EC institutional, and international system perspective. Together, these chapters provide a critique of the work's problematics, and serve to minimise the shortfalls associated with uni-disciplinary research analysis.

There are four main reasons why the research is centred on EC policy for semiconductors. First, to discern the extent to which the new diplomacy is manifest at an EC level, and which set of political actors - national governments or EC institutions - play a greater role in the new diplomacy. Second, to assess how policy emerging from this new diplomacy affects the competitiveness of a group of globally weak firms. Third, to investigate the degree to which EC policy for the European-based semiconductor industry contributes to the European integration process. The fourth rationale rests simply on the EC's economic importance as one pillar of the triad, and the world's largest trading entity. As such, its policy is worthy of study.

In chapter two, I draw together a number of eclectic theoretical constructs, discuss their meaning, and how they may be used individually as tools to further the work's analysis, and collectively as a framework with which to construct a coherent and logical argument. It is stressed herein that my research methodology is essentially a mélange of international political economy and international business concepts. Also, I describe how the work embodies three distinct levels of analysis - firm, EC institutional, and international system.

Chapter three looks at the early years of the semiconductor industry and investigates the power relationship between firms and governments during that period. Furthermore, I examine the affect which Cold War rivalries had on the development of semiconductor technology, and on the growth of the international semiconductor industry. In addition, the chapter's first section deals with the development of semiconductor technology, and reviews the technology's commercial development. The second section addresses the reasons for European firms early failure to maintain competitiveness. Part one focuses on the corporate strategy and industry structure reasons. Part two investigates the public policy reasons. The final section surveys the 'post-national champion' nature of the indigenous European semiconductor industry. The firms still involved in chip production shall be identified, and their product specialisation's and market shares will be established. The chapter also precipitates three important issues which will be examined in subsequent chapters. These are firstly, an analysis of the European level collaborative approach, as the fourth phase in European national policy for the semiconductor sector (and as the alternative to both 'national champions' and

'European champions'); secondly, an exploration of the reasoning behind the argument that for a government to target an industry for preferential policy treatment, or to use the strategic label as an excuse for discriminatory practices against foreign firms, is competitively redundant; and thirdly, an assessment of how the state-firm relationship for semiconductors has evolved (since its early state-dominant days), as the semiconductor industry has globalised, increased its user markets dramatically, and become the most technologically influential industrial sector in the modern international political economy.

In the fourth chapter there are two interrelated objectives. First, to determine, through innovation policy theory, how EC semiconductor policy is created and what are its varied elements. Second, to discern, through the Pentagonal Diplomacy model, the degree of influence exerted by each actor within the EC policy-making process for semiconductors. The intention is to determine which of the public and private sector players involved in the policy paradigm actually define and drive the policy. Furthermore, it is my hypothesis that the role of both large firms and intra-Commission ideological rivalries have the most profound impact on the development and direction of EC industrial policy for the electronics sector. This chapter is also designed to test in part whether EC policy for the semiconductor industry evolved as part of the Community's efforts to create a common area of action for industrial affairs. Finally, in chapter four I refer briefly to the Porter Diamond model of national competitive advantage. This allows us to comment on the consequences which EC policy has had for the European-based semiconductor industry's global competitive advantage.

Chapter five serves two purposes. The first is to assess the creation and control of EC semiconductor policy from the corporate perspective. I will investigate the corporate rationale for collaborating with governmental actors, and advance a firm perspective on the development, objectives, and outcomes of EC policy. The second purpose of this chapter is to provide a case study of EC industrial policy for semiconductors. A dimension of the policy set is dissected, with the aim of determining its origins, structure, and driving forces. The policy chosen is the collaborative research and development venture, JESSI. The relative competitive loss or gain accrued through JESSI is evaluated, and the programme is critiqued as a framework for collaboration and as a model for competitive enhancement. Also, through theories of corporate technology strategy, I establish that, from a firm perspective, the knowledge structure is the key pillar of structural power determining European collaboration. Moreover, as the knowledge network will show, the development and diffusion of technology is central to firms corporate strategies.

Chapter six has three main research themes. The first is to determine the effect which structural change in the global political economy has on the nature and direction of EC policy for a specific sector. This, largely theoretical line of analysis, involves an examination of the restructuring of power relationships in the global political economy, and the new role of the multinational corporation in international bargaining. From this, conclusions are drawn concerning the effect which this new diplomacy has on EC policy-making. My second objective herein is to assess the extent to which the semiconductor policies of non-Community governments (mainly the US and Japan) have an impact upon EC policy direction. The intention is to determine the ways and extent to which trade activities or trade tool utilisation's in or between non-Community countries, have affected the nature of EC policy. The central aim here is to establish whether or not the EC adopts a more mercantilist policy for semiconductors partially in response to external trade pressures and/or politico-economic alliances (e.g. the US-Japanese Semiconductor Trade Agreement). The third line of research in chapter six investigates whether or not the EC can learn - in policy terms - from other global government-firm policy bargains aimed at the competitive enhancement of the semiconductor industry. During the late 1970s and late 1980s respectively, Japan and the United States initiated policies for their semiconductor industries, which have involved varying degrees of state-firm bargaining and co-operation. In particular, the Japanese Very Large Scale Integration (VLSI) project and the American Semiconductor Manufacturing Technology Corporation (SEMATECH) are of interest. These shadow comparisons are intended to serve two purposes. Firstly, they highlight the nature of the state-firm power relationship in non-EC countries, and establish whether our arguments are valid outside of the European Community. Secondly, through identifying successful elements in these countries policies, we may consequently, discuss whether or not the EC can draw any useful policy lessons from the collaborative approaches adopted in the other corners of the triad.

The theoretical argument aside, this book recounts the following story. From the early 1950s until the late 1970s, European policy for the semiconductor industry was created and controlled in national capitals. Neither the European Community nor individual firms had significant input into the policy-making process. Since the early 1980s, firms rather than state actors, have set the terms of European semiconductor policy, within the broad constraints set by the structure of the international system. They have frequently done so in collaboration with the European Commission. Both firms and the Commission collaborate to keep apace of technological change. The Commission has a further, politicised purpose. It entered a policy partnership with large semiconductor firms in order to create a common area of action for a core technology, and thereby advance the economic integration process. It is impossible to say how the European-based semiconductor industry would have fared without EC industrial policy. Nevertheless, EC semiconductor policy does not appear to have been effective, due to institutional constraints, design flaws, and the dynamic movement of the international system. Although this study is analytical rather than prescriptive, it suggests that the use by the Community of trade instruments and R&D programmes can be improved. Lessons can be drawn in particular from American and Japanese semiconductor policies.

Notes

1   The notion of structural power is central to this work. It will be explained fully in chapter two. In brief, it may be defined as the unevenly distributed systemic ability to define the basic structures, or pillars, of the international political economy. These are security, credit, production, and knowledge (Strange, 1988, p.15).

2   Following the terminology of the Maastricht Treaty, the term European Community (EC) is employed throughout to denote the economic and social pillar of the European Union. This book does not deal with the other two pillars - common foreign and security policy and co-operation in the field of justice and home affairs. Moreover, the time frame examined is primarily before the Maastricht Treaty's implementation.

3   These figures are courtesy of Dataquest, the world semiconductor industry specialist.

4   This figure is cited in 'The Global Chip Payoff', *Business Week,* 7 August, 1995.

5   *Business Week* Special Report, 'Wonder Chips', 4 July 1994.

6   Ibid.

7   *Dataquest* 1990, cited in US Semiconductor Industry Association presentation, *The American and European Electronics Industries: Regaining the High-Tech Lead,* December 1991.

8   See also Van Tulder and Junne's (1988) description of core technologies, as described on pages 5-6; and Daniel Bell's (1979) conception of a meta-technology on page 6. In addition, see Prestowitz's (1988) argument that some technologies (such as semiconductors) can have a 'ripple affect' on the rest of the economy (page 7).

9   Several examples will illustrate the key role which semiconductor chips play within modern military systems. First, the Tomohawk cruise missile (much used in the Gulf War) contains 1,270 electronic part types. Second, roughly 35 per cent of modern fighter aircraft's is electronics. Third, microelectronic components comprise over one-third of a Poseidon missile. Fourth, other microchip defence applications include digital signal processing and radar control (SEMATECH, *Strategic Overview,* December 1991).

10   This quote is taken from a testimony given by William J. Spenser, President and CEO of SEMATECH, before the Subcommittee on Defence Industry and Technology, US Senate Armed Services Committee, 18 March, 1992.

11   For Bell, information technology is an integrated economic sector, comprising microcircuits, computers, and telecommunications.

12   For a more detailed account of these widespread innovations see Freeman and Perez (1988), in Giovanni Dosi (ed.), *Technical Change and Economic Theory*, pp.38-66.

13   This distinction is found in National Advisory Committee on Semiconductors, *A Strategic Industry At Risk*, A Report to the President and Congress, November 1989, Washington DC, p.7.

14 Background Report by the Secretary General, Concluding the Technology/Economy Programme C/MIN (91) 14, OECD 1991.

15 Nigel Lawson cited in *The Economist*, 'The myth of the powerless state', 7 October 1995, p15.

16 Alfred D. Chandler, Jr., *The Visible Hand: The Managerial Revolution in American Business* (1977), in Thomas K. McCraw (ed.), *The Essential Alfred Chandler*, p.387.

17 John Stopford and Susan Strange, *Rival States, Rival Firms,* 1991.

2 Perspectives and tools

Knowledge is of two kinds: we know a subject ourselves,
or we know where we can find information upon it.

Samuel Johnson

The theoretical basis of this volume derives from a mélange of international business (IB) and international political economy (IPE) approaches[1]. As Eden argues, international political economy needs a more precise focus on the transnational corporation as an institutional actor, if it, as a discipline, is to fully understand the use of power within the system, the nature of state-firm relations, and the effectiveness of government policy vis-à-vis the firm (1993, p.54). Therefore, IB analytical models must be fused with those of IPE, in order to achieve this comprehensive analysis.

Further support for the interdisciplinary approach as advocated by this author, has come from John H. Dunning (1993), one of the doyens of international business studies. Approaching the issue from a different disciplinary basis, Dunning is concerned with advancing the study of international business through broadening its methodological parameters:

> To understand the nature and practice of decision taking in international companies, one needed to develop a cross-disciplinary (or supra-disciplinary) paradigmatic approach (Dunning, 1993, p.25).

Thus, Dunning advances an agenda for international business studies in the 1990s which places more emphasis on disciplines which fashion the environment of international business. Among these disciplines, he includes political science and international relations. He cites an ideal type of interdisciplinary methodology as one which blends technology, business strategy, and international relations[2]. Such an approach fits closely with that utilised in this work.

1 Setting the scene

The purpose of this chapter is to select the lenses through which we may view our dependent variable (EC policy), and then proceed to delineate the heuristic tools with which we may examine and explain the constituent elements of the overall problematic. In pursuing this strategy, an eclectic approach will be adopted, drawing most heavily from the disciplines of international business and international relations. Having established the group of theories which are deemed relevant to this research, an attempt shall be made to link them together into an interdisciplinary social scientific framework of analysis. There are three levels of analysis (or perspectives) in this work. In order to fully comprehend and analyse EC policy, it is necessary to examine it at the following levels:

(1) Firm specific
(2) EC institutional
(3) International system

Specific EC policy must be analysed at both a firm and an EC institutional level, in order to understand how and why it comes about, and why certain policy options were selected above others (e.g. collaboration). This policy must subsequently be analysed at a third level, the international system, in order to assess the extent to which the allocation and exercise of power globally shapes EC policy. Let us begin this theoretical exploration at the EC institutional level.

2 The EC perspective

At the work's first level of analysis, the empirical evidence is collected and understood through one conceptual framework and is analysed with the aid of two theoretical tools. The framework of understanding is the Pentagonal Diplomacy model, developed by this author. The main analytical tools herein are the Porter Diamond of national competitive advantage; and the innovation policy model of industrial policy.

2.i. The Pentagonal Diplomacy model

This work attempts to expand the Stopford and Strange Triangular Diplomacy model of state-firm bargaining in specific applications. That is to say, when applied to the unique institutional structure of the European Community - which is an international setting, given that it consists of fifteen nation states - an extra dimension must be added to the bargaining process. In analysing, within an EC context, how firms and governments relate to and negotiate with one another over defined mutual goals, one must include another player or level of governance[3] within the paradigm - the European Commission. Thus, two other angles must be included, to transform Stopford and Strange's triangle into a pentagon[4]. Governments must thus negotiate not only with other governments and with firms, but also with the Commission; and firms must bargain with other firms, governments, and with the European Commission. Hence, what emerges is more along the lines of pentagonal diplomacy (fig.2.1), rather than triangular diplomacy.

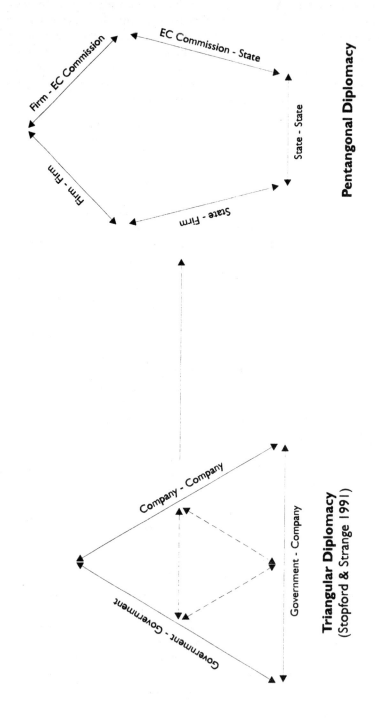

Figure 2.1 The Pentagonal Diplomacy model
Stopford and Strange's (1991) Triangular Diplomacy model is reproduced with the kind permission of Cambridge University Press. The author also wishes to express his gratitude to Dave Worth of the Policy Press for his modifications to this figure.

Such a five-sided bargaining structure is complex, because the interplay varies according to the specificities of a particular bargain. In effect, the Pentagonal Diplomacy concept is a framework for analysing and explaining how industrial policy develops within the European Community. It entails five inter-linked sets of negotiating bargains: state-state, firm-firm, state-firm, firm-European Commission, and European Commission-state. All five bargaining sets come into play for each industry. However, the policy impact of the individual sets varies according to the industry. Thus, for some industries, the firm-Commission interplay is negligible for instance; whilst for others, it may be the state-state bargain which has little input into policy development. The intention is to determine which bargaining set(s) dominate a particular policy-making process; which of the public and private sector players involved in the policy sphere actually define and drive a given policy.

Government-Commission bargaining (which is usually an intra-institutional procedure, between the Commission and the Council) can be a rigorous ordeal, or it may merely constitute a Council 'rubber stamping' of a particular policy. Similarly, Firm-Commission negotiating can be central to the development of a particular policy, or it may be peripheral, if not irrelevant, to the policy process. Thus, in order to cover all possible scenarios for EC level bargaining, the main actors can combine as follows:

[1]

| Firm-Firm |
| Firm(s)-Commission |
| Firm(s)-Governments |
| Government-Government |
| Government(s)-Commission |

[2]

| Firm-Firm |
| Firm(s)-Commission |

[3]

| Government-Government |
| Commission-Government(s) |

19

Competencies within the EC still vary, and firms can thus end up bargaining either with governments, with the EC Commission, or with both.

This state-firm bargaining concept is further supported by Dunning (1993), who argues that the entire nature of government-firm (or more precisely, multinational enterprise) relations has changed during the last three decades from one based largely on conflict, to one based primarily on co-operation. He gives the reason for this change as mainly due to states coming to view multinational enterprises (MNEs) as engines for national competitive advantage enhancement[5]. Thus, a bargaining situation develops on policy issues, within which the MNE has an equal, and sometimes dominant, position (Dunning, 1993; Blomstrom and Lipsey, 1993; Stopford and Strange, 1991). Again, the existence of such a model will be more clearly tested in chapter four, when the nature of the EC bargaining process will be examined.

2.ii. Prelude to industrial policy theory: an identification of strategic industries

Before discussing theories of industrial policy, we should clarify our understanding of strategic industry. This is a key concept in any analysis of EC policy for semiconductors, and in wider Community efforts to forge a common industrial policy. As we will see throughout this work, it is used by both the European Commission and national governments, as well as some large electronics firms, as a rationale for pursuing European level collaborative policy instead of, or in addition to, national industrial policy. The strategic industry notion is central to all studies of why European governmental actors choose to collaborate.

In the US, terms such as 'strategic industry', or 'economic security' for that matter, frequently have military/defence implications. However, in the European Community, such terms have more civilian and economic connotations:

> The governments of these [European Community] nations have accorded the semiconductor industry [and other 'strategically significant' industries] special promotional and/or protectionist treatment in the anticipation of several kinds of economic benefits, including: more productive, higher paying jobs for their workers; greater exports, as a result of an expanded share of growing world markets; the development of an indigenous technological infrastructure with spillover benefits for other industries; and the provision of linkage externalities - lower cost, higher quality inputs - for downstream user industries (D'Andrea Tyson, 1991, p.2).

It is this more European (and Japanese) usage of the term which shall be employed within this study.

For many academic commentators (Tyson, 1993; Krugman, 1986, and others), the concepts of strategic industries and high technology industries are coterminous. High technology industries, as discussed in chapter one, are, by definition, strategic in nature. Within, the European Community, it may be argued that this narrow definition of strategic industries is even more sector-specific. From the evidence of EC policy, strategic industries generally comprise industries within the information technology sector[6]. As Howell et al. **argue:**

> Europeans recognise that the cluster of industrial sectors which electronically manipulate, store, and transmit data are strategic, in the sense that the basic freedoms - political, industrial, economic, social, and cultural - depend on their survival (1992, p.462).

The criteria generally used to select a strategic industry in the non-military sense, have been most clearly charted by Krugman (1986). He argues that, given the much more important role that technological competition (economies of scale, innovation, and so on) plays in trade patterns, classical trade theory is increasingly outdated. This is, he continues, particularly true with regards to the concept of strategic industries. Classical free trade theory rejected this concept, on the basis that competition removes any substantial differences between what equivalent qualities of labour or capital can earn in different sectors. However, Krugman states that there are sectors that are more valuable to an economy than others. One of his main criterion[7] for what constitutes a strategic sector is:

> a sector where there is substantial 'rent', that is, where the return to labour or capital is exceptionally high (1986, p.16).

He defines the concept of rent as:

> A higher rate of profit in an industry than is earned in other industries of equivalent riskiness, or higher wages in an industry than equally skilled workers earn in other sectors (1986, p.14).

Krugman cautions that identifying strategic sectors is not done simply by comparing sectoral profit rate and wage rates over a given period of time. It must also involve a consideration of whether or not high value-added merely reflects high input; to what extent high rates of profit and wages among established firms within an industry reflect a periodical positive technological development, and consequent surge in demand; and to what degree (if any) high rates of return are attributable to counting only the successes within a given industry, whilst ignoring those firms which lost their investment.

2.iii. Theories of industrial policy and the innovation policy model

Central to explaining how a particular policy set comes about at an EC level, is an understanding of the bargaining process between the various governmental and corporate actors. As we have discussed, this may be conceptualised through the Pentagonal Diplomacy model. In addition, we must analyse why the policy set develops. This means studying not only why certain policy options were chosen above others, but also how they were formulated, who was most influential in shaping them, and why these policy choices were implemented at a collaborative, EC level. Further on, we will discuss the theoretical tools needed to assess the corporate rationale for choosing collaboration over (or in addition to) unilateral action. It is also necessary to find out why the national governments and the Commission of the European Community chose collaboration as a means for achieving their policy goals. We argue that this can best be explained from an international system level. However, part of the explanation lies at a purely intra-Community level. This can best be analysed with the aid of EC-level industrial policy

Industrial policy is utilised, in one form or another, by all industrialised and industrialising states. Is it possible though for such a policy to operate at an EC level? The answer would appear to be affirmative. Following the publication of a 1990 Commission paper[8] outlining a new Community approach to industrial policy, two consecutive meeting of the European Council[9] in late 1991 endorsed the approach, and thus, gave the EC - for the first time - an explicit mandate in industrial policy.

A criticism of industrial policy as defined by authors such as Tyson and Zysman (1983) and Audretsch (1993) is that they separate policies aimed at enhancing the competitiveness of a particular industry or sector, from those which intend to benefit the wider economy. They do not appear to consider that a selective policy framework can also, at least in official rhetoric, aim - through economic and technological spill-over - to raise the competitiveness of the wider economy. Such definitions do not adequately conceptualise what has been occurring at an EC policy level. Curzon Price (1981) acknowledges that, in recent years, a narrower sense of industrial policy has emerged in many countries. Her theory comes closest to (although not quite encompassing) the EC policy model which we are trying to frame. She argues:

> There has developed in recent years, a new attribute of government which is industrial policy in a narrower sense, and which can be defined as any selective government measure, or set of measures, to prevent or promote structural change on a specific *ad hoc* basis. Thus, modern industrial policy aims at more than merely setting a general framework (1981, p.18).

Curzon Price goes on to comment that:

> There are two basic types of industrial policy - whether broadly or narrowly defined. One is positive and forward looking: its aim is to assist the process of structural change either by promoting new industries and high technology or by helping old ones to restructure. The other is negative: it attempts to slow down, or even prevent, the process of structural change, or more bluntly, to keep declining sectors alive through artificial respiration (1981, p.18).

From this, it may be inferred that the National Champions policy pursued by many EC countries during the 1960s and 1970s was a negative type of industrial policy;

whereas, the positive form of industrial policy outlined by Curzon Price is more in line with the ongoing EC approach for semiconductors. Hence, it is argued here that it is this more focused, or as both Audretsch (1993) and Curzon Price (1981) term it, selective, form of industrial policy which is being employed as a policy framework by the European Community. However, given this prioritising nature, and the fact that the sectors of priority can be defined almost exclusively as high technology, it is conceptually desirable to proceed beyond categorising this policy framework as industrial policy in the traditional sense of the term. Therefore, in search of a more specific and applicable industrial policy theoretical model, we inevitably arrive at an examination of what the OECD first identified[10] as 'innovation policy'.

Ostry (1990) begins her exposition of innovation policy by stressing the fact that:

> innovation policy is not a given: it is a policy set, in the making, focused on the promotion and adoption of new technology (that is, the commercial development of the fruits of basic research). Thus however much the policy mix and institutional structure of industry vary from country to country, the government-corporate interface is an essential component (1990, p.53).

She continues by arguing that innovation policy has developed since the late 1970s as a progressive spin-off from, or logical extension of, traditional industrial policy. This is because it shifted the emphasis from ailing industries (what Curzon Price described as negative industrial policy) towards a new policy set aimed at improving international competitiveness. Furthermore, recent developments in economics (most notably, increasing support for the active role of government, espoused most eloquently through the US new trade theory), is creating a conducive environment for the fostering of new ideas. This new orthodoxy is establishing a middle way between the free trade model, and the protectionist school, concerning the role of markets vis-à-vis governments, in both trade and industrial policy, for leading-edge, high technology industries (1990, p.60). Ostry proposes that there is no longer an unchallengable belief amongst economists that trade liberalisation always leads to national gains.

The EC's mandate for co-ordinating trade, competition, and technology policies was finally clarified and legitimised with the creation of the European Technology Community, under the 1986 Single European Act. This mandate was, of course, most explicitly for the (strategically targeted) information technology realm, which became the locus of the EC's new innovation policy. Preoccupation with declining competitiveness -especially in the information technology sector- vis-à-vis Japan in particular, precipitated a heavy emphasis on the first of the three main domains of innovation policy - research and technological development (R&TD). This EC co-ordination of R&TD became the central pillar of EC innovation policy:

> The significance of the Commission mandate and of the ESPRIT model of industry-government, long-view targeting is far greater than that of expenditure in pointing a direction for EC innovation policy evolution (Ostry, 1990, p.73).

The other two policy instruments or structural pillars of EC innovation policy are trade, and market structure (competition policy)[11]. For the semiconductor industry, trade is most important, with a number of important policy tools being employed through which the overall objective of enhancing EC competitiveness is advanced. These tools are: informal pressures (so-called voluntary restraint agreements), rules of origin, local content requirements, the common external tariff, quotas, and most importantly, anti-dumping measures. All of these instruments are heavily politicised, and their enactment is generally at the discretion of the European Commission. It is not our intention to get into descriptive and critical detail on these policy tools at this time[12]. It is sufficient to say that increasingly the most utilised of these measures is anti-dumping. Strictly speaking, anti-dumping is independently arbitrated (by GATT panels), and is not under the jurisdiction of EC trade policy. However, in reality, it is a politically motivated judicial matter, where the accused firm is often guilty until proven innocent in the eyes of the European Commission. The usage of this measure will be of particular interest when empirically testing the innovation policy framework for EC policy towards a specific strategically-targeted industry (semiconductors).

To conclude, innovation policy is generally manifest only in industrialised countries. It is aimed more at revitalising or enhancing the competitiveness of an industrial (usually high technology) capacity which already exists (and may have been competitive previously), than with establishing an initial presence in a given industrial sector. Therefore, innovation policy - particularly with regards to the EC - is aimed at long-term, competitive revitalisation. Central to achieving this objective is of course an emphasis on science and technology R&D. We argue that EC industrial policy for semiconductors is best understood and analysed through the innovation policy model.

2.iv. Assessing EC competitive advantage

The concept of national (or European Community) competitiveness may be defined as:

> the degree to which a nation can, under free and fair market conditions, produce goods and services that meet the test of international markets while simultaneously expanding the real incomes of its citizens[13].

It is the nation's ability to stay ahead, technologically and commercially, in those goods and services likely to constitute a larger share of value-added in the future. The critical determinants of competitiveness are, according to Tyson (1988), productivity improvements, and technological innovation. Porter argues that the concept of a competitive nation is amorphous. In his words:

> the only meaningful concept of competitiveness at the national level is national productivity. A rising standard of living depends on the capacity of a nation's firms to achieve high levels of productivity and to increase productivity over

time...Sustained productivity growth requires that an economy continually upgrade itself. A nation's firms must relentlessly improve productivity in existing industries by raising product quality, adding desirable features, improving product technology, or boosting production efficiency (1990, p.6).

In line with the basic approach of this study, Porter goes on to argue that in order to explain the competitiveness of an economy, it is necessary to understand the determinants of productivity and the rate of productivity growth. Therefore, 'to find answers, we must focus not on the economy as a whole, but on specific industries and industry segments' (Porter, 1990, p.9). Furthermore, he states that competition *per se* is dynamic and evolving. Paraphrasing Joseph Schumpeter, he states that:

> competition is a constantly changing landscape in which new products, new ways of marketing, new production processes, and whole new market segments emerge. Static efficiency at a point in time is rapidly overcome by a faster rate of progress (1990, p.20).

Porter's theory of national competitive advantage provides an interesting vehicle through which we may firstly, link the competitive strategies of both industry and government; and secondly, discern the domestic variables involved in establishing competitive advantage for a country (or politico-economic Community).

At the core of explaining national advantage in any industry, must be the role of the home government in stimulating improvement and innovation. However, as previously indicated, Porter stresses the pre-eminence of industry in creating and sustaining a country's advantage. The method used to conceptualise this seemingly contradictory procedure, is the Porter Diamond[14], which graphically illustrates the four broad attributes of a nation that lead to competitive advantage. These attributes effectively mould the domestic competitive environment for corporate enterprises and, by extension, enhance or hinder the development of competitive advantage. In brief, these attributes are as follows:

(1) Factor conditions - the country's situation vis-à-vis factors of production needed to compete globally in any industrial sphere. Such factors include capital, an educated, skilled workforce, and so on.

(2) Demand conditions - the essential character of demand in the domestic economy for an industry's product. The size and consistency of a home market is crucial to national advantage, in particular, for sustaining competitiveness over time.

(3) Related and supporting industries - the indigenous existence or non-existence of globally competitive supplier industries and related industries. That is to say, the presence of industries which 'produce inputs that are widely used and important to innovation or internationalisation' (Porter, 1990, p.100), i.e. supplier industries; and the existence of industries in which 'firms can co-ordinate or share activities in the value chain when competing, or those which involve products that are complementary (such as computers and applications software)' (Porter, 1990,

p.105), i.e. related industries. This is a very important determinant with regards to our industrial focus. As Porter indicates, the semiconductor industry is an important supplier industry, due to the wide-spread usage and operational necessity of its products throughout an economy (such a conclusion is supported by the meta-technology argument in chapter one). Hence, it may be argued that an economy needs internationally competitive (and the word competitive should be stressed here) supplier industries, in order to enhance the competitive advantage of downstream industries, and by implication, of the wider economy.

(4) Firm strategy, structure, and rivalry - national conditions which, firstly, regulate the manner in which firms are established, structured, and managed (e.g. EC competition policy); and secondly, define the fundamental qualities of the domestic environment within which firms compete.

Therefore, the central argument to be construed from this model is that a national economy is most likely to succeed globally in industries where the above competitive attributes, as a set, are most favourable. That is to say, when an industry is most favourably reinforced domestically by the aforementioned four determinants, it will succeed in international competition.

Two final variables must be added to complete Porter's theoretical model. They are both outside of, but attached to, the Diamond. The first is chance events. These are defined as unpredictable occurrences which are beyond the control of firms (and usually governments also). They include civil unrest, major developments in core production technologies, natural disasters (such as the 1995 Kobe earthquake), and so forth. 'They create discontinuities that can unfreeze or reshape industry structure and provide the opportunity for one nation's firms to supplant anothers' (Porter, 1990, p.73).

The second, and very important extra-Diamond variable is government. Porter argued that government does not control national competitive advantage. However, he does concede that it can significantly influence it. The influence of government can be measured most accurately by examining the effects of its policies on each of the four determinants of the Diamond.

The central thesis arising from the Porter Diamond model of national competitive advantage is that 'competitiveness is born of fierce local rivalry, an active anti-trust policy, and avoidance of protectionism' (Stopford and Strange, 1991, p.8). This theory is tested against the empirical evidence advanced herein, and EC industrial policy for semiconductors is subsequently assessed in light of the findings.

The Diamond does have a number of important short-comings. The most important of these is Porter's failure to account for the influence which changes in the international system have on government policy and corporate competitive advantage[15]. Furthermore, as Stopford and Strange (1991) argue, the Diamond model views government as a monolithic actor, and does not account for the different political groups and interests of which it is composed[16]. A third criticism of Porter's model is that it does not consider the interaction between government policy and globally competitive home firms (Stopford and Strange, 1991, p.8). The Diamond does not facilitate a detailed analysis of state-firm bargaining (between governments and home firms) in the creation of policy for competitive advantage. Hence, the Porter Diamond is not a suitable theory for analysing and explaining the creation and control of EC industrial policy[17]. We therefore limit its applicability to evaluating the consequences which policy has for the competitive advantage of an industry.

3 The firm perspective

For a second level of analysis, the empirical material is conceptualised, analysed and explained with the aid of two theoretical tools. These are corporate technology strategy/knowledge networking, and the strategic alliance approach.

3.i. An understanding of collaboration

Keohane defines co-operation as a process whereby the actions of separate entities - which are not in pre-existent harmony - are brought into conformity with one another through a process of negotiation (1984, p.51). Although Keohane's definition is directed more at inter-governmental co-operation, it is broad enough to also encapsulate other international actors, including firms. Regardless of a firm's size and market strength, its corporate strategy has increasingly leaned towards various forms of collaborative activity with other firms and with government. This trend is particularly prevalent within high technology industries. Tucker supports this argument, citing the reasons for such intensification in high technology collaboration as:

> intensifying competition for global markets, rising development costs and rapid obsolescence of new products, and considerable uncertainties and risks regarding performance, schedules, and market size (1991, p.83).

Collaboration is construed in two different ways within this work[18]. It may take the form of an inter-firm collaborative venture, which is more commonly called an alliance. Alternatively, it may be manifest as a three-sided collaboration:

Firm A ↔ Government/EC ↔ Firm B

That is to say, a collaborative project or programme involving two of more firms, plus a public sector department(s). It is important to bear in mind that the concept, as it is used here, is developed from literature which considers such public-private alliances as exclusively occurring between corporate enterprises and governments. The work in hand is of course more interested in developing a model for firm-EC collaboration. Consequently, 'EC' will be substituted for 'government' wherever appropriate.

Corporate strategy was first formally delimited in terms of concepts, definitions, and methodologies, by Kenneth R. Andrews, H. Igor Ansoff, and Alfred D. Chandler, during the 1960s. Andrews has defined corporate strategy as:

> the pattern of decisions in a company that determines and reveals its objectives, purposes, or goals, produces the principal policies and plans for achieving these goals, and defines the range of business the company is to pursue, the kind of economic and human organisation it is or intends to be, and the nature of the economic and non-economic contribution it intends to make to its shareholders, employees, customers, and communities[19].

This work will use the concept in a manner which perceives strategy as long-term, high-level, corporate planning, intended to formulate the broad objectives of a firm, and to implement policies which are intended to achieve these objectives.

Established corporate strategy typologies such as that advanced by Porter (1980)[20], do not identify the strategy model with which we are most concerned, i.e. inter-firm collaboration. Hence it is necessary to proceed beyond the Porter analysis in order to discuss the more recent corporate strategy phenomenon of inter-firm collaboration. This shall be done in two phases: firstly, through a discussion of technology policy as an increasingly important aspect of firms broader corporate strategy; and secondly, by detailing the way in which firms have increasingly used this technology conscious corporate strategy process to select extra-firm collaboration as the most likely strategy option to enhance their overall corporate competitiveness.

3.iii. Corporate technology strategy

The argument for technology (developments and rapidity of application) as the most important contemporary factor of production, and, consequently, the central variable determining a nation's (or Community's) competitive position in the international economy, has been emphasised in the previous chapter. At this stage, it is further contended that technology is an equally important variable for the competitiveness of firms. Corporate evidence would appear to suggest that many transnational firms have come to this realisation and have consequently developed what may be termed a technology strategy. As Dodgson points out, such strategies have now been developed for firms as diverse as semiconductor manufacturers, and automobile producers. It may be argued that their only common denominator is a dependence on the development and rapid application of new technologies for competitive advantage. A technology strategy involves:

> an understanding within a corporation -manifest amongst senior management but diffused throughout the organisation- of the importance and potential of technology for its competitive position, how in the future that potential is to be

realised, and how this complements the other aspects of strategy, such as finance, marketing, and personnel (Dodgson, 1989, p.1).

Thus, technology strategy is an important part of a firm's broader corporate strategy, and should, according to Ansoff and Stewart (1967)[21], and Porter (1980; 1985), complement the other aspects of a company's overall strategy in developing and maximising firm-specific advantage.

Dodgson (1989) proposes a number of reasons for including technology strategy within a firm's overall corporate strategy. These include, firstly, the need to cope with problems posed due to the complexity and uncertainty of technological development; secondly, the failure of previous strategies which have not sufficiently integrated the technology factor; and thirdly, as a means of relating corporate strategy to public technology policies.

The rapid and complex development of information technology has created a certain degree of turbulence and uncertainty for firms. A key aspect of corporate competitiveness - especially within the microchip industry - is the rapid application of new technologies. Broad R&D competencies and skills are a means of dealing with the discontinuities and turbulence in technology development. New technological products and methods are often highly complex and both difficult and costly to operationalise within a firm. However, their rapid application is necessary if a firm is to be competitive. Hence, the necessity of including technology as an element of corporate strategy.

Strategic decisions must be made concerning how to overcome the complexities and application difficulties and costs of new technological developments, and ensure their rapid diffusion and application throughout the firm. An important element of such a technology strategy is deciding whether or not inter-firm collaboration is an effective means for the company to deal with technological complexity. This is a way of ensuring that the firm is aware of both incremental and radical technological developments, before (or at least at the same time as) its competitors, and as a means of sharing the risks involved in financing the development of new technological systems. Many firms have, since the beginning of the 1980s, decided that such alliances with other, often rival, firms, are an effective strategy option. Most companies within the semiconductor industry have pursued a collaborative form of technology strategy.

3.iv. The strategic alliance option

This conclusion leads us into a discussion of what may be perceived as the core aspect of this work's second level of analysis. An attempt will now be made, firstly, to define what exactly constitutes an inter-firm collaborative venture, or a strategic alliance as it is more fashionably termed, and secondly, to propose some reasons as to why such alliances have emerged as a viable and popular corporate strategy model for semiconductor manufacturers - in both theory and practice.

It is possible to propose two common features of strategic alliances. In the view of Mytelka, these are firstly:

agreements among independent firms, which involve knowledge-production or sharing activities, whether these are oriented towards the development of new products, new production processes, or new routines within the firm (1991, p.1).

Strategic partnerships are therefore about the dynamics of innovation and competition. Secondly, alliances are regarded as strategic when their aim is to improve the competitive position of the firm. Strategic alliances are generally of more significance within the context of a firm's long-term objectives (i.e. corporate strategy), rather than being perceived as a response to a company's short-term aims (policy goals).

Mytelka (1991) argues that there are two main forms of strategic partnering activity which involve the public sector: the first is of a pre-competitive R&D consortia nature, which can be either promoted by governments or privately initiated. Examples of this would include the European Strategic Programme for Research in Information Technology (ESPRIT) and SEMATECH. The second involves technological co-operation agreements, which contain arrangements for the equal distribution of equity or include development and production co-operation. Airbus and JESSI are prime examples of this form of strategic partnering.

Mytelka's argument is particularly significant in that it categorises this work's central case study, JESSI, as a different form of strategic alliance from other alliances of interest, namely Sematech and Esprit. The latter are classified as being of a pre-competitive R&D nature only, whilst the former goes further than this, to include co-operation in production and application also. If one consults the primary stated objectives of some of these programmes[22], this distinction basically holds true. These differences in alliance type will be analysed further in chapter five.

Why has strategic partnering emerged as an increasingly more favoured option to take-overs, mergers and acquisitions, intra-firm transfers of knowledge and skills, and other more traditional strategies of the firm? What are the corporate motives for participating in a strategic alliance? We will now turn to these questions.

Strategic alliances were not a common strategy option prior to the 1980s. Over the last decade or so however, (technology-driven) alliances have proliferated. Undoubtedly, activities at both the state and global level have partially affected this large increase. These will be analysed through the theoretical frameworks which shall be outlined further on in this chapter. This section is concerned solely with the corporate reasoning behind this large-scale change in strategy. For the firm, there are a number of prime motives for their participation in strategic alliances. These consequently help to explain the increased utility of the strategic alliance model of corporate strategy in recent years. According to Lorange and Roos (1992), there are two dimensions to the position of each potential partner. Firstly, the strategic importance (to the firm) of the particular business which the alliance is being considered for, i.e. whether or not this business is a central activity of the overall firm; and secondly, the position of the firm within the business sector with which it is primarily concerned. Its share of the market for that business will obviously influence its approach to any potential alliance.

Therefore, focusing on these two 'strategic positioning dimensions' (Lorange and Roos, 1992, p.6), a number of general motives may be identified to explain the emergence of strategic alliances. First, when the alliance is of central importance to the firm's overall business structure, and the firm has a large market share of the particular sector in question, the usual motive for participating in a strategic alliance is defensive. This defensive motivation for alliance is generally manifest in terms of a large market leader forging an alliance with a smaller, dynamic company, in order to keep in touch with new developments in a technology or to look for opportunities for further business divergence. In more militaristic terms, one could define this type of motive as one intended to create a defensive strategy to pre-empt being outflanked or outgunned by competitors. A further rationale for such defensive alliances is to secure raw material sources or cheap parts for the firm's products. This is particularly evident in the formation of alliances between transnational corporations and firms in developing countries.

Second, when the sector which the alliance is intended for is still central to the firm's general competence, but the firm does not have a significant presence in the constituent market, the leading motive for participating in a strategic alliance is, in the words of Lorange and Roos, 'to catch up'. This can be a very important motive for alliance because the very survival of the firm may rely on increasing its competitive position and hence, its market share.

A third motive for participation in strategic alliances arises when the business sector in question is not of central importance to the firm's overall corporate competence, but the company does have a dominant position within the constituent market. In this case, the major rationale is to remain in this position. The firm's primary objective is to maximise the efficiency of what it already possesses, rather than to improve its market position relative to its competitors. Maintaining or establishing the firm's position in a specific market is also an important part of the rationale for this type of strategic alliance.

Finally, if the business segment of interest is not of core importance to the firm's wider portfolio, and the relating market share is small, the primary motive for participating in co-operative ventures is to 'restructure the business' (Lorange and Roos, 1992, p.9). The intention of the firm is often to make a specific business sector, which is no longer of strategic importance to the firm, stronger and more appealing to other companies, in order to eventually remove it from the wider enterprise.

Given the above underlying motives, Lorange and Roos have identified four original models of strategic alliance which are typically utilised by firms. The main consideration which a firm must take into account before choosing which model it wishes to participate in, is the input of resources; that is:

how much of its resources should a firm put in to and retrieve from a strategic alliance (1992, p.10).

This decision significantly shapes the form that the alliance will take. Therefore, a short-term, minimum input of resources (all of which the firm regains), constitutes an *ad hoc* pool type of strategic alliance. A second pattern of alliance is that of the consortium. This is the most sensible option if the participants are willing to commit more resources than in the previous case, but the benefits created are still distributed amongst the members. For example, within an R&D consortium, each partner commits its best technologies, scientists, etc., but the benefits of any scientific discoveries return directly to the participants.

The third strategic alliance model outlined by Lorange and Roos is referred to as project-based joint venture. This form of alliance necessitates a minimum, short-term input of resources by the participants, who create a common organisation through which strategic benefits are jointly created. Unlike the previous two models however, the resources which are produced are not dispersed to the partners, except as financial results. That is to say, the co-operating firms embark upon such an alliance in order to generate revenue, rather than to develop a particular technology. A fourth and final alliance model is the full-blown joint venture. This alliance involves a significant level of resource input, and allows the resources created to remain within the alliance itself. This type of alliance effectively creates another autonomous organisation which has separate strategic concerns. It is used largely as a means through which partner firms can create a whole new business.

In summation, it is the firm's perspective regarding strategic positioning, in addition to the input/output of resources, that dictate the form of strategic alliance pursued. It should also be noted that strategic alliances can be formed to tackle any part of the firm's value creating activities - R&D, manufacturing, distribution, or service - or a combination of these.

In a study of 839 collaborative ventures, Hergert and Morris (1988) found that a majority of such agreements were carried out in high technology industries: aerospace (19 per cent), telecommunications (17.2 per cent), computer (14 per cent), and other electrical industries (13 per cent). Furthermore, they found that the largest proportion of the agreements were joint product development (37.7 per cent). Perhaps most startling was the revelation that the vast majority (71.3 per cent) of these ventures were formed between rivals[23]. Similar studies by Marti and Smiley (1983) and Zajac (1990), have proposed a number of factors which motivate firms to participate in inter-firm co-operative agreements. These are (1) an exchange or sharing of technology among the partners; (2) economies of scale in production and/or distribution; (3) risk sharing; (4) overcoming legal/regulatory barriers[24].

Ernst has produced such reasons also to explain the underlying logic for firm participation in strategic alliances. These are, firstly, the need to decrease cost and risk involved in certain projects; secondly, to increase economies of scale, without significantly increasing R&D costs; and thirdly, the necessity of reducing crisis vulnerability through increasing the ability of firms to react at all stages of production and to fluctuations in product demand (1983, p.112).

The goals of firms participating in a strategic alliance together need not be the same; they should however be complementary. The success of the venture is based largely on making the complementary issue the common driving force in the otherwise different strategic intents.

To conclude, Lorange and Roos argue that no form of strategic alliance is better than others. Rather, what matters is to make the appropriate choice of strategic alliance form, given the particular conditions at hand (1992, p.267). They also propose that strategic alliances are not decided on rapidly and in a clear-cut way. Instead they tend to be shaped over a period of time. Strategic alliances do not have to be defensive or last resort types of decision tools. In fact, many of the more successful alliances are offensive and proactive in nature. In addition, a strategic alliance is driven by selfish interests. If a prospective partner does not see 'whats in it for us', the alliance is unlikely to work (Lorange and Roos, 1992, p.272).

Therefore, for most high technology firms, the formulation and implementation of effective strategy necessitates the inclusion of technology strategy. From this process, such firms have increasingly chosen strategic alliances as the strategy most likely to enhance the competitiveness of the firm. Some of these alliances include governmental actors. The corporate rationale for collaboration with EC governmental players (namely the European Commission) will be developed further in chapter five. As mentioned previously, this section has, through the above process, endeavoured to construct a second level of analysis (the firm) for comprehending and analysing EC policy for the semiconductor industry. From this, we shall now proceed to level three - the international system.

4 The international system perspective

The third perspective from which we will view EC policy is the international system. Two conceptual frameworks are used here, and two theoretical doctrines combine to analyse and explain the empirical evidence. To facilitate our understanding of EC policy from a systemic perspective, we use, first, the concept of economic security; and second, the international state-firm bargaining framework. Our main analytical tools are strategic trade theory and structural power theory.

4.i. Economic security

The notion of economic security is employed to further our understanding of EC semiconductor policy from an international system perspective. This line of analysis will be developed in chapter six. A clarification of the concept's meaning and usage is necessary in advance of its implementation. This is because, although fashionable within international relations and international political economy circles, economic security is a somewhat grey area, analytically speaking. Definitions are frequently imprecise, and understanding is often blurred. Economic security does not represent any absolute value. Definitions vary according to the level of analysis (individual, firm, state, international), and according to the politico-economic system in question. Thus, for the purpose of understanding what is meant by a specific application of the concept of economic security, it is necessary to firmly establish such criteria from the outset. Therefore, for a precise definition of economic security with regards to the European Community, the international system must be taken as a level of analysis, and the concept is applied to the system of capitalism. Within such parameters, the first argument that may be established vis-à-vis EC economic security, is that relative security is possible but absolute security is not (Buzan, 1991, p.235). This is due, firstly, to the interdependent nature of the contemporary international system. To use a dictionary definition of the term, dependence denotes a state of being determined or significantly influenced by external forces. Interdependence simply means mutual dependence. Interdependence in international relations involves the reciprocal effects among countries or among actors in different countries. These effects often result from the flow of money, goods, and so forth. In what is generally considered the formative work on the theory of interdependence[25], Keohane and Nye (1977) challenge the core assumption of realism: that the nation-state is the primary actor in international relations and that military might is always a viable option with which a state can impose its will. They argue instead that since 1945, the continuous growth in the volume and breadth of international exchange has created a complex pattern of interdependence, which has made it increasingly difficult to define the national interest, and has subsequently made inter-state conflict resolution by force, less feasible and attractive. A multiplicity of interests have developed in the international system, both between states and between other international actors, such as multinational corporations. The reality of power is not discounted by interdependence theorists. However, they do (normatively) reject the use of military force by states in order to achieve power in the contemporary international system. Instead they advocate a bargaining process (the nature of which will be discussed in more detail in the third and final stage of this analytical framework), between market forces and the national political interests of states. This trade-off shapes the conventions or regimes governing monetary or commercial exchange, which in turn affects the substance of international economic relations. From these arguments it may be proposed that economic interdependence leads to a matrix of constraints on the formulation and implementation of all forms of policy. This is particularly so for an export-oriented economy. Interdependence implies a high measure of sensitivity to external forces, which in turn results in a high degree of vulnerability for trading units. Therefore, the economic security of the European Community cannot be absolute within an interdependent international system.

A second argument is that, in the words of Buzan:

> capitalism is by definition a competitive system, the whole dynamic of which depends on the interplay of threats, vulnerabilities, and opportunities within the market (1991, p.235).

Thus, it is unlikely that any units within such an environment could ever be meaningfully secure, when competition implies an ever present danger of becoming a loser.

From this premise, we may advance to a general concept of confederal economic security. Security may be equated with the two economic conditions necessary for the very economic survival of the EC and its member states. Knorr and Trager (1977) identified these as access to resources (raw materials and export markets) necessary for economic existence and the ability to adapt towards the most advanced and successful industrial practices elsewhere in the international system (new production and management techniques for instance) in order to compete successfully at the international level and prevent a loss of economic power relative to other states.

At a more specific level, EC economic security may be further subdivided, with a dichotomy of each of the previously mentioned conditions. The identification of these subdivisions is primarily derived from the works of Hager (1975) and Dell (1987). The first set of derivatives comprises the security of raw material imports, and the reduction of trade dependence:

> Growth, stable employment, and price stability can be adversely affected by Western Europe's dependence on both export markets and uncertain sources of supply (Hager, 1975, p.136).

In the first of these, is may be argued that the EC is dependent on raw material producers, often in less developed countries. Stockpiles exist for oil but not for other raw materials on which European countries are considerably more dependent, for example copper rubber, tin, and platinum. The potential risks to security of imports can often be much higher in these materials (Hager, 1975, p.136).

In the second derivative, economic interdependence and the high proportion of the EC's overall gross domestic product (GDP) represented by exports, is a large measure of vulnerability. Changes abroad which affect market access, can have implications for EC domestic welfare and employment.

The second set of derivatives are the maintenance or creation of international competitiveness, and restriction on the import of capital. The importance of international competitiveness for the well-being of an economy and society has already been discussed. Therefore, it is sufficient to say here that international competitiveness is crucial to economic security, not least in so far as it ensures low levels of dependency and thus ensures a higher level of independence of decision in policy-making. With regards to the final derivative, a number of observers argue that the imposition of restrictions on foreign direct investment (FDI) may be necessary for the EC's economic security. In the words of Dell:

> inward investment can become a drug of dependence (1987, p.105).

Dell goes on to argue that FDI restrictions would prevent foreign interests from 'retarding' the growth of indigenous industry in the same sector, and from taking over certain companies which the host government regards as technologically important from either an economic or military point of view.

Therefore, it may be summarised from the literature that EC economic security can be threatened by the creation of a condition of dependence upon another country or region for any one or combination of the following: raw materials, strategic imports, financial investment, export markets, and a failure to be at the forefront in high technology innovation and application.

The primary areas of insecurity for the economies of the EC have - especially during the Euro-pessimist years of the late 1970s and early 1980s - generally been perceived as the interrelated issues of increasing technological dependency and declining international competitiveness. Due to their enabling capabilities, semiconductors became a highly symbolic sector of insecurity for the EC. The details of these perceived insecurities for semiconductor technology will be explored further in chapter six.

4.ii. International state-firm bargaining

Our analysis inevitably confronts us with the question, 'who decides which industries are strategic and which are not?' One can argue that the answer is ultimately determined on a case-by-case investigation of the decision-making process involved in creating policies for individual strategically targeted industries or sectors. However, not even by this labour-intensive method can one reach a fully satisfactory answer - given the amount of implicit agreements and compromises which occur in such processes, and which are never documented. Therefore, the identity, first, of the actors within the strategic targeting process, and second, of the actor(s) which has the greatest input into the process at an EC level, may be conceptualised through the bargaining process framework. This in turn may be applied to individual cases of strategic targeting. The concept of 'bargaining' is taken here as meaning the process whereby 'an agreement or contract establishes what each party will give, receive, or perform in a transaction between them'[26].

As the evidence will show, although often diametrically opposed, and never identical, public policy and corporate strategy can converge at certain times, and in specific circumstances. Peterson supports this conclusion. He cites the Single Market programme as an example of such convergence. He states that it was launched largely because both European governments and industry reached consensus on its desirability (1993, p.8). A significant actor which Peterson omits is the European Commission. In certain cases, such bargaining takes place primarily between firms and the EC institutions - national governments participating via the EC Council of Ministers. How is this consensus reached though? How do public policy and corporate strategy converge? Strange and Stopford (1991) and Tucker (1991) argue that contemporary industry-specific policy is shaped through a process of government-firm bargaining. Thus, in effect, the entire nature of international economic relations has changed fundamentally, as the negotiating power of firms within the international arena, has increased significantly (see chapter one). As Strange notes:

> governments must now bargain not only with other governments, but also with firms and enterprises, while firms now bargain with governments and with one another (1992, p.1).

Hence, not only has the nature of government-industry relations changed, but as Strange and Stopford conclude, the entire nature of international diplomacy has changed as industrial policies and economic management replace conventional military-based foreign policies, as the chief form of inter-state competition (1991, p.1).

This concept of a new diplomacy within international relations will therefore be tested against the empirical evidence for the EC semiconductor sector, to discern what part it plays in competition with global rivals.

4.iii. Strategic trade theory

At an applied level, strategic trade theory is useful in analysing the extra-Communitarian elements of EC policy for semiconductors. It is proposed that elements of strategic trade thinking may be causally linked to strategic targeting, and consequently, to policies for competitive enhancement[27]. Let us therefore outline exactly what is understood by such policy thinking.

The first point to make, which extends from economic security rationale, is that, as Weber and Zysman (1992) have argued, trade is not always an activity concerning mutual gain; sometimes it involves inter-state competition where the stakes involved are the future technological development and economic prosperity of nations. As Tyson argues:

> new developments in trade theory have demonstrated that, under conditions of increasing returns, technological externalities, and imperfect competition, free trade is not necessarily and automatically the best policy (1993, p.3).

This argument is taken up by Paul Krugman, one of the theory's leading proponents, who asserts that the nature of trade has been fundamentally transformed: it has moved from a comparative advantage based system to a much more complicated system, involving numerous previously non-existent elements. This transformation necessitates a rethinking of traditional (liberal) trade policy (1986, p.9). Proceeding from this assumption, strategic trade policy assumes to redesign the structure and enhance the competitive advantage of oligopolistic industries[28] within the international economy. In pursuing this general objective, government is effectively targeting core sectors of the economy. From this identification of its corporate constituency, the model advances to an identification of its general composition and objectives:

promotional policies aimed at specific sectors can permanently alter the competitive balance in those industries and other industries linked to them. When governments provide subsidies or protection to firms competing in oligopolistic markets, the firms make use of those increased resources to pursue different market, pricing, production, and product strategies. Not all firms will effectively use those resources to build an improved and defensible market position, but those that do will have created comparative advantage (Weber and Zysman, 1992, p.182).

Thus, when imperfectly competitive markets exist (with heavy R&D costs, economies of scale, large, technologically advanced firms, etc.), strategic trade theory advocates government intervention in order to assist indigenous firms, at the expense of external competitors (Ostry, 1990, p.58). In addition to this competitive enhancement - or just simple protection, for economic security reasons perhaps - of strategic industries, the rationale for strategic trade policy has two further dimensions. These are, firstly, such policy can result in higher wages and profits, thus increasing the economic welfare of the nation; and secondly, there is often a spill-over effect, whereby benefits from such government supported activities as R&D, are diffused throughout the economy - especially to related and down-stream industries. The assumption is that if other governments do not pursue similar policies, the first government will have created advantage (Borrus et al., 1992, p.26).

From this discussion of strategic trade policy, it is possible to perceive the extent to which new thinking in trade can contribute to a more detailed analysis of strategically targeted government industrial and innovation policies.

4. iv. The selection of appropriate systemic theories

We cannot understand EC policy responses to systemic trade activities through classical realism. Early realist thinkers[29] stress that in conjunction with bargaining, the threat of force underpins all international processes. Obviously the present world order and the state of relations between the EC and its trading partners, combined with the Community's non-military nature, render redundant the notion of it threatening other international actors with military force. Yet, it continues to play an active role in international affairs and processes. Hence, realism cannot be employed to examine EC actions.

Keohane and Nye (1977) argue that the basic realist premises of the primacy of states in international relations, and the centrality of military force to international power, have been superseded by interdependence[30]. Non-governmental actors such as multinational corporations now compete with states for power in the international system; and state power through military might is frequently eclipsed by power through currency strength in international monetary negotiations for instance (Keohane and Nye, 1977). Thus, the emergence of new power relationships with which we are concerned - primarily the bargaining between firms and governmental actors - may be partially attributable to the accelerating pace of interdependence between national economies world-wide. Interdependence theory is however insufficient to conceptualise and analyse this work's problematic. Whilst we subscribe to the ideas that the system, in and of it self, affects the nature and control of power, and that power has been diffused beyond merely the system of states, we do not agree that states are increasingly irrelevant actors within the system, as interdependence theorists might suggest.

Within international relations theory, there is an ongoing battle between neorealism and neoliberalism, as to which explains the contemporary international system most accurately. According to Baldwin, both camps agree that anarchy exists within the international system (1993, p.4). However, the fundamental difference between the two groups concerns the extent of anarchy, and thus the degree of independence which powers experience in decision-making within this anarchical international system. Neorealists argue that states still determine their own policies, based on self interest. This includes decisions concerning whether or not to participate in international alliances. Neoliberals argue that state autonomy is a myth, due to global interdependence (Milner, 1991, p.70; pp.81-2). The neoliberal position may be interpreted as contending that states cannot - as neorealists argue - make decisions based solely on national interest; but that systemic factors impinge on these decisions and restrict a country's ability to negotiate and legislate independently. Thus, from this perspective, the neoliberal argument best fits the reality of international trade and investment in semiconductors. Evidence will be provided in chapter six to substantiate this position.

Some elements of neorealism are of analytical use to the work in hand. Neorealism focuses much more than classical realism on the distribution of power as a determinant of outcomes (Keohane, 1993, p.271). It accepts the existence of other international sources of power beyond that exercised by states through military means. Where neorealism is important to an understanding of EC actions is in the fact that it views states as behaving on the basis of their conceptions of their own interest:

> decision making in ambiguous setting is heavily influenced by the ways in which the actors think about their problem (Keohane, 1993, p.107).

Moreover, Keohane (1993) proposes that these subjective decisions are often made without thought to their implications for and interpretations by other systemic actors. As Conybeare (1987) has shown, trade conflicts sometimes arise from a state's underestimation of the effect which its actions may have on the activities of other trading states. Such is often the case between the EC, the US, and Japan. Furthermore, this idea that states act on conceptions, and not necessarily on fact, supports the notion that policy can be shaped by economic security perceptions. This linkage between policy direction and economic security will be investigated further on in this volume.

Keohane argues that although institutionalist theory became more commonly known as neoliberalism, its basis is moulded as much by realism as by liberalism

(1993, p.272). We contend that the EC has a political institutional legitimacy, a policy agenda, and a bargaining role of its own. Its actions are often constrained by its member states. However, in spheres such as trade, the EC is an international power player in its own right. Leading proponents of neoliberal institutionalism support such an argument (Grieco, 1993a, p.302; Moravcsik, 1993, pp.480-1). Such a position runs counter to the arguments of realism, which devotes little attention to the power of the EC in the international system. In addition, neoliberal institutionalism advances the idea that states seek to maximise their absolute gains, regardless of the gains which this conveys to others (Grieco, 1993b, p.117). Such an attitude would appear to denote EC trade policy, which rarely adopts a zero-sum, win-lose stance. Furthermore, the interdependence section of liberal institutionalism rejects realism's belief that states are the main actors in the international system. They argue instead that systemic power now rests more with actors such as multinational corporations and transgovernmental coalitions (Grieco, 1993b, p.119).

Neoliberalism / liberal institutionalism / neorealism are insufficient theories within which to frame the EC's industrial policy approach. They singularly under-rate the role played by non-state actors within international bargaining, and they fail to account for the impact which the system *per se*, and changes therein, can have on governmental trade and competitive positions.

This leads us to an examination of the utility of other, related models. In purely abstract terms, the model which appears most applicable to an understanding of the various facets of EC industrial policy is that of structural power. This model helps one to conceptualise both the role of the firm in developing this policy, and the impact of extra-Communitarian activities on its direction. The structuralist approach to international relations was developed during the late 1960s and early 1970s from Marxist interpretations of the world order (Frank, 1967; Wallerstein, 1974). The basic premise of this approach is that the proliferation of transnational cultural and economic interactions has led to the development of a global system. The structuralist school refer to this as the world economy (Palan, 1992, p.22). Their objective was, in the view of Wallerstein:

> to describe the world-system at a certain level of abstraction, that of the evolution of structures of the world system (1974, p.8).

The classical Marxist structuralist approach was however weakened by its underestimation of the role which states play within the world system. As Palan (1992) points out, a more balanced approach has since emerged which places the state centrally within any analysis of the international system. These scholars come from a disparate mix of disciplines, and adopt the view that the international system should not be approached as a one-dimensional, monolithic entity, but rather, should be viewed as a system containing numerous interlinked power structures (Braudel, 1979; Strange, 1988).Collectively, Palan describes them as the second structuralists:

40

Whereas the second structuralists agree that the whole is indeed different from the sum of its parts, and so merits distinct theoretical attention; they still believe that the whole needs to be explained in terms of its parts (Palan, 1992, p.25).

We subscribe to the approach of the second structuralist, or neostructuralist, school. Strange (1988) proposes that two types of power are exercised in the international political economy. These are identified as relational power and structural power. She describes relational power as the authority (or power) of a given international actor (always a state, according to the traditional realist approach) to force another actor in the system to do that which they would not do voluntarily. Structural power exists at a different level, being:

> the power to shape and determine the structures of the global political economy within which other states, their political institutions, their economic enterprises and (not least) their scientists and other professional people, have to operate...structural power, in short, confers the power to decide how things shall be done, the power to shape frameworks within which states relate to each other, relate to people, or relate to corporate enterprises (Strange, 1988, pp.24-5).

Strange (1988) proceeds to argue that the structural power approach is of much greater utility when dealing with the international political economy, given its non-distinction between economic power and political power. It is, in fact, a more actor neutral theory (compared with the relational power framework), and thus allows for the consideration of non-state actors in determining the nature and course of international relations. Strange develops her argument further by arguing that a number of separate but interdependent power structures exist within the international system. These may be seen as the four pillars of the international political economy. Strange argues that structural power is the unevenly distributed systemic ability to define the basic structures of these four pillars: security, credit, production, and knowledge (1988, p.15). All other elements of the international political economy (e.g. global issues such as trade or more specific sectoral items such as integrated circuits) are secondary structures, being moulded by the four fundamental power structures.

A final point worth noting is the claim that technology (stemming from the knowledge structure) is of central importance, both in gaining relational power, and in strengthening the other three pillars of systemic power. This will be important when this theory is applied to the empirical evidence, as the technology factor is central to any analysis of EC semiconductor policy. This primacy of technology and the knowledge structure within the contemporary international political economy corresponds to the rise of what Drucker described as the symbol economy (1986, p.781). Drucker describes this as the emergence of a global economy which is driven by flows of invisible assets such as capital and credit (and we might add technology). Such an information-driven economy has become intertwined with the real or tangible economy, i.e. the flow of goods and services

41

(Drucker, 1986, p.782). Thus, invisible assets drive the economy, and technology is the most crucial of invisible assets. The knowledge structure has therefore come to dominate other structures such as finance and production.

Both Strange's emphasis on technology as the catalyst of systemic change, and the changing role of the firm in international relations, concur with this work's interpretation of structural change and its impact on the international political economy. To analyse our dependent variable at an international system level, structural power theory and its associated notion of structural change are the most comprehensive heuristic tools. The (second) structuralist approach seeks to identify how international relationships are shaped by both state actions and systemic developments. The realist state-centric and the first structuralist system-centric approaches are therefore merged. As Palan puts it:

> They seek to identify the underlying configuration of forces which pattern the formal conduct of relationships between states (Palan, 1992, p.27).

This concurs with Drucker's (1989) argument that the society of states is now overlaid by a complex, interdependent, world economy[31]. In real terms, this means that we utilise the theory to conceptualise and analyse how, against the background of the international system, other politico-economic actors affect the nature of EC policy actions (which in turn, have an impact upon other actors within the system). This runs contrary to the more established notion that, as a tool of international relations research, structuralism denotes an interest in non-policy issues (Palan, 1992, p.28). Moreover, the notion of structural change enables us to understand why and how the power of firms has increased relative to governments, and consequently changed the nature of international relations. Strange argues that structural changes in finance, information and communications systems, defence equipment, and production methods, have together played the most important role in redefining the relationship between authority (government) and market (firms). The fundamental catalyst encompassing all of these changes is technology. The (rapidly) changing nature of technology has altered the allocation and exercise of structural power, through its transformative affect on the central pillars of structural power (1991, p.38).

To clarify the determinants of change at a systemic level, it is accepted that the state, the market, and technology, together comprise the three broad vehicles of transformation (Strange, 1991). Each of these three systemic players shapes the nature of the four pillars of structural power. However, the degree of influence is the key factor: government and market influence have, and continue to be, considerable, but the rate of change introduced by technology is, and continues to be, far greater in terms of its scope and depth. In addition, it is important to realise that although technology is the central player in structural change, it is not a tangible, structured entity. Therefore, one must attempt to determine who or what controls both its form and its results. Evidently, such direct control rests, for the most part (i.e. excluding government/military R&D laboratories), with corporate enterprises. From this one may concur that power or authority within the international system has been lost to the market, and thus, the role and strength of firms within the state-firm bargaining process, is significantly enhanced.

Therefore, emphasising the pivotal role of technology in structural change, strengthens this study's concern with the manner in which both firms and governments (or the EC) deal with technological development and application (through corporate technology strategy, government technology policy, and joint government-industry technology programmes). Also, it underlines the importance of semiconductors - as a (if not the) transformative technology - within the process of structural change. Technological change has a considerable impact on the nature of government power vis-à-vis other governments and with respects to firms, and consequently, shapes policy options and choices.

Thus, an analysis of the dependent variable through the structuralist view of the international system, will furnish a third and final level of analysis within the overall eclectic theoretical framework.

5 The theoretical agenda

To conclude, our theoretical agenda has three primary doctrines. These are, first, at the EC institutional level of analysis, the innovation policy approach; second, at the level of the firm, strategic alliance theory; and third, at the international system perspective, structural power theory. Innovation policy theory is necessary to understand EC choices; strategic alliance theory is the key to grasping firm choices; and structural power theory is essential to an understanding of the constraints imposed on both by the international system.

At each of these levels there exist several secondary doctrines, as well as conceptual frameworks. These are intended to complement the main heuristic tools, and facilitate a comprehensive analysis and explanation of EC policy for semiconductors. They include the Pentagonal Diplomacy model of policy bargaining and the Porter Diamond model of national competitive advantage (level 1); corporate technology strategy and the knowledge networking concept (level 2); and economic security and strategic trade theory (level 3).

Given this plethora of conceptual and analytical tools, it is important to ensure that one is applied throughout. This establishes a theoretical linkage between chapters, thus ensuring that the study follows a logical path of progression. It also allows us to view the work in its entirety, and extract a number of arguments deriving from the overall research findings. We advance the structural power doctrine as this research working theory.

Notes

1   Other approaches, such as government-industry relations, are referred to periodically, but are not deemed central to our theoretical framework. The reasoning for this selectivity will become evident as the work unfolds.

2   Dunning cites the work by Rob Van Tulder and Gerd Junne, *European Multinationals in Core Technologies*, as a perfect example of this interdisciplinary approach.

3   The inclusion of 'another level of governance and interaction (the European Commission)' into the Stopford and Strange model, was propounded by Maria L. Green in her paper, *The Politics of Big Business in the Single Market Program*, presented for the ECSA Third Biennial Conference, Washington DC, May, 1993. Ms. Green argued that such an inclusion was necessary in applying the triangular diplomacy framework to the Single Market programme. Her argument is in line with that which this author had been developing since 1991. She fails to get into the issue in depth however, and to expand the notion to policy bargaining realms beyond the Single Market programme.

4   European industry associations and European regional governments also feature in this EC bargaining process. For the purposes of this study, we include European industry associations within the firm perspective, given that such associations are seldom more than the sum of their parts. European regional governments can often conduct semi-autonomous bargains with firms and with the European Commission. However, in the creation and control of EC policy for the semiconductor industry, we will argue that the regions have little or no influence. They are therefore incorporated under the state actor side of the bargaining process.

5   John Dunning in Eden & Potter, op.cit., 1993, chapter 4.

6   The information technology sector is usually defined as being composed of electronics, telecommunications, computers, robotics, and the associated hardware and software to create the networks and systems which link them all together (Margaret Sharp in Juliet Lodge (ed.) *The European Community and the Challenge of the Future,* 1989, p202).

7   Krugman emphasises inter-industry linkage externalities and technology spill-overs as two other significant criteria in any identification of a strategic sector.

8   Commission of the European Communities, *Industrial Policy In An Open And Competitive Environment*, Brussels, 16 November 1990.

9   The European Council is a (usually) biannual meeting of the fifteen European Commmunity member countries heads of government (and head of state, in the case of France).

10 The term was first used in OECD, *Innovation Policy Trends and Perspectives,* Paris, 1982.

11 The main function of EC competition policy is antitrust. For further details see for example Howell et al., *Conflict Among Nations*, 1992, pp.412-9.

12   For a legalistic description of these policy measures, see in particular Howell et al., *Conflict Among Nations*, 1992, pp.412-19. Also, a detailed analysis of anti-dumping can be found in Ostry *op.cit.* 1990, pp.39-52.

13   This definition of competitiveness is taken from Cohen and Zysman (1987) and is based on a definition introduced in a report issued by a commission established by president Reagan in 1983 to study US competitiveness problems.

14   The Diamond model was created by Porter, 1990, as a means of conceptualising the interrelated components which together comprise a nation's competitive advantage.

15   This work acknowledges the important causal linkage between systemic changes and governmental policy and analyses this relationship in chapter six of the study.

16   In chapter four of this book, we analyse and explain the effect which differing intra-governmental interests and ideologies have on the nature and direction of EC policy.

17   This was of course never Porter's purpose.

18   We acknowledge that other forms of collaboration occur, beyond those discussed in this study. For instance, non-state transnational collaboration can occur between two (or more) cartels. In addition, transnational corporations can co-operate with other international organisations such as the IMF, the UN, or OPEC. Also, global firms can form alliances or co-operative agreements with non-state transnational authorities such as shipping conferences or the International Air Transport Association.

19   Andrews definition of corporate strategy is taken from J.I. Moore, 1992, p.9.

20   Porter identifies four forms of corporate strategy which business has utilised. He lists these as portfolio management, restructuring, transferring skills, and sharing activities. For further details see *Competitive Strategy*, 1980.

21   Ansoff and Stewart (1967), as discussed in Moore, 1992.

22   For example, the primary stated objective of JESSI is 'to advance Europe's position in the information technology industry's large and crucial submicron silicon sector by improving co-operation between the various European firms and research institutes on every level, from basic research to applications' (S. Radelaar, Vice Chairman of the JESSI Board, 1992).
      On the other hand, SEMATECH's central objective has been stated as, 'the development of integrated manufacturing systems using the most recent technologies, and to test them in an environment similar to the factory environment in which they will be applied', (quoted in Jean Claude Derian, *America's Struggle For Leadership In High Technology,* 1990, p.233).

23   Hergert & Morris, in Lorange and Roos (1992), ibid., pp.99-110.

24   Marti and Smiley, cited in Mytelka (1991), p.12, and Zajac cited in Lorange and Roos, ibid., p.14.

25   Robert O. Keohane and Joseph S. Nye, *Power and Interdependence: World Politics in Transition,* 1977.

26   *Collins English Dictionary*, London, 1979.

27   As Flamm (1991) points out, it is also possible to have a strategic trade policy for a non-strategic sector; or indeed, a nonstrategic policy in a strategic sector. That is to say, strategic trade policy can have a meaning other than that employed in this work. It may refer to government policy designed to induce change in the behaviour of a particular group of firms, or other governments. Most often this notion of strategic policy is employed to differentially affect the behaviour of 'domestic' and 'foreign' firms (1991, p.2). Thus, a government strategic policy may exist for bottled mineral water for instance, in an attempt to create a bottled mineral water cartel dominated by domestic producers. Conversely, it may develop for memory chip producers, but in the form of a tax credit for example.

28   An oligopolistic industry can be defined as an industry composed of a small number of firms, all of whom are able to exert a relative amount of power over their joint market .

29   E.H. Carr, as cited in Robert O. Keohane, 'Institutional Theory and the Realist Challenge after the Cold War', in David A. Baldwin (ed.), *Neorealism and Neoliberalism: the contemporary debate,* New York, 1993, p.270.

30   Keohane & Nye (1977) *Power and Interdependence*, critiqued in Crane and Amawi (1991), *The Theoretical Evolution of International Political Economy,* p.108.

31   Peter Drucker (1989), cited in Susan Strange (1994), 'Wake Up, Krasner! The World *Has* Changed', in *Review of International Political Economy,* p.212.

3 Industry and government: the early years

No army can withstand the strength of an idea whose time has come.

Victor Hugo

The main intention of this chapter is to place this work's study in a historical context. By providing *un peu d'histoire,* one may better comprehend the issues which are critically analysed within the following chapters. Thus, there are three primary objectives herein. First, to sketch the technological nature of semiconductor components. Second, to outline the development of the international semiconductor industry. Third, to assess what happened in terms of strategy and public policy for this industrial sector before the era of Euro-collaboration in the 1980s and 1990s, and how it affected corporate competitiveness. This chapter has one further research objective. It is to trace the genesis of state-firm relations for semiconductor production. The level of public policy priority attached to the industry in its nascent period will be assessed, and the reasons for this government attention will be discussed. Also, we attempt herein to determine the relative power positions of states and firms in policy bargaining during the industry's early years.

The information revolution began within the unassuming environs of Murray Hill, New Jersey, on 23 December, 1947. On that day, scientists working at Bell Laboratories[1] invented the transistor. This device used germanium semiconductor material to amplify or switch an electrical signal. It was the prototype of a new and more advanced form of electronics. Although the US federal government was, at this time, sponsoring a large research programme into the fundamental properties of germanium and silicon, the breakthrough actually came in a civilian funded laboratory. The transistor's military value was recognised immediately (components miniaturisation, more complex functions, etc.), and the US military subsequently funded - through both direct grants and indirect government procurement - much of the semiconductor R&D which occurred during the 1950s (Grunwald and Flamm, 1985, p.40). However, the problem of producing transistors at competitive prices was to prevent the rapid development and diffusion of the transistor for more than a decade after the initial discovery.

1 The development of semiconductor technology

Semiconductors are active electronic components which derive their technological importance from the fact that they can be used as either conductors or insulators. Their two basic elements are diodes and transistors. Diodes are very basic semiconductor devices, comprising forward and reverse biases and having an asymmetric flow. A transistor is a three terminal device which consists of the emitter, the base, and the collector (Grunwald and Flamm, 1985, p.13). Early semiconductors were primarily created from the element germanium. However, Texas Instruments introduction of silicon transistors in 1954 meant that silicon came to dominate, primarily due to its lower cost, ability to operate at higher temperatures, and the fact that it allowed semiconductors to be batch processed. Furthermore, crystalline wafers of silicon are the purest and most perfect solid material known to exist. Semiconductor product groups are divided into three groups: discrete devices (such as transistors), opto-electronics, and integrated circuit devices. This last group comprises microprocessors, microcomputers, and both standard and customised memory chips (Malerba, 1985, p.13). The most revolutionary of these three groups has undoubtedly been integrated circuits. Their market introduction initiated massive technological advances in information technology telecommunications, military hardware, production processes, aerospace, and in most other areas of business, government, and the wider society. The integrated circuit has had a dynamic impact on the national industrial base, international relations, and human society (Mackintosh, 1986, p.3). Thus, it is with this latter group of semiconductor devices that this work is primarily concerned. Hence, the term semiconductor will be utilised exclusively to mean integrated circuits throughout this book.

The process by which integrated circuits are created is well described by Mackintosh. By subjecting a silicon wafer to a very precise series of chemical physical processes, a complete electronic circuit of great complexity can be fabricated within an area as small as ¼ square centimetre. This can be reproduced all across the wafer, from wafer to wafer within a production batch of wafers, and from batch to batch. Thus, very large numbers of identical, complex circuits can be manufactured, and at a very low cost per circuit. These circuits each carry their own integral pattern of electrical connections (Mackintosh, 1986, p.3). These minute silicon circuits are more popularly known as 'microchips'. This more common term (or the shorter word 'chips') is generally used in this work when discussing integrated circuits. Memories, microprocessors, and microcomputers are all forms of digital integrated circuits, with varying capabilities and levels of complexity[2]. The density of integrated circuits increased from ten in the early 1960s, to more than 100,000 in the 1980s.

1.i. Government as patron

The first significant advancement in the new technology did not come until 1954. In that year, Texas Instruments announced that they had created the silicon transistor. Its ability to withstand much higher temperatures than germanium, further increased the interests of the Pentagon in semiconductor technology. An illustration of this was the fact that in the following year, 1955, the US government provided the semiconductor industry with $3.2 million for R&D purposes. In addition, defence requirements accounted for about one-third of total semiconductor sales during the mid-1950s (Braun and MacDonald, 1982, p.71). Thus, we see that in the US, the nascent semiconductor industry received considerable government attention, due to the application possibilities which it possessed for military systems.

This defence motivated federal government funding was of great significance in the early years of the semiconductor industry. As Maddock argues, the military economy can play a significant role in boosting technological progress (1990, p.119). The peacetime defence build-up broadly coincided with the first phase in the evolution of semiconductor technology. The renowned 1950 US National Security Council document outlining America's Cold War defence and foreign policy (NSC-68), signalled the beginning of the country's defence build-up. The US government believed that the threat which they perceived from the Soviet Union could only be contained by a very large increase in military spending (Maddock, 1990, pp.118-9). 1951 witnessed the beginning of just such a build-up. US defence expenditure for this year totalled $33.3 billion. This figure, compared with $14.5 billion for the previous year, signified an increase of 230 per cent (Kennedy, 1987, p.384). In 1952, the total increased to $47.8 billion. These figures were of course distorted due to the fact that the US was at war in 1951. Military demands caused by the Korean War naturally artificially inflated defence expenditure. However, the cessation of hostilities on the Korean Peninsula brought with it little reduction in US defence expenditure. This was in spite of President Eisenhower's efforts to reduce the influence of the military-industrial complex in American society. Between 1952 and 1960, the American government continued to spend an average of $45 billion per annum on defence. By comparison, the Soviet Union fell behind the US during this period in their total outlay on defence. From outspending the Americans in 1950 ($15.5 billion), the Soviets total defence expenditure lagged their Cold War rival for the remainder of the decade, averaging $28 billion per annum[3]. By the beginning of Eisenhower's second term of office, US military expenditure accounted for 44.9 per cent of the world total, versus 20.2 per cent for the Soviet Union. By comparison, the combined expenditure of NATO Europe accounted for only 19.2 per cent of global defence spending (Leontief and Duchin, 1983, p.6). These figures illustrate the disparity which existed between Europe and the US in the levels of corporate revenue generated by defence needs. More specifically, firms in fledging dual-use technology industries, such as semiconductors, received defence contracts in the US far in excess of those generated for their European rivals. This American government industry incubator served to give young US companies a competitive head-start vis-à-vis their European counterparts.

The Eisenhower administration's recognition of semiconductor technology's military potential, led to considerable government patronage for the fledgling industry. For instance, in 1956, the US Defence Department farmed out transistor production contracts worth $40 million to twelve semiconductor producers (Borrus, 1988, p.66). The government paid for engineering design and development costs, whilst the firms covered the costs of plant and facilities. In total, the semiconductor industry received at least $66 million for R&D and production from the US government between 1955 and 1961. This figure excludes integrated circuit R&D, and does not take account of indirect subsidies through subcontracting via weapons systems prime contractors. A Defence Department source estimated that government funds accounted for as much as one-quarter of total semiconductor industry R&D outlay, by the late 1950s[4].

The inherent ability of semiconductors to revolutionise computer technology, lay at the core of the government's projections for semiconductors military potential. As Flamm argues:

> The U.S. military invested heavy in both technologies, and the link between computers and semiconductors continues to be central to the question of why governments pay so much attention to the semiconductor industry (1990, p.227).

In addition, the military perceived the utility of semiconductor technology for advanced missile systems. Transistors (and later, microchips) facilitated weapons component miniaturisation, as well as the fact that silicon proved a more heat resistant and dependable material for weapons systems that previously used materials such as germanium. As Braun and MacDonald point out, this latter development of silicon transistors (by Texas Instruments in 1954) was of significant interest to the military, and helps explain their close relationship with the industry from the mid-1950s until the mid-1960s (1982, p.55).

This general emphasis on defence technology grew directly out of the Cold War tensions of the 1950s. Thus, the early development of the semiconductor industry was fostered by Cold War rivalries, and the US endeavours to maintain technological supremacy over the Soviet Union. Consequently, companies such as IBM and Fairchild were aided enormously in their nascent periods by no-downside-risk government contracts to supply electronic components for aircraft, missiles, and so forth. Initial risk-free markets were therefore provided for industries whose commercial viability was not immediately evident. This policy has been termed 'the incubator factor'. (Maddock, 1990, p.120). As Maddock points out, nowhere was this policy more evident than for integrated circuits. Initially, their production was too expensive for commercial exploitation. The US government therefore provided a military market for all integrated circuits produced, until production costs were reduced sufficiently to encourage private sector demand.

> Demand is sustained and research stimulated until eventually costs are reduced to levels where they become commercially viable to private corporations (Maddock, 1990, p.120).

Through this policy, the government created a potential semiconductor production capacity of more than ten million units by the late 1950s[5]. On that secure basis, such companies were able to develop highly competitive after-sales support and service that enabled them to capture a civilian as well as a military market.

Furthermore, Cold War rivalry helped nurture the culture of venture capitalism in the US electronics industry. A realisation emerged in the early 1950s that some government subsidy for R&D was not going to be enough to galvanise the private sector, and to beat the Soviets in military technology. The US government offered the prize of very profitable cost-plus contracts to those who offered a good price. One did not even have to be an established firm. This government policy derived from practices initiated during World War Two. During that period, the US government was conscious of the need to ensure equity in procurement between small and large enterprises, and to prevent large firms emerging after the war with considerably enhanced market positions, at the expense of their smaller rivals. This was particularly pertinent given that antitrust activity was suspended during wartime (Vatter, 1985, p.58). Consequently, in 1942 the US Congress established the Smaller War Plants Corporation, aimed at lending to small companies and aiding them in the battle for procurement contracts (Vatter, 1985, p.59). This war-generated government policy fostered American venture capitalism for the electronics industry. This contrasted starkly with the situation in Europe, where venture capitalism received no encouragement or government incentive. This is because European arms production had always been mainly either state-owned and run, or contracted out to old, established firms (such as Krupps and Armstrong Siddely) as a matter of course. What the Europeans did not realise was that American policy gave US firms a significant head-start technologically. This situation would seriously hinder the European industry's ability to compete from the early 1960s on, as the market focus shifted from defence to commercial end-users.

Later Japanese success in electronics may also be linked to the influence of international politics on industry and the market. With no military role, and practically no military budget, Japanese firms had no possibility to grow through dependence on protected military markets at home. Therefore, export for civil use, or as suppliers to original equipment manufacturers (OEMs) in the US or Europe, was their only option. Although also lacking a significant domestic military market, German firms did not experience the same growth rates as their Japanese competitors. In accounting for this, emphasis may be place upon the different market orientations of German and Japanese-based firms: Japanese firms globalised their sales virtually upon entering the market, whereas, until the 1980s, German companies generally focused upon their domestic and neighbouring markets.

New methods of production were developed in the late-1950s to produce devices which would increase the presence of semiconductors in the market. The result was market domination, when, in 1959, the first integrated circuit was developed by Texas Instruments. This innovation effectively marked the beginning of a decisive new phase in semiconductor technology. It highlighted the fact that the development of semiconductor devices had at this stage moved from a laboratory project to an industrial process. In the words of Braun and MacDonald:

> Unlike the transistor, the integrated circuit was a commercial innovation developed by scientists working in a technological industry (1982, p.88).

2 The commercial development of the semiconductor industry

As Cohen and Zysman (1987) have illustrated, the leading producers of electron tubes (the technology superseded by the transistor), such as RCA and General Electric, did not adapt successfully to the new semiconductor technology during the 1950s. Instead, new firms such as Texas Instruments and Fairchild were established, and rapidly became the market leaders. Later technological developments within the industry allowed even newer companies such as Intel and National Semiconductor, to enter the market. A further series of developments brought in Japanese firms such as NEC, Hitachi, and Matsushita (Cohen and Zysman, 1987, p.92). This trend is illustrative of the dynamic character and volatile development of the semiconductor industry. The ability to remain at the forefront in technological developments is critical to a firm's position. This is true for all types of firms. Pugel, Kimura, and Hawkins (1981) have identified three types of semiconductor firms. (1) Large merchant firms: these companies are aggressively market oriented in the production of semiconductors, e.g. Texas Instruments, Intel, Motorola; (2) smaller merchant firms: these are usually seeking a larger market share, e.g. Cypress Semiconductor; (3) electronic systems manufacturers: these are original equipment manufacturing firms which have integrated backwards to produce semiconductors. Such production is largely or entirely captive, i.e. it is oriented almost exclusively for in-house use, for instance, AT&T, IBM.

The small group of large established merchant firms which dominated the American electronics industry of the early and mid-1950s, were, by the end of the decade, beginning to be displaced by dozens of small, dynamic companies, which emerged as a consequence of the new technology. The top five companies immediately prior to the development of the microprocessor (by Intel) in the early 1970s were, IBM, Texas Instruments, Motorola, Western Electric, and Fairchild; none of which had been major commercial producers during the 1950s. As fig. 3.1 indicates, this ranking had changed somewhat again by the mid-1970s[6]. This leadership change-over resulted from several factors. First, the government-encouraged culture of venture capitalism made it easier for small firms in America to challenge large, established rivals. As already touched upon, this World War Two inspired, Cold War nurtured culture, meant that military contracts were open to competition between all firms, regardless of size or age. Given that such contracts comprised almost the entire demand source for

52

	Valves	Transistors (1955)	SCs[a] (1960)	SCs (1965)	ICs[b] (1975)	ICs (1979)
RCA	1	7	5	6	8	9
Sylvania	2	4	10	-	-	-
GE	3	6	4	5	-	-
Raytheon	4	-	-	10	-	-
Westinghouse	-	5	8	-	-	-
Amperex	6	-	-	-	-	-
National Video	7	-	-	-	-	-
Ranland	8	-	-	-	-	-
Eimac	9	-	-	-	-	-
Landsdale Tube	10	-	-	-	-	-
Hughes	-	1	9	-	-	-
Transitron	-	2	2	9	-	-
Philco	3	3	8	-	-	-
Texas Instruments	-	5	1	1	1	1
Motorola	-	9	6	2	5	3
Clevite	-	10	7	-	-	-
Fairchild	-	-	8	3	2	5
General Instrument	-	-	4	7	10	
Sprague	-	-	-	7	-	-
National Semiconductor	-	-	-	-	3	2
Intel	-	-	-	-	4	4
Rockwell	-	-	-	-	6	-
Signetics	-	-	-	-	9	6
American Microsystems	-	-	-	-	10	-
Mostek	-	-	-	-	-	7
American Micro Devices	-	-	-	-	-	8

Figure 3.1 Leading US merchant manufacturers ranked by share of world market

Source: I.M. Mackintosh, 'Large-scale integration: intercontinental aspects', *IEEE Spectrum*, vol.15 no.6, June 1976, p.54; and Dataquest, 29 February 1980, cited in Ernest Braun and Stuart MacDonald, *Revolution in Miniature*, 1982, Cambridge University Press, p.123. Reproduced with the kind permission of the Institute of Electrical and Electronic Engineers Inc., New York, © 19xx IEEE, and Cambridge University Press.

a Semiconductors
b Integrated circuits

semiconductors during their nascent phase, new American firms stood a better chance of gaining a foothold in their domestic market than did their European contemporaries.

Second, a more mobile employment structure in the US meant that established firms which failed to rapidly develop or commercialise new developments in technology, risked losing their technical staff to more adventurous, fast moving start-ups (Flamm, 1990, p.231). Frequently, such engineers began their own companies, building upon the knowledge they had accrued at one of the larger corporations. As Dosi contends, such start-up companies quickly diffuse new innovations, and take research risks which precipitate rapid, as opposed to incremental, change (1981, p.183). If they survive, these companies pose real market threats to slow moving, risk averse older firms. Most of the industry's leaders by the early 1970s emerged in this manner, Fairchild and Intel being just two examples. Europe lacked this tradition of human capital mobility. Consequently, European countries also lacked the vibrant start-up culture endemic in the US, and vital in a fast moving industry such as semiconductor components. Between 1961 and 1965, the number of companies producing integrated circuits rose from two to more than thirty. By 1972, there were one hundred and twenty firms world-wide producing semiconductors (Braun and MacDonald, 1982, p.122). A series of mergers and take-overs followed this period however, and the number of producers had declined by about 20 per cent within a decade. The second half of the 1970s also saw the demise of the American nature of the international semiconductor industry, as US dominance was significantly challenged by Japanese producers.

The 1960s was a decade of steady development and market expansion. This was again helped by massive government funding, due to the use of integrated circuits in both the Minuteman ICBM and the Apollo space programme (Grunwald and Flamm, 1985, p.40). Commercial use began to expand rapidly from the mid-1960s however, and the military market decreased from a high point of 48 per cent in the early 1960s, to only 10 per cent of total microchip sales by the early 1980s (Grunwald and Flamm, 1985, p.43). As prices dropped (from $50 per chip in the mid-1960s, to $0.005 by the end of the 1970s) and innovations increased, semiconductors became an increasingly important factor in the development of the computer industry. Cheaper and more advanced microchips meant cheaper and better computers, and consequently, a growing private demand for computer equipment. Semiconductor usage in computers tripled between 1963 and 1972. Microchips also established strong links with the telecommunications industry at this time; increasing the number of chips in various types of telecommunications equipment by up to seven times. It is argued that it is this important linkage with the computer and telecommunications industries, which led to the tough international competition that epitomised the semiconductor industry from the mid-1970s on (Grunwald and Flamm, 1985). The introduction of the microprocessor in 1971, was a decisive advance in microchip technology and application. The most important feature of the microprocessor was the ability of its on-chip memory to be programmed by software, after complete manufacture, to carry out a variety of different logical operations. It has been argued by Johnson that the mid-1970s was a significant turning-point in the semiconductor industry. The rate of major innovation which the industry experienced during the 1950s and 1960s, began to slow. Instead, smaller, more constant changes in chip design came to characterise a more mature industry (1984, p.151). These more incremental changes in chip design led to a diverse segmentation of the market. This was also largely due to a growing number of chip suppliers and users. A 1981 UNIDO study[7] identified five types of semiconductor devices on the market at this stage. The first were standard devices, which were usually technically indifferent to their final use; the second type were exclusive devices, which were indifferent to their final use but were supplied by a firm which possessed a technological monopoly. Thirdly, they identified specific devices as mass-produced for a pre-determined market. Customised devices were, as the name suggests, produced for a particular client. Finally, microprocessors were identified as circuits that can be mass-produced and used for many purposes. Furthermore, with the advent of very large scale integration in the late 1970s, the number of components per integrated circuit increased to more than 16,000. This development enabled the introduction of a number of some of the new chip types, particularly customised chips. Thus, by the 1980s, the semiconductor industry was of a dual nature. It possessed characteristics of both a 'mature, stable industry, and a young, innovative industry, at the same time' (Johnson, 1984, p.152). This division was primarily due to the fact that technological advances such as the development of Random Access Memories (RAMs) was being conducted by large, stable firms, whilst research into areas such as custom design technology was being carried out mainly by small, more adventurous companies. At least this was true for the US-based semiconductor industry. For structural and business cultural reasons, which will be touched on later, the division of labour within the European industry was not so clear.

3 The loss of European competitiveness in semiconductor production

3.i. Corporate strategy and industry structure reasons

During the period when the semiconductor industry was driven by transistor technology (1947-59), the native European semiconductor industry maintained relative competitiveness:

> During the 1940s and 1950s, European firms remained at this [technological] frontier and were internationally competitive (Malerba, 1985, p.3).

In fact, by the end of the 1950s, European markets were largely self-sufficient (Malerba, 1985, p.69). Philips and Siemens were particularly successful. During the 1950s, these two companies led the combined western European market in terms of market share and patents held (Malerba, 1985, pp.65-6). It is important to note however, that this relative competitiveness was restricted to European markets. The firms in question possessed no market presence outside of their home region.

The introduction of the integrated circuit in 1959, fundamentally altered the relative competitiveness of the European semiconductor producers. The enormous commercial (and military) utility of the integrated circuit semiconductor over the transistor semiconductor, completely transformed the technological basis of the international semiconductor industry. Those firms which did not rapidly adopt this new technology would be at critical - if not fatal - competitive disadvantage within their domestic markets, and would effectively stand no chance of establishing a market position within other countries. So it was with the European semiconductor producers. *En masse*, they missed the shift in the market (Flamm, 1990, p.232). Granted, the consumption of integrated circuits was considerably smaller, and their diffusion was much slower in Europe than in the US. A much smaller defence market for microchips in Europe was in part the reason for this disparity in consumption and diffusion. Nevertheless, the potential scope and scale of integrated circuit utility was evident almost from its inception. In spite of this, leading European firms such as Philips and Siemens, failed to rapidly adopt the new technology. Consequently, when the European integrated circuit market began to grow in the late 1960s, the main European semiconductor producers were poorly placed to take advantage of this expansion. American producers stepped in and quickly established their dominance within the European integrated circuit market. The European semiconductor manufacturers initial inability to both control their domestic markets and to firmly establish themselves within the world market, may be primarily attributable to their erroneous decision to focus on transistor technology for too long a period. Hence, European producers lost the opportunity to compete strongly with US competitors from the early stages of marketable electronic semiconductor devices.

Why did European semiconductor producers continue to lose market share, even after they had adopted integrated circuit technology? One of the core reasons was the failure of European firms to globalise. Unlike their American and subsequently, Japanese, competitors, European firms failed to realise that the nature of the industry necessitated internationalising their operations. Instead, they continued to concentrate their activities on obtaining greater shares of their respective domestic and neighbouring European markets. Furthermore, as Mytelka (1994) points out, a number of significant changes occurred within the wider information technology industrial sphere during the 1970s, to which European information technology producers did not (or could not) suitably adapt. Of prime importance were the interrelated issues of increased barriers of entry, escalating R&D costs, shortening product life cycles, and access to capital. That is to say, the dramatic increase in the costs associated with both starting-up a semiconductor fabrication facility, and in not only developing new generations of microchips, but developing them rapidly or risk obsolescence, necessitated a fertile venture capital culture. Access to capital for investment in R&D, microchip fabrication (fab) facilities, and so forth, was difficult in Europe though, and this fact became a serious hindrance and a disincentive within an industry which was attempting a catch-up strategy.

A further significant factor in Europe's relative lack of competitiveness may be attributable to the conservative structure of the European electronic industry. Unlike their American or Japanese counterparts, the European industry did not experience the shake-ups caused by regular challenges to the established order from home-grown market entrants. Dosi places particular emphasis on this as a reason for the US early lead over Europe in semiconductor development, production, and sales. He centres his argument on the vibrant start-up culture which has traditionally existed in America. Thus, once a semiconductor technology was developed, small start-ups proliferated (often founded by a member of the team which developed the new technology), and facilitated the rapid commercial exploitation and diffusion of the new technology. The number of these small start-ups diminished as the industry grew and matured, and as entry barriers rose steeply (Dosi, 1983, p.216). This lack of fertile start-up culture in Europe left slow moving older companies dominating the indigenous electronics industry. It is worth emphasising that American and European public policy differed substantively in their respective methods of fostering domestic semiconductor industry start-up enterprises. These different approaches may be likened to a horse-race promoter's efforts to stage a race. In order to attract a competitive field of jockeys, he discerns two courses of action. The first is to offer substantial prize money to the winning jockey; the second, is to offer to pay a portion of the winning jockey's wages. As an incentive to compete vigorously and strive to win, the former offer is much more likely to work. As we have seen, this was the course chosen by the US Government, both in securing high levels of venture capital for its semiconductor industry and in promoting a vibrant start-up culture therein. Conversely, the latter option was chosen by all the governments of those western European countries possessing native semiconductor producers. History has proven that the American policy approach helped to nurture a stronger, more diverse, and more independent industry than that fostered in Europe. In addition, direct competition was often timid. These firms rarely competed vigorously with each other for respective domestic market share. This is an important factor because, as Porter (1990) and Stopford (1993) have both argued (and as countries such as Japan have illustrated), domestic (or intra-EC) rivalry is a crucial factor in achieving national competitiveness in a given industry.

In addition to all of the above factors, as the competitiveness of European semiconductor producers declined in the 1960s and 1970s, governmental protectors resorted to traditionalist national and Community protectionist measures such as high tariff barriers on chip imports, and rigorous local content rules on information technology equipment:

Far from keeping the wolves at bay, [these policies] actually worsened the situation of Europe's semiconductor manufacturers by encouraging US and Japanese companies to leap tariff walls and increase their investment in Europe (Hobday, 1992, p.281).

Consequently, many fifth column production plants emerged, as US and Japanese firms began to increasingly supply the European semiconductor market from microchip fabrication facilities within Europe. Competition merely intensified for indigenous manufacturers.

A further reason for European firms competitive problems was that they saw their market as only national. Yet the number of existing or potential consumers for Philips in the Netherlands, or even for Siemens in West Germany, simply could not compare with that available to a company like Texas Instruments in the US. A common argument is that European firms failure to establish early competitive positions within world semiconductor production, was due to the lack of a large home market such as that enjoyed by American firms. As Hobday (1992) points out though, small countries such as Korea and Taiwan have since established competitiveness in semiconductor production, despite the small size of their respective domestic markets. The key factor is the rapid establishment of an export market. A strategy focus on exports was something European firms failed to implement during the 1960s and 1970s - unlike US companies. By contrast, American microchip producers during this period adopted an aggressive marketing strategy and a corporate culture which was innovative and not averse to risk-taking. Unlike their European counterparts, they invested quickly and heavily in new technologies. Also, they entered European markets early, and rapidly established production facilities.

From an early stage, European firms chose to be followers rather than leaders in semiconductor technology. They followed strategies of technological imitation rather than innovation, with the result that - in an industry where time is of the essence - they experienced three to four year time lags in commercial production, compared with American companies. This was a crucial miscalculation on the part of the European managers, and one which both the later national champion projects and the European collaborative programmes, attempted to redress (Dosi, 1983, p.217). By the end of the 1960s, European semiconductor producers had lost their dominant domestic market positions. From a state of self-sufficiency at the decade's outset, Europe moved to a position wherein its native firms controlled less than 60 per cent of the combined market[8]. This per centage continued to decline steadily in the subsequent decades, falling to just over 44 per cent by the mid-1970s, and under 40 per cent by that decade's close (Malerba, 1985, p.160).

3.ii. Individual firm strategy

Many British electronics firms expressed initial interest in microelectronic component development, but failed to follow-through with significant investment. GEC made many, usually short term, attempts at semiconductor development, but failed to achieve competitiveness. This was in spite of receiving generous government support with R&D. Other chip makers during this period, such as Plessey, Matra, and Ferranti, had tailored their production to niche markets. Their niche tended to be largely application specific chips for the capital goods sector and the supply of customised chips for military equipment (Charles, 1994). The commercial spin-off from this kind of product specialisation was minimum. Thus, these firms were poorly placed to compete when defence requirements were reduced and they were belatedly forced to seek more of their sales revenue on the commercial market.

By their own estimates, Siemens were ten years behind their American competitors in semiconductor technology by the end of the 1960s (Erker, 1994, p.15). This was at least partly attributable to the company's conservative corporate culture, and tendency to go with tried and tested products and processes, rather than with risky new innovations. This approach simply did not work for a technologically dynamic industry like semiconductors. Also, for both Siemens and Philips, there was a tendency not to let go of the old transistor technology. This was due simply to the fact that both companies had achieved very competitive and profitable positions within the germanium diode and transistor markets, right up until the early 1960s (Erker, 1994, p.25). Thus, Siemens and Philips both stayed with and attempted to further develop old technologies which had served them so well in the recent past. They soon found out that such technology allegiance was not rewarded within the international semiconductor industry.

By the late 1960s, Siemens, Philips, Thomson-CSF, and AEG-Telefunken were all captive-merchant producers, i.e. they produced mainly for user divisions within their own corporations. For instance, Philips Semiconductors produced a majority of their chips for consumption by other business units of Philips, such as consumer electronics (Hobday, 1992, p.281). This proved a major competitive hindrance for these firms. When chip technology changed in the early 1970s, and American firms moved into Large Scale Integrated (LSI) devices, European semiconductor manufacturers failed to do so (Van Tulder and Junne, 1988, p.32). This was partly because their in-house users still required the older devices, and had not yet adapted their manufacturing processes and product lines to the new technology. Thus, the European chip producers fell behind technologically and competitively.

In terms of industry structure, it is important to note the structural change which occurred in the international semiconductor industry during the 1970s. In short, the industry went from being a relatively large grouping of medium sized enterprises during the 1960s and early 1970s; to a small group of large, vertically integrated companies by the end of the 1970s (Van Tulder and Junne, 1988, p.33). This resulted from a vigorous acquisition strategy undertaken by the larger firms during the 1970s. The effects of this were also felt in Europe, where some of the largest producers were primarily following this strategy. Siemens and Philips - but also smaller producers such as Ferranti - acquired numerous smaller production houses, primarily of American origin. As market share statistics prove though, this acquisition strategy failed to significantly enhance the Europeans competitive position.

We have already stressed that west European nations were self-sufficient in semiconductors during the 1950s. Imports accounted for only a small percentage of total consumption of the countries of western Europe between the years 1952 and 1962 (Malerba, 1985, p.60). European firms had mastered transistor technology, and were also strong in passive semiconductor component production. Their competitive decline only began in the wake of the introduction of integrated circuit technology. According to Van Tulder and Junne, there were two main reasons that European producers failed to rapidly adapt to the new technology. As already illustrated, the first had to do with industry culture:

> European companies were good at managing incremental technological change, but had difficulties in mastering radically different technologies (Van Tulder and Junne, 1988, p.131).

The second concerned the nature of European end-users. On the whole this tended to be in less sophisticated areas such as consumer electronics, which did not require state-of-the-art semiconductor technology. For American chip makers the reverse was true: their end-users were largely the military and the computer industry. Both of these sectors demanded the newest semiconductor technology as soon as it was available. Thus, due in part to (Cold War inspired) customer demand, American firms seized the technological initiative and moved ahead of their European rivals.

An early lead in the semiconductor industry was important. As the technology developed, financial and technical barriers to entry escalated, thus making it increasingly difficult for European firms to recapture that which the Americans had previously attained (Hobday, 1992, p.281). Of course, it is not an industry where a firm can afford to sit back once it has achieved market leadership. Given the rapid pace of change in semiconductor technology, a firm must constantly innovate and improve on its products and marketing strategies, if it is to remain competitive. With the exception of a few who fell by the wayside (e.g. Sylvania and Raytheon) American firms did this, and thus maintained, and increased, their lead over European producers. By the late 1970s European firms had lost the competitive market positioning which they had shared with their American rivals two decades earlier. Worse, they were now being surpassed by East Asian based firms as well. A new corporate strategy option was evidently needed. This would, during the 1980s and 1990s, take the form of collaboration which did not stop at the borders of the firm's home country; it would expand to involve a tangled web of co-operative activities between firms, research institutes, and governmental institutions throughout both western Europe and the globe.

Dosi proposes that (prior to the 1980s) European government policy for the semiconductor industry can be divided into three stages. The first, dating from 1950 to the mid-1960s, witnessed limited intervention throughout Europe. That which did occur was directed at specific military-related areas, involved small amounts of public funding, and occurred largely in France and Britain. The second stage ran from the latter half of the 1960s until the middle of the 1970s, and concentrated on assisting native computer industries to innovate and compete. Computers, rather than their microelectronic components, were seen at this time as being a more important area of focus for public policy. Commercial benefit for the semiconductor sector during both this and the first phase of policy involvement was often secondary and usually limited. The third stage of policy went from the mid-1970s through to the 1980s, and involved, for the first time, the implementation of European government semiconductor policies (Dosi, 1981, pp.186-7). These were aimed at assisting the semiconductor sector particularly in research, development, and application. The early western European public policy approach for semiconductors was:

> to reinforce the existing strategies of the firm. This has meant, for the most part, a certain concentration of public support on computers rather than components. Only in the mid-1970s - notably in Britain, Germany, and France - was substantial active support given to semiconductors (Dosi, 1983, p.224).

This contrasted sharply with the situation in the US. As we have seen, Cold War rivalries spurred the US government to actively foster the growth of an American semiconductor industry from the early 1950s onwards. This large scale government support was particularly important during the early, and very costly phase of the learning curve. Deprived of this vast military market, European semiconductor producers lost competitiveness vis-à-vis their American rivals (Braun and MacDonald, 1982, p.159). By the close of the 1950s, they were beginning to fall technologically behind US firms. The American semiconductor industry was, until the mid-1970s, the only international semiconductor industry. Prior to this, the nascent microchip industries of other countries (particularly in western Europe) were content to retain a share of their own domestic and neighbouring European markets. It cannot be stressed too much that US federal government support for the semiconductor industry significantly aided the sector's development and growth during the formative years of the 1950s and 1960s. This support came primarily through indirect tools of industrial policy such as procurement contracts and R&D policies, via NASA and the Defence Department (Woods, 1987, p.69). Thus, as Pugel et al. (1981) have argued, a secure and profitable market was the major form of assistance. These government support policies were intended to develop and procure products of a strategic and military value. As Nelson observes:

there is no hint that anybody in government thought that he was creating an industry that would be a major economic asset (1984, p.43).

The American business culture is not, by and large, congenial to government planning. However, although co-operative government-industry strategy for international competitiveness was minimal, US government initiatives helped shape the environment within which the semiconductor industry evolved to become the world leader.

As noted earlier, the introduction of the integrated circuit changed the nature of Europe's position within the international semiconductor industry. The diffusion of integrated circuit consumption was much slower in Europe than in America. In addition, leading European firms, such as Philips and Siemens, failed to rapidly adopt the new technology. Consequently, when the European microchip market began to grow in the late 1960s, the main European semiconductor producers were poorly placed to take advantage of this expansion. Instead, US imports and foreign direct investment capacities came to dominate the European market. In the area of public policy, unlike their American and Japanese counterparts:

> European government policy neither strongly supported the domestic semiconductor industry nor protected the semiconductor market (Braun and MacDonald, 1982, p.139).

Public procurement remained small, and concentrated on a few large established firms. It was manifest mainly through military contracts. It ranged from a maximum of 15-20 per cent in Britain (largely for military purposes), to negligible amounts in Germany. Government funding of R&D was equally small. Again, it ranged from a maximum of 35 per cent in Britain, to minimal amounts in countries such as Germany and Italy (Braun and MacDonald, 1982, p.129).

Sharp has described the position of Europe within the new technology industry during the 1950s and 1960s, as 'playing second fiddle to the US' (1985, p.290). She argues that Europe's economies relied on large investments of American capital, technology, and management. Europe looked like being a follower rather than a leader in information technologies. Even worse, from the mid-1970s on, it looked like being relegated to third place. From this period on, the Japanese began to challenge the Americans within the international microchip market. They achieved incredible success, raising their market presence outside of Japan from virtually nil at the outset of the 1970s, to over 40 per cent by the mid-1980s. The Europeans were slower in internationalising their operations however, and even then, they continued to concentrate their activities on obtaining a greater share of their domestic market[9]. Consequently, as the U.S. Office of Technology Assessment declared in 1982, that with regard to global competition in integrated circuits:

> the battle for leadership in this industry is a battle fought between American and Japanese producers in US and European markets[10].

Most major innovations in microelectronics have originated in the US, and have been subsequently adopted by other countries. The delay in adoption is known as 'technology lag'. Woods expands this definition by expressing the concept in terms of the length of time it takes firms to bring competitive products and processes to market, following their introduction by rivals (1987, p.22). The notion of technology lag is tied to concerns about industrial competitiveness. The concept has become very fashionable in much of the contemporary literature on national industrial performances in leading-edge technologies. Many attempts have been made to measure such technology gaps or lags. For instance, Braun and MacDonald argued that there has usually been a delay of about two years between initial successful commercial production in the US and the first production in Europe (1982, p.151). The utility of microchips as a case study is sustained on this issue. As Woods states:

> microelectronics is probably the one high technology area where there is a clear technology gap between American and Japanese firms, and their European counterparts (1987, p.37).

When conceptualising a technology lag, one normally assumes it to mean the lack of know-how required to achieve a level of technological development commensurate with your leading competitors. Viewed in this way, much has been made of the technology lag issue in Europe - especially as a means to justify the expenditure involved in the massive collaborative R&D programmes begun in the 1980s. In fact, there is considerable evidence to support the contention that a technology gap, caused by insufficient technological know-how, did in fact exist for certain information technology sectors between European countries and firms, and their American (and increasingly, Japanese) counterparts. However, as the following chapters will illustrate, such a gap has since been reduced significantly, and can no longer be viewed as a main cause for European firms lack of competitiveness.

A technology lag can occur in two different ways (Sharp, 1985; Woods, 1987). Firstly, through inadequate scientific knowledge of how to produce a technology; and secondly, through the inability to rapidly adapt or apply this technology to business management and production engineering. It is this second form which from the early 1960s, adversely affected European firms ability to compete.

3.v. The era of national champions

Reasons for the creation of national champions are debatable. In the case of the semiconductor industry, the policy stemmed from a changing perception amongst European policy-makers of the importance of the industry. This change in perceptions usually involved the strategic and economic importance of the sector (as discussed elsewhere in this work), and Europe's initial technological dependence on the US. For policy-makers, the lack of international competitiveness in microchip production was increasingly seen as seriously impairing their country's technological capability and wider economic performance[11]. The protection and development of domestic production thus became a policy priority.

European national champion policy rested on two interrelated instruments: first, the construction of a protective wall (built of tariffs, quotas, rules of origin, and so forth) around the domestic market, to shield home companies from vigorous foreign competition; and second, substantial, direct and indirect, R&D assistance to native companies. Thus, an inordinate emphasis was placed upon developing the scientific base and the marketable technology needed for competitiveness. Therefore, one may argue that the rationale behind this second pillar of European national champion policies, was based in theory upon the Schumpeterian linear model. The linear model links science directly to economic growth. As *The Economist* wrote in 1963:

> Prosperity depends on investment; investment depends on technology, and technology on science. Ergo prosperity depends on science[12].

From a policy perspective, the view was that funding of basic science research would translate into technological developments, which would in turn, enhance national economic prosperity. During the early to mid-1960s, this linear model was, in effect, sold by civil servants to their national politicians in order to get science and technology integrated into the policy-making process[13]. It resulted in the creation of science and/or technology ministries in most western European countries, and the intrinsic policy linkage between science, technology, and competitiveness. Krige (1994) supports the contention that the linear model did affect European policy during the 1960s. He sees this as an evolutionary enlightenment however. For space policy, there was a gradual realisation within European governments that technological development and economic growth were intrinsically linked[14]. This notion developed further as the decade progressed, and blossomed into a policy framework that put science and technology policy as the core of government industrial policy for competitive enhancement.

The national champions policy of several European governments meant:
> giving preferential treatment to locally owned firms, through public purchasing and subsidies for research and development and other activities. The aim was to enable domestic firms to become large enough to champion the high technology needs of the given countries (Hobday, 1992, p.282).

Flamm adds a further element to European national champion policies. He points out that governments first erected high tariff walls to protect domestic semiconductor producers from external competition, and behind which they could pursue their nurturing policies (1990, p.232). These tariff walls were compounded by the imposition of a common EEC tariff of 17 per cent for semiconductor imports.

As Vernon points out, the development of a national champion was not entirely new. Such policies had been undertaken earlier in the century; for instance, the *Compagnie Francaise des Petroles* was created as a French national champion in 1924, to reduce French dependency on American oil (1974, p.11). The British government was actively involved in the creation of British Petroleum around this time for similar reasons. However, the national champion policies of the 1960s were different, particularly in structural terms. Most earlier national champions had been state-owned; whereas governments encouraged the development of the later champions through mergers between existing state, semi-state, and private enterprises.

Only in the US does the semiconductor industry contain a large number of independent chip-making firms. In Europe, by contrast, the industry is dominated by large integrated producers of electronic products. Therefore, such limited government policy intervention as existed in European countries during the 1950s and 1960s was aimed at firms which produced (in particular) computer hardware and peripherals, as well as microelectronic components.

During the late 1960s and through the 1970s, European public policy changed significantly. European governments began to concentrate support on their domestic semiconductor producers, through large and sector-specific policy measures (fig.3.2). The leading such policy tool was R&D assistance, through direct subsidy or low interest loans, or more indirect contracts. (Dosi, 1983, p.225). In effect, the semiconductor industry became the focus of European national champion policies. Ohlin argues that this approach can be distinguished by its emphasis on high technology sectors, the degree of commitment on the part of policy-makers, and by the close relationship between the government and the industry (1978, p.320). The national champion approach generally combines several instruments of industrial policy. These are (1) significant funding for R&D; (2) tax incentives; (3) public procurement; and (4) import restrictions and barriers to limit foreign competition and direct investment.

It is worth noting that semiconductors was not the first industry around which national champion policies were forged. In particular, during the mid-1960s, the computer sector was moulded by national champion policy. France created CII in 1966 as its national computer champion, and ICL became Britain's champion two years later[15]. As Hodges illustrates, emphasis was placed by the British government on the growth potential of the computer industry, and on the capacity of computer technology to invigorate the British economy (1974, pp.227-8). A major factor in the development of French, British, and other European national champion policies for the computer industries, was to counter the perceived threat of American technological domination. The latter half of the 1960s witnessed a fear of American industrial and technological hegemony comparable to that elicited by the rapid growth of Japanese foreign direct investment and market share in both the US and Europe during the second half of the 1980s. In France, works such as Jean-Jacques Servan-Schreiber's (1968) *Le Défi Américain*

	Period	Amount US $ m

Britain

1. Microelectronic support scheme	1973-79	21
2. Component Industry Scheme	1977-[a]	10
3. Microelectronic Support Scheme	1978-[a]	111
4. INMOS	1978-82	101
5. Microprocessor Application Project	1978-82	111
6. Suport for microelectronics under Product and Process Development Scheme	1979	54
7. Other (annual average)	1964-77	2-4 p.a.
8. Military (estimated annual average)	1970-79	4-6 p.a.
9. Non-business institutions and universities (estimated annual average)	1966-78	4-6 p.a.

Germany

1. BMFT support	1969-72	23
2. BMFT Electronic Component Programme	1973-78	118
	1979-82	74
3. 2nd Data Processing Programme	1969-76	32
4. 3rd Data Processing Programme	1977-78	N/A.
5. Synchroton Radiation Project	1981-82	26
6. Military and Space	1964-68	N/A.
	1969-76	33
	1977-82	N/A.
7. German Research Association	1964-76	22

France

1. 1st Plan Calcul°	1967-67	36
2. 2nd Plan Calcul°	1971-75	33
3. Plan Circuit Intégrés	1977-80	132
4. Non-business institutions and government laboratories (estimated annual average)	1964-75	10p.a.
	1976-82	N/A.
5. Military	1964-82	N/A.

continued...

	Period	Amount US $ m
Italy		
1. Technological Evolution Fund		
(a) grants	1968-78	1
(b) loans	1968-78	4
2. Electronics Plan (Law 675)[1]		
(a) grants	1980-82	96
(b) loans	1980-82	60
3. Military	1964-82	N/A.
4. National Research Council project on solid state physics	1964-82	N/A.

Figure 3.2 Government support for the semiconductor industry in Britain, France, Germany, and Italy, 1964-82

a Neither of these schemes had ended at the time when this chart was compiled (1983).

o Includes expenditure on other electronic components, but the bulk of the sums shown are believed to be attributed to semiconductors.

1 Grants, subsidies, and other transfers to the business sector only.

Source: Giovanni Dosi, 'Semiconductors: Europe's precarious survival in high technology', in Shepherd et al., *Europe's Industries,*1983, p.228, reproduced with the permission of Pinter Publishers, London.

prompted considerable debate concerning France's position as a leading industrial nation. Similarly in Britain, the Labour government of Harold Wilson advocated reducing Britain's technological dependence on American firms. In a 1967 speech, Wilson commented that:

> There is no future for Europe, or for Britain, if we allow American business...so to dominate the strategic growth industries of our individual countries, that they, and not we, are able to determine the pace and direction of Europe's industrial advance[16].

Furthermore, we have already seen the extent to which leading anti-Soviet Cold Warriors such as the US and Britain perceived computer technology as vital to the advancement of military technology. National security interests may thus be advanced as another dimension of British government national champion policy in sectors such as computers, and later, semiconductor components.

During the early years of the Brezhnev era, Britain's national champion policies focused on the computer hardware industry, and not on the microelectronic components sector. Initial attempts were made in the mid-1960s to extend the national champion policies to the development of integrated circuits in particular, but nothing substantial came of these endeavours until the following decade.

3.vi. Individual national champion policies

It was in France that a national champion policy for semiconductors was most decisively manifest. As Vernon stated:

> Bolstered by strong political leadership and a self-confident bureaucracy, France tested a number of different approaches to its national problems. The first approach, visible through the early 1960s, was the emphasis upon the comprehensive, rational plan, the efficient vehicle for the satisfaction of national demand; the second, ascendant through the middle 1960s, was the growing preoccupation with solving key sectoral and regional issues of a narrower and more specific sort, such as the question of catching-up in a lagging technology (1974, p.8).

This second, national champion phase in French policy was subsequently tried out in several other western European states. The very survival of an indigenous French semiconductor industry may be attributed to the national champion policy. However, mere survival was not enough in a competitive world market. What really mattered was the firm's ability to maintain a strong technological base and to attain world market share. Semiconductor components were perceived as strategic to French (political, military, and economic) national interests from an early date. From 1962, the French government invested heavily in assisting firms to conduct semiconductor R&D. Such assistance was ad hoc though, and no detailed government policy actually existed for the sector at this time. Instead, the government chose to focus its energies on aiding the survival of the computer industry. In the long term, it was hoped that this industry would reach international competitiveness. This was in line with the policy direction taken by all other large European nations during the second half of the 1960s. The *Plan Calcul* was launched in 1967, with the aim of establishing an independent French informatics industry through the creation of a large national champion company (CII), which the state would then support through preferential purchases and R&D funding. Public money estimated in the region of $1.5 billion was invested thus in the *Plan Calcul* between 1967 and 1975 (Mounier-Kuhn, 1994, p.21).

The poor competitive performance of French semiconductor makers, combined with a belief that a healthy chip industry would translate into a healthy information technology sector, prompted the French to gradually develop within the *Plan Calcul* a policy specifically aimed at assisting the semiconductor sector. The core element of this government strategic targeting of microchips was manifest through the Components Plan, whereby the government transferred almost $18 million over five years, to Thomson-CSF's chip producing unit, Sescosem. The money was to be spent on developing integrated circuits, mainly for computer applications (Oppenheimer and Tuths, 1987, p.88). However, despite this generous government support, Sescosem failed, both technologically and commercially, to achieve its objectives. France trailed even further behind the US. As the 1970s progressed, France was also overtaken by Japan in semiconductor technology. Thus, in 1978, the French government tried once again to build a semiconductor champion. A five year Integrated Circuits Plan was launched, aimed at enhancing the French chip industry's competitiveness, particularly in the area of telecom applications. A total of $55 million was designated in state aid. Of this, Radiotechnique Compelec and Thomson-CSF received $18 million, and Eurotechnique[17] received the remaining $37 million (Oppenheimer and Tuths, 1987, p.89). A second Integrated Circuits Plan was launched in 1981, with emphasis on VLSI and process technology. Both chip producers and semiconductor equipment manufacturers received financial assistance in this phase. The public expenditure was quite substantial, totalling $70 million in 1982 alone (Oppenheimer and Tuths, 1987, p.89).

Unlike in Britain and several other European countries, the French national champion policy did not die out completely in the early to mid-1980s. Albeit more low-key and financially scaled-down, the French government continued to pursue its own policy for semiconductors, in tandem with those policies pursued at a European level.

Britain is an unusual case in the European semiconductor national champions saga. This is because of its efforts to go beyond merely designating its chosen champion or champions. Instead, the British government created a champion to serve as its national flagship in the international race for leadership in semiconductor technology. As in the US, British government interest in the semiconductor industry was initially sparked, in large part, due to defence requirements. The Cold War climate was a crucial factor in Britain's semiconductor policy. The British defence industry (and standing forces) was amongst the world's largest, and Britain was a key US ally in the struggle to 'defend the free world from the Communist threat'. Thus, Britain had a strong interest in achieving superiority over the Soviet Union in military technology. This assertion is borne out by figures which show that during 1963 for instance (when Cold War tensions were high), half of all semiconductor sales in Britain were to the military. 50 per cent of semiconductors were for military use, as against 29 per cent in France, and 8 per cent in both Italy and Germany (Malerba, 1985, p.75). As the military uses of integrated circuits proliferated in the 1960s, British defence contractors and the Ministry of Defence began to buy large amounts of microchips from politically reliable sources. These sources took the form of American imports at first, and increasingly, of American chip production within Britain. Thus, American firms established a strong presence within Britain from an early period, due partly to British defence needs (Morris, 1994, pp.181-95). When British firms, with the aid of the government, attempted to enter the semiconductor market in the late 1960s, they found themselves unable to compete with the American producers located in Britain. Ironically, their competitors strength was partly attributable to the military market created by their own defence department. Thus, subsequent British Department of Industry attempts to create semiconductor national champions were unsuccessful, in part, because the British Department of Defence's contracts were often with American chip makers.

Until the late 1970s, the British national champion policy focused on computers rather than on semiconductor components. The computer champion policy commenced in 1965, when the Labour Government announced a four-point plan (including R&D subsidies and a Ministry of Technology directed Computer Advisory Service) to develop a healthy British computer industry, and to facilitate the diffusion of computer technology throughout the British private sector (Hodges, 1974, p.230). Three years later, with significant government encouragement[18], the largest British-owned computer makers, International Computers and Tabulation (ICT) and English Electric-Leo-Marconi (EELM), were merged to form International Computers Limited (ICL). The government rewarded this merger by allocating almost $20 million in R&D funding over a four year period (Hodges, 1974, p.242). Ostensibly, this cash injection was aimed at assisting the new company to overcome the technical incompatibilities arising from the merger. This example of a government encouraging electronics firms to amalgamate was common practice in western Europe during the latter part of the 1960s. We have already seen that the French government for instance, pursued the same approach vis-à-vis the creation of CII. Braun and MacDonald point out that the European policy ran contrary to that pursued in the US at the same time (1982, p.164). Although originally supporting the larger firms, US policy (as we saw earlier) assisted small start-up companies as well. Moreover, by the mid-1960s, as the industry was able to stand on its own financially, the American government was anxious to disperse its assistance to as many companies as possible, and to use antitrust law to challenge electronic industry oligopolies or an individual firm's hegemony (Braun and MacDonald, 1982, p.164). The failure of the national champions approach, together with the parallel market success of American semiconductor producers, indicates that the mid-1960s European government decisions to encourage bigger and fewer rather than smaller and more, was generally erroneous.

Government attention did not begin to move towards microelectronic components until 1972/73. The first concrete step was the establishment of the Department of Industry Research and Development Requirements Boards[19] in 1972. One of these boards dealt specifically with electronic components. The following year, £12.5 million was made available under the Microelectronics Support Scheme (Dosi, 1983), which ran until 1979. The main thrust of government policy for semiconductor components did not come until 1978 however. In that year, the British government gave priority to microelectronics in their industrial policy efforts. The Microelectronics Industry Support Scheme, the Microprocessor Applications Project, and the Electronic Components Industry scheme, were all launched - at a total estimated cost to the taxpayer of £250 million (Morris, 1994, p.187). The most important development in 1978 was the creation of INMOS. This, in effect, was the British government's attempt to create, rather than just choose a national champion in semiconductors.

Perhaps the most important decision taken in this field (microelectronics production and application) under the Callaghan Ministry was the establishment of INMOS, the semiconductor manufacturing firm set up as a subsidiary of the National Enterprise Board (NEB), with Government financial backing, in order to produce standard ICs of an advanced type (Morris, 1994, p.188). Inmos was a daring attempt on behalf of the British government, to establish a leading British presence in the world semiconductor industry. £50 million of public money was allocated to the fledgling company. However, Inmos failed to achieve commercial success, particularly with its flagship product, the Transputer parallel processor (Dyerson and Mueller, 1993, pp.77-8). In 1984, the British government sold its 76 per cent share of Inmos to Thorn-EMI, with a considerable loss on investment.

Germany's national champion policy proved, in the long term, to be less of an impediment to the competitiveness of its chip producers, than was the case elsewhere in western Europe. In fact, to an extent, it is incorrect to categorise the German policy as national champion, in the same way as France or Britain. It tended to be more even-handed than policy elsewhere in Europe (Dosi, 1983, p.227). Many firms - other than the flagship, Siemens - benefited financially from government intervention. Assistance was given to develop and improve data processing, applications, and software, as well as semiconductor components. Unlike in France or Britain, the semiconductor sector of a specific company was not targeted to develop a certain type of chip for particular applications. The German policy was much wider and more favourable to company initiative.

The first German government policy to have a significant impact upon the semiconductor sector, was the West German Data Processing Programme, instigated in 1965. As with other European countries, this was directed at assisting the native computer industry, as opposed to the semiconductor component sector. Although similar in form to the French *Plan Calcul*, the Data Processing Programme was a more equitable collaborative scheme, with each industrial participant receiving funding according to the amount of labour it contributed to a given project (Ziegler, 1994, p.3). The West German government first directly targeted semiconductors in the mid-1970s, when it established the four-year Electronic Components Programme - later enlarged as the Microelectronics Programme (Oppenheimer and Tuths, 1987, p.91). This programme diffused money throughout German corporations, universities, and private research laboratories, for R&D ventures. In addition, select firms (Siemens and AEG-Telefunken) received government financing for electronic component research. This research was conducted in mutually agreed, broadly differentiated areas (Ziegler, 1994, p.3).

As with France, the German government continued to finance semiconductor R&D within Germany, even after the European collaborative programmes had come into effect in the mid-to late 1980s. For example, the government invested $40 million during the second half of the 1980s to help German chip makers gain market share in gallium arsenide technology. In structural terms, the Megaproject was the most potent symbol of the German government's continued intervention, into the 1980s, on behalf of its indigenous semiconductor producers (Ziegler, 1994, p.3). Granted, it did involve collaboration with the government and electronics flagship of another country (the Netherlands and Philips, respectively). Nevertheless, its aim was purely to assist German industry attain the next level (one megabyte memory chips) in semiconductor technology. Such policy initiatives in Germany (and in France and the Netherlands) would seem to indicate a diminishing reluctance on behalf of large European states to pool technological resources completely, and reduce their own influence over industry. Thus, failed policies such as the national champion approach are not completely replaced; rather they are reduced in size and profile, and supplemented by new European collaborative policies.

4 The post-champion nature of the European based semiconductor industry

Finally, let us look at the corporate structure of the European semiconductor industry, as it has existed for the last decade or so. Which are the firms involved? What are their respective market shares? What segments of the semiconductor market are each of these firms involved in? What segments of the market are these firms strong or weak in or noticeably absent from?

The three main European actors in the semiconductor sector (that is to say, the only three who have managed to establish any presence internationally), are Philips, Siemens, and SGS-Thomson. Of these, Philips has maintained its position as Europe's largest indigenous semiconductor supplier, with over seven per cent of the European market during the early 1990s[20]. This was down almost five per centage points since the mid-1980s. In addition, the company was ranked tenth world-wide in 1994, placing it ahead of all other European-based chip producers. Figure 3.3 indicates the relative market positions of the other significant European semiconductor makers. Taken together, European chip producers consistently account for only 8-9 per cent of world semiconductor production. Furthermore, as Zysman (1993) has pointed out, more than 30 per cent of European use is supplied by foreign firms in Europe, with Americans providing 24 per cent and Japanese 7 per cent. European semiconductor consumption was $10.7 billion in 1990, and this figure increased to about $11.5 billion by 1992, and approximately $12 billion in 1993. This accounted for roughly 18 per cent of world-wide semiconductor consumption (compared to 26.6 per cent for the US and 36 per cent for Japan). Furthermore, perhaps more significantly, in 1993 and 1994, global semiconductor revenues increased by 29 per cent. This brought the value of the world market to more than $100 billion by the end of 1994[21]. These high growth rates continued, with global semiconductor sales reaching over $150 billion by the start of 1996. Such large world-wide

	EC (1992)	EC (1993)	World (1992)	World (1993)
Philips	9.3	7.1	3.24	2.7
Siemens	7.4	6.1	1.91	1.8
SGS-Thomson	7.3	6.5	2.46	2.4
GEC Plessey	1.59	1.0	0.58	0.3
Mietec	0.9	0.9	0.17	0.2

Figure 3.3 Main European-based semiconductor producers market share (%)

Source: Dataquest statistics, March 1994.

increases in chip consumption translated into European semiconductor sales of $28.5 billion by the end of 1995. This still constituted less than 20 per cent of the world market, behind the US (32 per cent), Japan (28 per cent), and Asia (21 per cent)[22]. Thus, it is obvious that there is a lot at stake in basic financial terms, and the projected high growth rates illustrate that a substantial market share is literally up for grabs. Hence, competition between European producers and their foreign rivals for European market share is likely to intensify further in the immediate future.

In the 1990s, only one European-based firm - Philips - has managed to figure amongst the world's top ten merchant semiconductor suppliers. Its global market share hovered around 2.6/2.7 per cent[23], making it the world's tenth to twelfth largest merchant chip producer. The only other European based firm in the top fifteen by 1994 was SGS-Thomson, at number thirteen, with a market share globally of 2.4 per cent (Dataquest, 1995). Siemens, Europe's third largest native producer, was ranked seventeenth, with a 1.9 per cent share. Comparing this with their respective position at the beginning of the decade, Philips was ranked ninth, SGS-Thomson twelfth, and Siemens sixteenth amongst world-wide semiconductor companies in 1990 (Dataquest, 1991).

Until 1993, all of the firms involved were either making only a small profit or, more often, a substantial loss, from the business. However, both SGS-Thomson and Philips semiconductor division announced respectable profits for 1994[24]. Combined sales for the European big three rose by 19 per cent during 1993 - at face value, a substantial increase. However, one must weigh such growth in light of that experienced by the industry world-wide. We see that the world semiconductor industry's sales grew by 29 per cent during the same period, thus illustrating that the European firms growth was still below that of their global competitors. Paradoxically, despite growing, the Europeans still lost market share.

It is advisable at this stage to identify which segments of the semiconductor industry each of these firms is primarily active in. Siemens is strong in application specific integrated circuits (ASICs) for industrial automation and in process technology. It also has a presence in commodity memories, primarily DRAMs, (Dynamic Random Access Memories). This is due to its strategic alliance with Toshiba and IBM (and before that, its alliance with Philips in the Megaproject). In effect, Siemens dominates European memory production. However, this domination does not amount to much in terms of actual market share. For example, in 4 Mbit DRAM sales in Europe, 96 per cent of sales are accounted for by one Korean, one American, and four Japanese firms. Furthermore, Siemens world market share in these memory chips generally hovers around 1 per cent. The company confirmed that it has no plans to retreat from strategic logic and memory chip markets though. Siemens chairman, Heinrech von Pierer has said that chips, particularly those integrated logic and memory systems on silicon, are a vital component in the Siemens systems strategy. In addition, the company reconfirmed that ASICs will remain a driving force in the Siemens strategy.

Philips has increasingly withdrawn from production of commodity chips, and swung its development and production focus towards consumer electronics. However, it is still a player in the production of SRAMs (Static Random Access Memories), much of which it uses in its consumer electronics products of course. The company's semiconductor division, Philips Semiconductors, based in Hamburg, has also targeted the fast growing automotive and telecommunications electronics markets for increased sales. In the automotive electronics market, Philips has introduced a new generation of power semiconductors that integrate all circuits on one chip. For the European Digital Cordless Telephone (DECT) system, the company has introduced an ASIC that will reduce the peripheral circuitry in a cordless handset by over 80 per cent.

SGS-Thomson Microelectronics has a discernible presence in two main areas of chip production - SRAMs, and Flash Memories (which it developed in alliance with Fujitsu). It has a significant presence in the flash memory market. The company also has an important share of the European ASICs market. In addition, the firm produces power amplifier integrated circuits, aimed at the consumer audio electronics market. It has also introduced three smart card memory chips aimed at industrial applications such as premises access control and banking applications. Furthermore, SGS-Thomson is marketing a low-voltage EPROM chip, aimed at the portable PC market.

In addition to these companies, three other European firms produce significant quantities of integrated circuits. These are Temic-Matra, GEC-Plessey, and Mietec Alcatel. Matra has traditionally produced customised chips for the defence sector. Thus far, there is no indication that it intends or is able to compete within the commercial semiconductor market. Similarly GEC-Plessey is primarily a supplier of chips for military applications. Its commercial market share is minimal. Mietec Alcatel is strong in ASICs, which are mainly used for telecommunication applications. The company's significant position in the field is obviously fuelled in part by France's strong position in the production of telecommunications equipment.

European integrated circuit producers play no part in the microprocessor market. An interesting fact is that a microprocessor chip has been developed by a European company - but not by any of the large integrated circuit manufacturers. Instead, a small German design company called Hyperstone Electronic, headed by a former Nixdorf computer scientist, introduced the Hyperstone microprocessor[25]. Financed largely by private venture capital, the company symbolises a nascent semiconductor start-up culture beginning to emerge in the Europe of the 1990s. Its first design-in was into an integrated services digital network PC module, developed at the German firm Intercope Electronics, and intended as equipment for telefax and teletext communications, local area networks, and videotext. The device has been sold for only $20 each in large quantities. As this microprocessor is only in the initial phases of commercial application, it is too early to predict its likely market share and overall affect on the competitive position of the European semiconductor industry. However, the mere fact that it exists and is being utilised commercially, bodes well for the future.

Maybe there is hope for the European semiconductor industry but perhaps it lies less in the traditional, large vertically integrated electronics companies, and more in small start-up firms where innovation is the main corporate driving force, survival depends on bringing products to market rapidly, and domestic inter-firm rivalry is vigorous. In addition, some of the larger firms have undergone harsh restructuring, which promise to produce leaner and more competitive enterprises in the medium term. Philips, SGS-Thomson, and Siemens have all significantly reduced their work forces and fabrication facilities[26]. The three have also narrowed their product lines and begun to specialise in niche markets. These have mainly taken the form of knowledge intensive, application specific chips, which are used in areas such as telecom and automobile electronics. As 1994 figures show, despite a decline in overall market share, SGS-Thomson was the first of the European-based firms to experience market success in the application specific chip market niche. The hardest options might indeed be the best for the large European producers.

5 Conclusions

One may view the technological evolution of the semiconductor industry as Borrus, Millstein, and Zysman have: in three distinct phases. The initial development and production of semiconductor devices, which essentially replaced the vacuum tube but did not fundamentally change the products into which they were incorporated. The second phase saw the substitution of electronic circuits for electrical mechanical functions. Thirdly, the advent of the microprocessor (and large-scale integration) opened up enormous new market developments (1982, p.43). Thereafter, incremental changes in chip design have contributed to the further development of the semiconductor industry.

Soviet technological leads such as the 1957 launch of the Sputnik space rocket, served as catalysts in the development of the semiconductor industry. They caused the US Department of Defence to increase its technological demands on and contracts with these firms[27]. The semiconductor component industry therefore became an integral part of what President Eisenhower termed the military-industrial complex.

European national policy for the semiconductor sector has evolved in four stages. The first, which stretched from the beginning of the 1950s until the mid-1960s, was largely one of non-intervention. During the second stage, which lasted from the mid 1960s until the mid-1970s, government policy focused on the computer industry, which gave some resultant stimulus to semiconductor R&D. The third phase, beginning in the mid-1970s and declining in the early 1980s, heralded a significant increase in the level of government involvement, with particular focus on microelectronics and telecommunications. The fourth phase, from the early 1980s to date, is dominated by the European level collaborative approach. This will be described and analysed in the following chapters.

Why did European firms lose competitiveness during the 1960s and 1970s? To briefly recap, there were first of all seven main corporate structure and strategy and business culture reasons: (1) remaining with the old technology for too long; (2) failure to globalise rapidly and to seek substantial export markets; (3) insufficient levels of venture capital; (4) the lack of a fertile start-up culture; (5) the wrong emphasis in applications; (6) choosing strategies of imitation rather than innovation; and (7) strategy restrictions due to in-house supply obligations.

In addition, public policy played a quite significant role in this loss of competitiveness. The national champion policies pursued by Europe's leading states during the late 1960s and the 1970s, hindered free trade and fair competition. These obstacles had the most negative impact upon the innovative spirit and market share of the very firms they were constructed to assist, and proved counterproductive in the long run. The main economic argument used to justify the national champion policy was based on the concept of establishing sufficiently large economies of scale to enable a company to compete globally. As subsequent research has proven[28], what matters for competitiveness is less the size and more the number of firms within an economy. Vigorous domestic rivalry between many firms will better enable a corporation to meet the challenge of international competition, than does the sheer organisational size of the enterprise. To compound this, national champion policy also had the negative affect of creating a cartel-like behaviour between the chosen few within a market. The international competitiveness of this domestic oligopoly declined further as the targeted firms became heavily dependent on government subsidisation.

It must be stressed that all of these causes developed against the back-drop of the Cold War. This, more than any other single factor, contributed to the competitive problems of European semiconductor producers during the industry's early years. The US Government's provision of a guaranteed market through military supply contracts, combined with the financial incentives it provided to help develop the semiconductor industry, gave US companies a definite competitive head-start over their European rivals. Moreover, the business environment fostered by American policy spawned abundant venture capital and a vibrant start-up culture for the semiconductor sector. This policy was driven entirely by the American Government's intention to achieve Cold War advantage through technological superiority in its defence systems.

As previously mentioned, European semiconductor production did not exist independently of the large integrated electronics firms. Individual (microchip) national champions included Siemens of Germany, Inmos of Britain, and Sescosem (a subsidiary of Thomson-CSF) of France. None of these national champions were successful in capturing significant market share from their established American or up-and-coming Japanese rivals. Only the more market-oriented German policy experienced some success. By the early 1980s, the utility of this policy was highly questionable. One alternative was to merge the individual national champions into one European champion. This had been proposed as early as 1974, with an attempt to create a European joint venture called Unidata, composed of Siemens, Philips, and CII[29]. Supporters of the Unidata idea failed to achieve a political consensus amongst the governments involved, particularly the French (Dang-Nguyen et al., 1993, p.14). It became evident then that the structural merging of champions was too fraught with political symbolism to receive governmental approval. Alternative policies seemed urgently necessary if a European presence was to be maintained within the international semiconductor industry. The following chapters will examine the development and results of these new policies.

In the introductory chapter, we discussed the importance of the semiconductor meta-technology to the electronics industry, the wider information technology realm and - by extension - to modern industrial economies. As Malerba argued:

> because of its crucial technological and economic importance for the electronics industry, and for industry as a whole, the semiconductor industry has also become a strategic industry for the international competitiveness of various economies (1985, p.11).

The notion of a strategic industry is frequently employed to serve as a rationale for protectionist policies implemented by a government. The concept can also have a benign function. To acknowledge that a specific industry constitutes the technological base of an advanced economy, can serve to prevent government from inadvertently impeding its growth, diffusion, and ability to compete with global rivals. However, it hinders competitiveness if a government targets that industry for preferential policy treatment, or uses the strategic label as an excuse for discriminatory practices against foreign firms. The reasoning for this argument will be explored in subsequent chapters.

As semiconductor technology has been diffused throughout national economies, and as the productivity rates and export performance of many sectors have become increasingly dependent on the rapid application of microelectronic devices, governments have come to recognise the core importance of the semiconductor industry. This chapter has shown that this recognition evolved earlier in some countries that in others. It was evident in the US from the very beginning of transistor technology. US Government interest in semiconductors was driven almost exclusively by Cold War rivalries in military and space technology. Through the Department of Defence, the state became actively involved in developing the young industry. This early and large-scale government intervention launched American semiconductor producers into the forefront of the world semiconductor industry, giving them a production capacity, ready market, and technological base which could not be matched by European rivals. They forged ahead through the 1960s, gradually shedding their military dependence, widening their commercial markets, and establishing an increasingly unassailable competitive lead over European-based semiconductor manufacturers.

Europe was a different story. There, governments went from virtually ignoring the new industry for much of the 1950s and early 1960s, to smothering it with attention in the late 1960s and through the 1970s. The exception to this rule was the British Government, which displayed an interest in semiconductors from an early stage. As with the US, ths was due to an interest in its military applications, sparked by Cold War rivalries. However, the British Government's early involvement was of little benefit to British semiconductor producers because of the state's tendency to source from American firms, rather than home-based suppliers.

Neither the laissez faire nor the national champion policy approaches helped European semiconductor makers in the battle with American producers for market share. Once the decision was taken to intervene, European governments adopted the wrong tactics to aid competitiveness. The state paid a portion of firms operating costs (such as R&D outlay) in advance, demanding little accountability for its expenditure. Rather than providing incentives to innovate and compete, as the American government did, European states gave financial assistance packages which served only to cushion European firms from the harsh reality of market competition, and dull their appetite to innovate.

The US government's nurturing of a new and weak industrial sector plainly illustrates the state-firm power relationship which existed. Similarly in Europe, the decision by governments to intervene in the sector - particularly with the development of national champion policy - was indicative of the state's power to act alone at this time. Although the potential economic and military impact of the sector was already evident, semiconductor firms were not yet in a position to negotiate with government on anything like an equal level. Government created policy and firms operated within its parameters. No bargaining existed: the state decided how it would shape the environment within which companies competed and industries evolved; and the individual firms sought to determine their corporate strategy under the influence of state intervention.

In the subsequent chapters, we endeavour to assess how this state-firm relationship has evolved, as the semiconductor industry has matured and developed into the most technologically influential industrial sector in the modern international political economy.

Notes

1   Bell Laboratories is the research wing of AT&T. Its interdisciplinary research co-operation provided an open scientific environment which was crucial to the creation of the transistor.

2   Digital integrated circuits have a binary (on/off) relationship between inputs and outputs. Memories are digital integrated circuits which can store information. Microprocessors are digital integrated circuits which can perform all of the functions of the central processing unit of a computer. Microcomputers are composed of both microprocessors and memories.

3   These figures are taken from Paul Kennedy, *The Rise and Fall of the Great Powers*, 1987, p.384.

4   Defence Department survey, cited in Borrus, 1988, p.66.

5   According to the US National Commission on Technology, Automation, and Economic Progress, *Technology and the American Economy*, 1966, pp.11-24, cited in Borrus, 1988, p.66.

6   IBM is not listed because it produced exclusively for in-house consumption.

7   United Nations Industrial Development Organisation report on the semiconductor industry. Referred to in Robert Ballance and Stuart Sinclair, *Collapse and Survival: Industry Strategies in a Changing World*, 1983, p.146.

8   Franco Malerba, 1985, p.112. This combined domestic market share for European semiconductor producers declined further during the subsequent decades, resting around 36 per cent by the early 1990s.

9   Philips was a notable exception to this rule. Due to the very limited size of its domestic market, it was forced to seek external markets for its products earlier than other European firms. However, initially, it tended to concentrate on attaining market share in neighbouring European states, rather than at a more global level. None-the-less, Philips subsequent position of leadership amongst European semiconductor producers may be partly attributed to its earlier adoption of an export-oriented strategy.

10 Quoted in Michael S. Steinberg, *The Technical Challenges and Opportunities of a United Europe*, 1990, p.69.

11 The recognition by governments that there is an intrinsic linkage between achieving global market share and sustaining good domestic living standards, has since been emphasised by Stopford and Strange (1991), *Rival States, Rival Firms*.

12 *The Economist*, October 1963, quoted in John Krige, 'Industrial and Technology Policy in the European Space Sector: How Ministers Saw the Problem', talk presented at the workshop *History of Science and Technology Policy in Europe, 1955-1970*, held at the European University Institute, Florence, 13-14 May 1994.

13 Comment made by Mr. Jean-Jacques Salomon, former scientific advisor to the French Prime Minister, at EUI *History of Science and Technology Policy in Europe, ibid.*

14 John Krige, op.cit.

15 Nicolas Jequier in Raymond Vernon, 1974, p.214.

16 Harold Wilson, British Prime Minister, cited in Michael Hodges, *Multinational Corporations and National Government*, 1974, p.228.

17 Eurotechnique was the product of a joint venture between Saint-Gobain of France, and NSC of the US, but was majority owned by the French partner.

18 Hodges argues that government support for the merging of Britain's largest computer makers stemmed from a perception that an indigenous British computer industry could only survive if it combined its resources and concentrated on competing with American firms, rather than with one another (1974, p.246).

19 For further information on these boards, see Morris, 1994, pp.186-7.

20 *Dataquest Europe Ltd.,* March 1994.

21 Robert D. Hof, 'The I-Way Will Be Paved With Silicon', *Business Week,* 9 January 1995.

22 *Business Week,* 'The global chip payoff', 7 August, 1995.

23 According to 1994 and 1995 Dataquest statistics.

24 During the first half of 1994 alone, Philips announced profits of $395 million for its component and semiconductor business, whilst projected 1994 profits for SGS-Thomson were $250 million, *The Economist*, 27 August 1994, p.54.

25 The Hyperstone microprocessor was discussed in the magazine *Electronics,* 25 January 1993.

26 Since 1990, Phillip's has reduced its workforce by a quarter and closed three fabrication plants. Since 1991, Siemens has cut its workforce by 1,500, and SGS-Thomson has shut down nine of its twenty-two plants, *The Economist*, 27 August 1994.

27 Walter McDougall perceives the launching of Sputnik as a pivotal point in American science and technology policy; leading to a more commanding role for the US military and a closer relationship between the Department of Defence and industry (1985, pp.5-10).

28 For example, Michael Porter, *The Competitive Advantage of Nations*, 1990, Keith Pavitt, 'The Nature and Determinants of Innovation', 1990 (cited in Hobday, 1992); and Margaret Sharp, 'Europe: Collaboration in the High Technology Sectors', in *Oxford Review of Economic Policy*, 1987.

29 Unidata was intended to be a high technology (electronics), European level, government-industry collaborative effort, on a par with Airbus and Ariane.

4 EC governance and policies for semiconductors

No man undertakes a trade he has not learned, even the meanest, yet everyone thinks himself sufficiently qualified for the hardest of all trades, that of government.

Socrates

From our historical discussion, we now proceed to the study of contemporary issues facing EC industrial policy-makers and the European semiconductor industry. The purpose of chapter four is to analyse EC semiconductor policy at an EC institutional level. This is one of three perspectives from which we view the creation and control of policy for the European semiconductor industry. The other perspectives - the firm and the international system - will be developed in the subsequent chapters. This chapter's main conceptual and analytical tools are, first, the Pentagonal Diplomacy model of policy bargaining; and second, innovation policy theory. The first facilitates an understanding of how collaborative semiconductor policy emerges at an EC level and who determines the shape and direction of the policy. The second enables us to analyse the nature of EC semiconductor policy: what are the primary policy instruments, and why were particular policy options (such as collaborative R&D initiatives) chosen above others. In addition, we refer briefly to the Porter Diamond model of national competitive advantage. This allows us to comment on the consequences which EC policy has had for the European-based semiconductor industry's global competitive advantage.

This chapter has two interrelated objectives. It aims to study how semiconductor policy develops within the EC, and to discern which actor wields the greatest bargaining power within the policy-making process. Two fundamental arguments are posited. Firstly, that both large firms and intra-Commission ideological rivalries have the most profound impact on the development and direction of EC industrial policy for electronics. Secondly, that the EC has developed a sectoral policy set for electronics, and that this policy set is fundamentally interventionist.

This section is also designed to test in part, first, whether EC policy for the semiconductor industry evolved as part of the Community's efforts to create a common area of action for industrial affairs; second, if there was a shift in policy emphasis in the early 1980s, away from the national and towards the EC level for semiconductors; and third, the extent to which semiconductors became the vanguard high technology industry in the post-Single European Act drive towards economic integration.

In line with the rationale advanced by Cawson et al., we undertake a sector-specific analysis of EC policy partly to reconsider, in light of the empirical findings, more general theories of the relationship between politics and economics and governments and industry (1990, p.4). This work is concerned with the role of both the European Commission and European electronics multinationals in the creation and control of EC policy for semiconductors. The objective is to understand and analyse the processes of Commission-TNC relations. This necessitates understanding how the various organisations interact; what goals they each pursue; how they construct their strategies; and how they influence one another (Wilks and Wright, 1987, p.275). This policy-making power interplay is best conceptualised in terms of the Pentagonal Diplomacy model which was described in chapter two. To briefly recap, the pentagonal diplomacy concept is developed from Stopford and Strange's (1991) triangular diplomacy model. It is a conceptual framework to assist in understanding how industrial policy develops within the European Community. It entails five interlinked sets of negotiating bargains: state-state, firm-firm, state-firm, firm-European Commission, and European Commission-state. All five bargaining sets come into play for each industry. However, the impact upon policy of the individual sets varies according to the industry. Thus, for some industries, the firm-Commission interplay is negligible for instance; whilst for others, it may be the state-state bargain which has little input into policy development. The intention is to determine which bargaining set(s) dominate a particular policy-making process; which of the public and private sector players involved in the policy sphere actually define and drive a given policy.

We acknowledge that other actors, especially national governments, are important players in EC industrial policy formulation. We argue that EC semiconductor policy is shaped and guided mainly by the Commission and a group of large firms. This process occurs through what Wilks and Wright describe as informal relationships (1987, p.286), the effects of which are often underestimated in analyses of EC industrial policy. Through the Pentagonal Diplomacy conceptual framework, the policy bargains can be understood and assessed. In this chapter and the next, national governments for instance, are seen to wield considerable influence in certain realms of EC microchip diplomacy. This is evident in EC policy areas such as Eureka co-ordinated semiconductor R&D collaborative programmes. It is also visible in EC policy variables, mainly the size of budget allocations and the scope of EC technology policy. However, the actual policy agenda-setting, trade tool utilisation, rules governing competition, and concentration of resources, remain largely the domain of the European Commission, in partnership with certain large corporate enterprises.

1 The development of EC policy for semiconductors

European Community policy for the electronics industry emerged in the late 1970s, as the failure of national champion policies was becoming widely evident. The symbolic starting point was the set of meetings initiated by European Commission Vice President, Viscomte Etienne Davignon, with the chief executives of Europe's twelve largest native[1] electronics firms. These round table meetings were the first serious attempts by the European Commission to establish a close working relationship with the European electronics industry. They signified a new departure in policy-making: both a new policy bargaining axis, and the genesis of European level efforts at competitive enhancement. This new departure in policy-making forms the basis of this chapter.

Three arguments are advanced herein. First, the past decade has witnessed a sea-change in the nature of the agenda-setting and policy-making processes for the EC electronics sector. EC policy-making has gone from being an intra-institutional consensus-building process, to a multi-sided bargaining process. This development may be seen as a move towards the Pentagonal Diplomacy framework for policy negotiation. The role of non-governmental actors in policy formulation and implementation has increased significantly since the early 1980s. In particular, large European high technology firms have significantly enhanced their policy bargaining position in relation to public sector actors. Firms have gone from policy outsiders to policy partners. In fact, EC policy for electronics substantially derives from bargaining between the European Commission and large European electronics firms - the firms frequently exerting the most influence over the final policy outcome.

Second, at a sub-pentagonal level, EC policy results in part from intra-Commission bargaining. Ideological cleavages exist as much within the Commission as they do within the Council of Ministers. Thus, policy is in part an outcome of intra-Directorate-General (DG) rivalries, and bargaining between those bureaucrats and Commissioners of different ideological persuasions.

Third, despite the rhetoric and the stated intention to move towards greater liberalisation, policy for electronics still has considerable interventionist elements. This is particularly prevalent in trade policy issues. The official Commission line on industrial policy advocates a middle-way between governmentally directed firm strategy, and free market competition. However, the result is a protective partnership, i.e. selective, firm requested government intervention. Although verbally shunning sectoral policies, the Commission has identified certain industries as strategic, and apportioned them special policy treatment. Most of Europe's large native electronics firms have been in such a protective partnership.

2 The firm-Commission bargain

Moravcsik (1994) acknowledges that non-state actors play a part in the EC decision-making process. However, he perceives nation-states and their diplomatic representatives as the most important actors within this process. He argues that 'non-governmental organisations rarely participate in decisive decisions; where they do, they rarely enjoy decision-making power' (1994, p.9). This work disagrees with such an assertion. Instead, we would argue that firms do (in specific circumstances) play a significant role in the EC decision-making process (Sandholtz and Zysman, 1989; Cawson et al., 1990; Green, 1993). One cannot ignore the changed role of the firm in the policy process. Large European high technology firms have significantly enhanced their policy bargaining position in relation to political actors. A central tenet of this chapter is that the thrust of EC policy for electronics industries has derived from bargaining between the European Commission and large European electronics firms. National governments (and the European Parliament) have generally only entered the process in a consultative way, or to give policy compromises final approval. It is argued that the role of business in EC policy-making increased further when Jacques Delors became Commission President in 1985 (Green, 1993, p.35). In the spirit of French social Catholicism, Delors always advocated dialogue and co-operation between industry and government.

The role of non-governmental actors in policy formulation and implementation has increased significantly since the late 1970s. In particular, large European information technology firms have significantly enhanced their policy bargaining position in relation to public sector actors. Firms have gone from being policy outsiders to policy partners. Grant advances five main roles that government has in relation to business. These are as a policy-maker, as a sponsor, as a regulator, as a customer, and as an owner (1987, p.36). Grant omits one key role of government however - that of partner with business. We argue that EC industrial policy is sometimes created and controlled by a partnership between the European Commission and transnational corporations. The policy partnership notion emerges from Richardson and Jordan's model of the policy community. These authors view policy-making as an obscure process, where traditional boundaries between government and interest groups become blurred. Policies are created and controlled through 'a myriad of interconnecting, interpenetrating organisations' (1979, p.74). They conclude that:

> it is the relationships involved in committees, the *policy community* of departments and groups, the practices of co-option and the consensual style, that perhaps better account for policy outcomes than do examinations of party stances, of manifestos or of parliamentary influence (1979, p.74).

Thus, Commission-firm policy partnerships emerge from this murky world of European-level policy communities. Firm-Commission negotiations are initiated by the governmental actor and policy bargains frequently cover a wide range of issues aimed at the competitive enhancement of the wider industry. For certain sectors, it is only through examining this relationship that we may best understand the EC industrial policy-making process.

The notion of policy partnership may be distinguished from mainstream theories of government-business relations such as corporatism, private interest government, and pluralism. It is substantively different from pluralist conceptions of lobbying or interest group politics.

The essence of neocorporatism, as applied to the EC, is that the future European political economy would be kept together through a 'web of dense and durable bi-, tri-, and multilateral bargaining relationships, involving public and private bodies alike' (Streek and Schmitter, 1992, p.199). Streek and Schmitter go on to argue that neo-corporatism assumes an underlying social structure which is effectively polarised between capital and labour (1992, p.212). Sargent (1985) supports the argument that this polarisation occurs at an EC level. She asserts that the Community institutions have endeavoured to develop a social partnership with representatives of labour and capital, and that this is indicative of EC level corporatism (1985, p.229). This fundamental feature of neocorporatism distinguishes it from the policy partnership which we identify within EC-industry relations for electronics. The Commission bargains only with capital, only with the management of Europe's large electronics firms. Labour does not enter the equation - certainly not at the policy-making level. As such, what we are describing for electronics cannot be conceptualised through neocorporatist theory. Furthermore, the nature of neocorporatist EC-level policy bargaining differs from that which this work describes. Although the European Commission consults with the social partners during the creation and implementation of reports and legislation, it does so neither at a high level (Commissioners are never directly involved), nor on an equal basis (Sargent, 1985, p.239). In effect, the neocorporatist interpretation of EC-business negotiation places private interest organisations in a subordinate role to EC institutional actors. This further distinguishes neocorporatism from the policy partnership notion, in that, first, consultation does not take place at the level of Commissioner-Chairman; second, these interest groups constitute only a part of the Commission's wide consultations on a particular issue(s); and third, neocorporatism refers specifically to organisations and not to individual firms or a small, autonomously grouped, alliance of firms.

A second theory is that of private interest government. In brief, the notion arises as an alternative to direct state intervention and regulation. It involves an attempt by government to use the collective self-interest of social groups as a means for achieving public policy objectives (Streeck and Schmitter, 1985, p.16). In effect, Streeck and Schmitter describe it as an attempt to maximise the overlap between the specific interests (categoric good) of particular groups, such as business lobbies, and the broader interests (collective good) of society. The policy bargaining which occurs between public and private interest government helps to define this overlap. Inherently, the theory involves a close relationship between interest associations and state or Community authorities, and a significant level of policy input from the private interest government actors (Streeck and Schmitter, 1985, p.20). However, this theory denotes a more liberal regime than that which presently exists for the European electronics industry. Being an alternative to state

ion - perceives
world market
y, emphasis is
velopment of
end in itself
Commission
Copenhagen
ployment in
and the way
technology
ategic trade
ategic trade
vantage of
1986, p.9).
electronics
nt market,
suing this
ors of the
ith heavy
ecessitate
pense of
form of
nce the
s. Such
ch and
a wider
effects,
sectors,
which
ut the
with

n put

have
nist
ing:
s a
an
her
ity

leory implies that government policy is
/ith free-market principles. Also, the private
s not adequately account for EC policy
ating instead on the national level. The
y is to devolve policy-making to the market.
exist to rubber stamp policy. Thus, the private
imilar to the policy partnership notion.

as of EC-business relations, pluralism does not
n occurring within the electronics/semiconductor
alism as being characterised by:

re-group politics and the lobbying of government
fragmented and competing interest groups, and by a
icipation by unions in policy-making (1984, p.62).

are no interest blocks which are sanctioned by
tiate on behalf of a business sector. The interests are
r controlled by the state', nor do they exercise a
icular business sector (Schmitter, 1977, p.9). It is more
n no real rules or central authority.
s (1979) policy communities model is a neopluralist
business relations. Neopluralists have:

le emphasis of some of the earlier discussions on interest
the consequent neglect of the various interlocutors with
cted, not least the state. In particular, the policy community
a framework for examining the behaviour of a whole range
articular political arena (1979, p.13).

cy partnership fits broadly within this neopluralist, policy
of government-business relations. It differs only in being
alist - arguing that EC industrial policy is often forged privately
executive officers of a group of large firms and individual
ssioners and their Cabinets. This modified version of neopluralist
ith Coates' argument that:

ationship of capital to government is of a subtler kind, less visible
otent than simply the interaction of lobbyist and lobbied (1984,

partnerships are a more actor-limited form of policy communities,
ave hidden agendas that make them more powerful relationships than
lly encapsulated by interest group theory.

3 Why target electronics?

The European Community - and particularly the European Commiss
a direct relationship between the ability to compete successfully fo
shares, and the economic well-being of a society. More specificall
placed upon high technology - both as a means to an end (e.g. the d
leading edge production processes for assorted industries) and as a
(the ability to produce and to export high technology products).
President Jacques Delors confirmed this rationale at the 1993
European Council meeting. He argued that the primary cause of unen
the Community was a lack of competitiveness with the US and Japan,
to combat this is through public investment in infrastructure and high
(Krugman, 1994, pp.28-9). Such an approach is in line with the str
thinking which has emerged as the globalisation process developed. Str
policy aims to redesign the structure and enhance the competitive a
oligopolistic industries within the international economy (Krugman,
Given the relatively small number of players within the European
industry, and their respective ability to exert relative power over their jo
electronics can safely be described as an oligopolistic industry. In pu
general objective, governmental actors are effectively targeting core sec
economy. The basic argument is that imperfectly competitive markets (v
R&D costs, high economies of scale, etc.), such as electronics, n
government intervention in order to assist indigenous firms, at the ex
external competitors (Ostry, 1990). This intervention should come in the
promotional policies aimed at specific sectors, which will enha
competitiveness of the targeted sector, as well as of related sector
promotional policies take the form of partial financing of resear
development activities, human capital training schemes, and so forth. In
perspective, it is hoped that this selective intervention will have spill-over
thus contributing both to the competitive enhancement of other industrial
and to the economic welfare of the broader society. Therefore, the industries
are targeted are perceived to impact a wide array of industries through
economy. Such is certainly the case with electronics, and particularly
semiconductor components.

Tyson and Yoffie argue that this targeted industrial policy has indeed bee
into practice by the European Community for the semiconductor industry:

> [Collectively] the governments of these [European Community] nations
> accorded the semiconductor industry special promotional and/or protecti
> treatment in the anticipation of several kinds of economic benefits, includ
> more productive, higher paying jobs for their workers, greater exports a
> result of an expanded share of growing world markets, the development of
> indigenous technological infrastructure with spill-over benefits for ot
> industries, and the provision of linkage externalities - lower cost, higher qua
> inputs - for downstream user industries (1991, p.2).

Traditional theories of industrial policy are not adequate to analyse this situation. Although EC policies are aimed at promoting the efficient performance of specific industrial sectors, mainstream industrial policy theory falls short analytically in a number of ways. Standard theories of industrial policy such as Tyson and Zysman (1983) and Audretsch (1993) separate policies aimed at enhancing the competitiveness of a particular industry or sector, from those intended to benefit the wider economy (what Audretsch defines as general versus selective policies). They do not appear to consider that a selective policy framework can also aim - through economic and technological spill-over - to raise the competitiveness of the wider economy. This has consistently been the stated aim of EC industrial policy. Curzon Price recognises this short-coming in much of industrial policy theory and advances the notion of positive or negative selective industrial policies. In this, government aims to either assist or prevent the process of structural change, often through promoting new industries and technologies (1981, pp.17-8). However, as we argue in Chapter two, this theory also fails to adequately analyse what is occurring at an EC policy level for electronics. Instead, we forward the innovation policy model as most appropriate to an analysis of the how and why EC policy for semiconductors emerges. This industrial policy theory, which emphasises the industrial promotion and adoption of new technologies, and has the government-corporate interface as its fulcrum (Ostry, 1990, p.53), comprehensively explains what has been occurring in European semiconductor policy. This argument will become clearer as the chapter advances.

Competitiveness, both as a corporate and as a national or EC phenomenon, has already been discussed in this work. However, again we are drawn back to the question of, who actually competes in the global market? If it is indeed firms, and not states (or the Community), should we not, from the outset of this chapter, condemn all EC policies for the microchip industry as unnecessary and undesirable? Krugman argues that competitiveness is a meaningless word when applied to national economies. Such a line of argument runs counter to President Clinton's soundbite that 'each nation is like a big corporation competing in the global marketplace' (Krugman, 1994, p.29). For our purposes, it is sufficient to advance two lines of reasoning which may cast doubt on both of these extremes. Firstly, it is accepted that there are transnational corporations (TNCs) which are autonomous actors in the international system and compete directly with one another for world market share (Stopford and Strange, 1991). Governmental actors tend to either be marginalised in this process, or to be adopted as partners, often merely to allow these TNCs to overcome political barriers or to gain public funds for R&D and so on. On the other hand, there are a sufficient number of firms (usually small and medium sized enterprises - SMEs) which cannot be classified as transnational enterprises, to warrant an air of caution by Krugman and other opponents of the idea that nations still compete in the global market. These firms have a distinct national identity and are largely under the regulatory jurisdiction of one state. Close co-operative links often exist between such firms and their respective government, in everything from R&D to marketing arrangements for foreign markets. They make an identifiable contribution to a country's employment, technology base, tax regime, trade figures, and so forth. The very citizenship of these firms shareholders, directors, and employees is generally homogenous. Hence, when these non-TNC firms export their products, it may be argued that both the individual firm and the nation are competing - given the clearly identifiable and strong ties between the firm and its national government and economy.

Secondly, access to market share globally is unequal. Free trade is widely accepted to be a misnomer, and firms often differ greatly in the government supported base level from which they compete. This is especially true in the age of co-operation, that is the last decade or so, since the proliferation of co-operative agreements and programmes between firms and firms, and firms and governmental actors. In addition, as chapter three illustrated, government has always played a role (either overtly or covertly) within either the fostering or the maintenance of competitiveness for information technology industries. This is a fact which applies equally to the US, Japan, and Western Europe. Government is part of the equation, whether desirable or not, and to advocate the complete withdrawal of governmental agents from the equation in one arm of the triad, is, firstly, naive, and secondly, risks weakening the R&D base of firms in a defined politico-economic region.

Therefore, it is suggested here that one should consider the existence of a two track process vis-à-vis global competition: i.e. on one level, the largely autonomous activities of TNCs, which compete for world market share largely on their own terms, and enjoy more than one legal national status; and on the other level, SMEs which have a more easily defined nationality and whose trade and investment activities are more securely policed by a given national government. In advancing the above hypothesis, there is no implicit value judgement. However, it is relevant to assess the extent to which the two-track competition process refutes or validates EC policies for the microchip industry. Probably the most rational assessment is that for track one - TNCs competing globally - supportive EC policies are unnecessary and undesirable; and for track two - SMEs competing outside of their domestic markets - some EC policies are necessary. Thus, for most of the indigenous European semiconductor sector, EC involvement should be kept to a minimum, given that the sector is dominated by TNCs. Where Community-level policy is perhaps most useful is by enabling small and medium sized start-up companies to reach a level of international competitiveness. This may be done primarily through creating a suitable competitive environment for them, through training schemes for instance, and assisting them in costly R&D projects, and thus overcoming high entry barriers.

4 Towards an understanding of European chip policy

Policy has been, and continues to be, a vital factor in the performance of the European semiconductor industry. Even as a business analyst, it is legitimate to examine public policy for solutions to corporate competitive problems. Semiconductors are a very special industrial sector for policy makers. In chapter one, we discussed the reasons for this special status, that is primarily the transformative affect which the technology has on economies and societies throughout the world. Thus, governments have seldom refrained from monitoring, if not directly interfering in, the structure and operation of this sector. Furthermore, the extremely high entry barriers have led to the emergence of a global industry where there are relatively few players, and these are all headquartered in a handful of west European and East Asian countries - in addition to the US of course. Thus, you have an oligopolistic global industry, which has always been a prime target for government interference.

Within the European Community, it would appear that much of the policy competence for semiconductors has shifted during the last decade from national governments to the European Commission. This is evident in two main policy realms: trade and R&D. The Commission's legal competence for the external trade affairs of the twelve, combined with the Research and Technology Community enshrined in the Single European Act, establishes it as the primary governmental institution dealing with the activities of the semiconductor industry. In addition, the Commission's business policing mandate, expressed through its competition policy, cedes further authority to Brussels in activities concerning industrial actors. These three policy pillars may be grouped together and analysed collectively as innovation policy. Thus, the last decade has witnessed a swing from national to EC policies for semiconductors. We will provide evidence to support this argument further on. Such a swing legitimises this work's concentration on EC rather than national government policy. It also allows for the consideration of a Pentagonal Diplomacy model of policy bargaining, as opposed to alternative bargaining systems (such as Stopford and Strange, 1991; Moravscik, 1994).

Tyson perceives a change in the nature of EC policy for the electronics sector, and attributes this change largely to the internal market initiative (1992, p.245). She argues that electronics is still accorded high priority in EC policy-making circles, but that there is increased disagreement about the objectives of policies for the sector, and the means through which such objectives are pursued. This line of argument is developed further by Sharp, who sees disagreement on policy goals and methods for electronics and other advanced technologies, manifest as a struggle between the minimalist and the maximalist approach. Sharp conceives of a twin track EC policy approach for advanced technology (1991, p.177). The first track, co-operation and concentration, consists of EC involvement in Community-wide and European-wide collaborative R&D programmes such as ESPRIT and Eureka. Sharp argues that the co-operative networks and transnational scope of such programmes has also led to a concentration of the electronics industry. By this she means that former national champions have been transformed into Eurochampions. A given number of national European electronics firms have become European multinationals, with an additional presence in extra-European markets. This metamorphosis has indeed taken place, and former national champions such as Siemens, Bull, or Olivetti, have decreased their dependence on domestic markets and increased their presence internationally - particularly at a Community level. However, Sharp attributes too much of this transformation to the effect of EC policies, and too little to changes in the international business environment, particularly the process of globalisation.

The second track is defined as deregulation and liberalisation. By this Sharp obviously means the Single Market initiative. Through phasing out impediments to intra-Community trade, and gradually developing a unified market, internal competitive rivalries between firms in different states will increase. In addition to raising European firms responsiveness to market forces, this would serve to better position European firms for global competition. This is a reasonable hypothesis, and the success of this system in the US and Japan, sustains its practical viability. However, it is not a smooth process, and much resistance has been displayed by certain EC member states on certain parts of the overall process. The single market programme illustrates vividly the ideological cleavages which persist within the Community, broadly speaking along *dirigiste*-liberal market lines.

As Sharp acknowledges, the relative weighting of these two tracks at an EC level reveals the tensions within the Community between those who favour a minimalist approach - seeing competition policy as the main or sole tenet of industrial policy - and those who prefer a maximalist approach - advocating an active, interventionist industrial policy regime. These tensions are evident not only at a European Council level, between member states of the Community, but also at a Commission level. A veritable battle rages between individual Commissioners and Directorate Generals, to determine policies for core technology industries. This argument is sustained by a number of senior Commission officials[2]. This conflict has been manifest in the public sphere during the 1990s in the form of a number of important policy papers. A critique and comparison of these and related Commission documents, plus their practical implementation, forms the core of the following evaluation of EC policy for the semiconductor sector.

5 EC involvement in R&D

In discussing the nature of the EC policy framework for microchips, one element emerges as the dominant policy tool. In fact, it may be argued that the other three pillars of the policy are often secondary to - and sometimes merely supportive of - the R&D activities. As previously indicated, this emphasis on knowledge creation and dissemination is the essential part of any innovation policy. R&D is perhaps the basket within which the Commission places most of its eggs. The sheer financial and structural scale of EC involvement in semiconductor research and development is indicative of this policy emphasis. For instance, the EC spends, in total, approximately $2 billion per annum on research, much of it on subsidies to collaborative industry programmes such as JESSI and ESPRIT. Also, it concurs with the Commission's stated objective of acting as a promoter rather than as a protector.

The 1980s witnessed a significant transformation in the nature of European industrial policies. As Sharp argues:

While the 1960s and 1970s could well be called the Age of the National Champion, the 1980s may earn the title the Age of Collaboration (1989, p.202).

As discussed in chapter three, during the late 1970s, large European firms, attempting to adjust to the new global competitive framework, began to perceive a need for co-operation and public policy involvement at an EC, as well as or instead of, at a national level. In addition, the European Commission, through individuals such as Commissioner Davignon, saw an increased role for it vis-à-vis large European firms. Consequently, the early 1980s proved a period of policy transition in the EC; with an expanded role for Community institutions - primarily the Commission. Such a role was sometimes in tandem with and often at the expense of, national governments - depending on the industrial sector in question. The power shift was most obvious within information technology industries - where the need for global competitively and greater economies of scale was most evident. Also, this was illustrative of an extension of Community research activities from more traditional industries such as coal and steel, into the new knowledge intensive industries. Thus, driven by the necessity of expanding their economies of scale and sharing R&D costs, western European states ceded considerable policy authority in information technology to Brussels. Business supported this power shift, seeing benefits to be had in a larger home market, greater trans-European co-operative linkages, and more sources of governmental R&D support. Finally, the European Commission actively sought this new policy competency, arguing that competitiveness could best be achieved if policy was implemented at a European level.

The special strategic role accorded to science and technology in general, and information technology (especially microelectronics) in particular, was described during the 1980s by EC Commission Vice-President, Karl Heinz Narjes:

It was not until 1980 that the Community was able to take a strategic view of science and technology. It was then that that the Commission first stated its belief that it was not possible to devise a new model for society, to secure Europe's political and economic autonomy, or to guarantee commercial competitiveness, without a complete mastery of the most sophisticated technologies (1988, p.396).

Furthermore, Narjes argued that the Community had a responsibility to strengthen the scientific and technological basis of European industry, in addition to actively encouraging industry to become more responsive to the global competitive environment. It is thus obvious that at the most senior levels of EC policy-making during the 1980s, an active interventionist view was taken towards European high tech industry's competitive enhancement.

It has been argued (OTA, 1991; Forum Europe, 1992) that the increased role of Community institutions in policy for high technology industries, had political undertones. Thus it is proposed that the Commission saw European high technology companies (particularly in the information technology sector) as potential allies in the advancement of an ever closer union. As outlined in various Community industrial policy documents[3], in Delors Copenhagen European Council speech of 1993, and in statements by numerous senior level Commission officials[4], the electronics sector (particularly semiconductor components) was seen as a priority industry for EC industrial policy. The proportion of R&D funding channelled to electronics under the EC Framework Programmes illustrates the industry's position at the vanguard of the Commission post-SEA drive towards economic integration. Hence, EC policy for electronics industries such as semiconductors was an integral part of the EC move to deepen industrial integration, and subsequently, to strengthen the economic basis of European political union. Working together, the Commission and large European firms could benefit one another. Commission efforts to enhance the firms global competitiveness, would be accompanied by a closer relationship between Brussels and corporate Europe, and therefore greater political authority for the Commission vis-à-vis national governments. The Commission decided that to convert Europe's largely sheltered, national high-tech companies into competitive multinationals, with a Europe-wide marketing base:

> would not only give them the size to stand up to the likes of IBM and Hitachi, but also the resources to turn an increased R&D effort into new, competitive products. One way to achieve this was to bring European companies together in research. Joint research would lead to joint ventures. A lot of small, national champions would become a few big, European ones, whose interests would lie with the Community, not with separate states. Once again, research was given a political role, this time through high-tech rather than nuclear power (Mckenzie, 1992, p.7).

In reviewing this powerplay over the last decade, at a superficial level, it would seem that the Commission strategy has been successful. However, it is important to consider the changed role of the firm in the policy process. Large European high technology firms have significantly enhanced their policy bargaining position in relation to political actors. From the Treaty of Rome until the creation of the first Framework Programme in the mid-1980s, EC policies for industrial R&D activities were focused - with the obvious exception of nuclear technologies - on traditional industries such as coal and steel (Dumont, 1990, p.70). Furthermore, during this twenty-five year period, firms were largely outside of the EC policy-making process (Green, 1993; Haas, 1958). This was partly due to the antipathy of EC founding fathers such as Monnet towards big business, which he viewed as too nationalistic to support a European project (Green, 1993, p.3); and partly the associated fact that such firms saw more benefit through their national political patrons, than through the Community.

As this chapter illustrates, this situation has changed significantly. Firms are now frequent policy partners - especially in high technology areas such as computers and electronic components. This partnership has come to the fore especially since the accession of Jacques Delors to the Commission presidency. Delors had, since his time as French Minister of Finance, been a great believer in the importance of cordial and co-operative relations between firms and public sector actors in the formulation of policy for industry. Thus, he began to increase the degree of consultation and collaboration between industry and the Commission in the creation of policy for sectors such as semiconductors.

5.i. EC technology policy for semiconductors

The Community's participation in semiconductor R&D has two separate and distinct manifestations: first, through its financial involvement in Eureka projects such as JESSI, which will be discussed in some detail in Chapter five; and secondly, through the EC's own ESPRIT programme, which we shall analyse in this chapter. With this two-pronged technology policy, the Community have pursued an active innovation policy for semiconductors - placing inordinate emphasis on knowledge creation and dissemination.

A symbolic starting point for large scale EC high tech industrial policy activity is Davignon's previously discussed 1979 meeting with the CEOs of Europe's big twelve electronics firms. As Sharp (1989) has argued, under Davignon's guidance, the Commission began to develop a more strategic approach to the IT sector. The creation of a round table, comprising both EC officials and industrialists[5], was intended to jointly devise ways in which the Community could help restructure Europe's high technology industries through research. If Community funded R&D was aimed at Europeanising nationally-based companies, it was necessary to have collaboration between researchers in different member states. However, this would almost inevitably mean that companies would be collaborating with firms that were their competitors (at least in some segment of the market). No company wanted to do that for fear of losing exclusive rights to the products that emerge from the research. The solution arrived at was the concept of pre-competitive research. This concept basically entails working on ideas so far from marketable products, that companies can save money and effort by pooling R&D resources without giving away trade secrets. As academic commentators such as Dumont argued:

> co-operation is therefore limited to research, and must not be extended to product development, industrial exploitation, or sales agreements (1990, p.71).

This was easier said than done. The concept was problematic for two reasons. No company wants to do research that is not, at some point, going to lead to products or processes. Moreover, the line between totally non-competitive and commercially interesting is ill-defined. However, the Commission chose to proceed with this concept and to limit its participation to projects which were only of this fuzzy pre-competitive nature.

The real surge in European technological collaboration began in the early 1980s. By 1982, the EC's research budget was Ecu 567 million, which was 2.55 per cent of the Community's total budget, and 2.2 per cent of the research spending of member states (Mckenzie, 1992, p.6). At this time, one could also witness the beginning of programmes aimed directly at promoting industrial competitiveness. From a legalistic standpoint, the formulation and enactment of the Single European Act, was a significant landmark in the development of EC technology policy, giving it a legal basis in the Treaty of Rome. Through the SEA, a European Research and Technology Community was established and the Community was given specific powers in the field of scientific and technical co-operation, primarily under the auspices of the Framework Programme of research and development. Although the Community's research and technology activities were to be both diversified and selective, they centred on a few large areas most notably the realm of information technology - semiconductor materials and components comprising the core of this area.

The first of the pre-competitive R&D Framework Programme's was officially launched in 1984, for a three year period. This extended joint research activities to cover a broad range of areas, and has since been followed by three other such programmes. EC funding normally covers up to 50 per cent of project costs. The Framework Programme was divided into eight strategic areas, which in turn were split into specific programmes such as Research into Advanced Communications Technology for Europe (RACE), Basic Research in Industrial Technologies for Europe (BRITE), and most notably, the European Strategic Programme for Research in Information Technology (ESPRIT).

5.ii. EC controlled R&D initiatives

ESPRIT was incorporated in the first Framework Programme in 1984, and is probably the best known of the EC joint research programmes. With a budget of ECU 750 million ($850 million approx.) for the first three year phase, its role was to sponsor collaborative research in information technology (Sharp, 1989, p.210). ESPRIT is itself subdivided into four areas, plus basic research. Of these areas, one of the largest is within the pre-competitive stage of microelectronics development[6].

The second, slightly delayed, phase of ESPRIT, which began in 1988, was roughly twice the size of its predecessor, with a budget of Ecu 1.6 billion. This figure was also three times the entire 1982 EC research budget. The ESPRIT II programme was streamlined into three main areas of research: microelectronics, information technology processing systems, and applications technologies. Although nominally still pre-competitive, ESPRIT II in fact came close to competitive research, as those involved in Phase I sought to develop some of the ideas promoted at that stage. The slight delay in launching ESPRIT II (and at a wider level, Framework II), was due to the first major reservations on behalf of a member state towards the whole idea. Britain delayed the second programme in an attempt to reduce Framework II's budget. A primary reason for this British ambiguity was the issue of additionality (Mckenzie, 1992, p.8). That is to say, the British had misgivings regarding the extent to which EC research funding was in addition to what a member state would have spent anyway on research activities, and not merely a means through which a state could reduce the amount of its regular budget[7]. The British wanted, in effect, to ensure that the national governments did not simply shift the financial burden of R&D to the EC. As the next chapter will discuss, these reservations may be extended to incorporate the firms participating in EC funded projects. Is EC money supplementary to their R&D resources already allocated, or do they merely substitute public money for their own corporate financing of R&D? Such misgivings, although usually difficult to prove, had some substance.

The UK succeeded in both delaying the introduction of Framework II and in reducing its budget, as requested by the Commission. Thus, Framework II was launched in 1988, with a budget of Ecu 5.7 billion, rather than the Ecu 7.7 billion initially requested. Even with the reduced total, this sum was still ten times greater than the EC research budget of the early 1980s.

Let us focus briefly on non-Eureka EC R&D policy for microelectronic semiconductor chips. In 1981, the Council of the European Communities adopted legislation[8] stipulating that each year thereafter, the Commission would forward a report to both the EC Council and the European Parliament on the development of Community projects in the field of microelectronics technology. The adoption of such legislation is significant proof of the EC's targeting of microelectronics as an industrial sector with special political and economic significance for the wider society (i.e. strategic). The two research areas covered by these reports were the Computer Aided Design (CAD) for Very Large Scale Integrated Circuits, and the Equipment for Manufacturing and Testing VLSI. These formed the core of the Community's early policy focus on microelectronics (often referred to as the MEL Programme). The programme was scheduled to run for four years, beginning in 1982. The programme's budget was Ecu 40 million, and was composed of 15 projects involving 62 organisations from different member states. The Commission covered, on average, over 40 per cent of project costs. According to official Commission documentation:

> The microelectronics (MEL) programme was prepared by the Commission in the late seventies and early eighties in order to take advantage of collaborative research and development to contribute to an increase in the competitiveness of Europe in the strategically and economically important field of microelectronics[9].

This gives further, strong support to this work's assertion that microelectronic components (mainly active semiconductor ones) were targeted as strategic by the EC from an early stage - in advance of and to a greater extent than all other high technology sectors. The industry was, from the outset, placed at the vanguard of the Community's efforts to enhance Europe's competitive position in information technology. As such, it accrued the political baggage associated with such an undertaking. In effect, semiconductors became the flag ship of EC efforts to co-ordinate European industrial affairs and further the Community's economic and political integration.

The MEL programme provided significant structural experience in the creation of the wider ESPRIT programme. In the fourth annual report on MEL's progress, issued in early 1987, it was argued that more co-ordinated efforts at Community level are needed for developing advanced equipment[10]. Hence, it is obvious that the Commission saw itself as playing the lead role in developing a competitive market presence for European semiconductor equipment producers. This is indicative of the overtly *dirigiste* information technology policy pursued by the Commission during the 1980s. At an inter-Commission level, DG XIII (then responsible for information and communications technology) was directly charged with implementing this interventionist policy approach. In fact, the MEL programme's implementation was primarily under the control of bureaucrats. The Commission implemented it, with the assistance of a Consultative Committee, comprised of member state representatives[11]. Thus, those who were directly affected by the research projects - the private sector players - had no substantial direct input into the MEL programme's decision-making and implementation process. This is illustrative of the top-down, big brother nature of early EC policy for semiconductors. Firms were consulted when the policy was being created, but were not always included in the policy's actual day-to-day operations. This remained solely the domain of the Commission.

5.iii. Assessing R&D policy: acknowledging the counterfactual

It is important to stress that we are aware of the limitations of theory. These limitations are most evident when assessing the affect of policy outcomes on industrial competitiveness. The counterfactual problem inherently arises for instance, when using theory to analyse and explain uncertain variables such as collaborative R&D programmes. For our purposes this means posing the question, if ESPRIT (or JESSI) had not been implemented, would the competitiveness of Europe's indigenous semiconductor producers have continued to decline? We must accept that we cannot argue that such programmes have adversely affected the competitive position of their industrial participants. Given the multitude of other variables, both internal and external to their industrial members, these programmes cannot be held responsible for any overall corporate competitive decline. However, it is possible to estimate the relative loss or gain accrued by firms through programmes like ESPRIT, in terms such as technological achievements and market share. A further, interrelated precondition which should be stressed is the difficulty in conducting any form of cost-benefit analysis for research and development vis-à-vis competitive enhancement. It is quantifiably precarious to weigh off the cost of a particular R&D programme against a company's relative gain in competitive position towards its market rivals. In addition, R&D programmes may often be a step in the right direction, but still comprise only a part of the overall requirements for competitive enhancement. Georghiou and Metcalf provide a useful analysis of the problems inherent in evaluating the impact of European Community research programmes on industrial competitiveness:

> An enhanced technological base still requires investment in plant and skills and successful entrepreneurial activity to support it. Products may draw upon multiple sources of knowledge and an R&D project may contribute to the development of the number of products and processes. Collectively these problems of attribution make it difficult to assess the economic return on R&D even in industry (1993, pp.161-2).

A further difficulty in evaluating R&D benefits is the time factor; that is to say, the competitive benefits of R&D often take longer to materialise than the life span of a particular R&D programme. However, generally evaluations occur during or just after a programme's running-time, and thus, its effects may not yet have been experienced (Georghiou and Metcalfe, 1993). Bearing these limitations in mind, let us advance an analysis of EC-controlled R&D initiatives for the electronics sector.

5.iv. An analysis of ESPRIT

Two influential reports on Commission-directed R&D programmes were released in 1989. One was a review of the overall Framework initiative, and the other was a more specific assessment of ESPRIT. Both were conducted at the behest of the Community, but by independent panels comprised of European scientists and industrialists.

The Framework Review Board[12] called for more research relevant to the Single Market and key technologies important to European industrial competitiveness[13]. Here, special emphasis was placed on information technology, due to the sector's meta-technology status. This lends further support to our argument that certain industries (particularly information technology industries such as microelectronics) were identified as strategic or key industries at an EC level, and were subsequently targeted by policy-makers for special attention. This translated as a greater share of R&D funding than other sectors, and more attention (read intervention) from governmental actors. The share of the total Framework budget dedicated to ESPRIT was, as already indicated, much larger than that dedicated to other industrial realms, and the EC established a separate directorate general (DGXIII) to oversee policy for information technology.

Most significantly, the Framework Review Board called for a less rigid structure for project definition and financing. They proposed that the budget should be divided between broad project clusters, rather than specific, individual projects. This would allow for a rapid and relatively easy transfer of financial resources between projects in the course of a Framework's duration, as particular projects became more tangible than others. In addition, the Review Board emphasised the ineffectiveness of conducting research projects across too wide a spectrum. In effect, Framework was trying to cover everything, and in doing so, was spreading its resources thinly across too many areas, rather than concentrating them on a few research realms.

The Review Board's criticisms of Framework II, and recommendations for structural change, were seen as valid by many policy-makers. Within the European Commission, there was a general consensus that the Framework Programme was in need of restructuring. In particular, most realised that Framework's project focus would have to be redefined and reduced. However, divisions arose on some elements of the proposed restructuring. The (then) Information Technology Directorate-General (XIII) was fully supportive of proposals to devote more attention to key technologies - most of which were under its jurisdiction. The Industrial Affairs and the Competition Directorate-Generals were critical of any policy favouritism and sectoral targeting[14]. The member of the Commission responsible for science and technology, Vice President Pandolfi, fully accepted the proposals for change, and immediately set about implementing them. However, he encountered opposition from the Council of Ministers - who, of course, have the final word on policy. The Community research ministers rejected the main recommendations of the Review Board because they wanted to know in advance what the Commission would spend their money on. Consequently, although already identified, serious structural problems have endured in Framework III and IV, particularly regarding issues of flexibility on funding allocation (Mckenzie, 1992, p.11).

The 1989 ESPRIT II Review Board[15] was a follow-up to its 1985 counterpart which reviewed the first phase of ESPRIT. Whilst praising the co-operative network established by ESPRIT, the Board acknowledged that in sectors such as microelectronics, the adverse balance of trade has continued[16]. Also, emphasis was put upon the necessity to place greater emphasis on economic exploitation, and to involve users more in the projects. Furthermore, it points out the possible weakness in developing an all-encompassing programme, rather than focusing on a few strategic themes (ESPRIT Review Board, 1989, p.9). In this respects, the Review Board targeted information technology as strategic, being of great importance to the Community's future[17].

Thus, EC policy for the semiconductor sector, as manifest through ESPRIT I, had no real success in improving European chip producers market positions[18], and in fact, their competitive decline merely continued through the 1980s, from a combined world market share of 16 per cent in 1980, to less that 10 per cent one decade later (Mytelka, 1993, p.1). This failure had two dimensions: firstly, much of the research carried out was too far upstream from the market to have any (short term) quantifiable affect on industrial competitiveness; and secondly, little emphasis was put on the need for European chip producers to move away from out-dated technologies, and adopt more competitive substances, processes and products. On this second point, Hobday (1992) has stated that:

Europe's IT firms were particularly weak because they were specialised in older less dynamic technologies. ESPRIT I did little to encourage a faster movement away from traditional technologies such as bipolar integrated circuits and silicon substrates and into CMOS technology, or Galium Arsenide and indium phosphide substrates, of particular importance in optoelectronic applications [19].

This fact began to hit home as the first phase of ESPRIT was wound down, and attempts were made to rectify the problem in subsequent phases[20].

Mytelka puts forward two interlinked arguments regarding the affect which ESPRIT has on competitiveness. She argues that the short term affect can lead into (and be outweighed by) the more long term affect:

> From a European perspective there are grounds for arguing that the ESPRIT programme has contributed both to the preservation of competition within Europe and internationally, while at the same time it has laid the bases for a future reduction in competition and the strengthening of an information technology oligopoly on a world scale (1991, p.20).

Indeed, ESPRIT has helped the cause of competitiveness through encouraging European information technology producers to adopt to the changing nature of market competition, and to adapt new design and production processes. Also, it may be argued that the continued existence of an indigenous European research and production base makes for more consumer choice and thus a generally more competitive global market in information technology. However, as correctly pointed out, there is a danger that this collaboration to compete could, over time and without the necessary vigilance, degenerate into uncompetitive collusion amongst European information technology producers.

At the beginning of the 1990s, the Commission's information technology division (DGXIII), which then administered ESPRIT, stated that the programme needed more time to produce results. However, officials elsewhere in the Commission[21], contended that the basic approach was flawed. These critics could be found predominantly in DGs III and IV (Industry and Competition). Specifically, they argued that:

(1) Large European electronics companies have become unhealthily dependent on EC subsidies and trade protection.
(2) The financial and management crisis at Philips and the weakness of other European industrial leaders, raises questions about the value and purpose of the programmes.
(3) Fujitsu's take-over of ICL and the existence of substantial US and Japanese manufacturing capacity in Europe, make it hard to limit EC support largely to European-owned companies[22].
(4) Though ESPRIT has improved technical information flows between companies, it has produced little commercially useful technology.
(5) EC technological support has been spread too thinly across too many projects.

Two additional observations which may be made at this juncture, are that:
(6) the EC's trade deficit in information technology products was continuing to grow.

(7) European-owned producers share of the market for chips and most electronics products had declined even further since the introduction of ESPRIT[23].

Some Commission officials were prone to blame industry for the above negativities of ESPRIT. These (largely DGXIII) individuals argued that companies had not carried out their part of the bargain, i.e. to rapidly and effectively utilise EC money to speed up product innovation and improve productivity. There is some truth in this assertion. However, it assumes that money always produces innovation, which is of course not true. Moreover, considerable blame for the above failures also lies with Directorate-General XIII of the Commission. Critics (often in other Commission DGs) accuse it of being more interested in 'empire building and forging cosy links with industry, than in devising effective technology policies'[24].

5.v. A critique of EC controlled R&D initiatives

In evaluating the EC's collaborative research and technological development policies, it is useful to consider external perspectives. The 1991 US Office of Technology Assessment report findings on these policies[25], provides a good example of a critical extra-Communitarian perspective. This report was written for the United States Congress, and intended to help establish the nature of American industrial competitiveness relative to the EC and Japan. In beginning to assess EC technology policy, the OTA correctly suggests that years of protection and government support for certain industries, has sapped firms competitiveness. However, it then makes the mistake of assuming that these firms are increasingly vulnerable due to the replacement of protectionist national policies with EC policies that forbid subsidising one member nation's firms at the expense of anothers. This assumption, firstly, underestimates the strong influence which national governments still exert within the EC policy-making process (for most industries), and their consequent ability to prevent or delay Commission attempts at industrial liberalisation which may adversely affect certain national firms. Secondly, it does not take into account the tendency of states such as France and Italy, to pursue dual level strategies for certain industries, i.e. to fully participate in technology policies implemented at an EC level, whilst continuing to fund specific domestic firms through national technology policies. Thirdly, and perhaps most importantly, it may be argued that, rather than creating a level playing field[26] within the Community, the co-ordination of much technology policy at an EC level merely changes the nature of government intervention and subsidisation, instead of reducing the degree of it. Thus, individual national champions often become collective European champions. A case in point is the European electronics industry.

The main conclusions of the OTA report on EC collaborative technology programmes are that previous EC protection of its internal market has effectively backfired, because it has often been circumvented by external firms establishing manufacturing operations within the Community. This has subsequently necessitated a response from the Commission. This response has come in three forms. First, common technology policy, which results in collaborative programmes such as ESPRIT and Eureka. Second, support (benign, not active) for transnational ventures such as Airbus. Third, a competition policy aimed at discouraging state ownership and the promotion of national champions. Following on from this, the OTA concludes that it is too early to fully evaluate the EC's collaborative technology policies. However, it does argue that they have at least succeeded in increasing the willingness to cooperate amongst EC firms and governments, and have helped to diffuse scientific and technical information throughout the Community. On the most important issue of competitiveness though, the OTA concluded that the aforementioned policies have thus far had little or no success in enhancing the international competitiveness of EC firms within policy targeted industrial sectors.

Numerous European policy-makers and computer corporate executives[27] argue that a *dirigiste* EC regime which supports European Champions, will lead to increased competitiveness for European firms. Two counter-arguments may be advanced. First, as academic commentators such as Porter (1990) and Stopford (1993) have argued, and as countries such as Japan have illustrated, successful national industries tend to be ones where intensely competitive domestic rivalries push each other to excel. By agreeing to deals that limit competition in its own chip or computer hardware industries, the EC deprives them of this incentive to innovate. Second, the creation of a European Champion obliges the Commission to support it if (and when) it runs into trouble. That means being involved in the type of centralised planning that has gone out of fashion even in Eastern Europe. It also means repeating the mistakes, made by national planners, on a pan-European scale. The fundamental counter-argument is that European business needs more competition, not less.

Woods (1987) argued that EC R&D policy during the 1980s had little or no positive effect on European firms market position, because it failed to address the real cause of Europe's competitive difficulties. That is to say, the problem was not a technology lag, but rather, structural obstacles which were present in the European economic environment. He argued that the competitive weaknesses of European firms lay not in basic technology, but in the marketing, commercialisation, and adaptation of technology (Woods, 1987, p.90). Woods acknowledges that both ESPRIT and Eureka are positive policy moves, in terms of overcoming the national champion approach (1987, p.96). However, as Mytelka (1991) also argued, there is a medium to long term danger that too much technological collaboration within Europe may adversely affect competitiveness. Furthermore, the attention which EC policymakers and corporate actors have given to collaborative research programmes, has eclipsed the more fundamental competitive problems facing most of Europe's information technology companies.

This work concurs with Woods analysis, and thus also stresses the need for shifting the spotlight away from research, and towards the European information technology producers central structural competitive hindrances, i.e. the inability to rapidly adopt new design and production processes, and get the resultant products to market faster. As the next chapter will illustrate, such a change of emphasis must occur at the corporate level, if it is to be effective.

6 Policy partnerships: the liberal policy mask

The European Commission argues that it has moved away from policies of sectoral preference and industrial intervention. The more recent policy statements emphasise a new commitment to creating a suitable business environment for all industries, and the establishment of a promotional partnership between the EC and corporations, in order to enhance European firms competitive advantage in the global market. Let us take a closer look at EC electronics policy this decade, and decide if the EC is indeed beginning to throw off the shackles of strategic targeting and interventionist electronics policy instruments.

A significant development in EC policy for electronics was the 1990 decision to clearly define and establish an EC industrial policy. As usual, this decision involved a proposal from the Commission, which was subsequently adopted by the Council. The official Commission communications surrounding the introduction of a *de jure* industrial policy were of a purposefully ambiguous nature. Constant stress was put on the concept of competitiveness and on the notion that the attainment of competitiveness is primarily the responsibility of enterprises. However, the role of governmental actors is far from weak in this process, and is more of an active partner than a silent spectator:

> The main question is no longer whether an industrial policy is opportune, since governments are increasingly aware that, in advanced economies, they have a major influence on industrial development and performance. The main issue, in the eyes of the Commission, is which conditions need to be present in order to strengthen the allocation of resources by market forces and thereby to accelerate structural adjustment, improve industrial competitiveness, and establish an industrial and in particular, technological, long-term framework (CEC, 1990, p.2).

The main policy document outlining this new and enhanced Community role in electronics policy, was the 1990 *Industrial Policy In An Open and Competitive Environment* report. Internal Commission sources[28] argue that this document was indicative of the more liberal tendencies within the Commission. It was seen as a victory for liberalism over interventionism. The document argued that a growing consensus has emerged on 'the type of policy needed to lay down the conditions for a strong and competitive industry (CEC, 1990, p.1). This consensus derives from the experience of Community policies operational since the mid-1980s. The implicit argument is that it has been recognised within the Commission that the top-down and heavily interventionist policies of the 1980s have not succeeded in enhancing competitiveness; and thus, a new post-interventionist policy set, with emphasis on global competitiveness, is needed. The communiqué goes on to state that the role of public authorities is above all a catalyst and path-breaker for innovation. The main responsibility for industrial competitiveness must lie with firms themselves, but they should be able to expect from public authorities clear and predictable conditions for their activities. There is nothing new in this argument. To say that the ultimate onus for competitiveness is on firms themselves, is to state the obvious. To say that this firm responsibility should be extensively supported by the public sector, has major public policy implications. The Commission acknowledges that firms compete for world market share but it argues that they cannot do so alone. Thus, a middle-way is advocated, between government directed firm strategy and free market competition. The result is policy partnership. Ross (1993) lends support to the thesis that EC industrial policy has been shaped by a Commission-large firm partnership. This applies in particular to policy for the electronics sector. He observes that EC policies for electronics have emerged during the 1990s as a result of large European electronics firms exerting pressure on the Commission to assist them:

Jacques Delors was frequently visited by the captains and generals of European industry. A select group of them thus alerted him in spring of 1990 to the clouds gathering around European electronics (Ross, 1993, p.21).

They exerted pressure through employing the economic argument, that, due to the strategic nature of electronics, if the European electronics industry was in difficulty, the wider European economy would also be adversely affected. In addition, the industrial leaders played the political card, intimating that the Community's *raison d'être* may be questioned amongst the European business community, if the Commission did not attempt to assist industry in times of stiff international competition:

Delors's corporate visitors proposed expensive bail-outs and protectionism and intimated, *sotto voce*, that if the companies sank deeper into trouble the Community might be held responsible, with dire consequences for business confidence in the Commission's efforts (Ross, 1993, p.22).

Such actions are in line with Richardson and Jordan's argument that:

as the relationship between groups and governments gets closer (more symbiotic), then it becomes easier for either side to 'lean on' the other in order to achieve a particular result (1979, p.120).

Although these authors developed their hypothesis with a view to the national policy-making arena, works such as Ross (1993; 1995) and Mazey and Richardson (1993) suggest that the same interest group pressure exists at an EC-level.

Not only did the Commission fear losing the confidence of European business (and thus losing power vis-à-vis national governments) but as several observers have argued[29], the Commission saw European industry - especially high technology sectors - as potential allies in the struggle to achieve a federal Europe. Again, this strengthens the argument that the Commission endeavoured to create a common area of action for European industrial affairs and that electronics was at the forefront of this undertaking. Moreover, the Commission purposefully courted big business, seeing them as important allies in the European integration process. As Flamm argues:

the EC seems embarked on a path toward technological integration of the Community (1990, p.284).

This objective - involving declining use of national R&D programmes and a much larger role for the European Commission in organising and administering national R&D initiatives - fits with that pursued tangentially for European semiconductor trade and investment (Flamm, 1990, p.284). As such, Flamm's arguments lends support to our assertion that the EC innovation policy model for the semiconductor industry is part of the Community's efforts to create a common area of control and action for industrial affairs. The success or failure of these efforts has important lessons for the practicality of European integration. One may conceive of the interventionist 1991 Commission Communication on policy proposals for the European electronics and information technology industry[30], directly resulting from such Commission-firm meetings in the 1990/91 period.

Therefore, in bargaining terms, it is the big firms that have the most influence. They are the real winners with respects to having the greatest input into public policy. Of course, they are the real losers in the long term, given that these policy outcomes often hinder rather than help their competitive positions. Let us illustrate this notion of a (protective) policy partnership with some policy reality. Several examples of policy instrument implementation may be advanced to support a partnership interpretation of EC policy. The most notable realms of EC intervention are R&D initiatives and trade.

6.i. R&D as an instrument of the protective policy partnership model

R&D activities emerge as the EC's dominant policy tool for electronics. We have already discussed the evolution of European level R&D initiatives in some detail. Official Commission figure show that in 1993, for instance, the Community spent, in total, over 2 billion ECU (roughly $2.4 billion) on research. This sum hovered around the $2 billion per annum mark for some years previous. Much of this sum goes to projects within the Commission directed Framework programme. According to a former Commission vice-president, Karl Heinz Narjes, the Community has a responsibility to strengthen the scientific and technological basis of European industry, in addition to actively encouraging industry to become more responsive to the global competitive environment (Narjes, 1988, p.396). Thus, it is obvious that at the most senior levels of EC policy-making during the 1980s, an active interventionist view was taken towards the competitive enhancement of European high technology industries such as electronics. In addition, this policy stance had a protective, big brother undertone, which implied that the Commission knew best how to tackle the competitive malaise affecting sectors such as electronics. Market reality indicates that this was not actually the case. As the US Office of Technology Assessment has argued, EC intervention and subsidisation through R&D has had little success in enhancing the international competitiveness of firms within policy targeted sectors (OTA, 1991). Numerous European policy-makers and electronics corporate executives[31] argue that an interventionist EC regime will eventually lead to increased competitiveness for European electronics firms. For instance, Alain Gomez of Thomson advances the argument that European electronics firms simply need an adjustment period, under EC protection, and with government financial assistance, from which they will eventually emerge as strong global competitors (*Fortune* 20 April 1992, p.159). The influence of Gomez and other leading pro-intervention electronics executives is implicit in EC policy practices. However, as numerous academic commentators (Porter, 1990; Stopford, 1993) have argued, and as countries such as Japan and the US have illustrated, successful national industries tend to be ones where intensely competitive domestic rivalries push each other to excel. By agreeing to deals that limit competition in its own electronics industry, the EC deprives these firms of their incentive to innovate.

The Maastricht agreement of 1991 heralded a significant change in EC R&D policy. Previous restrictions on the scope of EC research activities - limiting them to pre-competitive activities - were loosened, and the Community was also permitted to expand its activities into non-industrial research. Thus, the Commission's potential role in European wide R&D policy was expanded - on the unanimous decision of the Community member states[32]. At the same time however, problems were experienced on the issue of approving the budget for Framework III, which was scheduled to run from 1990 until 1994. Due to delays caused mainly by the European Parliament (which can veto Framework), the third Framework Programme did not get under way until late 1992 (McKenzie, 1992, p.12).

6.ii. Trade tools and protective partnership

> Governments should interfere in the conduct of trade as little as possible. Once bureaucrats become involved in managing trade flows, the potential for misguided decisions rises greatly (GATT Director General Peter Sutherland in a speech to the European -American Chamber of Commerce, New York, 1994).

The Community employs five significant protectionist trade tools. These are high tariff levels, local content rules, the Procurement Directive, rules of origin, and anti-dumping legislation. In spite of liberal overtones, numerous protectionist element remains in EC trade policy for semiconductors. One of the most controversial of these is the 14 per cent tariff which the EC imposes on semiconductor imports[33]. At a 1992 semiconductor production conference in Ireland[34], almost all of the world's leading chip makers expressed their dissatisfaction with what they described as the EC's unfair and inconsistent tariff policy. More specifically, the conference delegates highlighted two aspects of the overall policy for special criticism. First, the high duty on semiconductor manufacturing equipment, and second, the varying duties the EC imposes on components[35]. For instance, US chip giant Intel estimates that the 25 per cent EC duty on production equipment added $125 million to the cost of a wafer fabrication facility which Intel built in Ireland in the early 1990s. Intel Europe's director and general manager, Hans Geyer, describes the EC tariff system as another manifestation of protectionist policies, and states that such policies:

> make systems manufacturing in Europe more expensive...and by hurting our customers, the EC is hurting the industry[36].

As usual, there were a minority of firms in support of the EC's high tariff barriers. The most notable European firm in favour of import duties is SGS-Thomson. The next chapter will further develop this firm's position on EC semiconductor policy.

A related policy is that involving local content rules, i.e. that manufactured chips which have less than 50 per cent of Community value-added, are subject to tariffs. Most local content requirements in the Community are levied by member states, on their own initiative. However, there are EC wide requirements with regards to antidumping and preferential trade agreements. Here again, several of the leading global chip makers have had conflicts with the Commission (and with individual member states) regarding the very high level of local content required in the chips they sell in the EC. This policy is closely linked with another controversial and protectionist element of EC trade policy - the Procurement Directive agreed by the EC Council of Ministers in February 1990. The main thrust of this directive is that contracting bodies may refuse tenders, if 50 per cent or more of the value of manufactured products forming part of the tenders is of non-EC origin. A further dimension of this directive is that when EC and non-EC tenders are considered equivalent, the former must be preferred[37]. The US has expressed its reservations regarding the 1990 EC Procurement Directive, given its discrimination against non-EC manufacturers.

Another interventionist element of EC trade policy affecting semiconductors is rules of origin legislation. This trade tool is directly associated with local content requirements of course, given that local content rules cannot be implemented until the products country of origin has been determined. This procedure may sound overly bureaucratic: one might argue that it is a relatively simple task to determine where a product originates - in fact many have a 'Made In....' tag attached. This is true in textiles or in childrens toys for instance but it is not such a simple process when applied to semiconductors. Active semiconductor components go through a number of complex stages of production before they are ready for application. Due to production costs such as labour, the less complex but more laborious stages in this process are frequently carried out in countries other than those in which the chips were etched on the silicon for instance. This often means that the design and processing of chips will occur in a firm's home country, such as the US or Japan;

the assembly of these microchips will take place in a country where labour costs are low - frequently south-east Asia; and the final testing of the chips will be in the country where the export buyers are located, for example, EC countries. In 1989, Commission Regulation (EEC) No. 289/89 came into force, determining the origin of integrated circuits. This regulation (binding in all member states of course), adopted a clear and stringent approach in determining the country of origin for chips. Clear account is taken of the multi-leveled production process for integrated circuits, and of the fact that this entire process chain usually involves two or more countries. Also, most importantly, the Commission takes account of the difference in value between stages of production:

> Whereas Article 5 of Regulation (EEC) No.802/68 lays down that a product in the production of which two or more countries were concerned shall be regarded as originating in the country in which the last substantial process or operation that is economically justified was performed....Whereas, for integrated circuits, the variety of operations which come within the scope of manufacture makes it necessary to establish the last substantial process or operation[38].

Thus, the Commission stipulates that the manufacturing operations following diffusion (e.g. assembly and testing) do not - separately or collectively - constitute sufficient value-added to warrant country of origin status being given to the country in which they were conducted. Instead, the regulation determines country of origin as that country in which the knowledge-intensive chip creation stage occurs, i.e. where the microchip is given all its functional capabilities. In effect, this regulation severely limits microchip imports into the Community. It *de facto* requires non-EC chip producers to establish chip fabrication facilities within the Community - if they wish to avoid punitive measures on imported products, and enjoy full access to the EC market.

Taken together, import tariffs, rules of origin, the Procurement Directive, and local content requirements, are elements of an EC policy for semiconductors which has obvious and rigorous protectionist tendencies towards imports. As Tyson argues:

> European rules of origin combined with various local content tests to meet the rules, can determine the eligibility of foreign firms for the following benefits of the unified European market: exemption from residual national quotas, eligibility for government procurement, avoidance of antidumping duties, and eligibility for [EEA] and other preferential trading arrangements (1993, p.8).

A fifth protectionist trade instrument employed by the EC for electronics, is anti-dumping legislation. Anti-dumping is a legal instrument employed by the EC against companies which are alleged to be importing products into the Community at below market prices. Between 1987 and 1991 alone, fourteen anti-dumping investigations were initiated against electronics firms. The companies under investigation were mainly Japanese and South Korean (CEC, 1992b). Such East Asian firms were not necessarily dumping, but could simply have been producing at lower costs. As Ernst (1993) argues, Europeans have cried foul on this practice simply to protect more inefficient European producers[39]. It is difficult to establish the actual production cost of Japanese and Korean microchips. Thus, we cannot categorically prove whether or not these East Asian firms were actually dumping. To illustrate the increasing role played by antidumping legislation in EC trade policy, one can see that between 1987 and 1991, the Commission initiated 169 antidumping investigations, involving imports from 33 countries. Two leading semiconductor producing countries - Japan and South Korea - were at the top of the list in terms of antidumping investigations. The country most involved was Japan, with 21 investigated complaints; and South Korea was third, having 19 claims against its firms investigated by the Commission[40]. Of these cases, 14 concerned the electronics sector. More specifically, three were concerning semiconductors - two against Japanese and one against Korean producers. An example of one semiconductor antidumping case is the 1990 imposition of a provisional antidumping duty on Japanese DRAM imports[41]. The action was taken, based upon Council Regulation (EEC) No. 2423/88 of 11 July 1988, on protection against dumped or subsidised imports from countries not members of the European Economic Community. The complaint was initially lodged by the European Electronic Component Manufacturers Association[42]. The European complainant companies were Siemens, SGS Microelettronica, and Thomson Semiconducteurs[43], as well as - interestingly - Motorola (UK). Perhaps this latter complainant symbolises the good citizen seeking the complete protection of the welfare state, for which he has paid in full. The charges were levied at Fujitsu, Hitachi, Mitsubishi, NEC, NMB, Oki, Texas Instruments (Japan), and Toshiba. In fact, just about everybody who was anybody in the world of Japanese microchip production, was accused of dumping. Perhaps this is a further illustration of the Japanaphobia which, as chapter five will show, was prevalent within the European semiconductor industry. The complaint contained evidence of dumping of DRAMs originating in Japan, and of substantial injury in various forms. An interesting argument ensued, between the accused Japanese exporters and the Commission, concerning the allegation that the initial complaint was on behalf of practically all actual or potential Community producers of DRAMs. The Japanese pointed out that this was not true, since companies such as Philips and IBM had significant DRAM fabrication facilities within the EC, and yet were not listed amongst the complainants[44]. In addition, they pointed out that, under the rules of origin legislation applicable at the time the complaint was lodged, other firms which assembled DRAMs within the Community should be included in the term Community industry. Despite several counter-arguments, the Commission conceded that the term Community industry referred only to the actual complainant companies. This conflict is interesting because it may be interpreted either as resulting from the EECA misleading the Commission in its original complaint, or as a deliberate attempt on the part of the Commission to give its antidumping actions a semblance of widespread support and thus legitimacy. This latter interpretation would fit with the emergent image of EC trade policy as inherently protectionist and interventionist.

Were the competitive and financial difficulties experienced by the complainant firms due to the rapid increase in low-priced Japanese DRAMs coming into the Community? Alternatively, were they due to inappropriate corporate strategies, late market entry, and other structural and technical problems, particular to these firms? The Commission claims to have given due consideration to this point (OJ L, 20, p.20). However, little or no evidence or argument is offered to refute these other, non-dumping related factors in firm uncompetitiveness. Instead, the Commission focuses on dumping as the primary (if not only) cause of material injury and material retardation[45] to the complainant companies. A desire to justify an arduous and expensive legal investigation certainly appears evident. Furthermore, the Commission indicates again the value which it attributes to the semiconductor industry as a strategic, enabling industry, and indicates that the industry needs to be maintained (and if necessary, protected), for the benefit of the wider Community society and economy:

> The Commission is of the view that a viable Community DRAM industry will contribute to a strong Community electronics industry overall. First, DRAMs service as a technology driver for other more complex semiconductor devices. Second, the semiconductor industry of which DRAM production is a part, is a strategic industry in that ·semiconductors are a key component for the data processing, telecommunications, and automotive industries[46].

Thus, it may be argued that the Commission has also used antidumping legislation as part of a wider policy (already outlined) to protect product segments of the strategic European semiconductor industry from vigorous external competition within the EC market. This policy position was most fervently advanced by the Commission's Information Technology Directorate-General. It was adopted at the behest of a group of large electronics firms, through the EECA. This is illustrative of the protective partnership which has prevailed in EC innovation policy.

A two dimensioned Commission Measure was introduced as result of the above antidumping investigation. It involved, first, price undertakings between the offending firms and the Commission, whereby the Commission fixes a minimum reference price level for DRAM imports; and second, duty, whereby a provisional antidumping duty was imposed, to remove the injury caused to European industry. The duty was set at 60 per cent of the net free-at-Community border price before duty. Given the price undertakings offered by the accused Japanese firms, those firms were excluded from the duty.

It is interesting to note that, unlike semiconductor trade agreements between Japan and the US, the 1989 EC-Japan semiconductor price agreement was undertaken between a governmental actor (the European Commission) and a group of firms from a third country. The Japanese government did not sign the agreement and was not (directly) involved in its negotiation[47].

We have advanced evidence to suggest that a protective partnership exists in the nature of EC policy for semiconductors. This is evident in both the R&D and trade policy instruments which the Community employs. This reality is in conflict with the essence of Ostry's innovation policy model for industry. The essence of that model is to promote structural change and improve international competitiveness (1990, p.53). Our findings indicate that EC policy is actually distorting structural change and probably hindering competitiveness. The innovation policy approach does however fit with the official stated aim of EC industrial policy for electronics[48]. Thus, significant changes must occur if EC policy reality is to fit the rhetoric.

7 The interventionist consensus

In formulating an EC industrial policy, the Commission received strong support from the member states. In a meeting of November 1990, the EC Council strongly endorsed the Commission *Industrial Policy in an Open and Competitive Environment* communication:

> The Council warmly appreciates the document forwarded by the Commission. It approves the document's conclusions here attached, in view of achieving the goal of an industrial policy of the Community that would take into account the complexities of the situation both internal and external to the Community as well as a more balanced development and a greater economic and social cohesion within the Community. It calls on the Commission to continue its work and its studies in light of the discussion which has taken place (EC Council of Ministers, 1990).

The Commission declares that it wishes to escape from the traditional black and white approach to policy, i.e. liberalism versus interventionism, and forge a middle-ground policy (CEC, 1990). Such a government-business partnership has become very fashionable in the world of the 1990s. As we have seen, the most significant elements of EC industrial policy for electronics involve firms in a prominent role. Other studies have shown that large firms have, for instance, played a central role in launching the Single Market programme during the 1980s (Zysman and Sandholtz, 1992; Junne, 1992; Green, 1993; Peterson, 1993;). These big corporate players have a relationship with the European Commission which goes above and beyond that of any interest groups or lobbyists. They are frequently seen by the Commission as experts to be consulted on all policy decisions affecting their industrial sector (Junne, 1992; Ross, 1993). As Junne argues, 'representatives of MNCs get directly involved in political decision-making when either their interests are immediately at stake, or when the implementation of specific measures would need their direct co-operation' (1992, p.24). An example of the first kind of issue would be trade policy, and the second kind could be collaborative R&D initiatives. The Framework Programme, and especially ESPRIT[49], was established in consultation with large European high technology firms; anti-dumping investigations are undertaken at the request of firms. EC policy formulation has indeed become a more collective, public-private consensus-building process. It has, in effect, acquired a corporatist persona. Instead of imposing their will on the private sector, governmental actors are negotiating the nature and extent of intervention with their corporate constituents. This scenario is particularly prevalent for the electronics sector. Moreover, this policy-making model is not unique to the European Community. The Clinton administration excels at government-firm bargained intervention, and relations between the public and private sector in Japan and other East Asian countries have long been close and frequently consensual. This neo-interventionism is embodied in the Commission's 1990 industrial policy plan. The 1994 follow-up communication (*An Industrial Competitiveness Policy for the European Union*), emphasised the need to reduce levels of state aid for industry, and to address the unemployment crisis in Europe. Again, this document is touted as a new look industrial policy, which offers evidence of new thinking in Europe (*The Financial Times*, 15 September, 1994). Upon conducting a comparative analysis though, this later industrial policy document merely reiterates the earlier Commission objectives and methods. Thus, one can see that the neo-interventionist approach is still predominant amongst EC electronics policy-makers.

More concrete evidence for the Commission's interventionist tendencies is found in the 1991 communication on policy for the electronics industry. As we have seen, based on the rhetoric and policy statements of 1990, the Community appeared to be embarking on a more liberal approach towards information technology industries. The report, *The European Electronics and Information Technology Industries: State of Play, Issues at Stake, and Proposals for Action* (CEC, April 1991), directly countervened this ideological shift. Drawn up by DG XIII, the document's tone and content were criticised within the Commission (by DGs III and IV) as well as without. The official purpose of the communication, as outlined on page one, was to apply the November 1990 Commission defined concept of industrial policy, to the Community information technology and electronics industry. The report argues that the state of the European industry gives cause for concern in essential areas such as microchips. It goes on to propose that the root cause of Europe's poor competitiveness may be attributed to the fragmented nature of the European market. It may be argued that this particular attribution of competitive hindrances gave the Commission a green light to directly intervene in these essential areas of information technology - given that the implementation of the Single Market is primarily a Commission competence[50]. This report, in line with the 1990 EC industrial policy concept, advances a significant role for the Commission in the enhancement of European electronics producers competitiveness. The Commission effectively proposes what it terms, a fruitful dialogue, between it and producers, users, and investors - with a view to identifying conditions for a long term recovery, while respecting the roles of the various parties.

Five areas were targeted for Community action. These were demand, technology, training, relations with the main trading partners, and the business environment. Some of these action areas (training and the business environment for instance) are desirable for firms attempting to compete globally. They fit with Porter's (1990) model for policy factors which help to lay the foundations for firms to build competitive advantage. However, other areas, such as relations with the main trading partners, smack of managed trade and strong interventionism. In addition, the report declared that there would be no sectoral plan with massive injections of public funds (CEC, 1991). However, as witnessed by programmes such as ESPRIT, such a plan had existed since the beginning of the 1980s, with just such massive investment of public money.

One of the areas emphasised in this document in which the Commission can play a role as a competitive enhancer, is trade policy. Here, the Commission takes an aggressive tone, arguing that, in order to ensure fair conditions of competition and market access, it will have recourse to bilateral measures and will fall back on its customs regulations and trade policy instruments (CEC, 1991, p.4):

> In view of the enabling nature of [the IT and electronics] industries and their external effects on the economy as a whole, they are often regarded as strategic (CEC, 1991, p.1).

The report attempts to justify its interventionist bent in electronics through arguing that everyone else does it, so why shouldn't we? That is to say, it alludes to the government policies pursued in the US and Japan for the electronics sector, and argues that the EC should thus have no qualms about implementing such policies itself. Four pillars of this policy are outlined. They are the internal market initiative; competition policy, technology co-operation policy, and trade policy (CEC, 1991, p.3). This quadrangular policy fits with Ostry's (1990) innovation policy model. Moreover, innovation policy captures the Commission report's emphasis on R&D as the main instrument for competitive enhancement.

Ross (1993) identifies three main flaws in the 1991 Commission Communication on information technology. The first is its emphasis on technology rather than the market as the basis for industrial competitiveness. In fact, the document rarely refers to market mechanisms at all. The second major fault of the communication is that it is producer- rather than user- oriented. The third flaw is its preoccupation with the bigger the better solutions; only large, monolithic entities, aided by grandiose R&D programmes and Community-wide structural incentives, can successfully compete for EC and global markets.

8 EC strategic targeting of electronics

Although verbally shunning sectoral policies, the Community has in reality been pursuing just such a strategy. As has been illustrated, strategic trade thinking has led to a number of industrial sectors being publicly identified as strategic by the

Commission, and apportioned special policy treatment. This is particularly true for information technology industries. Witness the proportion of the total Framework budget which is allocated to that sector. In the aftermath of the 1991 Maastricht agreement, the Commission proposed to assess and redirect its R&D policy. The main stated reason for this change in policy was the realisation that although a strong technological base existed in Europe, serious problems existed in attempting to convert this knowledge into artefacts/products and in transferring these inventions into market shares and profits. These twin weaknesses were acknowledged to be particularly problematic in leading edge sectors such as semiconductors[51]. Thus, the change in policy primarily entailed a move closer to market for Community R&D activities, and the encouragement of better ways for industry to quickly and effectively exploit the results of such activities. This new policy had three elements: redirecting research activities, increasing resources, and strengthening the programmes.

On the first of these, the Commission introduced the notion of priority technology projects more directly linked to key generic technologies on which the competitiveness of European industry depends[52]. One of these priority technologies was of course semiconductors. Again, this is a clear case conceptually of lagging international competitiveness leading to economic security considerations, leading in turn to strategic trade thinking, which then leads to strategic targeting. Second, the new R&D policy involved an increased proportion of the Community budget devoted to research. In absolute terms, per annum, there was to be an increase from Ecu 2.4 billion in 1992 to 4.2 billion in 1997[53]. For Framework III (1990-94), ESPRIT received Ecu 1 billion 352 million, from a total budget of Ecu 5.7 billion (Buigues and Sapir, 1993, p.28). This represents almost 25 per cent of the total EC R&D budget being spent on information technologies. In addition, about Ecu 3.1 billion remained un-spent after Framework II, and this sum was transferred to Framework III, bringing the total five year budget to Ecu 8.8 billion[54]. This is a Community outlay of roughly Ecu 1.75 billion per annum, through the Framework Programme alone (Buigues and Sapir, 1993, p.25). Within this, microelectronics is top of the list of five areas of research (CEC,1992, p.5). For Framework IV (1994-98) the agreed amount of finance for information and communication technologies is Ecu 3 billion 384 million, from an overall budget of Ecu 12 billion[55] (CEC, 1994a, pp.3-4) This sum shows a significant increase in the proportion of the Framework budget which is apportioned to ESPRIT; the percentage share for information technology has been increased to about 29 per cent. Such an increase was partly in line with natural increases and partly to help fund the priority technology projects.

Finally, proposals were introduced to help overcome the inter-institutional disagreements which had delayed all three Framework programmes to date and resulted in detrimental funding gaps for particular projects. Here the Commission introduced the idea of funding extensions for framework programmes, in the eventuality of significant delays in ratifying their successors. Furthermore, a smoother Framework legislative procedure was advanced, establishing greater mutual recognition of each others prerogatives, between the Commission, Council, and Parliament. The fundamental effect of these changes (or at least the first two) is to increase the Community's influence on European collaborative R&D initiatives.

In addition, as we have seen, the EC utilises several trade policy tools to protect the sector from full exposure to global competition.

The Commission is not the only Community institution to overtly advance such a policy of preferential treatment for electronics. Both the Economic and Social Committee (1991) and the European Parliament (1994) have issued statements supporting sectoral intervention for electronics. Given its post-Maastricht budget approval mandate, the Parliament's view is particularly interesting:

> [The European Parliament] takes the position that, in view of this uneven competition in electronics, the European authorities (Commission and Council) should play an active role so that Europe does not lose control over, and access to, sub-sectors of electronics and does not become dependent on third parties in this strategic and dynamic area (European Parliament,1994, p. 5).

The ways advocated for playing this active role are the use of competition policy and trade tools to establish fairer rules of trade globally, within which European electronics firms can operate; and the rapid application of new Community powers gained in the realm of industrial policy to the electronics sector. These channels for proceeding are interesting because they reveal a highly interventionist tendency in the European Parliament approach to EC policy for the electronics sector. This is especially obvious in the Parliament's emphasis on trade tools as a means of enhancing the competitive position of Europe's electronics firms. Furthermore, in commenting on the Community's R&D programmes, the Parliament committee suggested that these programmes must be geared more towards strategic targets. On the basis of these recommendations, it is evident that the European Parliament policy stance on electronics closely correlates with the wider policy picture which is sketched in this chapter.

9 Intra-Commission rivalries in the creation of electronics policy

If we accept that the firm is indeed a leading player in EC policy-making for the electronics industry, it is further argued that the most significant public sector player in the policy process is undoubtedly the European Commission. Sandholtz (1992) has argued that ESPRIT represented both a major change in European policy-making for high technology, and an interesting case of international co-operation. The dismal past record of co-operation between governments in high technology sectors, added to the generally perceived sensitive, national security associated nature of semiconductors and computers, combined to make ESPRIT quite an unusual initiative. Furthermore, unlike other forms of government-government-firm-firm collaboration which had occurred in Europe, ESPRIT was unique given that its political leader was itself an international governmental actor, the European Commission (Sandholtz, 1992, p.2). Sandholtz argues that, through ESPRIT, the European Commission actually seized the initiative, and exercised policy leadership (1992, p.274). This concurs with George's notion of Commission leadership (1991, p.23) and Nugent's argument that the leadership capacity of the Commission has increased over time (1995, p.603). The Single Market initiative is cited as the most potent example of this Commission proactivism (Sandholtz and Zysman, 1989, p. 96; Ludlow, 1991, p. 85). Evidence exists that the Commission has acted as a policy entrepreneur in several other areas, most notably industrial policy (Lawton, 1997), regulatory policy (Pollack, 1994, pp.96-7), social policy (Cram, 1993), and environmental policy (Nugent, 1995, p.609). This is a rounded rejection of the realist argument that international organisations such as the European Commission, are irrelevant in any analysis of international co-operation.

Peterson (1993) argues that the 1990s have witnessed an increased transparency in the administration of EC R&D programmes. Due largely to pressure from the member states, the policy has become more exposed to outside assessment - conducted mainly by independent groups of experts (e.g. the ESPRIT Review Board). This development has seen a greater role (at least formally) for university and private research labs within the policy-making process. Thus, they must now be considered in any EC bargaining model. Peterson also supports the notion that Commission Directorate-General XIII (Telecommunications, Information Market, and Exploitation of Research) has been interventionist. Particularly during the early to mid-1980s, in collusion with the big 12 information technology firms, Directorate-General XIII dominated EC collaborative R&D programmes (1993, p.123). This central role of DGXIII has been significantly reduced, as the structure of Framework III (with increased emphasis on the role of SMEs etc.) has witnessed more administrative power swinging to less interventionist DGs such as DGXII (Science and Research).

Contrary to popular belief, the Commission is not a monolithic entity. As a multinational institution, it endeavours to contain several divergent political and economic cultures. The most prominent and vigorous intra-Commission schism is the divide between the open market, liberal trade cultures of the Community's northern members, and the more protectionist, Colbertist cultures of France and the Community's southern countries. This largely bipolar divide is particularly evident in industrial policy-making. Thus, tensions arise in both the Council of Ministers and the Commission, between those who favour a minimalist approach - seeing competition policy as the main tenet of industrial policy - and those who prefer a maximalist approach - advocating an active, interventionist industrial policy regime (Sharp, 1991, p.177). A constant struggle rages between individual Commissioners and Directorate-Generals, to determine policies for so-called core technology industries. This argument is sustained by a number of senior Commission officials[56]. Ross (1993) argues that Directorate-General IV (Competition Policy), is the most liberal, and has consistently been the most opposed to interventionist policies for the European electronics sector, and, indeed, has been opposed to the very notion of a strategic industry. It strongly condemned the 1991 *State of Play* report (which was developed within DGXIII). Directorate-

General III (Internal Market and Industry) is not as vigorously free market, but it does have more market-oriented tendencies than Directorate-General XIII, and it did disapprove of the aforementioned communication. It does not like the notion of strategic industries either. Directorate-General XIII has been the most interventionist DG, and the most collusive with big business. It has consistently supported strategic targeting. (Ross, 1993; 1995). None of these DGs can be discounted though when assessing the nature of intra-Commission policy bargaining (fig.4.1). These differences have been most evident in connection with the positions which DGs took at various points in time with reference to semiconductor/information technology policy.

Mason (1992) outlines a similar bargaining model of EC policy for the automobile sector[57]. For that industry, he found that the Commission (DGs I, III, and IV), the national governments, and the major European car-makers all had significant input into the policy-making process which led to the 1991 EC-Japan Automotive Accord. Together, they had to build a consensus on the nature of the accord, from the European side.

For semiconductors, some of the bargaining players tend to play a lesser role than others, the most important actors being: (a) during the 1980s - DGXIII, the big 12 European electronics companies, and national government ministries; (b) during the 1990s - DGIII, the antidumping unit of DGI, European chip makers and private research institutes, the European Parliament, and the EC Council. One can see that the process has become more complex, as the number of actors that significantly influence the policy bargaining procedure has increased. It may be argued that more checks and balances now exist on the Commission, and the general policy-making process is more transparent and inclusive. However, this fact does not appear to have exposed the weaknesses inherent in this policy, nor altered its broadly interventionist nature.

Directorate-General XIII is traditionally viewed as a bastion of *dirigisme*. Thus, perhaps the late 1993 movement of information technology R&D responsibilities from there to Directorate-General III was a symbolic move, intended to illustrate a desire on the part of the Commission to finally move in reality towards a more liberal regime for information technology. The policy reality does not fit with this alleged development though. Interventionist elements remain powerful within the Commission policy-bargaining process, and *de facto*, continue to determine policy. This decade has witnessed the strengthening of Commission liberals, and the attempt to incorporate their approach within the Commission agenda for electronics. More recent policy statements contain a much greater liberal flavour than previously. However, the interventionist policy tools implemented during the 1980s have not been repealed or superseded. If anything, they are often enforced more rigorously than during their ideological prime.

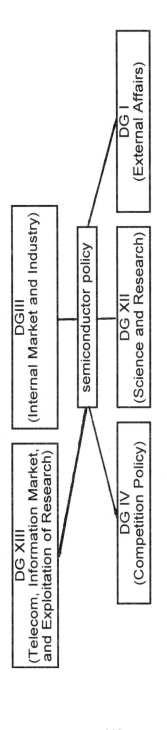

Figure 4.1 Intra-Commission rivalries in the creation of EC industrial policy for semiconductors

10 The main policy actors for electronics

Mason (1992) argues that for cars, EC policy-making is a member state-dominated process. Thus, in theoretical terms, he comes down on the side of the neorealists, perceiving the EC as a loose network of inter-state bargains, controlled by national governments. Governments dominate the European Commission, and not the other way around, as neofunctionalists might have you believe. We subscribe to a different principle from both the neofunctionalist and neorealist schools. Influence must be attributed to both sources of political authority (EC and national), within the policy bargaining process. However, for the electronics industry, the process is dominated by EC institutions, in conjunction with large firms. As Green (1993) argues, neither intergovernmentalism nor neofunctionalist theory takes account of the firm as an actor within EC policy-making[58]. Neither is sufficient to analyse recent EC policy-making for industry, as neither can adequately explain the increased influence of the firm within this process. Other works support our emphasis on the central role that firms play within (EC) policy-making. From their study of European government-industry relationships in both the telecommunications and consumer electronics sector, Cawson et al. found that:

> even where governments were acting strategically in the promotion of industries and products, outcomes were ultimately decided by the strategies of firms (1990, p.361).

Individual firms such as Philips, Thomson, GEC, and Siemens have long been important political players in their national arenas and extended this influence to the European stage on issues such as the development of High Definition Television (Verwey 1994; Van Schendelen 1993). Firm bargaining power was particularly strong in situations where governmental actors set performance objectives, such as the competitive enhancement of the domestic electronics industry. In these situations, government is trying to set both the policy means and ends - a situation which gives more bargaining power to the corporate actors, without whose specific actions the policy ends could not be achieved (Cawson et al., 1990, p.362). This supports our argument concerning the role of firms in EC policy for electronics industries such as semiconductor components. Such policy has specified performance objectives (competitive enhancement), thus giving semiconductor producers greater policy bargaining strength relative to EC governmental agents.

Similarly, Junne argues that large firms occupy centre stage in the creation and control of EC policy for areas such as trade and the environment. He argues that they influence policy-making both through their economic activity, and through their political interventions (1992, p.23). These transnational corporations get directly involved in policy development when their interests are at stake, or when their co-operation is needed in order to implement specific measures:

Their relationship with the Commission (and national political bodies) implies more than that of the normal lobbyists who try to impose their vision on government. Representatives of MNCs are often called in by government (or the Commission, for that matter) because of their in-depth knowledge of specific affairs which civil servants would lack (1992, p.24).

As we have already seen, Ross (1993; 1995) substantiates this argument. As an observer within the Delors Cabinet during 1991, he witnessed first-hand the direct and high level relationship which existed between the Commission and the European electronics industry. Frequent meetings occurred between President Delors and the Chief Executive Officers (CEOs) of some of Europe's industrial giants[59]. The overall objective for both parties was to halt the competitive decline of the indigenous European electronics industry. Delors participated in such meetings because he believed in the need for a corporate input into industrial policy formulation. He listened even more attentively to the electronics firms because of their implicit threats to withdraw their political support for the Community (and thus for the integration process) if their views were not adequately accounted for in the policy-making process (Ross 1995, pp.115-6).

It is evident that a complex set of bargains exist between firms, firms and the Commission, the Commission and the member states (usually through the Council of Ministers), member states themselves, and states and firms, in order for EC electronics policy to emerge. However, the empirical evidence shows that two other, more peripheral actors must now also be accounted for in the bargaining process. They are the European Parliament and non-governmental, non-corporate members of the scientific community (i.e. from university or private research labs). The European Parliament's function in approving EC R&D spending, and its increased willingness to use this role to question and delay related policies, means that it must be considered within certain parts of the policy-making process. The existence of independent R&D policy assessment panels, and the European Assembly of Science and Technologies[60], indicates that university and private research labs also influence policy choices at certain times in the policy-making process.

We are thus faced with the option of expanding the Pentagonal Diplomacy model to incorporate two further actors. However, given the fact that neither of the two players have a significant impact upon the policy bargaining process, and generally only influence certain parts of the policy set (mainly collaborative R&D initiatives), it is not deemed necessary to include them within the pentagon. Instead they may be viewed as linked external variables, which influence certain sides of the pentagon at particular times.

In summation, the EC bargaining process which has been outlined comprises five categories of actors (fig.4.2): first, on the Commission side, Directorate-Generals XIII (Telecommunications, Information Market and Exploitation of Research), III (Internal Market & Industry), XII (Science & Research), and to a slightly lesser extent, I (External Relations)[61], X (Audio-visual Affairs, Information, Communication, and culture), and IV (Competition Policy); second, on the

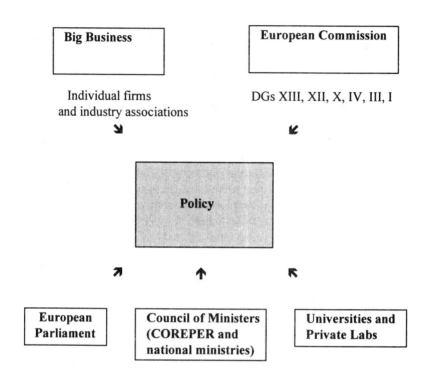

Figure 4.2 EC policy-bargaining for electronics: the actors

Council of Ministers side, assorted national government departments and COREPER (national permanent representatives to the Community); third, the European Parliament, on budgetary issues; fourth, university and private research laboratories; and finally, most of the leading European-based electronics firms. Of these the most important actors are Directorate-Generals I, III, IV, and XIII of the European Commission, and the large European electronics firms. The process has become more complex, as the number of actors that influence the policy bargaining procedure has increased. It may be argued that more checks and balances now exist on and within the Commission, and the general policy-making process is more transparent and inclusive. However, this fact does not appear to have exposed the weaknesses inherent in this policy, nor altered its broadly interventionist nature.

11 Policy and competitiveness

Zysman (1993) argues that, whatever its political benefits, EC R&D policy has not been an industrial success. Our findings in this and the subsequent chapters lend support to this argument. Zysman contends that the policy emphasis in the EC has been wrong: you need to move away from a focus on improving technology (which he argues is an excuse for subsidising producers) and towards a focus on user needs. That is to say, the Community should support areas in which there is obvious market demand, rather than those in which the Commission perceives the need for a supply. The focus of European policy for IT and communications technology industries in the last decade has been to correct weaknesses rather than to build on strengths. Elements of this move towards focusing more on user needs have emerged in recent years - witness the *Industrial Policy in an Open and Competitive Environment* report for instance. Zysman's arguments are valid though, as the root cause of Europe's lack of competitiveness in semiconductors and related industries has not been insufficient technology. In emphasising the technology gap, European policy-makers have been diverting attention away from the real problems. Also, as Zysman points out, European policy has been producer rather than user driven, and such an approach fails to comply with market demand.

How can one rate the partnership between EC governmental actors and industry in creating competitive advantage for specific European information technology sectors? More particularly, how is EC policy affecting the competitiveness of European chip producers? Let us return to Porter's competitive advantage model, as outlined in chapter two. How does the current EC policy approach compare with Porter's Competitive Diamond[62]? The Porter Diamond was created as a means of conceptualising the interrelated components which together comprise a nation's competitive advantage. For Porter (1990), government's role in establishing competitive advantage for an industry is to stimulate improvement and innovation domestically. He stresses that it is ultimately up to the industry alone to actually compete. Thus, the Diamond advances four attributes which shape the domestic competitive environment for corporate enterprises, and by extension, enhance or hinder the domestic firms competitiveness in the global market. Chapter two contains a detailed discussion of these attributes, which is not necessary to go into again. In brief, they are factor conditions (e.g. skilled workforce), demand conditions (e.g. sufficient domestic economies of scale), related and supporting industries (e.g. having a software industry in addition to a computer hardware industry), and firm strategy, structure, and rivalry (e.g. regulatory systems such as EC competition policy)[63]. As the evidence in this chapter proves, these four Porter Diamond attributes comply perfectly with EC policy for semiconductors, and electronics in general. This is not surprising. In searching for a more acceptable policy structure, the Commission set upon Porter's model, correctly seeing it as *en vogue* amongst large segments of the international business and governmental community. One can see Porter's concepts throughout the 1990 *Industrial Policy in an Open and Competitive Environment* Commission report. Indeed, his competitive advantage model is mentioned by name in the document. Policies have been implemented for human capital development (factor conditions), sufficient economies of scale, through the Single Market programme (demand conditions), developing links between enterprises at different stages in the production cycle, and encouraging the development of indigenous semiconductor design and equipment manufacturers (related and supporting industries), and, through competition policy, to regulate corporate structure and behaviour (firm strategy, structure, and rivalry). So, if one sees any utility in the Porter model. and if it has been applied to the EC policy structure, why has competitiveness not improved? The answer lies in the important extra-Diamond variable, government. As argued previously, government (or governmental actors such as the Commission) should not attempt to control competitive advantage. If it does, the competitive diamond will be distorted. Although unable to control competitive advantage, there is no denying the influence which public policy can have on this phenomenon. Therefore, the argument here is that the overall thrust of EC policy has failed to enhance the global competitiveness of the European semiconductor industry because it has been overly interventionist and frequently directed at the wrong areas. Using Porter's model, one can argue that the nature and extent of EC policy has upset the balance of the Diamond and adversely affected the competitiveness of European microchip producers. This chapter has suggested a number of ways in which the Community could change its overall policy structure. These include the abolition of trade tools such as antidumping, rules of origin, and import tariffs, which merely protect uncompetitive European-based chip makers; the phasing out of large collaborative R&D programmes which are administered by the Commission; greater emphasis on funding of basic research within the framework of the industry-led Eureka initiative; and more promotional assistance - through training schemes, technological diffusion, etc. - for start-ups and young SMEs within the semiconductor industry. Such changes may reinforce the Diamond and finally permit the creation of a viable domestic competitive environment for European semiconductor producers. After that, it is up to the firms themselves to build competitive advantage and capture greater global market share.

12 Conclusions

The innovation policy model of industrial policy enables us to conceptualise EC policy for semiconductors as comprising four pillars. These are R&D, trade, competition policy, and the Single Market. We have chosen to concentrate our study on the first two of these - R&D and trade. This selective analysis results in part from the EC's policy emphasis on these pillars, and in part because we see these two as illustrative of a strong and enduring interventionist element in EC innovation policy for electronics.

In considering the scale of EC policy for the semiconductor sector, one can see that the policy emphasis is on collaborative R&D initiatives. This would suggest that in labelling such a policy set, one cannot use traditional industrial policy notions. Instead, the innovation policy model is more applicable to this situation.

Further research is necessary to examine the importance of TNC agenda-setting in triangular diplomacy (Green, 1993). This is precisely what this work is attempting to do at a sectoral level, and from that sector analysis, draw a bargaining model (Pentagonal Diplomacy) for the wider electronics and information technology. Thus, to relate this chapter's findings to the Pentagonal Diplomacy model, we emerge with a slightly modified version of the original model. It is evident that a complex set of bargains exist between firms, firms and the Commission, the Commission and the member states (usually through the Council), member states themselves, and states and firms, in order for EC microchip policy to emerge. However, the empirical evidence shows that two other, more peripheral actors must now also be accounted for in the bargaining process. They are first, the European Parliament; and second, non-governmental, non-corporate members of the scientific community (i.e. from university or private research labs). The European Parliament's function in approving EC R&D spending, and its increased willingness to use this role to question and delay related policies, means that it must be considered within certain parts of the policy-making process. The importance of independent R&D policy assessment panels, and the aforementioned European Assembly of Science and Technologies, indicates that university and private research labs also influence policy choices at certain times in the policy-making process.

We have argued in this chapter that intra-Commission rivalries effect the nature of EC industrial policy. This notion that ideological conflicts between different departments of a single governmental actor partially shape policy, is not especially new. As Wilks and Wright argue, the notion of intra governmental and intra-bureaucracy policy disputes is a recurrent theme in research findings (1987, p.288). Non-Community examples of governmental fragmentation include that of the acrimonious dispute between the Japanese Ministry of International Trade and Investment and Ministry of Posts and Telecommunications, over the sponsorship and regulation of Nippon Telephone and Telegraph; and the fierce rivalry in the US between the federal departments of defence and justice (to name only the main protagonists), for control of telecommunications policy (Wilks and Wright, 1987, p.288). Consequently, to argue that differences of opinion within the European Commission bureaucracy must be considered when analysing the EC policy-making process, does not set a theoretical precedent. Evidence from studies of the policy-making process of other governmental structures suggests that such intra-institutional clashes are quite common.

The Community has continually argued that its role is largely that of a competitive facilitator - the instigator of structural adjustments and the catalyst of innovation. Competitive enhancement *per se*, is the job of firms themselves. This is a very thin dividing line between realms of responsibility. For instance, as the changing structure of the Community Framework R&D programme has shown, it is increasingly difficult to delineate between Commission and corporate sponsored Community-wide research projects. Furthermore, consider the overall expanse of EC policy for the electronics sector: elaborate and expensive R&D support structures; competition rules which police and judge corporate structure and practice; a wide array of policies aimed for instance at assisting firms to comply with international environmental standards, to adapt to new production and management techniques, and to have a well trained and flexible manpower pool at their disposal; trade tools which serve to restrict the impact of global competition on Community-based firms. The Commission encompasses all areas of activity which affect the competitiveness of European electronics producers. Furthermore, it is there with the support of a majority of all other actors in the paradigm - national governments, the European Parliament, universities, private research laboratories, and firms. It may be argued that there is nothing unusual or unprecedented about this fact, particularly when viewed in a global context. Relations between the public and private sectors have long been close and consensual in Japan and Korea for instance. In the US, there are many cases of government-firm negotiated intervention, e.g. the 1986 Semiconductor Trade Agreement. Interestingly though, in relation to semiconductors, such partnerships do not appear to have adversely affected corporate competitiveness in these third countries. Chapter six will look at policies pursued for semiconductors in both the US and Japan, and attempt to draw lessons for European policy from their experiences.

The point is that the widely espoused liberal approach which the Community is supposed to have adopted since the early 1990s, has not come to full fruition. Intervention - manifest through everything from semiconductor product development activities to managed trade - persists, and shows no sign of abating. The main transformation has simply been, as illustrated in chapter three, a large-scale shift in policy initiation and control from the national to the Community level. In applying the principle of subsidiarity to microchips, one finds that most governments and firms have decided that activities are best consummated, conducted and controlled at a Community level.

The other important change in policy has been the nature of the agenda setting and policy-making processes. EC policy-making has gone from being an intra-institutional consensus-building procedure, to a multi-sided bargaining process. The role of non-governmental actors, particularly firms, has increased significantly since the beginning of the 1980s, and now frequently has an equal say in the formulation and implementation of policy. As Peterson argues:

> Taken together, [the Framework Programme and Eureka] have provided industry with a significant and unprecedented role in decision-making about the goals, organization, and funding priorities of European collaborative R&D (1991, p.271).

In effect, a Community-firm policy partnership has developed for information technology industries such as semiconductors, coinciding with and overshadowing (although not completely replacing) the incestuous nationally based government-firm relationships of the 1960s and 1970s. As we have seen, this new partnership is even evident in the Framework programme, the former bastion of public sector driven policy for industry. Sandholtz lends support to the notion that ESPRIT developed from a firm-Commission bargaining process:

> With the help of company representatives, the Commission drafted a proposal for ESPRIT, including the strategic rationale and specific objectives in the work programme. In this sense the Commission/industry alliance was moving ahead of governments (1992, p.308).

Moreover, Sandholtz's findings reveal that the individual large electronics firms involved in the ESPRIT negotiations, played a vital role in convincing their respective national governments to accept the European collaborative programme (1992, p.310). Thus, their influence on the policy bargain was evident at both the national and the European level of government, displaying these firms pre-eminent power position as both policy shaper and governmental mediator.

Neo-interventionism is the *de facto* EC policy format for electronics. However, it does contain more liberal elements than its 1980s predecessor. This is based in part on the fact that the administrative competencies and decision-makers for trade and for R&D are separate (DGI versus DGIII, DGXII, and DGXIII). Thus, whilst (units of) DGIII and DGIV are trying to advance a more market oriented, liberal policy regime for chips, elements of DGI (the antidumping unit for instance) or of DGXIII traditionally, are pushing a more interventionist and protectionist line. The Commission has to facilitate better co-ordination between these different policy jurisdictions for the same industrial sector, to avoid conflicting policies and to formulate a clear and unified policy set for each industry. If one believes the official Commission line, as put forth in the 1990 and 1994 industrial policy documents for instance, there is an aspiration towards a purely supportive, environment enhancing role for the Community. In developing the four attributes of the Porter Diamond for building competitive advantage, this aspiration is beginning to take shape. However, EC policy does not stop at this business environment enhancement role. In directing collaborative R&D initiatives such as ESPRIT, and in employing several protectionist trade tools, it goes beyond this liberal, promotional mandate.

On a final point, this chapter has shed some light on the neofunctionalist assertion that the any shift in policy emphasis from the national to the European level deepens economic integration and strengthens European political union. Cawson et al. argue for instance that:

> It is possible that the current period is one of transition where national policies are giving way to European-level initiatives, and that it is not state intervention itself that is waning but the salience of the nation-state level within Europe (1990, pp.377-8).

The evidence herein tends to support large parts of this neofunctionalist position. The Commission's success in creating a common area of action for information technology affairs, has helped to solidify Europe's industrial integration.

Moreover, it appears to have translated into greater political unity. This is evident in the secondary role of national governments in creating and controlling EC policy for electronics industries. However, the Commission has achieved this success through a policy partnership with large firms. Neofunctionalism fails to account for the role of large firms in EC policy bargaining. As a theory, it does not therefore go far enough in explaining the creation and control of EC semiconductor policy.

Notes

1   This chapter does not intend to debate the issue of corporate nationality. For analytical purposes, this work applies the term native simply to those electronics firms which have their corporate headquarters within a European Community member state.

2   The vigorous intra-Commission rivalry in creating policy for electronics and information technology was brought to this author's attention in interviews conducted with several senior Commission officials, Brussels, February 1994.

3   These include the definitive CEC industrial policy documents, *Industrial Policy in and Open and Competitive Environment* (1990), and *An Industrial Competitiveness Policy for the European Union* (1994); as well as the Commission's (1992), *Research After Maastricht* report.

4   Some of these statements were made in private, in interviews conducted by this author with European Commission officials; others were made in public, for instance in a speech given by former Commission Vice President Pandolfi at the *Horizons of Research* conference, 1992, Brussels.

5   The corporate members of Davignon's round table were ICL, GEC, Plessey, AEG, Nixdorf, Siemens, Thomson, Bull, CGE, Olivetti, STET, and Philips.

6   Paul Taylor, writing in *The Financial Times*, 17 March, 1992.

7   It is important to remember that a member state's contribution to the Framework budget was in direct proportion to its share of the overall EC budget. Thus, a country such as the United Kingdom, which is a net contributor to the EC budget, would most probably contribute more to Framework than it would receive in return. Consequently, it is understandable that the country should raise questions regarding additionality.

8   EC Regulation No. 3744/81, adopted on 7 December 1981.

9   Commission of the European Communities, *Communication from the Commission to the Council and the Parliament concerning the final programme assessment of the Microelectronics Programme*, Brussels, 5 April, 1988, p.1.

10   Commission of the European Communities, 'Community Action In The Field Of Microelectronic Technology', Council Regulation (EEC) No.3744/81, *Fourth Report by the Commission to the Council and the European Parliament*, 1987, p.6.

11 Commission communication to the Council and the Parliament, April 1988, p.18.

12 The Framework Review Board consisted of Pierre Aigrain, adviser on research to the CEO of Thomson; Sir Geoffrey Allen, then head of research at Unilever; Eduardo de Arantes e Oliveira, a Portuguese scientist; Umberto Colombo, head of the Italian state energy corporation, ENI; and Hubert Markl, then head of the DFG, the German research council.

13 Report of the Framework Review Board, cited in Debora McKenzie, 1992, p.10.

14 Interviews with European Commission officials, Brussels, 1992 and 1994.

15 The ESPRIT Review Board was comprised of Dr. A.E. Pannenborg, retired Vice-Chairman of the Board of N.V. Philips (Chairman); Professor H. Durand, professor at the University of Paris, and former Assistant Secretary General of NATO; Professor U. Colombo, Chairman of the Italian energy agency, ENEA; Dr. J.R. Forrest, director of engineering, Independent Broadcasting Authority, UK; Prof. P.L. Olgaard, Institute of Electrophysics, Technical University of Denmark; Prof. J. Peracaula, Technical University of Catalonia; and Prof. I. Ruge, Director of the Fraunhofer Institute for Solid State Technology, Munich.

16 The Report of the ESPRIT Review Board, May 1989, p.7.

17 Ibid., p.9.

18 Of course the counterfactual is relevant here, as we do not know whether without ESPRIT, things would have been worse.

19 Mike Hobday (1992), cited in Mytelka, 1993, p.9.

20 ESPRIT II and III witnessed a deliberate move towards more commercially viable projects, and project clusters were formed, wherein assorted aspects of a particular technological problem were worked upon. In addition, ASIC design and production projects were embarked upon.

21 European Commission *functionaires* cited in *The Financial Times*, 22 October 1990.

22 In chapter five, we discuss the issue of why, if at all, support should be restricted to European-based firms.

23 European-based companies combined share of the world microchip market declined from 16 per cent in 1980, to just over 8 per cent by 1994.

24 *The Financial Times,* 22 October, 1990.

25 Congress of the United States, Office of Technology Assessment, *Competing Economies: America, Europe, and the Pacific Rim,* Government Printing Office, Washington DC, October 1991.

26 That is, establishing a competitive environment from which firms may compete on the strength of their corporate strategies and market achievements, relatively unhindered by public policy.

27 Most notably former Olivetti CEO, Carlo de Benedetti, and Alain Gomez, CEO of Thomson.

28   Interview conducted with senior Commission official, Brussels, February, 1994.

29   Most notably, the United States Office of Technology Assessment in their 1991 report on competitiveness, and Forum Europe in a 1992 document released by them.

30   CEC, *The European Electronics and Information Technology Industries: State of Play, Issues at Stake, and Proposals for Action,* 1991.

31   Most notably former Olivetti CEO, Carlo de Benedetti, and Alain Gomez, CEO of Thomson.

32   Commission of the European Communities (1992), 'Research After Maastricht: An Assessment, A Strategy', *Information Memo,* Brussels.

33   It is important to note though that under the Uruguay Round of the GATT, EC tariffs on semiconductor manufacturing equipment imports are now scheduled to be phased out by 1996. This tariff removal is not applicable to the actual semiconductor components though.

34   In 1992, Dataquest Ltd. organised a conference on European semiconductor production in Dublin, at which most of the leading international chip producers were represented (*Electronics*, 13 July 1992).

35   *Electronics*, 13 July 1992, p.10.

36   Quoted in *Electronics,* 13 July 1992, p.10.

37   Internal Commission document, *General Overview of EC/US Trade Relations*, 1992, p.21.

38   Commission Regulation (EEC) No. 288/89 of 3 February 1989, *on determining the origin of integrated circuits*, OJ No L 33, 4.2.89, p.23.

39   Dieter Ernst interview, UC Berkeley, March 1993.

40   Data gained from Commission of the European Communities, *Tenth Annual Report From The Commission To the European Parliament On The Community's Anti-Dumping and Anti-Subsidy Activities (1991),* Brussels, 27 May 1992.

41   Commission Regulation (EEC) No. 165/90 of 23 January 1990, *Imposing a provisional anti-dumping duty on imports of certain types of electronic microcircuits known as DRAMs (dynamic random access memories) originating in Japan, accepting undertakings offered by certain exporters in connection with the anti-dumping proceeding concerning imports of these products and terminating the investigation in their respect,* OJ L 20, 25 January 1990.

42   As the name suggests, this is an industrial association whose membership includes most European-based microelectronics makers. Chapter five discusses the nature, role, and trade ideology of the European Electronic Component Manufactuers Association.

43   The complaint was lodged in February 1987, just before SGS and Thomson merged.

44 This argument is rather spurious as IBM, unlike Motorola, was not a merchant chip producer, and Philips in 1990 was in the process of reducing its chip manufacturing capacity.

45 'Material injury' being defined primarily as financial loss, and 'material retardation' being defined as delays caused in the adoption of decisions that would have occurred in a fair market environment.

46 Commission Regulation (EEC) No 165/90, op.cit., p.22.

47 For further details of this agreement, see OECD Trade Committee, *Restrictions on Trade in Electronic Components,* draft copy, 16 March 1992.

48 The improvement of European firms international competitiveness is a stated objective of all Commission industrial policy communications since the 1990 *Industrial Policy in an Open and Competitive Environment* document.

49 The Framework Programmes, initiated in 1984, are successive structures through which the European Commission administers research and development programmes in various technological fields. The first venture conducted under the auspices of Framework, was the European Strategic Programme for Research and Development in Information Technology (ESPRIT).

50 Actual involvement is not the issue here: even economic liberals admit that there is a role for the state in eradicating barriers to competition and so forth - that is what the 1992 programme was all about. We are more concerned with the nature and extent of EC involvement, and see these factors as illustrative of the EC's interventionist tendencies.

51 EC Commission Spokesman's Service, *Research After Maastricht: An Assessment, A Strategy*, Brussels, 8 April 1992.

52 Ibid.

53 Ibid.

54 ESPRIT projects received Ecu 180 million of the Ecu 3.1 billion remaining from Framework II (*Innovation & Technology Transfer*, Vol.14, No.1, March/93, p.8).

55 This amount may be increased during the course of Framework IV.

56 The vigorous intra-Commission rivalry in creating policy for electronics and information technology was brought to the this author's attention in interviews conducted with several Commission officials, Brussels, 1994.

57 Mark Mason, *Elements of Consensus: Europe's Response to the Japanese Automotive Challenge,* paper presented at the 1992 Annual Meeting of the Academy of International Business, Brussels, November 1992.

58 Neofunctionalism does propose a coalition between supranational organisations such as the Commission, and business interests. However, this approach envisages a political alliance between the European Commission for instance, and business associations. This alliance would be primarily intended to supersede the nation-state and further the development of a federal Europe. There is no real conceptualisation of individual firms, or an alliance of

individual firms, attempting to advance their own agendas through bargaining with political actors.

59 George Ross (1995) describes the high level Commission-industry relationships, in *Jacques Delors and European Integration*, pp.115-6.

60 In 1994, the European Commission moved to create the European Assembly of Sciences and Technologies. This assembly comprises about one hundred senior scientists and industrialists, and functions in the same manner as the US National Research Council and the Japan Research Council. Its stated aim is to ensure that there is a direct and permanent contact between the European Commission and Europe's scientific and industrial community (CEC, DGXIII-D, *Innovation and Technology Transfer,* Vol.3/94, June 1994, p.4). The Assembly is both representative in terms of enterprise size, discipline, and geographical location; and is independent of Community and national government (direct) influence. It functions mainly as an advisory body on EC R&D policy, but can also publicly comment on such policy on its own initiative.

61 Directorate-General I is included here due to its competency for trade tools such as anti-dumping.

62 Michael Porter, *The Competitive Advantage of Nations*, 1990.

63 For further details on these attributes, and on the Porter Diamond in general, see chapter two, section 2.iv.

5 Firm strategy and
European collaboration

Ability is nothing without opportunity.

Napoleon Bonaparte

This chapter serves two purposes. The first is to assess the creation and control of EC semiconductor policy from the corporate perspective. As initially proposed in chapter two, the analysis of this work's dependent variable has three constituent parts. The second of these is the firm. In what way(s) and to what extent has the firm influenced EC policy for the microchip sector? What is the firm logic for collaborating with national governments and the European Commission? The following section endeavours to address such questions, and to advance a firm perspective on the development, objectives, and outcomes of EC policy. It is our opinion that EC industrial policy cannot be comprehensively analysed and understood unless firm actions are explained.

The second purpose of this chapter is to provide a case study of EC industrial policy. The theory of industrial policy has already been discussed, as has the role which technology plays in determining its nature. We have also shown how industrial policy developed for the semiconductor sector, both in the US and in Europe, and the relative power positions between states and firms during the industry's early years. In the previous chapter, we analysed the nature of the EC policy-making process, and the role which large firms play within this process. In the next chapter, we will account for other actors and factors within the policy-making process, and draw lessons from the US and Japan for the nature and competitive impact of EC policy for semiconductors. Therefore, in this chapter, a dimension of the policy set is dissected, with the aim of determining its origins, structure, and driving forces. In so doing, we will also provide some indications as to the implications which policy has for industrial competitiveness. The dimension chosen is that part of EC technology policy directed at the Joint European Submicron Silicon (JESSI) programme. The reasons for this focus will become evident as the chapter unfolds. Briefly, its collaborative nature (firms, research labs, national governments, and the European Commission), the large financial outlay involved, and its position at the vanguard of European policy efforts to

133

enhance semiconductor capabilities, all contribute to JESSI's importance as a study.

Nowhere is it argued that studying JESSI will provide insights which are applicable in all areas of EC industrial policy. Neither is it asserted that EC policy for semiconductors is limited only to JESSI. Other elements of this policy set - such as trade - are also studied in this work, so as to obtain a rounded analysis of Community policy for the sector. Nevertheless, the policy insights gleaned through analysing JESSI are relevant. R&D assistance is shown in this work to be the central pillar of EC policy for semiconductors. JESSI is the single most ambitious collaborative semiconductor R&D project undertaken to date by European governmental actors, in co-operation with private sector players. In studying the nature and effects of this project during the first five years of its existence, lessons will emerge for the wider EC policy set. Our time frame for analysis is 1989 to 1994. Thus, we chart the course and effects of JESSI from its inception as Eureka Project 127, until the midway point of JESSI Phase II (1992-96). Five years is considered an adequate time frame within which to pass preliminary judgements on a collaborative R&D programme's relative contribution to competitiveness.

The corporate perspective on EC policy is framed by strategic alliance theory. It is the key to understanding firm choices. To comprehensively analyse the semiconductor firm perspective, corporate technology strategy and the knowledge networking concept are also utilised in this chapter. These are especially applicable when studying the corporate rationale behind policy initiatives such as JESSI.

Two main arguments are advanced herein. The first is that firms choose to participate in European collaborative programmes mainly to obtain access to the 'knowledge network' (Mytelka, 1991) which it provides. Technology is at the centre of European semiconductor producers competitive strategies. To maximise their knowledge network, firms participate in a specific form of strategic alliance, which we label the bottom-up European collaborative programme option. Through this, firms endeavour to strengthen their long-term competitive advantage through reducing the risks and costs of R&D, and widening their access and exposure to new ideas and innovations.

The second argument is that JESSI's relative contribution (as a dimension of industrial policy) has not been significant. It has in fact been a failure with respects to its main initial objective: it has not produced any competitively successful products or processes. Also, the combined market share of its corporate participants did not increase during our period of study.

1 Corporate collaboration

Hamel, Doz, and Prahalad (1989) talk about the concept of competitive collaboration, by which they mean joint ventures, outsourcing agreements, product licensing, and co-operative research. Firms, collaborate to compete - they pool resources and exchange knowledge in order to develop new products, gain entry to new markets, and/or increase market share in established markets. However, a danger of such collaboration - especially if it is of a bilateral nature - is that one partner may end up being competitively weakened vis-à-vis the other. This can emerge if the gains of collaboration are balanced too heavily in the favour of one partner - as is often the case in transnational inter-firm strategic alliances[1]. Perhaps this weighted outcome is not as severely imbalanced - and thus not as significant a threat to competitiveness - for firms that participate in European collaborative programmes. The multitude of partners and linkages, combined with public sector monitoring of activities, causes a wider diffusion of results and precipitates a form of 'social censor' for firms who might otherwise pursue more mercenary and aggressive strategies.

In collaboration, 'the partners strategic goals converge while their competitive goals diverge' (Hamel et al., 1989, p.135). That is to say, international business research[2] has found that the merging of corporate objectives - manifest in inter-firm collaborative activities - leads to an unwillingness amongst the partners to then compete directly with each other for market share. Often a type of gentleman's agreement emerges between corporate collaborators, not to invade the others market. In the European context, this development serves to consolidate a long-standing competitive hindrance, i.e. the *de facto* avoidance of vigorous competitive rivalry between indigenous firms (particularly in our sector of interest) for respective home markets. Therefore, it is important to bear in mind that collaboration which is intended to enhance the competitive position of its industrial partners, can also have a negative effect on competitiveness. This may be applied in particular to Eureka and the Framework Programmes, given the breadth and depth of collaborative linkages which they incorporate.

Van Tulder and Junne advance six reasons for the predominance of collaboration as a corporate strategy choice for high tech Europe during the last decade (1988, pp.217-20). With respects to the JESSI/Eureka model, a number of these may be deemed relevant. The pertinent motivating factors are, first, risk sharing: this has a number of dimensions, and can mean sharing risk vis-à-vis development of a new technology, or with regards to patent litigation, or market share and access, or the risk of one's product not being accepted by the market. Basically, high technology R&D is both very risky and very expensive. Thus, it makes business sense to share both burdens. Second, complementary developments in different technology clusters. This argument proposes that firms are increasingly forced to collaborate in R&D, in order to gain access to product or process technologies which are complementary to their own product development. Basically, they sometimes cannot proceed with the development of a technology or product, if they cannot master another (or others) related technology. For example, European computer makers must collaborate with component producers or process designers, in order to develop state-of-the-art personal computers. This collaborative motive can lead to both horizontal and vertical alliances within a product food chain.

The third motive is precipitated by on-going technological developments. The evolution of product systems necessitates regular and close R&D collaboration between European information technology firms in particular. Interactive technologies currently being developed - which involve telecom, computer hardware, electronic components, and sometimes robotics technologies - require ever closer co-operation between the firms in these sectors.

A fourth reason for collaboration is the desire for a number of companies (particularly those based within a common geographical region or politico-economic system) to create common standards. This is a form of risk aversion, as opposed to the earlier risk sharing. It can take two forms. The first, involves firms collaborating in the development of a common standard in order to avoid developing a product independently which may not be based on the dominant standard which emerges. The second, is a type of 'defensive' collaboration, whereby a number of companies attempt to formulate alternative common standards as a means of excluding a dominant competitor from their domestic markets. A good example of European firms attempting to establish common standards is the Eureka HDTV project (Mytelka, 1994, p.10).

The final reason given for collaboration is simply that 'co-operation has become a strategic tool to improve a company's competitive position' (Van Tulder and Junne, 1988, p.220). This argument supposes that who you co-operate with can be more important than what you co-operate for. This is a concept which may have two different strands. One strand would consist of small and medium sized enterprises (SMEs), who participate in collaborative agreements and programmes in order to acquire know-how from larger, dominant companies and thus enter a given market which those larger companies already occupy. A second strand would comprise large firms, who collaborate with both their most competitive peers and with highly innovative SMEs as a means of ensuring that they remain at the cutting-edge of particular technologies and thus either increase or maintain their market share[3].

Other academic commentators[4] adhere to some of the above underlying motives for strategic alliances, whilst also adding to the list. Thus, a further set of reasons consists of firstly, escalating barriers to entry during the 1970s and 1980s, as in industries such as microchips, the life-span of each generation of chip began to shorten dramatically, and concurrently, the cost of development increased rapidly. European companies attempting a 'catch-up' strategy within this industry, were increasingly dissuaded from attempting this on their own, as investment capital was more difficult to secure, and the amount of capital required for such investment was very high. Secondly, broadening barriers to entry, as the essence of competitiveness shifted towards 'newer, intangible investments in R&D, management, and marketing' (Mytelka, 1991, p.8). This shift necessitated microchip manufacturers to establish closer ties with both their users and with related sectors such as design houses. The rapid acquisition and implementation of new production techniques became increasingly central to a firm's competitiveness, as design systems (and therefore product types) proliferated, and consumers became more demanding. Thus, it became vital for a chip maker to establish new networks for knowledge access, with respects to both user demands and state-of-the-art design techniques. In effect, access to knowledge became crucial to a firm's survival, as knowledge became the key factor of production, eclipsing traditional core factors such as labour and raw materials (Drucker, 1986; Stopford and Strange, 1991).

A third reason for collaboration was uncertainty caused by rapid technological change. Changes - such as shortening product life cycles and the increasing integration of previously separate industries - increased the value of production flexibility and monitoring the new technologies. This rapid change and constant uncertainty (with respects to product marketability, choice of design technique, and so forth) weakened the business reasoning behind vertical integration and product-based oligopolies, and increased the corporate rationale for moving towards strategic collaboration for R&D. This development in the business environment increased the incentives especially for European semiconductor firms (and other sectors of European information technology) to collaborate, because their individual resources of investment capital for R&D and production could not reach the market share level of American and Japanese competitors (comparisons with such resources available to Japanese companies undertaking a catch-up strategy in the 1970s, illustrates this reality). Also, it could be argued that poor economic indicators[5] in western Europe during the early 1980s, were causal factors in the difficulties encountered by European firms in matching the investment levels of their global competitors, and thus further contributed to the move towards alliance. National champions were not the answer in such an environment, as a large share of one's national market was not sufficient to compete within an industry where global market share was what really counted and kept you competitive. Also, these champions could not construct the type of user-producer links which were necessary within the aforementioned new mode of competition.

Building on Van Tulder and Junne's explanations of business reasons for pursuing collaborative strategies, a number of motives may be advanced to justify the type of collaboration with which this work is primarily concerned, i.e. technological collaboration. Dodgson provides five corporate objectives in undertaking technological collaboration (1993, p.11). These are, first, increasing efficiency in the product chain. Vertical information exchanges can help firms to improve the 'fit' between stages two and three of a product development chain for instance, thus allowing for a greater understanding of specification requirements between development stages, and often reducing the time-to-market. Second, improving the development process. This generally consists of both horizontal and vertical exchanges of design and process know-how within an industry. Again, it is at an inter-firm level. Third, merging elements of previously separate technologies and disciplines to create a new hybrid technology. Perhaps the best contemporary example of such collaboration is biotechnology, where biology, physics, and chemistry firms have fused activities to collectively develop a new technology. Fourth, information exchange, with both other firms and with public sector agencies. The intention here is to discern who is worth collaborating with, and what types of collaborative activities exist already. Fifth, technological collaboration may also be perceived as a means for advancing other elements of a firm's overall corporate strategy. For example, it may be used by a number of competitor firms within a given market, to consolidate their joint control over the

137

market, and exclude other competitors. The enthusiasm expressed by individual European microchip producers towards European collaborative programmes such as JESSI, may be partially interpreted as a means through which some of these firms may maintain such a cartel-like behaviour within the European microchip market.

2 Corporate technology policy

The argument for technology (developments and rapidity of application) as the most important variable in corporate competitiveness, has been touched upon in chapters one and two. Dodgson (1989) argues that most transnational corporations have developed a technology strategy within their wider corporate strategies. This development is based on the assumption that competitive advantage rests in large part on the development and rapid application of new technologies. Dunning (1993) also places emphasis on the increased importance of technology both to firms and to governments. The essence of his argument is that technology has played a significant role in the globalisation of business, and is thus a central variable not only in the corporate strategy of multinational corporations, but also in the economic policy of most national governments. He bases this hypothesis on four factors: the rapid increase in the level of trade based on knowledge and information goods or techniques, and the fact that this technology derived trade is not controlled by any one nation; the transnational mobility of technology; the need for firms to 'go global' and to seek various forms of strategic alliances due to escalating product and process costs; and finally, the new information based technologies have changed the organisational structure of international trade, making geographical boundaries less relevant, and consequently, transformed the entire nature of long-term national economic policies. What evidence emerges in this work to support the existence of technology strategy and its importance in determining the actions of European microchip manufacturers? Is it possible to establish a causal linkage between technology as a strategy variable, and firm decisions to participate in European collaborative programmes such as JESSI? These questions will be addressed as this chapter develops.

At a more abstract level, three groups of strategy options can be delineated for Europe's microchip firms (Fig.5.1). We label the first group unilateral options, that is, strategies which a firm can pursue either between business units within its wider corporation (e.g. skill or resource transfer or sharing activities), or towards other enterprises outside of its corporate structure (e.g. acquisition or merger)[6]. In all cases, the firm acts independently and does not rely on external actors to achieve its objectives. The second group can be called bilateral options, and consists mainly of co-operative arrangements either between two firms, between a firm and a university or private research institute, or between a firm and a government. This group of strategy options is normally geared towards R&D activities or technology transfer, and can be of a specific, limited nature, or a less-defined, unrestricted form.

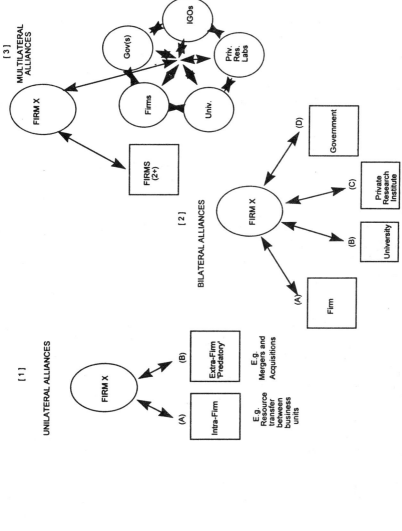

Figure 5.1 Collaborative strategy options for European semiconductor producers

139

The third group is therefore identified as multilateral options. Here one can include all forms of extra-firm collaborative strategy options, which involve more than two partners. Generally, such options involve both public and private sector players, and are manifest as research and development projects or larger programmes.

The first of these groups of strategy options can be largely disregarded. As subsequent evidence will support, they have not been relevant to either the environment or the objectives of European chip producers. Competitive enhancement, resulting ultimately in increased revenue and market share, was the primary objective; R&D activities leading to state-of-the-art semiconductor design processes, materials, production equipment, and end products, was the approach chosen to achieve these objectives; and a fiercely competitive global market and sphere of production, combined with escalating R&D and manufacturing costs, was the environment within which strategy options had to be selected. Given these operational parameters, the firms in question[7] all realised that the unilateral strategies which they had previously focused on, were not enough and all of them chose to pursue some form of collaboration. That is not to say that unilateral actions were abandoned[8], they were simply complemented, and to an extent, overshadowed, by bilateral and multilateral activities. Put simply, such strategy options were not perceived by European semiconductor manufacturers as being sufficient to address their profitability, technological, and production problems, and to enhance their competitiveness in the global market.

The second and third options have thus come increasingly into play. They form two forks of an overarching concept, that is, the 'strategic alliance'. What makes an alliance strategic? Mytelka (1991) gives two interrelated reasons: it is created as a means through which the future competitive position of the firm is enhanced; and it is structured in a long-term, gradualist perspective, rather than as a direct response to possible short-term market gains. From these basic criteria, both bilateral and multilateral options fall within the strategic alliance strategy model. At a more applied level, one may talk about a strategic R&D alliance. That is to say, bilateral and multilateral strategic alliances which function through R&D collaboration. Thus, to dissect the alliance concept further, four different kinds of R&D alliance have been identified[9], which expand on the typology constructed by Mytelka (1991). These are (1) private inter-firm alliances, organised without government involvement; (2) firm-university alliances, which involve two or more firms and have some government funding (e.g. Sematech); (3) inter-firm collaborative agreements which emerge as a result of intergovernmental agreements (e.g. Airbus); and (4) national or international collaborative programmes. Within this category, one can list the EC Esprit programme, Eureka, and ICOT in Japan.

This typology is applicable to the work in hand, but needs some modifications. The fourth classification could be further divided, into three sections (Fig. 5.2). The first of these would be consensual public-private national collaborative programmes; the second, top-down international collaborative programmes; and the third, bottom-up international collaborative programmes. Three variations of R&D collaboration generally emerge, with respect to the technology variable. It

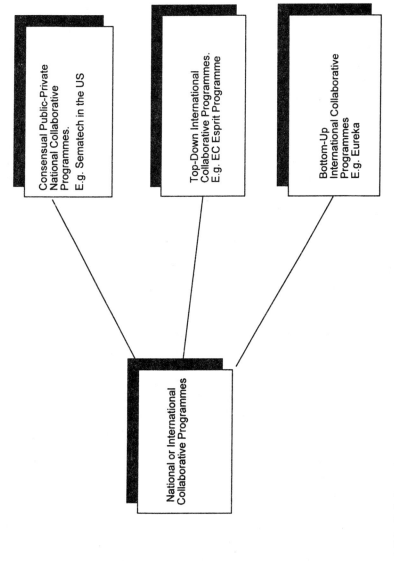

Figure 5.2   R&D Alliances: typology of national and international collaborative programmes

Consensual Public-Private National Collaborative Programmes.
E.g. Sematech in the US

Top-Down International Collaborative Programmes.
E.g. EC Esprit Programme

Bottom-Up International Collaborative Programmes
E.g. Eureka

National or International Collaborative Programmes

may involve the exchange or pooling of existing technologies, or the development of new technologies (Dunning, 1993), or indeed a mixture of both. Let us proceed to analyse JESSI, in light of these conceptual classifications, and determine the extent to which technology defines the strategy options of large European semiconductor producers.

3 JESSI: a study in chip collaboration

At the time of writing, the JESSI programme was undoubtedly the most ambitious collaborative research and development activity ever undertaken by the European information technology industry. The largest programme within the Eureka framework, it involves fourteen European countries, as well as the European Commission, who participate in its development and contribute towards its project costs. JESSI was founded by fourteen companies and research institutes in Britain, France, Italy, the Netherlands, and Germany, and scheduled to run for eight years (1989-96). The initial budget was set at more than 3,000 million ECU ($3.5 billion approx.) However, this sum has since been pared back to $2.4 billion. Of this, 50 per cent is provided by the firm and institutes participating, 40 per cent by national governments, and 10 per cent by the European Commission.

The programme's non-governmental participants can be divided into four groups: first, all major European electronic equipment manufacturers active in consumer and telecommunications equipment and automotive electronics; second, all merchant European semiconductor manufacturers, i.e. firms producing microchips for sale on the open market; third, the main semiconductor production equipment and materials manufacturers; and fourth, major European research institutes and universities.

By the mid-1990s, the number of countries involved in the programme had grown to include, Austria, Belgium, Denmark, the United Kingdom, Finland, France, Germany, Ireland, Italy, Liechtenstein, the Netherlands, Portugal, Sweden, and Switzerland. The overall number of participants totalled more than 150 firms, universities, and research institutes. The number of project clusters came to fifteen, and within these, there were around seventy projects in operation[10].

3.i. The organisational structure

JESSI began as an eight year R&D programme on silicon based microelectronics and its integration into systems. It deals with submicron silicon, that is silicon devices with details smaller than one thousandth of a millimetre:

> JESSI is the first European co-operative programme in which the development of microelectronics components (or chips as they are often called) together with the equipment and materials needed for the production of them and the subsequent applications of these chips, are all included[11].

142

The definition and planning phase for the JESSI programme started actively at the beginning of January, 1988. The programme was launched one year later, on 1 January, 1989, and officially installed as a Eureka project (EU 127) at the Eureka ministerial conference in Vienna on 19 June, 1989. It was agreed that the programme would run from 1989 until 1996. Its founder members comprised fourteen companies and research centres from Germany, France, Italy, Netherlands, Belgium, and Britain. Assigned costs for the three year implementation period totalled Ecu 550 million[12].

The organisational structure of JESSI is dominated by the participating firms, with governments in a more consultative role, primarily on issues of funding. The executive body of JESSI is the industrial JESSI board, which has ten members. The functions of this board symbolise the industrial, rather than governmental undertaking of JESSI. Its responsibilities include monitoring the overall progress of the programme towards its objectives. The JESSI board is supported by a small permanent staff, which is based in Munich. Representatives of the subprogramme management boards are members of the JESSI board. These management boards are comprised of representatives from the major participating industries. They issue calls for proposals, sort out and examine the submissions, and refer their conclusions to the JESSI board. In addition to these two forms of interrelated industrial administrative boards, the national governments and the European Commission are represented on a Joint Council or Committee, which decides on programme and proposal acceptance for funding, with the help of one international Expert Group per subprogramme. As we shall see subsequently, the organisational structure of JESSI is one area in which the Europeans could learn from other international semiconductor consortia. The next chapter examines the structure of both the US Sematech organisation and the Japanese VLSI initiative. From this we will advance several ways in which the organisational structure of JESSI is inferior to its global counterparts.

A number of (vague) criteria were outlined during the JESSI planning phase, for both firm and institute participation in the JESSI programme[13]. For firms, these criteria were, first, sufficient technical experience and capability, second, new technical concepts, third, an economically sound 'European' company, and fourth, the company had to be internationally competitive. The third criterion on this list raises an interesting question, which is relevant not only to JESSI, but also to this work's wider themes such as the nature of European collaboration and competitiveness. The question is, 'what is a European firm?'. Interpretations are rather broad, but more-or-less consensual, on the issue of what a European firm actually is in the contemporary global economy. A senior European Commission official[14] cites five (somewhat ill-defined) conditions necessary, in the realm of high technology, in order for a firm to be referred to as European and thus permitted to participate in EC supported research. These conditions are, firstly, the existence of European Community partners; secondly, establishment in Europe, i.e. substantial research and manufacturing facilities in Europe; thirdly, the payment of taxes to EC governments; fourthly, the generation of employment in EC member states; and fifthly, a significant contribution to the improvement of the scientific base and competitiveness of the wider European industrial sector on the world market[15]. He thus argued that IBM, Ford, and ICL[16] all fulfil these conditions, and consequently participate in collaborative programmes such as JESSI. Another Commission perspective[17] has simplified the definition by arguing that location of R&D is the central criteria for European corporate citizenship. Any company that operates and is registered in the EC, and that conducts a large portion of its R&D within the Community, may be regarded as a European company, and consequently qualify for membership of collaborative European programmes.

The concept of a European firm (frequently prefaced by the word indigenous or native) shall be used in this chapter, primarily to prevent analytical ambiguities. That is to say, when assessing EC policy and European collaborative programmes, one must accept that, in certain instances and for specific purposes, a European and a non-European firm can be defined. It is not of central importance whether the author considers a firm to be European, American, or global. To avoid any further uncertainties, the core understanding of European corporate nationality herein, rests on the existence of a firm's global headquarters within the territory of the European Union.

The main ambiguity with the previous Commission definitions is the lack of set levels for R&D activity. No official EC guidelines exist to determine the amount (measurable both as a per centage of total corporate R&D activity, and in terms of absolute financial outlay) of R&D which a company should conduct within the EC in order to qualify for membership in European collaborative programmes. Decisions are arbitrary, and thus open to both lobbying from individual firms, and to discrimination against firms due to country of origin for instance. However, no evidence has been found to support such possible discriminatory practices on the part of the Commission. Rather, as ICL argues[18], it is the European firms and their representative organisations that are more likely to discriminate on such grounds.

Institutes and universities co-operating within JESSI have also to fulfil certain requirements. These include the guarantee that long-term research shall develop new methods and processes, thereby satisfying the prerequisites for future products; the assurance that supporting and alternative research will be carried out under industrial orientation; and the promise that research findings must be made available to industry.

3.ii. Why JESSI was created

Within official JESSI publications[19], emphasis is placed firstly on the technology factor, and the importance of microelectronics, not only to the wider electronics sector, but to modern society in general[20]. It is correctly argued that microelectronics are an engine behind economic growth, and a support for our standard of living. Then the argument switches to one of condemnation - condemnation of what is termed 'aggressive competition' (presumably meaning the Japanese in particular), and the way in which this 'disturbs' the European and even the global supply situation for microelectronics. From this position, the JESSI

144

organisation advances the proposition that Europe runs the risk of losing control over its microelectronics industry. This would, the argument continues:

put Europe's future at stake, placing it in the hands of other regions[21].

Such a line of argument is not only alarmist, but also inaccurate. Reference is made frequently in official JESSI documents to 'Far Eastern industry', as if this was some monolithic entity, with a calculated plan to desecrate European industry. It is argued that Far Eastern global market success is attributable to a well defined strategy combined with a unique set of economic, political and social conditions - which Europe simply could not compete with. This magic formula strategy is described as being tri-faceted. Firstly, Far Eastern industry systematically acquires knowledge, penetrates markets, increases market share, and finally dominates a given market. Secondly, a strong position in one industry is used as a springboard from which to attack the next dependent industry. Finally, the Asian aggressors keep their domestic markets virtually closed, whilst consolidating their control over the wide-open European market[22].

This entire thesis is not only flawed, but is also blatantly bigoted, and ignorant to the differences between both Far Eastern countries and companies. The first element of the strategy could be as easily attributed to an American or a European firm, as to an East Asian one. Knowledge acquisition, market access, and subsequent growth in market share, are variables in the strategy of any firm attempting to establish a presence in a given industry and market. The second facet of the so-called Far Eastern strategy is simply rational business strategy - if you are a vertically integrated Japanese company and your semiconductor division successfully competes within and establishes a strong market position in a given country or region, it is only natural that other business units of your wider corporation will then attempt to compete with their product sector counterparts within that market also. To propose that this is some form of malicious strategy, aimed at conquering a particular economy, is preposterous. On the third dimension of the strategy, it is true that Far Eastern markets (particularly the Japanese) are proving highly resistant to foreign penetration (one need only to have followed the mid-1990s US.-Japan trade conflict in the press to be aware of this fact). It is not the intention here to enter that debate, as it will be dealt with in the following chapter. The European market, although more open than its East Asian counterparts, is not wide open, as the JESSI organisation would have one believe. The extensive system of trade regulating tools employed by the EC (discussed in the last chapter), combined with certain national government discretionary measures vis-à-vis import restrictions, makes for selectively restricted market(s) for importers. Although Japanese and Korean (in particular) markets still do not facilitate significant foreign presence, they are gradually opening up to American and European competitors. This will be discussed further in the following chapter. Officially, the core aim in setting up JESSI was to:

ensure that European system houses have early access to leading edge technology and will not be dependent on their, often vertically integrated, competitors for the realisation of advanced products[23].

A further rationale for the creation of JESSI was to increase co-operation - both vertically and horizontally - within the European semiconductor sector. This would serve to increase the industry's overall competitiveness in this fast moving area. In this respects, JESSI has certainly increased the level and nature of co-operation. The reasoning offered to justify public support of JESSI is that investment in the microelectronics industry is beneficial for the whole of society. The rationale employed to explain the need for public support of such a venture, begins with the two-level assertion that no individual European company has the resources (either financial or technological) to undertake the long-term development of new leading-edge technology; and, if left unaided, the numerous small and fragmented R&D efforts would lead to under investment in future technology. Within this rationale of course is the explicit assertion that public funding of R&D is needed only for long-term basic research - thus delegitimising the EC's involvement in the other subprogrammes of JESSI. Moreover, American and other global corporate competitors can afford such long-term research, without receiving any overt[24] government support. There is also the matter of government sharing of risks which would be too high for the collaborating industrial partners alone. A final justification proffered for partial public funding of JESSI, is that it helps to create a level playing field of sorts within the global economy. European public funding of such programmes merely evens out the competitive parameters for European firms in competing with American or East Asian firms. Granted, there is a certain degree of public money being channelled, through different means, to semiconductor R&D in all of the countries where such products are produced[25]. However, the total amount is often quite small, and it is frequently conveyed indirectly, through public laboratories for instance. However, in terms of scale and overall amount, no one comes even close to the Europeans with respects to such funding. In addition to the $1.2 billion of public money which is being poured into JESSI, further millions are being spent on related research, both within the EC's ESPRIT programme, and within various national R&D projects.

The central reason for creating JESSI was, according to the chairman of the original JESSI Planning Council, Professor Veltman, Europe's 'technological dependency' on the US and Japan in the crucial area of microelectronics. He has argued that Europe needs to bring the balance of the chips trade in equilibrium, in order to secure Europe's industrial and economic future. In slightly less alarming prose, the Eureka secretariat has argued that trade was the main determinant in the establishment of JESSI[26]. They have stated that semiconductor production was projected to double in value during the first half of the 1990s, from 55 billion ECU in 1989, to more than 110 billion ECU ($143 billion) by 1994[27]. These calculations proved to be largely accurate, with world semiconductor sales topping $150 billion by the end of 1995[28] Of this sum, Europe has under ten per cent . Europe meets less than half of its needs, and incurs a trade deficit of nearly 2.5 billion ECU.

Hence Eureka argues that Europe's import-export deficiency in microchips was an important determinant in the establishment of JESSI.

Mr Radelaar, former vice chairman of the JESSI Board, has stated that JESSI had five main objectives. These were to (1) reduce the fragmentation of Europe's industrial and research landscape; (2) improve vertical co-operation between companies at different levels along the development and production chain, and subsequently, shorten development time; (3) integrate all relevant industry sectors by means of a broad approach to microelectronics (he argued that the division of the programme into four different but complementary subprogrammes, could achieve this integration); (4) procure national and supranational (EC) funding at an early stage, in order to emphasise the political importance of Jessi and its European character; and (5) orientate the programme towards industry, since its ultimate objective is to improve Europe's market position in microchips. This is an important point, which shall be returned to further on.

Therefore, to summarise, the fundamental mission of Jessi was to secure the availability in Europe, of resources for the design, manufacture, and application of microchips; and strengthen the whole European microelectronics industry chain - the electronics systems industry, the microelectronic components industry, and the semiconductor equipment and materials industry - to an extent whereby they could compete effectively in the global market[29].

3.iii. The technological objectives

The original structure of JESSI was divided into four subprogrammes: technology, equipment and materials, applications, and long term research (fig.5.3). The objectives of these four subprogrames has been outlined in the results of the JESSI Programme Planning Phase (1989) as follows. First, the goal of the technology subprogramme is the development of the production process. Its aim is to develop a flexible, competitive manufacturing technology for advanced systems application. Second, the goal of the equipment and materials subprogramme is to develop manufacturing equipment and materials for microelectronics in selected areas of the European supply industry. Third, the applications subprogramme is intended to establish competitive system-design procedures and tools, with which to develop highly complex microchips, and facilitate their integration into systems. Finally, the objective of JESSI's basic and long term research subprogramme is complementary applied research for the long-term future, in order to increase interaction between industry and universities and to secure a European knowledge base in core technologies.

The applications subprogramme was originally the real driving force behind JESSI, with eighty firms and research centres participating in twenty-two projects. The ultimate goal of the projects was to deliver prototype chipsets. The applications chosen (Europrojects) had to demonstrate a high sales potential. Projects selected have included high definition television (HDTV), automotive electronics, and advanced telecommunications. The second major focus of this subprogramme was the development of leading-edge CAD tools, to meet both the

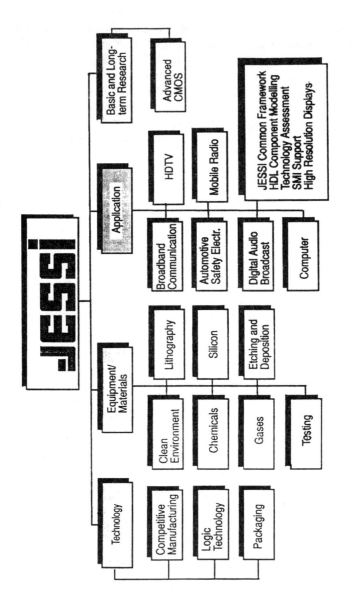

Figure 5.3 JESSI programme structure

Source: JESSI official publication

requirements of Europrojects, and general market demands. To look briefly at one of the projects within the JESSI applications subprogramme, we can see how JESSI formed part of a much wider set of what Mytelka and Delapierre term, 'networked, knowledge-based oligopolies' (1994, p.10). For HDTV, four competing alliances strove to control the international television market[30]. One emerged in Japan, comprising several leading Japanese electronics firms, in co-operation with the Japanese Ministry of Post, Telephone, and Telegraphs (Mytelka and Delapierre, 1994, p.11). A second consortium developed in Europe, composed of Philips, Thomson, Bosch, and Thorn Emi, the main European-based TV makers.

148

This group worked under the aegis of Eureka (thus bringing in public money also), and was chosen as a JESSI applications project[31]. The other two consortia emerged partly in response to the Japanese and European alliances: one consisted of American firms in partnership with the US government, and the other, comprising both US and European firms, developed from the industry's technological shift in the early 1990s[32]. Due to technological lag (caused by staying with analog, rather than switching to digital standard) the Japanese consortium withdrew from the HDTV competition in early 1994:

> A cluster of firms tied together by the development of common technical specifications was thus put into a position from which they could shape the direction of technological change in an emerging sector. Gone were the days when a single dominant firm, could, through its own R&D efforts set the rules of an industry (Mytelka and Delapierre, 1994, p.11).

The HDTV case illustrates how JESSI has, through its applications subprogramme, contributed to a new form of international competition. This is one based on 'strategic families' (Albach, 1992) - knowledge-based networks of global firms, collaborating to enhance their collective competitiveness. Such co-operative corporate networks are, by their very nature, oligopolistic, and serve as market industry barriers. Through the alliance network, the partners can, collectively, set industry standards, shape the nature and pace of technological development, buffer themselves from the full force of market competition, and maintain a steady access to both knowledge and markets (Mytelka and Delapierre, 1994, p.10).

This example shows how, through JESSI and its related, applications projects, large firms have constructed international networks of power. These networks shape technological change and international industrial standards, as well as the rules which govern the market itself. It lends support to our argument that acting in unison, large firms must be seen as credible international actors, influencing the terms of global competition, and negotiating with governmental agents from a position of relative strength.

The equipment and materials subprogramme became increasingly important as JESSI developed. A chairman of the Equipment and Materials Board has commented that:

> in advanced microelectronics, the manufacturing equipment and materials play just as important a role as do the production technologies themselves[33].

Equipment and materials are key factors in achieving quality and competitiveness at all levels of the microelectronics sector. This subprogramme essentially complements its technology counterpart, and works in close co-operation with progressive European microchip producers.

The basic and long-term research subprogramme contained five projects, working on the resolution of technological problems in each of the three previous subprogrammes, and on exploring long-term trends in microelectronic technology:

This subprogramme helps to explore long-term trends, and map out the alternative paths which may perhaps replace todays technologies and processes[34].

JESSI encountered several problems during the first three years of its operation. Not least amongst these was the 1990 decision by Philips, one of JESSI's founders, to withdraw from the project it was to have led - to develop static, random access memories (SRAMs) - citing its dismal financial performance that year. Philips also argued that the market for SRAMs was not developing encouragingly. The withdrawal of Philips from one of JESSI's vanguard projects, was widely perceived as a decisive blow to European co-operation in microchip development. However, officially the JESSI board played down the event. Raimondo Paletto, chairman of the board at that time, argued that JESSI would not be held back by the decision; it only concerned a small number of the JESSI projects, in a very well-defined sector. Anyhow, he continued:

the Dutch company continues to be a major participant in several fields, and especially in applications linked to HDTV[35].

4 JESSI: the private sector participant perspective

The impossibility of conducting a rigorous scientific analysis of economic variables was discussed in chapter two. For reasons already outlined, it is impossible to carry out a cost-benefit analysis of R&D activities, or to definitively prove their success or failure. Hence, we can merely advance a critique of JESSI, as a dimension of EC industrial policy for semiconductors, based in large part on the opinions of the participants and on the extent to which the initial objectives of the programme have been achieved. From this evaluation of the empirical evidence to hand, one may comment on the relative utility and effect of JESSI.

The opinions of JESSI's private sector participants are obtained through analysing both their individual comments and reports, and those of industrial organisations which represent all or part of JESSI's non-public membership. Thus, the following section will examine the opinions voiced by:
(1) Individual firms and research institutions
(2) The European Round Table of Industrialists (ERT)
(3) The European Electronic Components Manufacturers Association (EECA)
(4) The EUREKA Secretariat
(5) The JESSI Secretariat

This work bases its individual corporate perspective largely on the positions of two companies: ICL and SGS-Thomson (although assorted comments and arguments are included from a number of other companies also). This selective emphasis is due to the facts that (1) ICL is a chip user and not a producer, whereas SGS-Thomson (ST) is a producer and not a user; (2) ICL has made the transition from national champion to free marketeer, whereas ST is still heavily reliant on government support; and (3) ICL is owned by non-European parties, whereas ST is owned by two European governments.

4.i. SGS-Thomson: the view of a microchip producer

SGS-Thomson, a Franco-Italian microelectronics firm, and Europe's third largest indigenous producer of microchips, views European collaborative programmes for semiconductor R&D in a very favourable light. According to Dr Enrico Villa, Director General of SGS-Thomson:

> We believe that JESSI has substantially contributed to the improvement of the microelectronics industry in general, and to our company in particular. From that point of view, we value JESSI as a successful project[36].

High praise indeed. Why does ST support JESSI so enthusiastically? What reasoning does the firm provide for the financial and human resource emphasis which has been placed on the semiconductor industry? How does the company assess JESSI's achievements to date? ST condones a public sector strategic targeting of the semiconductor sector. The core reasoning behind this position has been explained as the following:

> No advanced industrial society can exist without controlled access to an advanced electronics industry, which in turn cannot exist without controlled access to an advanced semiconductor sector[37].

Pasquale Pistorio, President and CEO of ST, has long been a leading advocate of the necessity of maintaining an indigenous European presence within microchip production. His argument is premised on the supposition that, given the fact that most semiconductor producers are part of a larger vertically integrated corporation, it does not make business sense for such producers to supply state-of-the-art chips to its competitors, before the other business units of the wider company have exploited the competitive edge gained through early access to the chip technology. This argument may be somewhat relevant for Japanese and Korean producers, but it is problematic when one applies it to the US suppliers. This is because most of the leading US merchant chip suppliers are not part of a larger vertically integrated corporation, but are self-contained business enterprises. Also, in view of the dynamism of the technology and the rapid pace at which new developments spread, this internalisation issue is evidently misleading. It is highly improbable that competitors based outside of the EC can protect intellectual property rights by means of patents for instance, due to the slow and transparent nature of such processes.

Pistorio continues by arguing that within any defined macroeconomic system (the EC in this case), it is vital that users have an independent, indigenous supplier. He rejects any suggestions that such a supplier could originate from another macroeconomic system, on the grounds that their strategy is dictated by the needs and competitive drive of external interests - often to the cost of Europe. He further rejects transnational strategic alliances as an option, on the grounds that they benefit only a few large firms, at the cost of the many smaller operators.

In proposing the necessity of indigenous chip producers, Pistorio appears to suggest that such producers grant competitors access to their leading-edge technologies, on the basis that they are fellow Europeans. The reality is that this would in fact be the case, but not as a consequence of any Europe first corporate strategies. Rather, the complex technology lock-ins which exist between European-based firms had to be consolidated in the 1980s, as a result of the increased need for producers to improve their knowledge of user requirements (Mytelka, 1994, p.4). As Ernst and O'Connor (1992) argue, the shift in emphasis from price to product differentiation necessitated closer links between chip manufacturers and chip users. Those firms which have close ties and frequent communication with their users, have been able to gain competitive advantage through incorporating system design requirements early on in the development of new product generations[38]. As Pistorio acknowledges, JESSI did succeed in providing the 'new institutional arrangements for improving knowledge about user requirements' (Ernst & O'Connor, 1992, p.27), and facilitated technology lock-in amongst European chip makers and users. This in turn was meant to enhance the competitive advantage of the chip manufacturers[39].

A related advantage to being part of an R&D network such as JESSI is the ability to 'window' (Mytelka, 1994, p.4). The disparate knowledge accumulated within the JESSI framework allows member firms to hypothesise, with greater accuracy, on the future nature of the market. This reduces the risks (and time) involved in pursuing particular lines of R&D activity, and increases a firm's chances of being first-to-market with a product. This notion is implicit in Mr. Pistorio's arguments in support of JESSI. ST evidently saw benefit to be had through windowing in JESSI.

At a market applicable level, ST argues that the most illustrative examples of the way in which JESSI has played a major role in helping some of its industrial participants to make new integrated circuits, are in the area of non-volatile memory chips. With its 16 MBit EPROM devices, developed in part through JESSI, SGS-Thomson has demonstrated the technological advances which the programme has achieved in an important part of the memory chip market. Commercial success has accompanied technological success within this market, as SGS-Thomson achieved the world's number one position in EPROM sales at the end of 1993[40]. To what extent were these advancements within this particular market segment really achieved because of JESSI though? It would appear instead that they could be largely accredited to ST's own strategy of choosing to hinge the firm's future on this product area. This is indicated by figures which show that in 1993, EPROMs represented 31.2 per cent of ST's total world-wide corporate revenue[41]. It may therefore be argued that JESSI functioned more as a vehicle for ST's product concentration strategy, allowing the company to conduct subsidised R&D into EPROMs, in place of solely in-house R&D for that product family. Thus, JESSI's only clear area of successful product development occurred largely because one firm clearly wanted it and had already targeted this product for development. In the absence of one or more companies driving a product-oriented project, the projects often fail. As the next chapter will illustrate this notion of a company-led project structure dominated the Japanese VLSI project, and was one of its most successful structural dimensions. The case of EPROMs, where a member firm pushed for quick and specific results, was rare within the JESSI structure.

The SGS-Thomson argument continues that the competitive success of the semiconductor sector rests on the balanced input of producers, commercial users, and public authorities (especially at an EC level). There are three areas in which both national and Community policy should play a central role: innovation; restructuring of the industry; and flexibility[42]. Of these, emphasis is placed especially on the first - innovation being referred to as the main fuel for growth. It is also seen as the vehicle through which semiconductor manufacturers can move significant portions of their product range to the more knowledge-intensive, specialised niche markets - where it is argued that competition is less cut-throat, and the lower margins involved allow a company to minimise losses caused by market slumps or corporate strategy miscalculations.

In relation to the role of the indigenous semiconductor industry in enhancing competitiveness, ST cites five main action items. First, as with policy actors, chip producers should also place particular emphasis on innovation. R&D activities are high-lighted as the most fundamental factor in the survival and growth of the semiconductor industry. Second, strategic alliances are emphasised. Both vertical and horizontal alliances are advocated for Europe's chip producers. The third item is globalisation. This is emphasised for the purpose of creating adequate economies of scale to compensate for high input costs. Also, it permits a firm to reduce its dependency on one or two national markets, and thus avoid the financial losses involved if the national market(s) experience periods of low or negative growth. The fourth issue which the producers can address is dimensions of scale. In this, it is argued that the present fragmentation of the industry should be eradicated through a process of restructuring and concentration. Such dimensions of scale may always be achieved by proxy, i.e. through horizontal alliances. Finally, the issue of productivity needs to be tackled. In this respects, it is advised that a continuous improvement process must be conducted within each chip producing firm, and at every stage in the product development cycle.

ST representatives have argued that JESSI addresses, in some way or another, all of the above items - with the exception of the fourth, which is of course an internal corporate matter. In line with the previously discussed input balance, ST argues that JESSI provides the ideal framework within which semiconductor producers, the wider electronics industry (commercial users), and national and EC policy sectors, can all contribute, in a balanced and co-operative manner, to the competitive enhancement of the industry. Perhaps most importantly, JESSI addresses the need for innovation, which is, as already pointed out, the very essence of competitiveness. The questionable existence of a technology lag between Europe and the U.S. and Japan was the subject of intense debate during the first half of the 1980s. Whether or not such a gap actually existed is still contentious, but regardless of this, the fact is that innovation is something which is central to the semiconductor industry. The need to innovate constantly, is a core dimension of maintaining or increasing corporate competitiveness within such a rapidly changing industry. Thus, JESSI's emphasis on innovation is important and supportable.

ST's third argument in support of JESSI, is that it fosters a co-operative environment between users and makers, and between firms and research institutions at a horizontal level. This co-operation helps especially in tackling the previously mentioned dimensions of scale factor, but also, at a psychological level, in simply creating a spirit of co-operation amongst European researchers, producers, and consumers. Co-operative networks have evolved through JESSI, and empirical evidence illustrates that most of JESSI's participants acknowledge it as one of the programme's main successes. In addition, it signifies the achievement of one of JESSI's initial objectives.

A further point advanced by ST is that JESSI contributes to manufacturing science, and is helping to develop new product design. Therefore, indirectly, it is benefiting productivity in other, related sectors. True, numerous technical achievements have so far emerged from various JESSI projects. However, the question is, 'were these generally developed ahead of extra-JESSI competitors, or were they merely duplications of existing technologies?' If the former is true, the logical assumption is that their market introduction would rapidly translate into increased market share. In general, this is not the case.

Finally, it is argued that JESSI is furthering the globalisation process. This is done through the greater international credibility which JESSI has given its corporate participants in terms of technological achievement. This argument is supported by market share statistics which indicate that the combined extra-EC sales of the JESSI partners increased from 36 per cent to 43 per cent of their total sales between 1989 and 1993[43], JESSI's first five year period of operation. These figures prove little, apart from the fact that the JESSI partners have slightly reduced their dependence on home markets. This process may be viewed as inevitable given the external competitive pressures on them to globalise. What ST fails to do is translate these extra-EC sales percentage increases into European and world market share (fig.5.4). Taking 1992 and 1993 alone, the JESSI partners combined European (EC and EFTA together) market share declined from 29 per cent to 24.6 per cent, whilst their share of the world market fell from 9.1 per cent to 8.1 per cent[44]. During 1994 and 1995, these figures appear to have remained static[45]. It is worth noting though that several of the JESSI partners declined in their overall market ranking in the 1993-95 period, whilst others failed to improve their ranking, despite strong growth in revenues. Philips dropped from third to fourth in terms of individual share of the European market; whilst Temic-Matra went from fourteenth to sixteenth. ST failed to move up from its fifth overall ranking (*Dataquest,* 1995, p.4). ST's figures show that Europe's chip makers have increased their global presence somewhat since JESSI's inception, but the reality is that this increased presence in the global market has not translated into gains in total world market share. These market share statistics suggest that during the first

European Semiconductor Component Market
1992	29%
1993	24.6%
1994	26%[46]

World Semiconductor Component Market
1992	9.1%
1993	8.1%

Figure 5.4 JESSI partners combined market share

	Europe			World		
	1992	**1993**	**1994**	**1992**	**1993**	**1994**
Philips	9.3	7.1	6	3.24	2.7	2.6
Siemens	7.4	6.7	7	1.91	1.8	1.9
SGS Thomson	7.3	6.5	6	2.46	2.4	2.4
TEMIC-MATRA	N/A	2.2	2	N/A	0.7	N/A
GEC Plessey	1.59	1.0	N/A	0.58	0.3	N/A
Mietec	0.9	0.9	N/A	0.17	0.2	N/A
ES2	0.21	0.2	N/A	0.05	0.0	N/A

Figure 5. 5 JESSI partners individual market share
(these figures remained largely constant during 1995)

Source: Dataquest statistics, 1995.

four years of JESSI's second stage of operation, it had little or no obvious positive affect on its industrial partners combined market share. This is true both at a European and at a global level. It appears that ST attribute a significant degree of success to JESSI. Pistorio argues, convincingly, that true success can only be measured in terms of world market share and profit, in conjunction with the ability to secure technological independence for European users. The third element in this equation may be measured on the basis of broad acceptance by electronic systems companies. In this respects, ST asserts that JESSI has played a key role. ST proposes that true success has indeed been attained, as all of the above three criteria are satisfied. It is argued that the combined world market share of European chip suppliers has halted its decline, and is now stable at about 10 per cent. Moreover, from the end of 1993 on, many European manufacturers began to show a profit (including ST). Finally, indigenous European chip makers are increasing the acceptability of their products and processes at a steady rate, and are forming numerous alliances with European and non-European systems manufacturers. ST cites a number of examples of increased credibility leading to transnational agreements with systems houses for them[47]. These include a product development agreement with Mitsubishi in the Flash memory area. It is argued that such co-operation maintains the independence of ST and does not affect its participation in JESSI. Also, an agreement was signed to supply Northern Telecom with customised chips for telecom applications. ST again attributes this deal largely to its enhanced international stature achieved through participation in JESSI.

Let us tackle the three pillars of true success, as delineated by Pistorio. On the issue of world market share, the figures cited by ST are inaccurate. In 1992, the combined world market share of the European chip makers fell below Pistorio's ten per cent, and declined further thereafter. As illustrated earlier, the combined share of JESSI's chip producing partners declined from 9.1 per cent to 8.1 per cent during the 1992-93 period and although improving slightly during 1994-95, failed to reach the magic ten per cent mark (Dataquest figures). Furthermore, corporate profitability cannot be attributed to a particular R&D consortium - the inability to conduct a cost-benefit analysis for R&D, has already been discussed. In addition, vis-à-vis increased corporate profitability, one must consider external demand factors caused by an upturn in the European and global economies, which leads to increases in chip consumption (there is a history of such demand cycles within the semiconductor industry). This was evident during 1994, when increased demand for memory and application specific chips increased world-wide profitability in these markets. As a Dataquest survey shows, the major participants in the DRAM market experienced the strongest revenue growth during 1994 (1995, p.2). Companies such as Siemens and SGS Thomson, who have comparative strength in the most recent high growth areas, naturally benefited from this global demand surge. This at least partly explains the growth experienced by such companies during 1994, compared with previous years.

Also, successes achieved through transnational strategic alliances are probably linked with profit increases. The increase in Siemens 1994 profitability and market share (both at a European and a world level) is largely attributable to the aforementioned surge in demand for DRAMs during 1994[48]. These products form the core of Siemens semiconductor production. It is likely that Siemens DRAM development global partnership with IBM and Toshiba played a part in this relative market success. Moreover, on this final measure of success, it is difficult to make a causal connection between membership of JESSI and the formation of product development alliances or supply contracts with extra-EC systems houses. In fact, it might be argued that membership in such a consortium may prevent such international agreements rather than cause them since Mitsubishi, for instance, may not relish the possibility of its knowledge in a given area (such as Flash memories), seeping out to global competitors allied with ST in JESSI. For international supply contracts, the counterfactual argument can be invoked: if ST had not been a member of JESSI, would Northern Telecom (for example) have contracted it to supply customised chips? It is by no means clear that the answer to this question would have been negative.

SGS-Thomson did improve its competitive position during the 1990s. It is in fact one of the fastest developing firms in the industry, growing by 26 per cent in 1993-94[49]. It has had particular success in the Asia-Pacific region, where its 1995 turnover totalled $925 million. Of this, the Japanese market accounts for roughly 20 per cent. As of the end of the third quarter of 1996, ST's sales in Japan had risen to $180 million, up from $102 million the previous year[50] It is now the leading world producer of EPROM chips. This success in specific product areas has yet to transfer into significant overall corporate market share gains though, either in Europe or world-wide. It is inevitable that there will be companies within all such collaborative ventures that succeed, at least in particular market niches. This can be in spite of, rather than because of, such collaborative ventures. These firms may have strategic weaknesses which JESSI does not address, and which they overcome themselves. They may have strengths which JESSI complements, rather than creates. Such firms might be more focused than their R&D network partners, and know better what they want from collaborative R&D projects. ST appears to have been one such company: it possessed a basic technological strength in non-volatile memory chips, knew exactly what it wanted to achieve in this product area within JESSI, actively sought these developments in specific projects, and achieved them. This would suggest that EC policy can enhance corporate competitiveness, but almost in an unintended manner. Market success can be attained by a firm which uses a project partially funded by the EC to achieve specific product development. The key point here is that the particular instrument of EC policy merely complements a firm's ongoing development plans, and is not a means for achieving market competitiveness in its own right.

To summarise his argument at COMPONIC 93, Pistorio argues that microelectronics is a cornerstone of the electronics industry, which in turn, is the cornerstone of modern industrial society. He goes on to propose that European electronics producers must assure access to an indigenous supply of state-of-the-art semiconductor components if they are to compete with global competitors. The only way in which such an indigenous source can be provided, according to

Pistorio, is through an R&D based co-operative triad involving the producers, users, and public authorities. He concludes that JESSI is a perfect example of such a three-way co-operative system in action, and succeeding. He footnotes this positive assessment though by asserting that:

> in such a rapidly evolving scenario as that of microelectronics, with technological innovation and market cycles sweeping the industry at each new product generation, it is hard to tell the difference between true success and just hitting close to a moving target[51].

This is a very telling footnote, and a conditionality which effectively renders all of Pistorio's previous arguments questionable. After publicly describing JESSI as a perfect co-operative system and a complete success, ST's CEO acknowledges that JESSI's projects may merely be scoring near misses rather than direct hits on the constantly mobile and changing target of technical and market success.

4.ii. ICL: the user perspective

According to ICL representatives, the firm's approach to European collaborative programmes is pragmatic[52]. That is to say, closer inspection of particular programmes will only follow an affirmative response to three main questions: is it relevant for us?; can we afford it?; and is it necessary to meet market demand? ICL proposes not to be against European collaboration *per se*. The firm sees many structural and co-operative benefits from it. However, they argue that they adopt a pragmatic, non-ideological stance, that is to say, they are not really interested in overall frameworks, but rather, in individual projects. To quote an ICL executive:

> ICL supports the principle of European co-operation in R&D but will only join a specific programme where they are confident that each project fits ICL's overall R&D strategy rather than simply co-operating at the European level for the sake of it or to gain access to external funding[53].

This position is contradicted by the nature and extent of ICL's early participation in the ESPRIT programme. As Mytelka (1991;1994) shows, ICL was one of twelve key corporate players in the development of the ESPRIT network. The last chapter touched on this process, which began with the 1979-80 round table meetings between Commission Vice President Davignon and the leaders of twelve of Europe's largest electronics firms. Playing an instrumental role in the creation of EC-level collaborative R&D networks would indicate that ICL was originally interested in more than just a few specific collaborative projects. The firm was of course interested in specific projects which would fit with its overall R&D strategy, but at the same time the company was a central player in the creation and direction of the ESPRIT collaborative framework (Mytelka, 1991, pp.201-5; 1994, pp.5-7). The contradiction may be explained by events subsequent to the first two stages of ESPRIT. Enthusiasm for collaborative frameworks may have been dampened in the early 1990s, in the wake of the company's majority take-over by Fujitsu. After the Fujitsu acquisition, in 1990-91, ICL was ejected from the European Information Technology Round Table[54], and excluded from several JESSI and ESPRIT projects. It is rational to assume that this treatment, at the hands of its long-time industrial partners, would cause ICL to modify its position concerning European co-operative frameworks. Despite its exclusion from some of JESSI's R&D activities, the company continued to assert its support of JESSI as an idea. However, it states that it has not yet seen concrete, competitive products emerge through JESSI.

Regarding interest in individual projects rather than wider programmes, with respects to JESSI, ICL is particularly interested in projects for the further development of computer aided design (CAD) for chips. This of course is due to the fact that ICL designs chips for its range of mainframe computers, and does not produce them. Thus, it is interested only in design techniques which they implement when commissioning advanced semiconductor technology from their mainframe technology partner (and majority shareholder), Fujitsu. ICL is also a major consumer of commodity semiconductors, mainly for its range of personal computers and mid-range computers, which it purchases from the most competitive sources of such technology, regardless of regional or company origin. At a fundamental level, ICL supports the JESSI venture simply because it provides more choice in the marketplace. This, ICL believes, in and of itself makes it a good idea. However, to reiterate an important point, ICL is sceptical of the actual success of JESSI, because they argue that they have not yet seen the product.

On a broader level, ICL supports most forms of R&D collaboration within the EC, primarily due to the technology transfer which it facilitates:

ICL remains strongly committed to collaborative R&D because it provides a straight forward, practical and effective method for technology transfer between research bodies, industry, and society as whole[55].

In outlining its view of the best form of collaborative R&D methodology to pursue, ICL supports the involvement of end-users at all stages in such collaborative programmes. This is of course to ensure that those products which the customers require, actually do result from the R&D. As has already been shown, the system houses do indeed participate within the JESSI structure. ICL supports government funding of basic, long-term research, arguing that this is R&D which otherwise might be neglected because of market driven business pressures.

The firm cites three other pertinent benefits of EC (and national) collaborative R&D. These are, first, the co-operative spirit and concrete links which such R&D programmes foster within the European electronic sector, and between the sector and universities/public research institutes, and governments; second, these programmes facilitate the involvement of small and medium sized enterprises (SMEs) in long term research - something which might not otherwise occur, due to their relative lack of financial or human resources for such research; third, a political vision is provided by these programmes, within which the industrial and academic participants can develop co-operative initiatives focused on solving real world problems.

The ICL perspective is, on the whole, refreshing and clear. Unlike ST, ICL does not attempt to declare JESSI a success - nor, for that matter, does it try to label it a failure. The firm acknowledges the programme's successes in terms of the technology transfer which it facilitates, its funding of basic, long-term research, its inclusion of SMEs in long term research projects, and the co-operative network which it has created. However, a rational approach is adopted, and thus ICL is sceptical about JESSI's relative success, due to the programme's inability to provide tangible, competitive artefacts.

4.iii. A research institute perspective

Although a member of JESSI, the Belgian research centre, IMEC[56], harbours reservations about its utility - especially in the realm of chip development. It acknowledges that Europe is weak (or non-existent) in the production of large volume commodity components - memories, microprocessors, and gate arrays. Furthermore, the centre believe that such commodity components possess a strategic importance, and thus European firms should maintain some presence in them. However, it does not support attempts to maintain a presence and/or enhance competitiveness in these product areas through European (particularly EC) collaborative R&D programmes:

> The decision making process within the European Community is very slow. Combined with the struggles for funding, we lose a substantial amount of valuable time before we can even get started on new projects[57].

Rather, due to the global nature of production in these areas, IMEC advocates transnational strategic alliances between European firms and US, Japanese, Taiwanese, and Korean firms, as the best strategy for European producers. Also, emphasis is placed on Europe's strengths in ASICs and in a number of niche markets, and it is indicated that IMEC favours this concentration of resources and strategy on such areas, rather than on such markets as memory chips. Despite its reservations regarding the utility of European collaborative R&D programmes for large volume commodity components however, the research institute supports such programmes for other microelectronics sectors, such as semiconductor equipment development and design techniques. In pursuing these R&D objectives, IMEC is completely supportive of collaborative European initiatives[58]. Hence it is a member of both ESPRIT and JESSI. The centre still stresses the necessity to maintain global research links though, in tandem with any European co-operative activities.

The IMEC perspective is particularly valid in its emphasis on collaboration to enhance semiconductor equipment development and design techniques. These are both areas within which Europe has a very weak domestic presence. As the Americans realised in the mid-1980s (through Sematech), it is necessary to build-up strength in these sectors first, if you wish to increase your competitiveness in actual microchip component market segments. State-of-the-art design techniques, coupled with the most efficient chip-making equipment, will almost inevitably translate into better and more marketable microchips. This is an argument which shall be returned to further on.

4.iv. The equipment manufacturers opinion

ASM-Lithography, a joint venture between Philips and the Netherlands Merchant Bank (ING), was founded with the objective of tackling lithography issues in the manufacture of very-large-scale integrated (VLSI) circuits[59]. It controls 10 per cent of the world market for wafer steppers. The company is a JESSI partner, as well as being involved in ESPRIT and in Dutch national R&D programmes, but also has R&D facilities in the US and in East Asia. Furthermore, it has numerous private inter-firm R&D alliances. ASM Lithography's managing director (MD) argues that Europe could not do without JESSI, due both to increasing development costs, and to the rapid development time within JESSI. On this latter point, he argues that the JESSI structure facilitates quick and easy knowledge transfer between its industrial partners, and thus allows for shorter development time overall. However, ASM Lithography's managing director is sceptical about relying entirely on JESSI for European corporate competitive enhancement. He stresses that global alliances are indispensable:

> It is insufficient to think that European co-operation is enough to keep up with developments. In the future there simply has to be something broader than just European co-operation[60].

ASM Lithography displays strong support for the JESSI ideal and structure. The firm seems to believe that JESSI is a necessary but not sufficient condition for competitive enhancement. A central problem with the ASM Lithography perspective, is its belief that JESSI is crucial for helping European semiconductor firms to cope with escalating development costs. Certainly, it is one framework through which firms can deal with such costs. However, its desirability as the primary or only co-operative system of this kind, is questionable. Public sector involvement should always be monitored, since there is a constant danger that the availability of public finance for corporate R&D will be abused. As SGS-Thomson illustrates, public money can become addictive. Thus, for specified areas (such as basic, long-term research), and for a set time period, public-private collaborative frameworks can be of benefit to firms. However, firms can, and should, be able to survive without such mechanisms also. The strange thing is that ASM Lithography's logic seems to be disjointed: whilst emphasising the indispensable nature of transnational inter-firm strategic alliances for competitive enhancement, the company fails to perceive this co-operative option as an alternative framework through which firms could jointly tackle rapidly increasing development costs. A question mark also hangs over ASM's second justification for JESSI's necessity.

Granted, JESSI has facilitated less complex and more rapid transfers of knowledge between its industrial partners. Has it rapidly decreased development time though? Given the importance of the time factor in an industry such as semiconductors, such a development would be considerable. Doubts are raised on this claim however, because decreased development time should mean the ability to get one's product to the market faster (traditionally a major competitive problem for European chip producers), and consequently, capture greater market share. As already proven, this is not the case.

4.v. A collective business opinion: the European round table of industrialists

Since its inception in 1983, the European Round Table (ERT) has been one of the most influential forces in industrial lobbying at an EC level. Its voice has been particularly relevant in relation to collaborative programmes. Its membership comprises forty European industrial leaders[61], who, together, negotiate with both the European Commission and national governments on policy issues. The Round Table's stated objective is:

> to create the right environment for European industry to achieve economic growth and prosperity[62].

Established largely as a forum through which big business could publicly promote its own agenda and solution to various Europe-wide economic problems (Green, 1993, p.8), the ERT also received strong backing from the European Commission, as a means to raise political support for Commission industrial policies[63]. It pursues this objective primarily through identifying and studying the key issues, and promoting wider awareness of Europe's most urgent problems (ERT, 1993).

The ERT structure is compact and efficient. It operates through Policy Groups[64], each of which is chaired by a member, who is assigned responsibility to study an area of policy which the ERT's members perceive to be important to their combined interests. Proposals are subsequently made to the EC and/or national governments, which detail the Round Table's position on specific policy issues.

In more recent times, the ERT has maintained a constant pressure on the EC to incorporate its demands into policy. These demands have been largely consistent. Several influential documents released by the ERT have detailed these demands, as well as indicating the position of the ERT's industrial members vis-à-vis the utility of European collaborative programmes. One such report[65] lists seven conditions for competitiveness for European industry. These are, in brief, total priority to innovation and new technology, education and training, favourable financial conditions, trans-European infrastructure, a balanced approach to environmental issues, competition policy based on market realities, and an open world economy. In addition, the report proposes the establishment of The European Competitiveness Council[66], along the lines of the US Competitiveness Policy Council, to advise on implementation and to keep competitiveness at the forefront of policy debates.

As illustrated, the first condition for competitiveness listed by the ERT, is a prioritising of innovation and new technology. This emphasis is of particular importance to this research, given the core linkage which is drawn throughout this thesis between innovation and competitiveness. Thus, the basis of the ERT's most recent opinions on this area is that:

> Governments and industry should work together to identify strategic areas which meet the needs of society and embody those enabling technologies where a major industrial society must be strong[67].

Top of their list in terms of strategically important enabling technologies is microelectronics. From this strategic targeting phase, the ERT argues that industry and science should then combine to examine those areas which have been targeted, and to select the areas which are relevant to the needs of the market. The Round Table indicates that questions must be asked at a corporate level, including: 'what is technically feasible?'; 'what can be done by companies on their own?'; 'what needs a joint commitment of major resources?' To solve these queries, it is proposed that all actors in European R&D - public and private, national and EC - should pool their knowledge and efforts.

The ERT basically argues for innovation initiative and collaborative R&D structure to emerge at an industry level. However, what is interesting is the framework for government participation which the organisation forwards. The first point to note is their argument that the state, in conjunction with universities, should be primarily responsible for the conduct and funding of basic research, whilst leaving technology application to individual companies. Thus, jurisdiction for the two opposite outer limits on the R&D scale is assigned separately to the public and the private sector. It is the large area in between that the ERT sees as the domain for public-private sector collaboration:

> between the two extremes lies a broad area where the industrial clusters can share responsibility with the public sector, including the funding and management of joint projects[68].

Within this realm of co-operation, the ERT's industrial members seem to agree that the role of government should be more supportive, i.e. providing what they term 'scientific infrastructure' (human, technical, and financial resources) geared towards supporting the long-term development of European industry. It is emphasised that government should not design or manage programmes themselves. In addition, it is suggested that the public sector should act in a co-ordinating role for collaborative R&D, and avoid the dilution and duplication caused by maintaining separate national and Community programmes within the EC. If governmental agents are to be collaborative co-ordinators but not active participants in the definition or direction of collaborative projects, what type of framework should be constructed? The ERT fails to forward any details regarding the organisational technicalities of their proposal. It would appear though that what

163

they are advocating is quite similar to the Eureka framework. It must be presumed that they were aware of this similarity when drafting their reports.

Further government functions propounded by the Round Table include a facilitator for firm participation in collaborative projects, as well as a promoter of new technology dissemination through reasonable levels of regulation and public advocacy of these nascent technologies.

A final interesting point made by the *Beating The Crisis* (1993) report vis-à-vis government's role in R&D collaboration, is its support for public procurement. This is important because it most cogently illustrates the continued existence of more interventionist tendencies within large European industry. The ERT attempts to justify its support of public procurement by arguing that many new markets reflect the needs of society as a whole, rather than those of individuals. Such markets include the environment, transport, and energy. For these large, society-based markets, government should be active at all stages of the research, development and application cycle, and should use its purchasing power wisely so as to drive the pace of change (ERT, *Beating The Crisis,* 1993).

Prior evidence of the ERT's protective partnership[69] approach, can be found in their action plan for Europe, released in late 1991[70]. Here again, emphasis is placed on the development of the previously mentioned scientific infrastructure, within which firms can collaborate to develop and exploit new technologies. Furthermore, electronics (and biotechnology) is again targeted as strategic, that is as critical to the health of European industry. Thus, within this realm, public sector involvement in R&D is strongly advocated, at both a national and a Community level.

A major ERT criticism of Community R&D policy is its original emphasis on pre-competitive co-operation, which is argued to be out-dated, given its failure to consider rapidly changing technologies and short product life cycles. This argument is particularly pertinent to microchips[71].

Thus, this work supports the ERT's long-standing advocation of getting the results of research rapidly into the market place; and concurs with criticism of the EC's pre-competitive research approach - given the reality that such an approach cannot succeed for product groups such as active semiconductor components, where the technology is changing rapidly and the products become quickly obsolete within the market. In such cases, R&D must - with the exception of a certain level of basic research - always be conducted with a view to its rapid adoption and competitiveness in the market place.

With regards to ERT support for the Eureka system, and by extension, JESSI, the most clear evidence is found in the organisation's 1990 report, *Bright Horizons*. The importance which the Round Table attributes to microelectronics and to collaborative European programmes for their research and development, is evident throughout the document:

Access to advanced micro-electronics and information technology gives nations a competitive advantage at every stage of the economic chain that links suppliers and users. A major European effort is therefore needed to meet the challenges from Japanese and U.S. producers of IT hardware. Europe must respond to these challenges not only by competing head-on, but also by launching many more co-operative joint ventures and partnerships[72].

Regarding public sector involvement, the *Bright Horizons* report advocates a more flexible ad hoc financial support from European governments, with public funding of R&D being awarded to specific firm-proposed projects. This system is in line with that operating within the Eureka framework. Also, it is worth noting that although a pan-European form of collaboration is advocated, the European Commission is attributed a secondary role to national governments in terms of public sector involvement. Following a line of argument previously discussed, the 1990 report recommends that EC-level rules concerning pre-competitive R&D collaboration should be reviewed - especially with respects to rapidly evolving technologies and decreasing product life cycles. This may be interpreted as a further condemnation of the original basic premise of the EC Framework Programmes, and a subtle line of support for the close-to-market Eureka system.

Support for an industry-led, government-supported collaborative framework, in line with the Eureka structure, has been evident in all of the major R&D related reports released by the ERT during the first half of the 1990s. Furthermore, given the Round Table's constant targeting of microelectronics as a strategic industry, which needs special attention within such a collaborative framework, it may be concluded that the ERT has consistently supported the structure and objectives of JESSI.

4.vi. The Eureka Secretariat and EECA perspectives

In terms of technical achievements, the Eureka Secretariat claims that JESSI has thus far produced several useful products and processes[73]. These include: (1)16 Mbit DRAM; (2)16 Mbit EPROM; (3)design and production techniques for logic chips with 0.7μm structure widths; (4) world-wide achievements in production lithography equipment; (5) the first version of a common framework for full integration of CAD tools for microelectronic circuits; (6) the first CMOS structures with dimensions of 0.3μm.

One cannot dispute the existence of these products and processes, and the fact that they were achieved through JESSI projects. However, again the questions must be raised: Were these technologies developed ahead of JESSI's competitors? Have they translated into increased market share for their corporate developers? Was a European capacity in these new technologies really necessary? Whilst uncertainty remains concerning the answers to any or all of these questions, one cannot declare JESSI a success, based simply on technical outputs.

According to the trade lobby association, the European Electronic Component Manufacturers Association (EECA)[74]:

European [firms] cannot live with niche markets; they must have volume production[75].

This argument does not generally hold true. Volume chip producers (particularly in the memory market) rarely reap a satisfactory return on their investment - relying for company profit on other product areas. It is much easier - and economically sound - for European chip-makers to cede volume production to American and East Asian rivals. For European users, the vigorous competitive rivalry which exists within volume chip markets, means that they can pick and choose amongst several potential suppliers. Alternatively, European firms might maintain volume production in memory chips through a transnational memory development strategic alliance with world market leaders. Siemens pursued this latter option when they entered into a DRAM development alliance in 1992 with IBM and Toshiba. The EECA takes a very hard-line, interventionist approach. Its rhetoric is tough, and its actions are aggressive (witness its leading role in launching anti-dumping cases at an EC level against two Japanese and one Korean memory chip makers for instance). It constantly emphasises the need for unity amongst European component manufacturers in the face of foreign competition, and, at an EC-wide level, the necessity to maintain (through what ever measures necessary) a local European electronic components industry. In providing a rationale for this position, the association constantly plays the strategic industry and economic security cards:

> When thinking of suppliers, electronic components can be compared to ammunition. In a war, no one would dream of depending on the enemy for supplies. To do so would be suicide![76]

In the highly unlikely case of a trade war between the EC and Japan for instance, memory chips (for example) can simply be purchased from Korea or the US. Perhaps the EECA foresees a trade war with all of these countries simultaneously.

Regarding JESSI in specific, the EECA argues that JESSI was unfocussed originally, with too many participants, too many projects, and too much dilution of funds. It recognises that the programme has changed in part, and become slightly more focused. However, the EECA remains somewhat dubious about the achievements of JESSI.

5 JESSI: a self-evaluation

At a detailed, technical level, the JESSI Secretariat lists a number of JESSI results to date. Without going into the nuances of electronic engineering, it is sufficient to briefly name these technical achievements, and sketch their commercial/industrial significance.

The first such result cited by the secretariat, is the development, within a JESSI project, of 16Mbit EPROM chip[77] engineering samples, for delivery to customers. What does this mean for the customer? The 16 Mbit EPROM chip offers a memory capacity equal to the content of 1000 written pages, with access time of less than 120 nanoseconds per bit, and the possibility to erase and rewrite the information on the chip, as one needs. EPROM cells can also be included in logic circuits for new systems and applications. The main benefit of this is that the performance of products can be changed or customer wishes implemented without modification of the hardware[78]. The development of the 16Mbit EPROM technology is part of that JESSI cluster labelled Competitive CMOS Manufacturing. The activities within this cluster are intended to strengthen the know-how of the European semiconductor companies in the field of advanced volume production for memories and logic circuits[79]. In the flagship-project of this cluster, Advanced Technology for Volume Production, SGS-Thomson and Siemens, together, focus their efforts on non-volatile memories (EPROMs and FLASH memories[80]) and on application-specific DRAMs.

A second development which official documentation cites as proof of JESSI's success in terms of technological achievement, is the High Precision Optical Wafer Stepper. The steppers,[81] developed through the JESSI project i-line production lithography for 0.5 µm, are enabling ASM-Lithography to increase its world market share, due to their highly competitive product features. This may be perceived as an important advance, in a market currently dominated by Japanese manufacturers.

A third achievement of JESSI is the development of flexible, powerful mixed signal VLSI testers[82], by one of its industrial participants, Schlumberger. It is important to note here that the JESSI office states that the presence of mixed testing capabilities is of strategic importance. This is due to the fact that applications requiring mixed signal IC - such as telecommunications and multimedia - are important future growth markets.

A fourth tangible result of the JESSI projects is the JESSI Common Frame, an open framework for computer-aided engineering applications[83]. The purpose of a framework for CAD applications, is to provide a so-called environment for integrating and running computer-aided design programmes. In terms of users, the framework serves tool developers, and designers from system houses, and chip manufacturers. Perhaps the most crucial advantage which can be gleaned from this technological development, particularly when related to one the central arguments espoused by this work on Europe's competitive hindrances, is that this framework could help to reduce the time to market.

A fifth JESSI technological development to-date, is the transfer of basic know-how on process modules for 0.35µm IC-technology to industrial pilot lines. The knowledge has been transferred from Philips Research to GEC-Plessey's and Siemen's pilot lines. The process modules in question are Nitrided Gate Oxide and LATID[84]. These more sophisticated forms of process technologies are necessary in order to overcome impairments to semiconductor device performance, caused by, for instance, short channel affects on new, submicron dimensioned MOS transistors.

All of these achievements mean little if they do not ultimately contribute to the profitability and market share of chip producers. Establishing such linkages between technology and competitiveness is beyond the scope of social scientific analysis. However, we have established that in an industry such as semiconductors, competitiveness is largely determined by a firm's ability to rapidly adapt technological innovation into marketable products and processes. Time is of the essence in an industry which is characterised by short product life cycles and rapidly evolving manufacturing processes. Our evidence would indicate that JESSI has had little success in bringing its products and processes to market quickly. This fact undermines the JESSI organisation's claims to project success.

6 The restructuring of JESSI

In 1991-92,there was a national government led push which culminated in the reorganisation of JESSI[85]. During the 1991 Eureka Ministerial Conference in The Hague, EC Ministers decided that JESSI should focus on a few main objectives and not spread out funds over a multitude of projects. Following on from this, the EC Research Council of October 1991, decided that Commission subsidies in specific, should go directly to the part of JESSI devoted to research on integrated circuit development. Due to budgetary restrictions, and this national government-initiated restructuring of the JESSI programme, JESSI was obliged in late 1992 to redefine a number of its subprogrammes. In order to decide which projects should be continued and which should be axed, a number of guidelines were established. With respects to the Basic and Long-Term Research subprogramme for instance, these were: first, that research topics in the field of technology should be given priority; second, that research projects should be selected with a view to their potential value to the overall JESSI programme; and third, that results should be readily available throughout the course of JESSI. As a general rule-of-thumb, the JESSI Subprogramme Management Board decided that, for the technology and the basic and long term research subprogrammes:

the highest priority should be given to those themes most likely to result in urgently needed solutions[86].

To decide which themes should be selected, the technology development departments of eight leading chip companies were consulted, to ascertain their needs and demands for research.

Greater attention is now given by governments of the participating countries to the joint interface with JESSI. Such an interface has been provided for since the inception of JESSI, through the JESSI Committee, which is composed of senior officials from the member countries appropriate ministries. The JESSI organisation and the respective governments stress that the Committee does not influence the technical strategy of JESSI - which is controlled entirely by the corporate participants, through the medium of the JESSI Board. Rather, the JESSI Committee tackles issues of a procedural and operational nature, and helps to harmonise and synchronise JESSI activities and effects in the various member countries. The JESSI Committee is, in turn, supported by the Governmental Action Team (GAT), which is a working group of national experts[87]. The British member of the GAT[88] stresses the importance of JESSI meeting its world competitive goals. This is possible, he argues, as JESSI is shaped for success. That is, JESSI is structurally strong, and appears to function efficiently. On the issue of the British government's view of JESSI, the same GAT member states that:

> the UK is executing only a small part of the JESSI programme, but we fully subscribe to the importance of it[89].

Arguably the most important development in JESSI's overall restructuring, occurred vis-à-vis memory chips[90]. This particular change in direction had two, interrelated elements. Firstly, the JESSI Board chose to pull-out of all multi-megabit projects. This symbolised the beginning of a phased withdrawal from all volatile memory research, development, and production. However, because of volatile memory inclusion in many applications, some DRAM research has been maintained to date - exclusively for applications purposes though. The second element in JESSI's redesigned plan for memories, involves a switch in focus towards non-volatile memories. This is manifest in the various FLASH and EPROM projects currently underway. Associated with this revamped memory chip policy, JESSI's product development began to concentrate on application specific integrated circuits (ASICs). Thus, there are JESSI R&D projects in operation which illustrate the above redirection. JESSI-developed EPROM and Flash-EEPROMs are already on the market. The JESSI research into advanced CMOS technology focusses on DRAM and EPROM/Flash technology. The project Advanced Technology for Volume Manufacturing, which includes the development of advanced technology for next generation EPROM and Flash memories and the development of application oriented DRAMs, is the flagship of the JESSI cluster, Competitive CMOS Manufacturing. The participants within this cluster include GEC Plessey, ES2, TEMIC-Matra, IBM Europe, Mietec, Philips, SGS-Thomson, and Siemens. This indicates the leading corporate involvement within and support for the change in project focus.

Why are these changes of importance? It is contended here that JESSI's phased withdrawal from the volatile memory chip area is a positive move. There are two pragmatic reasons for this assertion. The first is based upon the fact that European based companies have consistently failed to establish a competitive position within bulk volatile memory markets. The second rests on the premise that volatile memory chip production is not a very profitable sector, and in fact, many of the firms competing in that market are actually making a loss on their sales. In addition, volatile memories are not very complicated, knowledge-intensive commodities, and have many supply sources. Thus, there is little or no market advantage to be had for a producer to provide them to certain users (e.g. the personal computer division of its own vertically integrated firm) before others. Also, the economic security variable is lacking in so far as there is no need to become dependent on a particular corporate or national supply base, simply because there are so many supply sources, and users can not only choose from a variety of producers, but they can also play them off against each other (in terms of cost for instance) to their own advantage. Therefore, if individual European chip producers wish to remain involved in volatile memory chip technology, they can do so through transnational inter-firm alliances, e.g. Siemens DRAM alliance with IBM and Toshiba.

The next chapter will investigate the role which collaborative R&D programmes (namely Sematech) have had in the rebuilding of the US semiconductor industry. Concentration was on improving equipment and process, rather than developing end products. American firms within this industrial sector have been rapidly increasing their market share, both domestically and internationally, since the early 1990s. Most of the U.S. semiconductor equipment and component manufacturers attribute a large part of this market success to Sematech[91]. Thus, here is an important part of the semiconductor industry which is often forgotten by policy-makers and by economic analysts, but which has potential for new market entrants to establish competitive positions fairly quickly. Most importantly though, as the Americans realised almost a decade ago, leading-edge, market competitive microchips derive from high quality materials, state-of-the-art design techniques, and fast and efficient production processes. The US collaborative gamble appears to have been correct. The reassertion of US strength in semiconductor components has been seen since the end of 1992, as American firms regained the top positions globally in most chip product markets. Lessons may be drawn for JESSI strategy and structure from the American experience. Moreover, design technology (customising the chips) is increasingly diverging from process technology (making the chips).This is a realm within which JESSI could help firms to meet the high costs and risks of R&D. There is concrete reason to believe that European firms could compete globally within the semiconductor design sector. For instance, a small start-up called Advanced RISC Machines (ARM) exists in the UK, which develops and sells RISC (reduced instruction set computing) design technology for making tiny, low energy chips which run faster than average microprocessors. ARM is carving out a lucrative market, and could be set for fast growth[92]. However, its market is likely to become very competitive in the near future, with large global firms such as Motorola poised to enter it. Hence, the firm may benefit from participation in a knowledge transfer co-operative framework and from assistance in undertaking further high cost R&D.

7 JESSI: critical conclusions

JESSI has been primarily important in three directions since its introduction in 1989: first, it has built upon the technology networks fostered by ESPRIT, and focused European R&D resources on closer-to-market orientations. Second, it enables, through public support, technology transfer amongst European firms; and helps these firms to conduct high-risk, high-cost R&D. Third, it illustrates how European chip makers and users, along with national governments and the European Commission, can combine to create partnerships amongst competitors. The important objective of improving co-operation between European industry and research institutes has certainly been achieved. However, in terms of market share, this success does not, as originally intended, seem to have translated into an significant advance in Europe's position in the submicron silicon sector. As already mentioned, the global market share of JESSI's chip producers declined further during 1992 and 1993, from 9.1 per cent to 8.1 per cent and has since remained relatively static and under 10 per cent (Dataquest, 1994).

JESSI was reworked in 1991-92 in large part because a common recognition emerged that a catching-up strategy was doomed to failure. Thus, there was a shift from concentration on bulk volatile memory chips, to more specific technologies, such as ASICs. The result of such a rationalisation of JESSI for the corporate participants could be the ability to produce leading-edge application-specific and other more complex chips, at a faster rate and higher volume, which should consequently transfer into increased market share.

One cannot argue that JESSI has failed. Apart from the problem discussed in Chapter two, relating to scientific evaluations of success or failure for R&D, there are other reasons, based on empirical evidence. Firstly, many of the corporate participants simply do not concur with such a conclusion. Secondly, the gap between initial objectives and results to date is not so easy to identify, as the initial objectives were often vague and general, and because some of them actually have been achieved. Therefore, failure is most visible only in terms of budgetary allocations and market share. Most of Europe's large native merchant chip producers experienced a decline in their world market share during between 1989 and 1994. Those that experienced some market success (in certain product areas at least) did so largely on the strength of focusing their R&D and marketing efforts on specific component areas where in-house technological strength already existed.

A further criticism of JESSI's relative success concerns first-to-market products. All of the arguments concerning technological advances made through JESSI are fine. However, how many of these technological developments were made by JESSI before global competitors, and how many were simply duplications of already existing technologies? This issue is worth considering when attempting any analysis of JESSI's relative success or failure.

In terms of scale and overall amount, no one comes even close to the Europeans with respects to funding for semiconductor R&D. In addition to the $1.2 billion of public money which is being poured into JESSI, further millions are being spent on related research both within the EC's ESPRIT programme, and within various national R&D projects. The Japanese government did in the late 1970s and early 1980s, but their involvement has declined steadily since then. The Korean government invested significant sums in semiconductors in the mid to late 1980s, but most of it was directed through public research laboratories. The US government has been involved in partially funding equipment and materials R&D (Sematech), but not actual chip development *per se*. The evidence suggests that the EC pursues what was defined in the last chapter as a maximalist policy approach[93] to the semiconductor industry. This maximalist approach was adopted in both Japan, during the late 1970s, and Korea, during the second half of the 1980s.

However, it was pursued for a relatively short time, and only whilst domestic firms were attempting to internationalise their sales. Such an active, widely interventionist policy has not existed in the US since the early 1960s. European public policy for semiconductor R&D is both too extensive and too late in the industry's life-span to be effectively implemented. The European semiconductor industry is gone beyond the nascent period - the EC is not trying to help establish market presence or build up an industry from nothing - and the amount and extent of funding involved at this stage in the industry's development could adversely affect competitiveness. This is achieved through diverting firms attentions to a perceived technology gap and away from more close-to-market contemporary competitive hindrances. When coming late into a market, as with the Japanese or Koreans, one needs to rapidly establish a complex and costly technology base and production capability. In order to do this, and coming from a very low or non-existent knowledge and capability base, it is necessary for government and firms to work closely. However, when the thresh-hold is reached, that is when the industry reaches a level of technological capability and production capacity comparable to international competitive firms based in other countries, their is considerably less market rationale to support continued active government intervention.

JESSI will not, nor could not, save the European semiconductor industry. As a senior Philips executive has commented:

A co-operative R&D programme like JESSI, in itself, cannot save the microelectronics industry. R&D is important, but it is no more than an enabling factor, a necessary prerequisite. The real question is whether the European microelectronics industry can exploit the new dimensions offered by JESSI on the European market[94].

The scope of JESSI is far more sweeping than Sematech or any Japanese joint R&D project. JESSI has attempted to revitalise the entire value-added chain for semiconductors, rather than particular sectors. Although partly addressed in the 1992 restructuring, this dilution of effort and resources continued subsequently, and remained its main weakness. The fate of JESSI in the post-1996 period, is tenuous. Channels of communication have been opened and co-operation has been fostered between firms and between firms and research institutes. It is likely that this co-operative network would continue without the JESSI framework. Thus, it is doubtful that the expenditure involved can be justified in the future without important technical developments which transform into a significant increase in market share amongst JESSI's main European corporate partners.

8 Eureka/JESSI as frameworks for inter-firm collaboration

Eureka is a pan-European network which promotes market driven R&D projects in all fields of advanced technology[95]. Eureka may be perceived as a third and unique

R&D framework involving both the public and private sector within Europe. It is complementary to both national R&D programmes and to the EC Framework Programmes. This is defined by two basic organisational principles: firstly, Eureka is very market oriented, focusing on downstream, product oriented, near-market research, within a collaborative framework involving participants from different member countries; and secondly, Eureka's bottom-up principle, through which private sector participants have total responsibility for defining and implementing their particular project. This principle ensures that Eureka projects are motivated by sound commercial and technological interests, and are run by those most affected by R&D results i.e. private enterprises.

In terms of the nationality of participating firms, the borders of the Eureka system are more fluid than either the EC Framework Programmes or collaborative programmes elsewhere, such as Sematech. Eureka is however aimed at European co-operation. Also, Eureka has a much looser structure than the EC Framework Programmes. Funding is not guaranteed. Eureka may effectively be seen as a counter-balance to centralised Brussels funding of projects which Commission officials select.

The main differences between the EC Framework Programmes and Eureka are as follows: European Commission Framework Programmes must look at the overall benefit of particular projects to the Community and its member states and industries. This is not necessary within the Eureka system, where benefit to individual or groups of firms is most important. An example is silicon materials production. If, for instance, the German silicon company, Wacar, proposed a specific R&D project, and there was no natural collaborator for it, the EC Framework Programme cannot fund the project (as the benefit would be only to a specific company in a specific country). Eureka would consider funding such a project [96].

Eureka consists of nine broad areas of R&D[97]. Of these, JESSI falls under the technological subprogramme, 'information technology', which also comprises system development and software. However, despite the position of information technology as only one of nine areas of concentration, in overall financial and resource terms, it accounts for nearly 50 per cent of the total Eureka budget[98]. Furthermore, in spite of its sub-section of a sub-programme status, JESSI is Eureka's biggest project, accounting for almost 30 per cent of the total Eureka budget[99].

It is interesting to note that JESSI has not been the only Eureka project developing faster chips. In EU 16, ES2 (European Silicon Structures), several major European semiconductor firms have developed specialised software to design and test ASICs, which are then produced using electron beams to make the submicron-scale patterns on the silicon wafer. The fast and flexible process can deliver customised chips within a few weeks. Thus, the emphasis is on design techniques for ASICs but the stated wider objective is to enhance semiconductor design expertise in Europe. The total cost of ES2 is ECU 84.3 million. ES2 has penetrated the U.S. market, securing contracts from such American champions as Boeing and McDonnell Douglas. In 1992, it was recognised by the market research organisation Dataquest as the outstanding European niche vendor of the year. ES2 now participates in a number of JESSI projects, and is generally regarded as a JESSI partner. Furthermore, despite its above successes, its market presence is still minimal, and not increasing. In 1993, ES2 controlled 0.2 per cent of the European semiconductor market, and under 0.1 per cent of the world market. This signified a decline in European market share from the 1992 figures of 0.21 per cent, and no change in its global market share[100].

Another project, EU 102, EPROM, has produced the fastest 4Mb EPROM chip on the market, as well as prototypes of 16Mbit EPROMs. The partners aim to develop 256 Mb chips by the end of the decade[101]. Among the immense variety of memory chips, EPROMs are unique and cost effective. They are non-volatile, meaning that they can store programmes and data without a constant voltage supply. They are used in personal computers, mobile phones, laser printers, and robotics. EU 102 was a consequence of the 1987 merger between two of Europe's leading EPROM producers - SGS Microelectronics and Thomson Semiconductors. The offspring, SGS-Thomson Microelectronics, has conducted much of its R&D - with the participation of the CEA-Leti laboratory in Grenoble and some Italian universities - under the auspices of JESSI.

Further projects concerning chip design, process technology, and manufacturing equipment, exist within Eureka, but not under the JESSI mantle (although usually closely allied). The most significant are, first, the Joint Analogue Micro-system Initiative of Europe (JAMIE), aimed at new CAD design techniques for ASICs; second, the development of an all dry single layer photolithography technology for sub-micron devices (DESIRE), which develops new optical lithography techniques for transferring circuit patterns onto silicon; and third, ION-PROJECTION, a project working on ion beam lithography machines for manufacturing integrated circuits[102].

8.i. An assessment of Eureka

The Eureka assessment panel was established in 1990 by the Eureka Ministerial Conference, in order to evaluate the first five years of Eureka, and suggest any procedural or structural changes needed to improve the programme. The panel was composed of senior figures from a number of European research centres and from European business [103]. The central fact which can be taken from the ensuing report is that the panel concluded with a fundamentally positive view of Eureka. As a concept and as an instrument for technological co-operation, Eureka was perceived as an important framework for European business, government, and research institutes. Also, the panel had a favourable view of the technological and commercial results of Eureka's first five years. At a structural level, three strengths were identified in the programme. First, the bottom-up nature of Eureka, which has facilitated a great variety of projects being advanced and accepted (in fact there is no limitation of the technological areas covered by Eureka). Second, the flexible and decentralised structure of the programme has prevented the project selection and implementation process from becoming overly bureaucratic. Third, its market orientation has begun to accelerate the pace at which certain new technologies are transferred from the laboratory to the market [104].

The main weaknesses of the programme were identified as, firstly, a lack of transparency and secondly, insufficient synchronisation of procedures. Interestingly, the latter of these is evidently a consequence of Eureka's decentralised structure, which the panel previously outlined as a major strength. Overall though, these defaults were seen as not posing a serious problem to the smooth operation of Eureka, and an acceptable price to pay for the vitality of Eureka[105].

A further recommendation of the panel related to the participation of small and medium sized enterprises (SMEs) within the Eureka framework. Although the number of such firms participating in Eureka projects was increasing, greater involvement was encouraged. On the issue of competitiveness, the panel concluded that:

Eureka has contributed to the strengthening of the competitive position of individual European firms by stimulating co-operation in research and development, by accelerating the introduction of new technologies, and by creating business opportunities. The panel is confident that ultimately this will have a positive effect on the competitive position of Europe[106].

The main fault of the 1991 assessment is its support for strategic targeting. It is argued that strategic projects which would give Europe an additional competitive advantage, have not materialised on a large scale. From this premise, a recommendation is advanced that European governments should encourage industry to integrate a number of strategic projects into their overall R&D strategy. In addition, governments should be prepared to create any supportive measures necessary for the introduction of such projects. Finally, the best structure through which these twin measures can be implemented in a complementary and co-ordinated manner, is the Eureka programme.

What the panel understands by strategic is not evident, thus we shall employ the concept as it was defined in chapter two of this volume. Therefore, to dissect the hypothesis, we argue the contrary: firstly, many strategic projects may be identified within Eureka - most notably JESSI, but also ES2, EPROM, HDTV, AIMS. Given that these projects (especially JESSI and HDTV) together constitute almost half of the total Eureka budget, it is logical to argue that strategic projects are in fact a very important and large scale part of Eureka.

Secondly, the idea of governments encouraging firms to conduct co-operative R&D in areas identified by policy-makers as having strategic importance for the wider society and economy, simply does not fit with the otherwise market-led nature of Eureka. In fact, the advocation of such a top-down approach for certain sectors, directly contradicts that which the assessment panel initially identified as a core strength of Eureka: that is, its bottom-up character. To incorporate such selective interventionism would not only remove that core element which differentiates Eureka from both the EC Framework Programmes and national R&D

collaboration programmes, but also seriously impede the competitive enhancement ideals of Eureka.

A follow-on to the so-called Dekker Report (1991 assessment) was published in 1993. It concentrated on the extent to which Eureka achieved its initial objectives, rather than on evaluating Eureka as an initiative. Thus, its findings and conclusions are of some interest to this research, in terms of analysing Eureka as a framework for collaboration. However, the report is not relevant vis-à-vis microchip collaboration, or more specifically, JESSI, as the large strategic Eureka projects (JESSI being the most prominent) are excluded from this evaluation. This evaluation was conducted in 1992-93, by an international expert group, which comprised teams of national experts from fourteen Eureka member states[107].The evaluation constituency comprised 70 projects, 1170 industrial and 487 non-industrial participants, large and small firms, and nine different technological areas[108]. Many Eureka participants were found to be involved in other forms of R&D collaboration, particularly those projects funded by the EC and by national governments. Collaboration within Eureka was found be largely based on prior business links, rather than on organisational assistance measures to find partners for firms. Corporate reasons for collaboration included (1) access to complementary expertise (central motive); (2) sharing of costs and risks; (3) acceleration of the time to market. Large firms participated more often horizontally, with direct competitors- especially in more up-stream projects. SMEs tend to pursue more vertical collaboration, and at a closer-to-market stage. A high level of interdependence was charted amongst collaborators. Over 70 per cent of respondents believed that partners were crucial both for achieving results and for their subsequent exploitation.

The 1993 evaluation found that there was a high level of agreement concerning gains in knowledge base of firm, accrued through involvement in Eureka projects. 76 per cent of firms reported moderate to large increases in their knowledge bases. 42 per cent expected increased sales, and 38 per cent expected a similar increase in market share. However, only 15 per cent had actually achieved sales increases whilst participating in Eureka projects.

Further studies of the Eureka initiative[109] reveal a generally positive attitude towards the programme, particularly with regards to its success in bringing an increasing number of SMEs in to collaborative ventures, contributing to changes in the competitive environment within which European high tech firms operate, and facilitating both inter-industry and inter-state technology transfer. On the down-side, attention is drawn to Eureka's frequent administrative inefficiency (it is hampered by insufficient means to achieve its ends), often conflicting objectives on the part of its public sector participants (which can lead to costly delays in project funding decisions), and a persistent lack of transparency.

It is rational to argue that collaborative strategy has derived from a combination of all the motives outlined at the chapter's outset. Which factors are the most important, depends on the firm in question and the industry within which particular firms are grouped. This work regards Mytelka's (1991) set of reasons as the most relevant to choices made by European semiconductor producers. However, other motives such as risk sharing, the development of product systems, and the need to gain access to knowledge and technologies which are complementary to the successful development of a firm's own product, are also important - although secondary - variables in their selection of a collaborative strategy.

What are the primary perceived benefits to the firm in collaborating? In the view of Mytelka :

> Gains from partnering thus derive more from learning and the future positional advantages that innovation in products, processes or internal routines brings, than from static allocative efficiency (1991, p.9).

Mytelka stresses that the production and sharing of knowledge is the core element within a strategic alliance, and not actual product manufacturing or sales. She further emphasises that transformations in the nature of production now indicates that knowledge does not mean simply techniques and technologies generated within the realm of R&D, but is instead a concept which must be applied at all stages in the product life cycle. Given that knowledge is the primary factor of production for high technology industries (Drucker, 1986, p.34), when applied to the long-term competitive well-being of a firm, this argument is sustainable. Thus, Mytelka's argument is that firms participate in strategic alliances primarily for the knowledge network which it entails. This is certainly a core element in firms decisions to participate in European co-operative programmes such as JESSI. Michalet (1991) sustains this argument. He stresses the central role of technology within global competition, and links this factor to the proliferation of strategic alliances. Michalet points out the fact that knowledge intensive high technology industries (such as electronics) are thus, of course, particularly prone to selecting such alliance options (1991, p.46).

A further central variable in this decision is the R&D subsidies which such programmes entail. Given the level of public funds available through programmes such as JESSI ($1.2 billion in total), it is logical that firms should choose to participate. Escalating R&D costs pressure firms to seek extra finance outside of their corporate structure. This is particularly pressing for SMEs, but large enterprises are also tempted by the lure of public money. The fifty percent of project operating costs offered by national governments and the European Commission through JESSI, allows firms to maintain or often increase their R&D activities. Therefore, the widespread approval of JESSI amongst its private corporate and institutional members, may be partly attributable to a rational desire not to kill the goose that lays the golden egg. It does not make sense to publicly condemn that system which is providing one with capital and a co-operative framework through which one may pursue expensive R&D projects, which may (or may not) translate into improved corporate revenue and market share.

9.i. Corporate technology policy: the concept applied

Is Dodgson's thesis concerning technology strategy, valid for our sector of interest? The empirical evidence advanced in this chapter indicates that it is a practically applicable concept. It is evident that all of Europe's home grown semiconductor producers have realised the importance of technology to their overall corporate competitiveness. Consequently they have developed technology strategies within, or at the core of, their wider corporate strategies. Both the bilateral and multilateral groups of strategy options previously discussed, are heavily weighted towards co-operative arrangements in the sphere of technology development and/or exchange. Hence, the theory fits the practice because technology is indeed at the heart of European semiconductor companies competitive strategies.

Returning to a second element of the industry optic defined in chapter two, does strategic alliance theory provide a useful heuristic tool in analysing firm behaviour vis-à-vis European collaborative programmes? Again, the evidence provided in this chapter would indicate that activities pursued by Europe's semiconductor producers to strengthen their long-term competitive advantage, do fit with the strategic alliance model. However, as argued earlier, these firms involvement in Eureka, and more specifically, JESSI, is indicative of a very specific type of strategic alliance. This is what Buckley (1993) defines as an international collaborative programme. More specifically though, this alliance model is described in our work as a bottom-up European collaborative programme. Therefore, in examining firm strategy through this very particular form of strategic alliance model, it is possible to discern the reasons why European chip makers choose certain options in specific circumstances, and thus, why they choose to collaborate with both direct competitors and with governmental actors. Using this alliance model as a perspective through which firm strategy may be viewed, let us proceed to examine the corporate rationale for collaboration. The most pertinent questions at this point are: as a structure for corporate competitive enhancement, why was the Eureka/JESSI framework chosen by its corporate participants? What are the perceived benefits of the collaborative model above other strategy models? What are the problems which collaboration can bring? Is JESSI a framework with which to proceed?

Working together through the ERT, many of Europe's large IT firms began to reach a consensus on the idea that collaborative R&D served their collective interests (Peterson, 1993, p.8). The central reasons that European high technology firms moved towards collaboration during the 1980s, have been described by Peterson as:

178

firms thus seek joint ventures, collaborative agreements, or sub-contracting arrangements with other firms which possess complementary assets in terms of knowledge...R&D is particularly ripe for collaboration because it can reduce risks and costs and promote 'multi-technological' innovation. There is thus an economic logic to collaborative R&D for firms in industries where there is a high knowledge input (1993, p.7).

Returning to our earlier concept of bilateral versus multilateral alliances, at an intra-European level, why did the indigenous chip producers choose multilateral collaboration over bilateral alliances? The answer to this question is that they actually tried both, consecutively. The Big Four European chip producers created two separate bilateral alliances in the mid-1980s. Siemens and Philips launched the Megaproject in 1984, with the intention of jointly developing 1 megabit and 4 megabit RAMs. Philips was to work on developing a 1 MB SRAM, to be marketable by 1987, whilst Siemens was to develop 4 MB DRAMs, for sale by 1989. However, Siemens maintained a chip development alliance with Toshiba at the same time, to develop 1 MB DRAMs. Halfway through the Megaproject, Siemens decided to simply buy the 1 MB technology from Toshiba, and subsequently began production of the chip. Involvement in the Megaproject promptly took a back seat, and the alliance with Philips began to decline. During this period also, Thomson Microelectronics and SGS-Ates began to move towards an alliance for chip development. This corporate flirtation ended in wedlock, as the two producers merged their activities in 1987. Thus, partly in response to this fragmentation of research efforts, all four firms were brought together in the combined JESSI effort.

A second question at this stage must consequently be, are the two strategies mutually exclusive? If so, should European semiconductor producers select one above the other? Rather than being mutually exclusive, bilateral and multilateral collaboration options are actually complementary. This is because most European multilateral co-operative networks are in R&D, whilst most of the bilateral alliances are close to the market or aimed at direct commercialisation. In addition, the former generally has a longer time frame within which to operate, as well as a broader set of objectives; whereas, the latter usually has a set time frame and a very specific objective or objectives. Working within this assumption, it is perfectly natural, and strategically acceptable, for European chip producers to pursue both forms of co-operation in tandem.

There are several reasons as to why intra-European co-operation cannot be exclusive of transnational inter-firm alliances. Fundamentally, this would weaken the competitiveness of European firms in the long-term because it would lead to (1) a further monopolisation of the European market; (2) a protectionist attitude towards non-European competitors; and (3) a lack of expansion into markets outside of Europe. Moreover, transnational inter-firm alliances cannot be exclusive of intra-European co-operation. This would also mean that long-term competitiveness would be weakened, because it could imply, first, a one-sided penetration of the European market; second, a permanent status of the European firm as junior partner; and third, the eventual possibility of the decline of European potential in R&D - which could of course have spill-over effects on other information technology sectors (Van Tulder and Junne, 1988, p.252).

An interesting observation made by Dunning (1993) is that vis-à-vis some forms of collaborative programmes, criticism can be levied at the political management and organisation rather than at the actual concept (or application) of R&D collaboration. Using this distinction, one could distinguish serious faults at a management and organisation level within both of the European collaborative R&D frameworks. The only real level for evaluating them becomes essentially that of technical product and process output deriving from the actual R&D. This is too narrow a system of evaluation though, as it provides little insight into the structure and management of collaborative programmes. It is posed here as an option, primarily to indicate the emphasis which this study places on viable technological and commercial results as an evaluative tool.

10 Conclusions

During the initial phase of JESSI (1990-91), the Community contributed Ecu 102 million to its operating costs, i.e. 18 per cent of the total budget. In total, between 1990 and 1994, the Commission contributed Ecu 302 million to JESSI[110]. Since its inception, the Community has funded four of JESSI's projects[111]. Officially, the projects chosen were those which were perceived to have the greatest potential benefit to the Community as a whole. Following on from this, within the working document of the Fourth Framework Programme, the Commission once more accorded special priority status to microelectronics. According to the intellectual property rights clauses of the JESSI Framework agreement, a reciprocal agreement exists between JESSI and ESPRIT regarding the exchange and exploitation of results[112]. This allows for a wider dissemination of project results than might otherwise occur.

The Commission (or at least DGXIII) is fully supportive of JESSI, and sees it as a structural example for some future collaborative initiatives. A rationale for this public affirmation of the Commission's support for JESSI may be political. As a senior Commission official has stated:

> The Commission believes that if it were to contemplate a reduction of its presence in JESSI, this could lead to a split of the cohesive forces which have been developed, and send the wrong message to the international community[113].

Therefore, one may speculate on the extent to which Commission policy vis-à-vis JESSI exists as part of the effort to enhance corporate competitiveness; and how much it exists as a symbol of increasing European integration. Also, in the widely publicised Delors White Paper on Employment[114], an emphasis is placed upon European collaborative R&D as a means of tackling the Community's growth and employment problems. It is stressed though that such collaborative initiatives should have clearly defined economic goals and effectively implement and diffuse the technological results of the research.

As we emphasised from the outset, the counterfactual involved in an analysis such as this, means that one cannot conclusively argue that JESSI has adversely affected the competitive position of its industrial partners. Given the many other variables, both internal and external to the private sector members of JESSI, the programme cannot be held responsible for an overall corporate competitive decline. However, it is possible to measure the relative loss or gain accrued through JESSI, in terms such as technological achievements, participant satisfaction levels, and market share. In terms of technological achievements, a number of artefacts have been developed but have yet to translate into increased industry market share[115]. Reasons for this include the slow development time within JESSI projects, and the inability of European microchip firms to rapidly apply new technologies and products to the market. Time is of the essence for the micorchip industry, and time is where European firms are weakest.

A further means of evaluating JESSI's relative utility is in terms of the extent to which it has achieved its initial stated objectives. Here, there are mixed opinions, particularly amongst corporate and governmental actors. To select one opinion above the others necessitates deciding whether success in this respects means achieving all the original aims, or merely some of them. The simple answer, as propounded by a European Commission official[116], is that JESSI has not been a success, at least in terms of achieving its initial objectives. This is particularly true for the ultimate objective of JESSI, which was defined by the vice chairman of the JESSI Board in 1992, as being to improve Europe's market position in microchips[117]. However, one should be careful not to over-emphasise objectives when evaluating such programmes as JESSI. In addition to restructuring due to dissatisfaction with achievements, they may be revised in the light of changing circumstances (including changes in technical or market conditions). Such changes should be noted in any evaluation.

Returning to previously discussed models for evaluating the contribution of collaborative programmes to competitive enhancement, the following findings emerge. At a fundamental level, the Georghiou and Metcalfe (1993) framework proposed that a programme such as JESSI should be evaluated in terms of knowledge, skills, and artefacts resulting from it. At this level, there has been a mixture of success and failure. As the opinions of private sector JESSI members have illustrated, it has certainly created a valid cooperative network, and has facilitated technology and skills exchange. JESSI has enabled many SMEs to participate in research and technology transfer activities which it would not otherwise have had access to. It has focused European public R&D resources on closer-to-market orientations. On the down side, few of the artefacts which have emerged from JESSI projects to date, have succeeded in capturing significant market share. Reasons for this failure are numerous, but stem largely from development time delays within JESSI, as well as the inability of the European microchip industry to rapidly apply new innovations to the market - rather than from any fundamental weakness in JESSI's technology base.

Applying our findings to the other elements of this evaluatory model, the following can be concluded: (1) Project failure (in technological and market terms) has led to a narrowing of project variety within the programme. This would indicate a realisation amongst the JESSI Board, that competitiveness is not being improved. (2) Acknowledging that competitiveness is a relative concept, one can place JESSI's achievements as claimed by its corporate participants, in a comparative context vis-à-vis the relative position of its market rivals. Here, the key characteristic for distinguishing competitive enhancement, is the rate of change of market share. When placed in a global comparative context, an overall decline in market share is evident on the part of the JESSI partners since the programme's inception, whilst their main global rivals have generally remained static or increased their shares. (3) There is no evidence that JESSI has increased the autonomy of chip producers from their umbrella enterprises. Consequently, the strategy choices and use of R&D results for these chip producers remains restricted by their obligations to supply other areas of the wider corporation. Such a relationship can adversely affect competitiveness.

A final tool in analysing JESSI's relative contribution to competitiveness is budgetary. We have touched on the fact that between 1989 and 1994, JESSI's budget was consistently reduced, relative to original cost estimates. The $3.5 billion total outlay envisaged in JESSI's planning phase did not come to fruition, being pared back to $2.4 billion after three years of activities. Governmental members have been increasingly reluctant to pay for a programme from which they perceive little direct, tangible benefit. Moreover, one should consider the fact that there has been no funding approved for JESSI in the post-1996 period. Thus, unlike Sematech for instance, there appears to be no intention to extend JESSI once its initial running time has ended. One may speculate on a two-dimensional cause for this apparent waning in governmental support for JESSI. Firstly, perhaps it symbolises a realisation that JESSI is only partially achieving its aims, and/or is costing far too much to achieve what it has achieved. Secondly, due to wider EC budget constraints, one may argue that in this area of European semiconductor policy, the state-state dimension has come to dominate the Pentagon (witness the role of national governments in the 1991-92 Eureka restructuring). Therefore, the firm-Commission dimension has been weakened, as states increase their bargaining position within Pentagonal Diplomacy[118], leading to a reduced commitment to European public-private collaborative initiatives such as JESSI.

One may conclude by arguing that it is not possible to say that JESSI has failed, but its relative contribution has not been significant. This is particularly true when one considers the sheer scale of finance, manpower, and organisational effort which has been put into the initiative. It is doubtful that the expenditure involved can be justified in the future without important technical developments which transform into a significant increase in market share amongst JESSI's main European corporate partners.

Notes

1   Evidence for this assertion is provided by Gary Hamel, Yves Doz, and C.K. Prahalad, in research conducted between 1984 and 1989, on strategic alliances around the world. For references see Prahalad and Doz, *The Multinational Mission,* 1987, and Hamel, Doz, and Prahalad, 'Collaborate With Your Competitors - and Win', *Harvard Business Review,* January-February, 1989.

2   Ibid.

3   Support for this hypothesis is provided in *Evaluation of Eureka Industrial and Economic Effects,* 1993. A survey of industrial respondents within Eureka showed that the single largest group gave their main reasons for pursuing collaborative options as being to reinforce existing core technologies. An example given was of large firms seeking process or material improvements, that are often being developed by an SME supplier. The second most frequent group here was found to comprise firms (sometimes SMEs) seeking to diversify within existing business lines and acquire a new core technology.

4   Lynn Krieger Mytelka, 'Dancing With Wolves: Global Oligopolies and Strategic Partnerships' in J. Hagerdoon, *Internationalisation of Corporate Technology Strategies,* 1993.

5   These include rising real interest rates, declining national savings rates, and slow rates of growth - which were especially prevalent in the larger western European economies.

6   These four forms of corporate strategy were identified by Porter in *Competitive Strategy,* 1980.

7   When 'the firms' are referred to, we mean Europe's large indigenous semiconductor producers - namely Philips, Siemens, and SGS-Thomson, but also GEC-Plessey, Mietec Alcatel, and Matra MHS.

8   Traditional unilateral strategies continued during the 1980s and early 1990s. For example, the previously discussed merger between two European chip producers - Thomson Microelectronics and SGS Microelectronics - in 1987, and Siemens take-over of Nixdorf during the same period.

9   Buckley, 1993, cited by John H. Dunning, *The Globalization of Business,* 1993.

10   Official Eureka publication, *What Is JESSI?*

11   Ibid., p.4.

12   Results of the Planning Phase of the JESSI Programme, Itzehoe, 1 February, 1989, p.1.

13   Ibid., pp.36-7.

14   Dr Rainer Gerold, Director, DGXII, Commission of the European Communities.

15   Comments obtained from a paper delivered by Dr. Gerold on the issue of 'Is EC Level R&D For Europeans Only?, at *Horizons of Research* Conference, organised by Forum Europe and DGs XII and XIII, Scandic Crown Hotel, Brussels, 2 April,1992.

Dr. Gerold is director, DGXII, responsible for Science and Research and Development.

16 In including ICL in this list of companies which fulfil the requirements needed to be considered European, he is of course referring to ICL post-Fujitsu investment. After all, ICL's UK/European roots stretch back into the 19th Century.

17 Interview conducted with Mr Tsalas, Microelectronics Division, DGXIII of the European Commission, Brussels, 6 April, 1992.

18 In an interview conducted with a senior ICL executive (London, December 1993), it emerged that the firm perceived a thinly veiled 'Japanophobia' amongst many of its peers within the European electronics sector in the late 1980s and early 1990s. ICL's expulsion from the European Information Technology Round Table and from three out of five of the JESSI projects with which it was involved, is attributed by the firm to an anti-Asian sentiment which existed amongst other IT producers based in Europe. This is of course due to the fact that the exclusions occurred shortly after Fujitsu took an eighty percent controlling stake in ICL in 1990. Also, ICL attributes its removal from the JESSI projects to the other corporate participants, and not to the national governments or the European Commission. The firm acknowledges that this attitude has dissipated somewhat as more and more European companies have entered into partnerships with Japanese and other Far Eastern companies.

19 Official organisation document, *Why JESSI?*, Munich, 1993.

20 These ideas are explored in greater detail in chapter one.

21 *Why JESSI?*, op.cit.

22 This argument can be found in its entirety in *Why JESSI?*, op.cit., p.4.

23 Ibid., p.5.

24 The word 'overt' is emphasised here because it may be argued that US Department of Defence contracts indirectly provide funding for such research.

25 For figures relating to government expenditure on semiconductor R&D in the United States and Japan, see chapter six.

26 *Eureka News,* (Quarterly official publication) No.11, January 1991, 'Jessi Dossier'.

27 Figures for 1994 show that the world semiconductor market did in fact increase at a tremendous rate, although not quite as much as that predicted by the Eureka secretariat. As of the last quarter of 1994, the total global market was valued at $109.7 billion (almost 90 billion ECU) *Financial Times,* 10 January, 1995. This means that the industry grew by of one and a half times, rather than doubling, over the five year period specified by the Eureka organisation.

28 World semiconductor sales figures cited in *The Economist,* 'that astonishing microchip', 23 March 1996.

29   This is the official JESSI organisation mission, as detailed in *What is JESSI?*, 1993, p.6.

30   The product technology objective was to produce high resolution television sets.

31   In 1994, this alliance became the Eureka Consortia in Advanced Digital Television Technologies.

32   During the race to produce high definition TV, the industry's technological standard switched from one based on analog to one based on digital. This had the effect of rendering obsolete much of the research conducted by the Japanese and European consortia, and permitting the other two alliances to enter the game.

33   Mr. Kamerbeek of the Dutch firm ASM, quoted in *Eureka News*, op.cit.

34   Mr. Lazarri, LETI Research Centre, and former chairman of basic and long-term research subprogramme.

35   *Eureka News*, No. 11, January 1991.

36   This quotation is taken from a letter sent by Dr Villa to this author, on 11 March, 1994.

37   This argument was advanced by Pasquale Pistorio, President and CEO, SGS-Thomson Microelectronics, at COMPONIC 93, Paris, November 17, 1993.

38   Ernst and O'Connor (1992), cited in Mytelka (1994), *Dancing With Wolves*, p.3.

39   As Levy and Samuels (1991) argue, these new institutional arrangements for increased technology linkages between European electronics firms had the added attractions of sharing the costs of R&D, production, and marketing. These factors were seen as further contributing to these firms' ability to compete.

40   *Dataquest* figures show that SGS-Thomson achieved the number one ranking in world EPROM production in 1993, with a market share of over 20 per cent and a full range of products, topped by 4 and 16 Mbits.

41   Figures extracted from *Dataquest* statistics.

42   Ibid., p.3.

43   Dataquest 1992 figures.

44   These figures are obtained through the author's analysis of data received from *Dataquest Europe Ltd.* The statistics were compiled in March 1994.

45   Please refer to the next footnote for an explanation of this apparently contradictory statement.

46   This figure is misleading as it represents total European share of the European semiconductor market, and not just the JESSI partners. Thus, it accounts for the sales of roughly forty European-based semiconductor manufacturers. On the evidence of 1990-93 market shares, we estimate that the non-JESSI chip makers account for less than 2 per cent of total European output (*Dataquest*, 1994). This implies that the market share for the JESSI partners has remained at about 24 per cent.

47   SGS-Thomson internal company report, op.cit.

48 Dataquest Alert (1995), *Semiconductors Worldwide,* report issued by the Dataquest Corporation, UK.

49 Ibid.

50 *Financial Times,* 'Europe's chip sales to Japan up', 8 November 1996.

51 Pasquale Pistorio, speaking at COMPONIC 93, Paris, November 17, 1993, p.7.

52 Interview conducted with senior ICL executive, London, 17 December, 1993.

53 Interview conducted at ICL, London, December 1993.

54 The European Information Technology Round Table is an industrial association, which draws its membership from European information technology firms. ICL, a founding member, was forced to withdraw from the association soon after Fujitsu acquired a majority share in its ownership.

55 *The Case For Collaborative R&D,* Memorandum by ICL Plc, December 1993.

56 IMEC (Inter-university Micro Electronics Centre), based in Leuven, was founded in 1984 by the Flanders government, as a centre for performing scientific research to anticipate the needs of industry by five to ten years. It is an independent organisation, headed by a board of directors, and employs 480 people.

57 According to Prof. R. van Overstraeten, president of the IMEC, in *Jessi News,* Vol.2, No.1, October 1992.

58 IMEC (1990), *EC R&D Policy: Evaluation and New Priorities,* work-session presentation.

59 ASM Lithography was founded in 1984, has annual revenues of over $100 million, and a world-wide staff of more than six hundred.

60 W. Maris, quoted in *JESSI News.* Vol. 2, No.1, October 1992.

61 Information dated November 1993, lists the ERT's current Chairman as Jerome Monod, Lyonnaise des Eaux-Dumez, and the Vice-Chairmen as Andre Leysen of Gevaert and Floris Maljers of Unilever. Other members include Umberto Agnelli of Fiat, Etienne Davignon, Société Generale de Belgique, Carlo de Benedetti, Olivetti, Pehr Gyllenhammar, ex-Volvo, Heinrich von Pierer of Siemens, and Jan Timmer of Philips.

62 Cited in European Round Table information pamphlet, Brussels, 1993.

63 See Chapter four for a more detailed discussion of this politicised relationship which exists between the European Commission and a group of large European electronics firms.

64 The ERT has six Policy Groups, which are: Education, Competition Policy, Industrial Policy, Infrastructure (within the EC), Infrastructure (between Eastern and Western Europe), and Research. It also, has four International Groups: Central and Eastern Europe, Japan, North/South, and Trade & GATT. Furthermore, the ERT has five Expert Groups, consisting of Environment, Export Controls, Young Managers Development Programme, EC-US Relations, and Industrial Relations and Social Policy.

65 *Beating the Crisis: A Charter for Europe's Industrial Future,* a report from the European Round Table of Industrialists, Brussels, December 1993.

66   In the words of the ERT's *Charter for Europe's Industrial Future,* the proposed European Competitiveness Council would be comprised of representatives from industry (both employers and employees), from government and from science. It would be established by, and under the direct jurisdiction of, the EC Council of Ministers. Its mandate would be to firstly, advise the European Council and the Community institutions on the development and implementation of policies for competitiveness within the framework of the Charter for Industry; secondly, to identify priorities, monitor progress, and report back to the European Council at regular intervals; thirdly, to encourage continuity in the development of policies and consistency between the actions of member states and the Community as a whole; and fourthly, to stimulate a well-informed public debate.

67   ERT, *Beating The Crisis,* Brussels, 1993, p.18.

68   Ibid.

69   The concept of protective partnership, developed extensively in Chapter four, is used to describe government-industry partnership, with government protecting industry when and where the industry requests.

70   The European Round Table of Industrialists, *Rebuilding Confidence: An Action Plan For Europe,* Brussels, December 1991.

71   The European Round Table of Industrialists, *Reshaping Europe,* Brussels, September 1991, p.39.

72   The European Round Table of Industrialists, *Bright Horizons,* Brussels, May 1990, p.13.

73   *Eureka Information Technology, 1993,* official report of the Eureka organisation, Brussels.

74   The EECA is the association that represents electronic component manufacturers in the countries of the EC, and, if they wish it, those countries committed to joining the EC. Its members are the electronic component manufacturers associations in the various member states. EECA operates through four main bodies: the General Assembly and Council (the executive and policy making bodies of the association), the President's Committee, Specialist and Product Committees and Working Groups, and the Secretariat (which is responsible for overall co-ordination, for processing decisions of the General Assembly and the Council, and for liason with the European Commission, the European Parliament, and with other international organisations and associations inside and outside Europe.

75   This statement was made by Mr. E. Runge, Secretary General of the EECA, in a personal meeting, Brussels, 4 February, 1994.

76   European Electronic Components Industry Report, 1992, EECA, Brussels.

77   EPROMs (Erasable Programmable Memories) are memory chips where information is stored in the form of an electric charge on an isolated gate. The charge can be removed to erase the memory, by exposing the chip to ultraviolet light. As part of the family of non-volatile memories, EPROMs are

currently the most popular type of memories for programmable storage, and have numerous applications.

78   Official documentation from the JESSI Secretariat concerning project results to date (October, 1993).

79   Projects within this cluster include 200mm Wafer Diameter Manufacturing, Special Tools and Methods for Assessment of High Reliability, and Support Tools and Systems for Advanced IC-Production.

80   FLASH memory (electrically erasable programmable memory) the information has the same high density as in EPROMs, but is erased by applying a high electric field across the gate oxide, a method which makes erasing and rewriting of the memory in the application possible.

81   The structuring of silicon is done through a process which involves transferring the required pattern from the mask to the silicon wafer, and it is one of the most important steps in the production process of integrated circuits. This step has to be repeated as often as twenty times for advanced microchips. The industry presently uses optical pattern transfer, called photolithography, for the transfer process. As the silicon wafer is exposed stepwise, i.e. chip by chip, the manufacturing tool used is called a wafer stepper.

82   Testing is a central part of the chip production process. It is basically part of the manufacturers quality control. The equipment must fit into an IC production environment, and have user friendly software to allow fast test programme generation and to provide ease of use. In addition, given the need to follow developments in integrated circuits, the equipment must now have the features of both digital and analog automatic test equipment, without any trade-offs with regard to standard requirements, such as productivity and user friendliness.

83   To employ the official, technical description, for the user, the most important part of the framework is the Design Manager, which consists of the Process Manager and the Framework Utilities and Functions. Design data and administrative data are stored and managed in the Object Management System, which is an object oriented data base. The system has a graphical uniform user interface, based on the international industry standard. The project manager can configure his project workspace by defining the users, structures and flows. By combining users and flows with elements of the product structure, he can ensure that the right person is working on the right element in the process flow.

84   Nitridation of thin oxide gates improves the performance of small dimension transistors. Know-how on nitridation is being transferred to Siemens and GEC-Plessey, who use this technology in their pilot-lines. The nitridation of thin gate oxide slows down the diffusion of boron atoms into the transistor channel and improves the transistor characteristics. LATID (Large Angle Tilted Implanted Drain) is used to increase the transistor lifetime of small transistors. The strength of local electrical fields can reach high values where

electrons get hot. Consequently transistor characteristics deteriorate and lifetime is reduced. By adjusting the doping profile in the transitional areas of the transistor between the channel and the source and drain region, the electric field can be tailored to reduce the damage. The LATID process minimises hot-electron effects and increases transistor lifetime tenfold.

85   According to a source in DGIII, CEC.

86   *JESSI News*, Vol.3, No.4, October 1993.

87   The GAT meets about ten times per annum, and more than half of these meetings are held jointly with the JESSI Organisation. In addition, there are several GAT working groups, to deal with special issues, such as publicity and funding.

88   Mr John McAuley, Deputy Director, Technology Programmes and Services Department, Department of Trade and Industry, London.

89   John McAuley, ibid., quoted in *JESSI News*, October 1993.

90   The MOS memory hierarchy can be divided into volatile Random Access Memory [Dynamic Random Access Memory (DRAM), and Static RAM (SRAM)], and non-volatile Read Only Memory [Electrically Programmable Read Only Memory (EPROM), Flash-Erasable EPROM (Flash-EEPROM), EEPROM, SRAM with incorporated battery back-up, and Mask ROM]. The most significant difference between the two groups is that non-volatile memories will retain data and programmes, even when the equipment is disconnected from the power supply.

91   This assertion is based on interviews with senior executives at a number of US semiconductor equipment and component manufacturing firms (May 1993). The results of these interviews shall be further analysed in chapter six of this volume.

92   *The Economist*, February 19, 1994.

93   Sharp (1991) describes the maximalist approach as an active, interventionist industrial policy, having large collaborative R&D programmes as its basis.

94   Comment from Nico Hazewindus, director of product development, Philips, at a *Forum Europe* Conference, Brussels, 1989.

95   Eureka was launched by seventeen European countries and the EC Commission in Paris in July 1985. Its basic objectives were set down as, to improve the productivity and competitiveness of Europe's industries and economies on the world market, through collaborative projects directed at developing high technology based products, processes and services, with world-wide potential. The initiative presently comprises around 700 projects, with a total value of around ECU13 billion, and involving approx. 4000 companies and research organisations. The present Eureka member countries are the EC twelve, the six EFTA states, Turkey, and most recently, Eureka has continued to expand geographically, and incorporated Hungary in 1992 and the Russian Federation in 1993 as full members. A number of other Central and Eastern European countries are participating in several specific Eureka projects also.

96   This comparison was developed in a conversation with an European Commission DGIII official.

97   The nine technological sub-areas of Eureka are Biotechnology and Medical, Communication Technology, Energy Technology, Environmental Technology, Information Technology, Laser Technology, Material Technology, Robotics and Production Automation, Transport Technology (*Euro Abstracts,* CEC, DGXIII, Vol. 31, No.11, 1993).

98   In overall terms, information technology accounts for ECU 6,012 Million, from a total budget to date of ECU 13,507 million, *Euro Abstracts,* ibid., 1993.

99   The total JESSI budget currently stands at ECU 3,800 million (*Euro Abstracts,* ibid.).

100 Dataquest statistics, March 1994.

101 *Eureka Information Technology 1993,* official report published by the Eureka organisation, Brussels, 1993.

102 The technical details concerning these projects is taken from Eureka information sheets for projects EU 579, EU 38, and EU 50.

103 The Eureka assessment panel was composed of: Dr. Wisse Dekker, CEO, N.V. Philips, the Netherlands (Chairman); Mr. Henrik Ager-Hannssen, Senior Vice President, Statoil Group, Norway; Sir Geoffrey Allen, Executive adviser to the President of Kobe Steel Ltd., U.K.; M. Philippe Desmarescaux, Executive Vice President, Groupe Rhone-Poulenc, France; Prof. Antonio Garcia-Bellido, Research head developmental genetics section CBM, Universidad Autonoma de Madrid, Spain; Mr. Yrjo Toivola, President, Vaisala Oy, Finland; and Prof. Dr. Ing. Hans-Jurgen Warnecke, Director, Fraunhofer Gesellschaft fur Produktionstechnik und Automatisierung, Germany. The panel was assisted by the Eureka assessment secretariat, composed of Mr. Bert van Duyvendijk and Mr. Emile Louzada, Ministry of Economic Affairs, the Netherlands. This secretariat in turn received assistance from Andersen Consulting, The Hague.

104 *The Report of the Eureka Assessment Panel,* 1991, p.6.

105 Ibid.

106 Ibid., p.7.

107 The evaluation was conducted under the French Presidency of Eureka. The International Expert Group was chaired by Dr. E. Ormala, Science and Technology Policy Council, Finland, and the national experts came mainly from universities and research institutes, but also from business.

108 The technological areas examined were biotechnology, communication, energy, environment, information technology, laser, materials, robotics, and transport.

109 For instance John Peterson (1993), *High Technology and the Competition State.*

110 Commission of the European Comunities, DGXIII, *Community Participation in JESSI,* Information Note, Brussels, 22 March 1993.

111 These four projects are as follows: (i) the Joint Logic project, intended to develop the next generation of generic CMOS technology suitable for ASIC applications; (ii) Research into subsequent generations of CMOS technology, using even narrower line-widths; (iii) A project on manufacturing science and technology, aimed at developing more cost effective production tools, methods, and materials; and (iv) the JESSI Common Frame, which is developing, amongst other things, a common computer engineering environment which would incorporate a broad range of co-operative design tools, and allow for design-flow management covering the entire system design process (*Commission, DGXIII Information Note, ibid.*).

112 Ibid.

113 Commission of the European Communities, *Community Participation in JESSI*, Information Note, DGXIII, Brussels, 22 March 1993.

114 Commission of the European Communities, *Growth, Competitiveness, Employment: The Challenges and Ways Forward into the 21st Century*, White Paper, COM(93) 700 of 5 December 1993.

115 With the exception of 16 MBit EPROM chips. The unique nature of that project makes it difficult to count it as a definitive successful product development achieved through JESSI. As already argued, SGS-Thomson's overall R&D focus on this product resulted in the company using JESSI to partially achieve this aim.

116 Conversation with a European Commission *functionaire*, Brussels, 1994.

117 Conference Report on public presentation of the JESSI programme: S. Radelaar, vice chairman of the JESSI Board, *JESSI for the main phase - European microelectronics on its way*, CeBIT Hannover, 16 March, 1992.

118 We acknowledged in chapter four that national governments are important players in EC industrial policy formulation. Our evidence has indeed shown that, for JESSI and for budgetary decisions, states are the most influential governmental actors within the pentagonal diplomacy policy-bargaining model. However, this does not detract from our argument that in all other areas of the EC semiconductor policy set (ESPRIT, trade tool utilisation, competition policy, agenda-setting, etc.), the European Commission remains the most influential governmental actor.

6 Power and policy in the international system

It is not the policy of the government in America to give aid to works of any kind. They let things take the natural course without help or impediment, which is generally the best policy.

Thomas Jefferson

Peterson argues that the growth of collaborative R&D schemes necessitates a reassessment of existing models of EC policy-making. The model he proposes is based upon employing policy networks to analyse European R&D collaboration (1993, p.208). However, Peterson's model is inadequate for an assessment of EC collaborative policy for high technology industries such as semiconductors. This is because the analytical framework advanced by Peterson is too domestically or intra-Community oriented to account for all of the factor inputs in certain EC decision-making processes. Given the global nature of the producers, production base, and markets for semiconductors and other information technology industries, one can only adequately understand the policy which emerges for them, if one examines it in an international context. We argue that external determinants in and influences on EC policy-making for microchips are crucial in determining the nature and direction of the resultant policy. Thus, our third level of analysis is an attempt to understand the interplay between governmental and corporate actors in the creation of EC policy at the level of the international system. It is here that perhaps the most comprehensive understanding of this interplay can be achieved. Given that the semiconductor sector is a global industry, with firms producing for and selling on world, rather than national or regional markets, one may best understand the extent of their bargaining power relative to governmental actors, through a systemic analysis. Implicit in this chapter is the idea that that the global nature of semiconductor firms means that the boundaries of their activities are beyond the control of any one state; hence, their independence and bargaining strength is enhanced vis-à-vis governments.

This chapter has three main aims. The first, which is a major objective, is to examine the nature of international state-firm bargaining for semiconductor policy. The hypothesis advanced is that the ability to determine structural change gives an actor structural power, which in turn translates into relational power. Large semiconductor producers, possessing such influence over structural change, through their influence over the knowledge structure, have a stronger bargaining position vis-à-vis governmental actors than do other industries. From this, conclusions are drawn concerning the effect which this 'new diplomacy' has on EC policy-making.

The second research objective seeks to investigate whether or not the EC can learn - in organisational terms - from other global government-firm collaborative initiatives for the competitive enhancement of the semiconductor industry. In particular, the US SEMATECH programme (1987-92) and the Japanese VLSI project (1976-80) are of interest. These shadow comparisons are intended to identify successful elements in these countries policies, and consequently, whether or not the EC can draw any useful policy lessons from the collaborative strategies of other corners of the triad. It should be noted that the intention is to study only government policy in these countries, and not firm strategy.

The third and final purpose is an assessment of the extent to which the semiconductor policies of non-Community governments have an impact upon EC policy direction. The national policies with which we are most concerned are those of the US and Japan. The intention is to determine the ways and extent to which trade activities or trade tool utilisation's in or between non-Community countries, have affected the nature of EC policy. The central aim here is to establish whether or not the EC adopts a more neomercantilist, protectionist policy for semiconductors partially in response to external trade pressures and/or alliances.

Structural power theory (Strange, 1988) is this chapter's main theoretical tool. It has as its main premise the notion that the international system has four interdependent structures or pillars (security, credit, production, and knowledge), and that structural power is the systemic ability to define the basic structures of these pillars. All other elements of the international political economy, such as trade, are shaped by the four fundamental power structures (Strange, 1988, p.15). Within this model, knowledge/technology is seen to be the driving force of change within all other structures.

A secondary theory employed herein is that of neoliberal institutionalism. Its main purpose is to facilitate a structural power analysis of EC trade policy. Neoliberal institutionalism provides two important insights into any analysis of EC power and policy in the international system. First, states seek to maximise their absolute gains, regardless of the gains which this conveys to others (Grieco, 1993, p.117). Second, systemic power can rest with non-state actors such as the EC or transnational corporations (Grieco, 1993, p.302; Moravcsik, 1993, pp.480-1). Furthermore, the EC has its own institutional legitimacy, policy agenda, and bargaining role. Let us proceed to analyse the empirical evidence and establish the extent to which the theories provide useful tools for conceptualising, analysing, and explaining the reality.

The following division of policy realms into national and systemic fits with two main policy tools. At the national bargaining level, R&D activities are the favoured policy instrument for governments. At the international bargaining level, trade policies are the primary instrument employed. Thus, a division of analysis exists in this chapter, roughly concurring with the dual pillared R&D and trade policy set.

In the first, we can examine two countries policy approaches separately, and individually compare them with those of the EC. For the second, policies become more intertwined, and the policies of the largest non-European players - the US and Japan - tend to dominate. Thus, a comparison is made between EC policy and the inter-linked policies of Japan and the US. All are framed by events in the international system however, and the analysis is not a clear comparison of national trade policies. Rather, it is an analysis of how international state-state and state-firm bargaining and collaboration, along with change wrought in the system by technological change, can have an impact on a given actor's policy outcomes. Therefore, individual technology polices and domestic government-firm bargains for the semiconductor industry shall first be examined. We begin with the US.

1 Government-industry collaboration in the United States

Although some academic commentators (Philips, 1992, p.109) argue that recent US administrations refused to develop an industrial strategy for semiconductors, this work contends that such was not in fact the case. Beginning in the late 1970s, the US government was involved in partially funding chip development programmes. The Department of Defence sponsored the Very High Speed Integrated Circuit (VHSIC) programme begun in 1979, and running until the late 1980s at a cost of $1 billion (Fong, 1990, p.273). About twenty-five American microchip makers (both captive and merchant) received R&D contracts through this scheme. As Fong (1990) argues, this was the largest and most expensive effort undertaken by the government in semiconductors, since the mid-1960s. American federal government policy for the semiconductor sector emerged in a clear and deliberate way during the mid-1980s. For analytical purposes, a clear distinction may be made between trade and R&D. These policy pillars may best be analysed through examining their main emphases: in trade, the Semiconductor Trade Agreement (STA), and in R&D, the Semiconductor Manufacturing Technology Corporation (SEMATECH). The former shall be studied in the next section of this chapter. For now, let us look at SEMATECH, and the role of corporate players in developing US federal government technology policy.

1.i. The role of the firm in US technology policy

Phillips (1992) argues that as the Reagan years progressed, a shift occurred within corporate America regarding public policy. At the beginning of the 1980s, the most vociferous corporate advocates of government activism were firms in declining sectors. In plain terms, these firms were seeking government protection for their sectors. However, as East Asian competition intensified, those industries seeking government activism increased. In part, this was due to a perception that the competitiveness of East Asian companies may be partially attributable to the government-industry partnerships which existed in their home countries. Thus, similar firm-state alliances should be experimented with in the US. Those firms which were now feeling the pressure caused by East Asian competition were largely in more advanced sunrise sectors such as computers, automotives, and electronic peripherals. As George Fisher, CEO of Motorola argued:

> Our principal rivals today are no longer military...they are those who pursue economic, technology, and industrial policies designed to expand their share of global markets. This is the way it is. US policy must reflect this reality if we are to remain a world leader and a role model[1].

The political influence of these corporate players cannot be underestimated. At the time of this statement, Fisher was also chairman of the business led Council on Competitiveness[2]. Members of the Council include the CEOs of some of America's largest corporations, and the organisation has issued reports urging strong government-business ties in developing and commercialising so-called critical technologies (Branscomb, 1992, p.26). It is this concept of critical technologies that is central to the political influence held by the semiconductor sector. Without the industry's ability to affect a wide array of other industries, as well as the defence sector, its bargaining position vis-à-vis government would be significantly less. As Yoffie points out, the actual design and manufacture of semiconductors is a small industry by most traditional standards. The numbers employed in the industry are low compared with industries such as automobile or steel making for instance. Also, the industry is geographically concentrated, being located mainly in the states of California, Arizona, and Texas (1988, p.83). This means that the number of congressional districts and senate regions influenced by the industry are relatively few. This situation would normally translate as little political influence for an industry at a federal government level. However, this has not been the case. America's political leadership subscribed *en masse* to the notion that semiconductors were indeed a critical technology and vital to America's economic and military future. Thus, the industry's pleas for activism - if not assistance - did not fall on deaf ears. Yoffie argues that the formal campaign began in June 1985, when the Semiconductor Industry Association (SIA) filed for relief under Section 301 of the 1974 Trade Act, against Japanese chip manufacturers (1988, p.83). A little over one year later, the US and Japan came to an agreement which benefited American producers both in terms of regulating the prices of chips coming into the US; and guaranteeing American producers a share of the Japanese domestic semiconductor market. This deal had teeth also: in 1987, believing that a number of Japanese firms were violating the agreement, the Reagan Administration approved $300 million in punitive sanctions[3]. Such fines marked the first against Japanese firms since World War Two.

This SIA action was followed by individual negotiations between government and both semiconductor producers and users. Japanese competition was viewed with such alarm (and hostility), that the CEOs of companies such as Intel, Digital Equipment, Harris Corporation, AMD, and Texas Instruments, all made pilgrimages to Washington[4]. Their objective was simple: to bargain with government and build-up the political advantage of their firms and the semiconductor industry.

During the course of the Bush Administration, both the US Congress and the White House voiced their support for government-industry R&D partnerships. Tellingly, presidential approval was given to government support for pre-competitive R&D in generic[5] and enabling technologies[6], as advocated by big business. This followed an earlier Congressional initiative which, in 1988, created a government-firm R&D partnership for high risk generic and enabling technologies, called the Advanced Technology Programme (ATP). The ATP received $10 million from Congress in its first year of funding (1990), and this was raised to $36 million the following year (OTA, 1991, p.63). The first round of ATP partnerships actively began in 1991. Of the eleven grantees (selected from 249 proposals), five went to private sector consortia. Most of the technologies selected for funding were related to microelectronics and computers (OTA, 1991, p.66).

Government support for enabling technologies increased under the Clinton Administration. In November, 1994, the *Los Angeles Times* brought attention to the fact that the fastest growing agency in the federal government during 1994, was a previously little-known institute called the National Institute of Standards and Technology. The role of this agency is outlined as:

> boosting American international competitiveness by making large grants to private companies exploring high risk, enabling technologies and then actively promoting joint ventures and alliances[7].

This is further evidence of the continuing power which enabling technology firms such as semiconductor manufacturers have in American policy-making. Thus, although US government agencies vehemently deny that this Congressional and Executive sanctioning of government-firm collaborative R&D favours particular firms or industries (OTA, 1991, p.13), favouritism does actually exist. Enabling technologies are specifically highlighted by both branches of the American federal government as warranting special treatment regarding government sponsorship of collaborative R&D. As this work has consistently stressed, and as the ATP project selection has supported, semiconductors are just such an enabling technology. Thus, the semiconductor sector was in fact implicitly targeted by the US government for an R&D partnership. This lends further support to our argument that firms which control an enabling technology - most notably semiconductor technology - have more power relative to governments than do firms in industries which are not built upon enabling technologies. This power is further enhanced by semiconductors dual-use applications, increasing their utility to encapsulate both the military and the commercial spheres of a nation.

The Office of Technology Assessment (OTA) accepts that two primary reasons governments select industries for protective partnerships are, firstly, that an industry has the political leverage to attain such a selected position; and secondly, that certain critical industries are important for national economic security (1991, p.73). Electronic components - mainly active semiconductors - are a prime example of such an industry. As 1990 US Department of Commerce and Department of Defence lists illustrate, semiconductors are officially considered to be both a national critical technology and a defence critical technology[8].

An important industry voice which influences US policy-making is the Semiconductor Industry Association (SIA)[9]. Founded in 1977, and representing a solely corporate constituency, the SIA has consistently advocated greater government activism for the semiconductor industry. To achieve this, the SIA plays upon both the enabling and dual-use nature of semiconductors. In a 1992 report, the SIA accepts these as given features:

> It is assumed that the semiconductor industry is a *strategic* industry, which directly and profoundly affects all aspects of economic activity and national security[10].

Through a variety of reports, technology workshops, and policy statements, the SIA endeavours to 'encourage government attention to top-priority needs' (SIA,1993, p.1). The SIA has supported both the Semiconductor Trade Agreement (STA) and SEMATECH as positive dimensions of government-industry collaborative policy. In fact, the creation of SEMATECH was partly due to the efforts of the SIA, and - as will be illustrated further on - the association played a significant part in setting-up the government supported semiconductor consortium. Also, as previously discussed, the STA developed largely from SIA action. Perhaps the most important forum through which the American semiconductor industry influenced federal government policy, was through the National Advisory Committee on Semiconductors (NACS). Established by an act of Congress (1988 Omnibus Trade and Competitiveness Act), the Committee comprised senior members of both industry and government[11], as well as academic and scientific advisors. Its goal was to 'devise and promulgate a national semiconductor strategy' (OTA, 1991, p.73). The Committee helped to raise the visibility of the semiconductor sector within the highest ranks of government. Members of the Committee met periodically with the President's Chief of Staff, the Office of Management and Budget Director, and the Chairperson of the President's Council of Economic Advisors. Such broad access to senior administration officials is not commonplace in American business circles. It is evident that semiconductors attained a special position in the upper echelons of American politics.

During its existence (1988-92), the NACS issued several documents arguing for an industry-government alliance to offset the declining market share of American semiconductor manufacturers:

> It is imperative that US industry, in co-operation with government, develop a strategy to retain a strong semiconductor capability[12].

These reports were submitted directly to the US President and Congress. The NACS based their argument for the necessity of a government-industry partnership on two premises: firstly, that the industry was vital to US national security; and

197

secondly, that the very nature of the industry as an enabling technology gave it a strategic importance for the wider information technology sphere, and indeed, for society as a whole. The Committee's proposals for action included promoting capital formation, reforming trade law, protecting intellectual property, improving the antitrust climate, developing an information superhighway, and increasing support for Sematech[13]. Since the first report's release in 1989, most of the NACS policy recommendations have been enacted. Some, such as the inclusion of intellectual property protection in the Uruguay Round of the GATT, the promotion of capital formation, and increased funding for Sematech, were initiated under the Bush Administration. Others, such as the creation of an American fibre-optic superhighway and a more activist stance on trade issues, were at the forefront of President Clinton's policy goals. Upon the expiration of the NACS mandate, the SIA took charge of administering its programme.

2 SEMATECH: the domestic partnership

Perhaps the most prominent illustration of semiconductor manufacturers bargaining strength in the US, may be found in Sematech. As government agencies admit (OTA, 1991, p.65), semiconductor firms lobbied hard for the creation of Sematech. This programme became the vanguard for American contemporary government-industry collaboration, and emerged at a time when the US administration publicly professed an antipathy to such activist government policies. As already discussed, American semiconductor makers built political advantage in Washington, and reached a position whereby they were shaping the policy agenda. Given the hostile conservative capitalist Reaganite environment of the time, the very creation of Sematech is evidence of the bargaining strength which semiconductor firms had relative to government. US government policy measures, most notably the 1986 US - Japan Semiconductor Arrangement and the formation of SEMATECH research consortium, provided the means for an industry initiative to halt and partially reverse, at least temporarily, the erosion of the US competitive position in microelectronics that was rapidly unfolding by the mid-1980s (SIA, 1992). The way was legally opened for the creation of SEMATECH in October 1984, when President Reagan signed the National Co-operative Research Act. This Act eased antitrust restrictions against joint research and development (Yoffie, 1988, p.85). Coming as it did during the height of Reaganism (and in an election year), this Act proved a significant symbol of the importance which the US government attached to semiconductors.

This section shall be approached as follows: first, a brief description of how and why Sematech was established; second an identification of how it differs from JESSI (its focus on semiconductor manufacturing and equipment, not on actual microchip development); and third, an evaluation of Sematech.

Founded in 1987, Sematech emerged at a time when many American information technology firms were losing both domestic and global market share to Japanese competitors. It became commonplace within US political, business, and academic circles to lament the decline of American technological might. Such melancholy was accompanied by equally strong feelings of hostility towards Japanese firms, who (in collusion with their government) were perceived as employing unfair practices to win market share. The legitimacy of this argument is largely irrelevant now; what matters is that American decision-makers perceived such a state of play. It was from this perception that Sematech emerged. Despite the widespread belief that American-based firms were being exposed to unfair competition from their Japanese adversaries, the US electorate generally remained hostile to government intervention. Such intervention would countervene the society's traditional view that government should not involve itself in assisting industries experiencing competitive difficulties. Thus, in order to garnish public support for government assistance to the semiconductor industry, Congress and the Reagan administration, in association with the SIA[14] and individual corporate leaders, evoked the national security cloak. As Derian argues, national security justification for government involvement in technology development allowed the public authorities greater room for intervention (1990, p.251). We have discussed the nature of this approach earlier in this section, and outlined how semiconductors were targeted as a strategic, enabling sector. To lend the connection legitimacy, the Defence Science Board[15] issued a report in early 1987, warning that:

> without a semiconductor manufacturing base in the United States, future weapons systems would depend on our ability to secure semiconductors from foreign suppliers, a situation best avoided especially in wartime[16].

This was the kind of jingoistic rhetoric which elicited either active support or passive acceptance of federal government involvement in American industries. Once again, it achieved its objective. In August 1987, the Defence Advanced Research Projects Agency (DARPA) of the Department of Defence, in collaboration with a group of leading US semiconductor manufacturers, and supported by a number of universities, founded Sematech (see fig.6.1[17]). Another partner is also acknowledged in all of Sematech's public documents. In line with the American desire for accountability to the taxpayer, the American people are always included in listings of Sematech's partners. Perhaps this is merely paying lip service to the notion that those who spend public money should constantly be aware of and accountable for that fact. It is easy to be cynical concerning such acknowledgements. However, such notions are rarely, if ever, even mentioned in European collaborative R&D documents. This may be attributable to different cultural norms. It may also be due to a tendency among those who direct programmes such as JESSI to inadvertently omit the public from their organisational chain of responsibility. In this respects, whether due to cultural

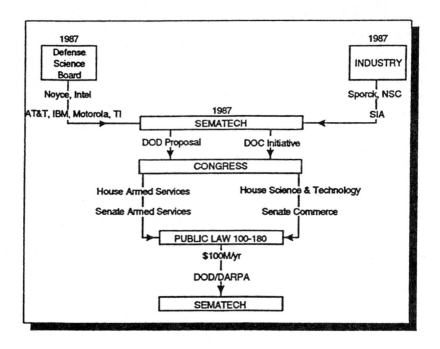

Figure 6.1 The genesis of SEMATECH
Reproduced with the kind permission of the SEMATECH Consortium

differences or superior organisational style (if one can separate the two), Sematech is more attuned to providing taxpayers with constant proof that their money is well spent. European consortia should draw organisational lessons from this attitude.

The first head of the US consortium was Robert Noyce, one of the co-developers of the integrated circuit and a founding father of the semiconductor industry. Over one third of Sematech's total staff comprised individuals seconded from member companies. Most of the organisation's professional research staff were on assignment from the corporate members (Grindley et al., 1994, p.729). Sematech's original member companies numbered fourteen[18]. These companies together accounted for more than 80 percent of US based semiconductor component capacity. They were drawn from all segments of the semiconductor component industry: ASIC, memory, and logic, military and civilian, captive and merchant[19]. Two of these firms (LSI Logic Corporation and Micron Technology Inc.) withdrew from the consortium in 1992, followed by Harris Semiconductors in 1993[20]. At face value, such defections would appear to indicate dissatisfaction with the consortium. However, LSI Logic for instance, argues that this was not the case. Rather, company sources[21] indicate that Sematech and LSI Logic's technological trajectories diverged, as Sematech focused more on DRAM technology and LSI's core technological constituency is ASICs[22]. The company therefore dropped out of

200

Sematech, but remained supportive of it - seeing it as beneficial, from a broader industry perspective.

In parallel with Sematech's creation, a group of the largest American semiconductor materials and equipment suppliers formed SEMI/SEMATECH. The intention was to solidify connections between them and Sematech. SEMI/SEMATECH participates in joint research projects with Sematech, and permits technical and managerial interaction between the two bodies. This group accounts for about 85 per cent of US semiconductor materials and equipment sales (Grindley et al., 1994, p.730). SEMI/SEMATECH's president is a member of Sematech's board, and a joint meeting of the two organisations boards is held four times a year.

2.ii. SEMATECH's objectives

Sematech's core objective was to enable US firms to regain leadership in semiconductor manufacturing technology[23]. Herein lies the fundamental difference between Sematech and government-industry collaborative initiatives for semiconductor R&D in all other countries. Sematech was intended to re-establish US market pre-eminence within the semiconductor materials, processes, and equipment sectors - not to establish a market presence through developing semiconductor components[24]. The emphasis was on manufacturing capability, not on device design. The rationale was twofold: strength in the equipment and materials manufacturing sector per se was desirable; and strength in manufacturing technology would enable the rapid development of state-of-the-art semiconductor components. More specifically, the latter objective was to develop the manufacturing technology needed to produce new generations of memory chips such as the sixteen and sixty-four megabit DRAMs and four megabit SRAMs. Thus, in technical terms, the essential objective of Sematech was, according to Derian:

> to develop integrated manufacturing systems using the most recent technologies, and to test them in an environment similar to the factory environment in which they will be applied (1990, p.234).

Under the National Defence Authorization Act, the Department of Defence was authorised to make payments to Sematech of $100 million per annum, for an initial five year period[25]. This would be matched by the combined contribution of Sematech's member companies. This total annual budget of $200 million was minuscule compared with the $8 billion spent by US manufacturers on R&D and new facilities and equipment each year; and the $1 billion committed by the Department of Defence to R&D and technology demonstration of electronic device technology[26].

One year after its inception, Sematech established its headquarters in Austin, Texas. The intention was to have a complete state-of-the-art production process located at its Austin facility. Individuals would be loaned to Sematech for a fixed time period, and would form scientific and engineering teams working on all stages of the semiconductor production process. It was thus that the consortium produced its first silicon wafers in 1989. The decision to locate the bulk of Sematech's activities in one facility, can be viewed as a positive element in its organisational structure[27]. Such a move minimised the time wastage and risk of experimental duplication incurred through geographically fragmented collaborative R&D activities. As has been frequently emphasised, time is of the essence in an industry where there is a rapid rate of technological change. As Sematech evolved and encountered fresh threats to the American semiconductor sector, and new needs among its corporate constituents, its main objective changed. As Sematech entered the 1990s, the central objective switched to strengthening the semiconductor manufacturing equipment industry (Grindley et al., 1994, p.730). This transformation of Sematech's technical mandate was directly initiated by the consortium's corporate members (see fig.6.2). Each firm employs its own form of process technology, and due to its direct connection with the firm's competitive advantage, firms are hesitant to share it with others. Amongst other reasons, the free rider syndrome is cited for this reticence. Therefore, Sematech members began to question the practicality of having an industry consortium based on process technology. Instead, they supported a shift in emphasis towards technologically assisting the ailing semiconductor equipment makers, whilst encouraging greater co-operation between equipment suppliers and users (Grindley et al., 1994, p.730). Sematech's revised technological mandate may best have been described by President and CEO, William J. Spenser:

> We develop the tools and equipment necessary to manufacture semiconductors. We do not design chips; we do not build product for sale. Our sole product is knowledge (Sematech strategic overview report, 1991, pp.1-6).

It is important to note at this juncture, the role of the government in defining Sematech's research agenda, and its position concerning the above sea-change in the consortium's objectives. Alic et al. (1992) argue that government and the firms have often taken divergent positions within the decision-making structure of Sematech. The goals of Pentagon officials and semiconductor executives were frequently divergent after 1987. Creating a fit between civilian and military needs in semiconductor technology proved to be more difficult than anticipated[28]. DARPA[29] voiced its disapproval of the shift in Sematech's research agenda towards equipment development and away from more fundamental, long-term research into manufacturing process technology[30]. Its corporate partners did not agree. Thus, bargaining between the public and private sector actors was vigorous. On the basis of events, it would appear that firms gained the upper-hand in this bargaining process, and defined Sematech's focus for much of its lifespan. This corporate leadership in decision-making has also been evident at a more micro level. Specific technical goals and timetables are established by Sematech and member firm managers, who meet throughout the year to review ongoing projects and define future technological needs (Grindley et al., 1994, p.733).

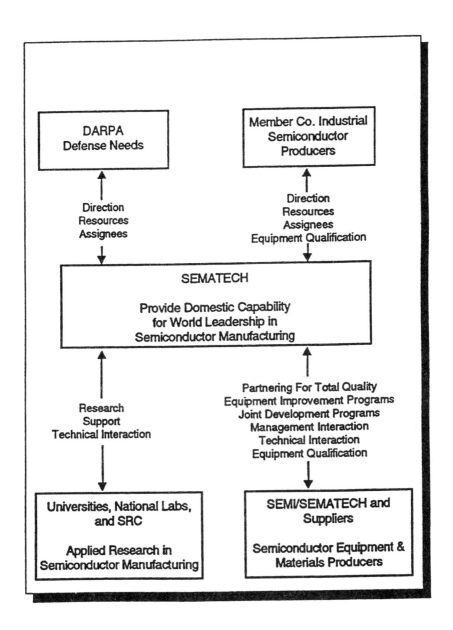

Figure 6.2 SEMATECH operational concept
Reproduced with the kind permission of the SEMATECH Consortium

As with our analysis of JESSI in chapter five, it is difficult to say whether Sematech has been a success or failure. This is due to the evaluatory problems inherent in any study of collaborative R&D initiatives (see chapter two). Instead, a number of evaluatory conclusions from different sources shall briefly be posited, and we will comment on Sematech's commercial utility. These evaluations all date from between early 1991 and late 1994. Five sources are used: federal government, individual semiconductor firms, the press, academic commentators, and the Semiconductor Industry Association.

First, through a 1992 report issued by the US General Accounting Office (GAO), we obtain a view from the federal government, particularly DARPA. This survey was conducted towards the end of Sematech's first phase. Most significantly, the GAO questioned DARPA on the progress made by Sematech towards achieving its original objectives. The conclusion was that Sematech appeared to be on schedule for achieving its primary technological objectives of 'demonstrating the capability to manufacture 0.35-micron semiconductors using only US equipment, by the end of 1992' (GAO, 1992, p.8). A number of other technical achievements[31] were also advanced to testify to Sematech's success. DARPA implicitly stated that its main motive for participation in Sematech was to provide a source of federal assistance for efforts to improve the American semiconductor manufacturing base. The transfer of semiconductor manufacturing technology to military purposes was only a secondary motive (GAO, 1992, p.19). However, as the GAO report proceeds to illustrate, the Department of Defence can benefit from Sematech without any direct technology transfer. Seven of Sematech's founding members rank in the top ten microchip suppliers to the US military. Combined, these firms account for 70 per cent of all chips used by the Defence Department (GAO, 1992, p.20). Hence, any technological gain accrued by Sematech's corporate members automatically translates into a technological gain for the military. In addition, direct links between Sematech and the defence agencies do exist. Sematech has worked with the National Security Agency and Naval Command for instance, on developing design, manufacturing, and application technologies[32]. DARPA did concede that it was intending a gradual phasing out of federal financial input into Sematech. Rather than indicating waning moral support, DARPA argued that this action was based on need: now that the industry consortium was up and running well, it no longer needed government financial assistance. DARPA affirmed its opinion that Sematech had been a 'tremendous success, resulting in broad infrastructural changes within the industry' (GAO, 1992, p.23).

The views emanating from Sematech's corporate members appear generally supportive of the consortium, and relatively positive concerning its achievements. As Craig Barrett of Intel stated, 'Sematech is one of the more intelligent creatures of our government'[33]. AMD adopts a similar position. It argues that Sematech helped to support the US semiconductor industry in its time of competitive crisis, and thus filled an important role. AMD sees the consortium's main success as helping to improve the technological basis of equipment manufacturers[34]. This is important as it provides access for US chip manufacturers to leading-edge tools. Executives at National Semiconductor also confirm that their company is a strong supporter of Sematech[35]. The firm has been especially enthusiastic about Sematech as an organisation for pooling research in order to develop more advanced manufacturing technologies.

Applied Materials has an interesting corporate perspective. It is a semiconductor equipment manufacturer, and was therefore one of the corporate targets for Sematech's emphasis on developing equipment technology. More specifically, Applied Materials regained the number one position in terms of world manufacturing equipment sales during 1992-93. Hence, it is important to assess to what extent the company attributes this market success to Sematech. According to the firm's director of product development and strategic planning, Sematech has played an important role in facilitating the interplay between companies, and creating linkages between public laboratories and industry. However, he is very critical of Sematech's actual benefit to industry in terms of enhancing their competitive positions. No part of Applied Materials market success is attributed to Sematech. Rather, the company sees the consortium as having achieved nothing vis-à-vis market enhancement for individual firms[36]. This is an interesting divergence from the otherwise positive views which has been cited here. Also, it runs contrary to the credit which Sematech itself has taken for the growth in equipment makers market share[37]. It serves to illustrate that not all semiconductor manufacturers have been happy with Sematech - either in terms of its concrete achievements, or as a collaborative framework. It is worth noting that Applied Materials is not a Sematech member, whereas the other companies assessed above, all are. Perhaps there is something to be learned here from the proverb that one should not kill the goose which lays the golden egg. It is not in the best financial interest of Sematech's corporate members to publicly criticise that which provides them with R&D resources. Non-members like Applied Materials, on the other hand, stand to lose nothing through openly stating their misgivings about Sematech. There are divergent views on whether or not Sematech serves a purpose, and has succeeded in achieving its technological and commercial objectives. However, more firms view the consortium favourably, than do not.

Although not a member of Sematech, the research and assessment company, VLSI Research, provides another private sector angle. The company's president, G. Dan Hutcheson, has argued that Sematech 'did an excellent job at saving the equipment industry, and US semiconductor manufacturing'[38]. He stated that Sematech set out to regain market leadership for US semiconductor manufacturers, and it did just that. Market share statistics provide strong support for this thesis. Dataquest (1994) figures show that US firms lost their leadership position in world semiconductor market share to Japanese competitors in 1985. Between 1985 and 1989 (Sematech's infancy), this market share continued to decline, from just over 43 per cent in 1985 to 39.1 per cent in 1990. This downward spiral was halted in 1990, and by 1992, American firms had regained parity with the Japanese. The last quarter of 1992 saw the combined US market share overtaking the Japanese again. Figures for 1993 put the US share at 43.6 per cent, versus 40.2 per cent for

Japanese firms (Dataquest Inc., 1994). By the close of 1994, American market leadership had further strengthened, with US-based companies controlling 45.4 per cent of the world semiconductor market[39].

The press on both sides of the Atlantic were cynical about Sematech from its inception. However, they have conceded certain gains achieved through the consortium. In 1991, *The New York Times* stated that 'Sematech is beginning to bear fruit' (19 April, 1991). In particular, they pointed to individual cases of product improvement achieved through Sematech's advances in manufacturing process technology. Also, the paper drew attention to the co-operative environment which the organisation developed within the US semiconductor industry (although the merits of creating a cartel enhancing, co-operative framework amongst long-standing competitors are dubious). In addition, Sematech was perceived as enabling greater vertical dialogue, between equipment suppliers and users (*The New York Times*, 19 April 1991). This facilitates a better understanding of user needs amongst the equipment manufacturers. In a 1994 survey, *The Economist* acknowledged that Sematech has achieved significant advances in line-width technology[40], allowing more and faster integrated circuits on a silicon chip, as well as more productive wafer fabs. Such technology is capable of producing DRAM chips two generations beyond those which have just been introduced (*The Economist*, 2 April 1994). However, *The Economist* sounds a note of caution concerning Sematech's success. It argues that the consortium has proved adept at fostering technology, but that alone is not enough. For instance, some of the technologies which it has helped develop have been late to market - such as GCA's 0.35 micron wafer stepper, introduced one year after its rivals. Another problem has been the unavoidable factor of picking winners (often unsuccessfully) through its allocation of research funds. A further possible neutraliser of Sematech's achievements is the notion of the consortium's main phase merely coinciding with a cyclical upturn in the economy. As *The Economist* points out, other American industries have regained competitiveness without the assistance of consortia. Overall, it is conceded that the goal of revival has been met, and it is difficult to establish exactly how great a role Sematech played in this. As an organisation, it is 'well run, and appears to have done some good' (*The Economist*).

The SIA credits Sematech with being one of the means through which US semiconductor firms reversed their competitive decline[41]. This has been achieved mainly through Sematech's achievements in improved manufacturing technology. Furthermore, contrary to the arguments of Applied Materials, the SIA argues that Sematech helped to prevent the collapse of the US semiconductor equipment industry (SIA, 1992, p.xvi). In a 1992 report[42], the SIA outlined four major Sematech contributions to the restoration of a competitive, self-sufficient American microelectronics infrastructure. First is its funding of new semiconductor equipment development; second is its role in establishing industry quality standards, and in fostering collaborative development initiatives between equipment makers; third, the SIA credits Sematech with encouraging greater vertical co-operation within the industry, between equipment suppliers and users; and fourth, Sematech is commended for its success in improving manufacturing equipment technology, and encouraging US chip component manufacturers to purchase American equipment. Being one of Sematech's initial sponsors, the SIA has a vested interest in supporting the consortium. Nevertheless, it is representative of a majority of American semiconductor companies, and its reports do give significant examples of Sematech's achievements.

Finally, a word from some leading academic commentators. Industry expert Michael Borrus stated that Sematech 'hasn't accomplished by any means all that was hoped for'[43]. He does believe the consortium to be an important experiment in collaboration. Borrus argues that Sematech succeeded in providing firms with a structure through which they could pool portions of their R&D budgets and focus them collectively on specific technological objectives. However, he concludes that Sematech did not really help US firms to increase their market share[44].

A 1994 survey[45] conducted by Grindley, Mowery, and Silverman reveals that:

SEMATECH's original aims of developing next-generation manufacturing technology proved hard to achieve, and the program has refocused on generic technology and the equipment industry infrastructure. Though more modest, these new objectives have produced significant tangible results (Grindley et al., 1994, p.723).

In line with Borrus, Grindley et al. reject the thesis that US market share resurgence in microchip components has been due to Sematech. Instead, they attribute this competitive revival to changes in both the American and global industry structure[46]. These changes included, most notably, the price advantages held by American producers due to their domination of market segments such as microprocessor. Thus, the vigorous international price competition which developed in the early 1990s (spurred by Korean memory producers), had little impact upon overall American industry revenue, given this American strength in the more knowledge-intensive segments of the market. Similarly, gains made by semiconductor equipment manufacturers in global market share, is not due to Sematech, but to world industry changes - particularly the competitive problems experienced by Japanese firms (Grindley et al., 1994, p.740). In fact, arguably, the consortium failed to prevent the decline of one important segment of the equipment market - lithographic wafer steppers[47]. This is despite the fact that this sector was the flagship of Sematech's equipment development programmes, accounting for 38 per cent of its 1988-92 research budget (GAO, 1992). It would therefore appear that Sematech has had more success in strengthening the technological base of industry segments which already possessed relatively strong manufacturing techniques and market positions. It has been unable to assist firms within those sectors of the industry which had weak technology bases and poor market positions. To conclude on a positive note for Sematech as an organisation, Grindley et al. (1994) argue that the consortium passed a critical market test of viability, in so far as eleven of its original fourteen members (accounting for about 80 per cent of total US chip output) continue their financial and moral commitment to the venture.

In terms of the government-firm bargaining to create Sematech, and to define its research agenda, the evidence suggests that firstly, large firms within the semiconductor industry, in conjunction with the SIA, were the main driving force in creating the consortium[48]. Government had to obtain public support and provide legal and political approval for the venture. Thus, by employing the notion of national security considerations, the federal government achieved this, and in doing so, gave the appearance of being the main driving force behind Sematech's creation. Secondly, the large semiconductor manufacturers also dominated the bargaining process after Sematech's inception. As we have seen, these firms had - and continue to have - the lead role in defining the consortium's research agenda. Therefore, in all major aspects of US government-firm bargaining for collaborative semiconductor R&D consortia, large firms have displayed the most power, relative to other actors.

Sematech has achieved some successes, and has also failed in some of its core objectives. As we have seen, there are various opinions concerning what Sematech has actually achieved. One thing which is far from certain is the extent to which Sematech played a role in the revival of semiconductor component and equipment manufacturers market shares during the first three years of this decade. Although difficult to prove that Sematech played no part in regaining market leadership, many corporate executives and industry analysts argue that this was the case. The counterfactual involved in such an assessment makes it difficult - if not impossible - to reach a definitive answer. Hence, we base our argument on other factors, most notably, improvements made by Sematech to manufacturing process technology, and to fostering dialogue between equipment suppliers and users. Here we may discern a more widespread positive reaction. Sematech is seen by all interested parties as having made significant contributions in both of these areas.

Perhaps the most symbolic factor testifying to the utility of Sematech is the continued support which it receives from its corporate partners. This is especially relevant given that government funding finished at the end of 1996:

> At a news conference in Washington, leaders of the [Sematech] consortium politely thanked the Government and said they would wean themselves off Federal financing - now $90 million a year - by 1997. The group, to be financed solely by industry money, intends to concentrate not on 'national industrial policy' but on the nuts and bolts, and microscopic circuits, of the chipmaker's art (*The New York Times*, 'A Declaration of Chip Independence', 6 October 1994).

More importantly, this withdrawal by the government appears to have been a prearranged, amicable separation, rather than a sudden and acrimonious divorce suit. A statement made by Bill Spenser, President and CEO of Sematech, to the US Congress in September 1994[49], testifies to this impending termination of federal funding for the consortium. He cites the intention of Sematech's industry members to assume full responsibility for financing its operations as of 1997. This follows from a July 1994 resolution of the Sematech Board of Directors[50], outlining a 'new model of co-operation' for the near future. This effectively entails continued co-operation with government agencies in implementing federal technology policy. This interface will occur largely through the Semiconductor Technology Council, a public/private sector advisory body established by Congress in 1993. Thus, Sematech will continue as a purely privately funded operation but it will compete periodically with other private sector enterprises for federal research grants for specific projects. As the *Washington Post* confirmed, the consortium's eleven member companies have pledged to continue supporting Sematech once government funds cease ('Chip Research Consortium to Drop US Subsidy', 5 October, 1994). As Intel's chief operating officer argues, the semiconductor industry is doing well and now can 'afford to pay its own way'. The industry will, he states, continue to strongly support Sematech[51]. This industry commitment is supported by the Sematech Board's July 1994 resolution. Therefore, as a framework for firm-firm and government-industry R&D co-operation, Sematech appears to have broad support, and to have been relatively successful. As a worthwhile collaborative model, we may thus draw structural lessons from Sematech for European chip consortia.

2.v. Structural advantages of SEMATECH

European collaborative programmes for semiconductor R&D could learn from Sematech in a number of structural/organisational way. These are as follows:

(1) The organisation's relatively centralised structure has facilitated a flexible and industry responsive research agenda (Grindley et al., 1994, p.749). The more hierarchical and bureaucratic command structure of European collaborative ventures reduces European firms collective ability to rapidly change the research agenda, according to market demand.

(2) The definition of a feasible agenda - this is something which Sematech dealt with successfully; when the original agenda began to appear unfeasible, the consortium rapidly refocused its research objectives. JESSI attempted this also (in 1992) but in a much less decisive and focused way than Sematech.

(3) Sematech's objectives were, from the start, much more specific than JESSI. Like the Japanese VLSI programme, Sematech sought to strengthen a relatively narrow array of capabilities in which the US semiconductor industry was weak in the late 1980s, rather than attempting to reconstruct an entire industry (Grindley et al., 1994, p.753). It did not attempt to establish a presence in existing microchip markets, to develop new generations of chip technology, or to conduct basic research into semiconductor component technology. This ability to focus both its financial and human resources in on specific areas of weakness was an important structural advantage of Sematech. Such an approach was more likely to achieve concrete results, quickly. JESSI could learn from this, rather than attempting to cover all areas of the industry. As William J. Spenser, President and CEO of Sematech argues, Sematech established itself as the centre for manufacturing

technology research, and could thus focus its resources for maximum impact[52]. JESSI could draw significant structural lessons from such an approach.

(4) Sematech was, from the beginning, geographically centralised. The bulk of its activities were originally conducted in its Austin labs. This had the advantage of minimising decision-making time, and eliminating the risk of communication misunderstanding within its research teams.

(5) Sematech's budget was relatively small, compared to European collaborative programmes ($220 million per annum, versus a projected per annum median of almost $600 million for JESSI). Thus, project goals had to be well-defined, and there was no room for risky experimentation or costly delays in project start-up (a factor which plagued JESSI in its early years).

(6) Due to the nature of American business culture, and its inherent dislike of collaboration/consortia, Sematech has been under continuous scrutiny from both its corporate and political partners. Its very *raison d'être* has been constantly questioned. A sizeable number of members of the US Congress - mainly Republicans - along with senior executives in the US semiconductor industry, opposed the consortium from the beginning. Consequently, Sematech has been obliged to meticulously account for its expenditure, and to provide detailed cost-benefit analyses on a regular basis. This contrasts significantly with European initiatives such as JESSI. It has been reviewed periodically by independent panels, and has some political and corporate opponents. It also releases regular progress reports. However, its level of accountability and the degree of criticism encountered, do not compare with that experienced by Sematech. Hence, one may argue that Sematech is more directly accountable to its fiscal masters, and operates more like a business enterprise, than does its European counterpart.

(7) Unlike JESSI, Sematech has no politically motivated project alliances. Governmental sponsors of JESSI - particularly the European Commission - frequently allocate project money to partnerships which enhance European industrial and technological cohesion. Larger firms from industrially advanced parts of the EC are often required to take as partners small or medium sized enterprises from economically less developed regions of the Community, before public money is handed over. No such political factors exist within the SEMATECH structure. Instead, all collaborative activities are determined purely on their business merit. The US Department of Defence (DoD) has been involved in funding the consortium, and one may thus argue that military requirements have restricted some aspects of Sematech's project selection. No evidence exists to prove that this is the case. The DoD appears to have been a silent partner, content in the knowledge that SEMATECH's commercial results may frequently be adapted for military purposes.

On a critical concluding note, as Grindley et al. argue, a flaw which Sematech and JESSI both share, has been the shift in emphasis away from more long-term research towards more short-term, market applicable research goals. In terms of the long-term utility of such consortia, it may be better for them not to enter this close-to-market realm, and leave such endeavours to individual firms or university-industry alliances for instance.

3 Government-industry collaboration in Japan: the VLSI project

In assessing government-industry collaboration for semiconductor R&D in Japan, it is evident that these activities were concentrated in the late 1970s, and have since declined. During the 1980s and into the 1990s, the role of government in such activities has become negligible. In effect, the relationship became skewed: it went from being a government-firm partnership aimed at attaining competitiveness, to a situation where the firms had achieved this competitiveness, and no longer needed government. Sporadic and/or low-scale collaborative activities continued to occur, but nothing to compare with either Sematech or JESSI. Returning to the 1970s, we find a venture which does bear comparison with American and European collaborative efforts. Perceiving a need to catch-up with their global competitors in semiconductor technology, the Japanese government and industry came together in 1976 to create the Very Large Scale Integration (VLSI) programme. Given the causal factors, objectives, structure, and government-firm relationship inherent in this consortium, it is the closest which Japan has come to a collaborative model such as Sematech or JESSI. Therefore, any analysis of Japanese government-firm collaboration for semiconductor development, must focus on the VLSI project. This work adopts such an approach.

There is one reason why less analysis is given here to the VLSI project than to Sematech. The reason has to do with time. The Japanese VLSI project ended a considerable time ago, and almost a decade before Sematech or JESSI commenced. This relative antiquity of the VLSI project is important in a rapidly changing industry such as semiconductors, as it means that causal factors and project objectives differ considerably for more contemporary consortia initiatives. Economies of scale have escalated tremendously; concurrently, product market prices have been significantly reduced, semiconductor applications have proliferated, and thus the user market is much more diverse than during the 1970s. Competitors have emerged from newly industrialising countries such as Korea and Taiwan, forcing older chip makers to be more sensitive to the needs of their customers, given that they now have a wider choice of supplier; and so forth. Therefore, the Japanese case is interesting for our study of EC collaborative initiatives, but many of its features are not relevant in today's world. Hence, we shall approach it more as a historical example, from which we may draw some structural lessons; rather than as a contemporary case, from which we may derive directly applicable organisational examples. As with our analysis of Sematech, there are two objectives in briefly looking at the VLSI project. The first is to understand how government-firm bargaining has developed in Japan. The second is to draw structural lessons from the VLSI experience.

In the wake of the 1973 oil crisis, a fundamental shift occurred in Japan's industrial balance:

> The entire industrial structure shifted towards an energy-saving, technology-intensive, and high-value-added one. Energy-intensive industries scaled down

and high technology industries expanded rapidly (Odagiri and Goto, 1993, p.89).

Government supported this shift, and began to devote large amounts of R&D money to facilitate the growth of these new industries. As the basis of the entire information technology sector, the semiconductor industry became a primary test case for this new departure in Japanese industrial policy. As Tyson and Yoffie argue, the industry is a very successful example of 'infant industry promotion and protection' (1991, p.12). They also emphasise the fact that this policy was a means to an end, rather than an end in itself, as the ultimate objective of the government was the establishment of a world class computer industry. Hence, as in the US and the EC, the industry was targeted more for its enabling capacity, than for its own economic merits.

3.i. The genesis of the project

The Japanese semiconductor industry was (and remains) a virtual oligopoly of vertically integrated companies, which both manufacture and consume microchips[53] (Howell et al., 1988, p.50). In this respect, it is structurally similar to the European industry. In addition, there are no significant market players within the Japanese industry which specialise only in the production and merchant sales of semiconductor components (Kikkawa, 1983, p.254). In this way too, the Japanese industry is like its European counterpart in terms of composition (and unlike the US industry). At the firm level, a significant weakness existed in semiconductor R&D. This may be partially explained by low rates of R&D investment by the major Japanese electronics firms. During the first half of the 1970s for instance, the combined semiconductor R&D outlay of Hitachi, Fujitsu, and NEC was less than Texas Instruments R&D budget (Tyson and Yoffie, 1991, p.12). The early 1970s witnessed the Japanese government intervening to provide finance for joint semiconductor development initiatives with industry. As Borrus, Millstein, and Zysman (1982) show, during the first half of the 1970s, the Japanese government invested several hundred million dollars into sixty semiconductor R&D projects. Thus, from its inception, it was a government-firm partnership. Commentators[54] agree that at no stage in Japan's history of government-industry relations for the electronics sector, did the government dominate the private sector players. As Howell et al. argue, the relationship is best described as a 'partnership between central bureaucrats and entrepreneurs' (1988, p.43). Both partners have a good deal of power within the policy bargain. Government sets the agenda, but industry works with government in defining this agenda. For semiconductors, government - working mainly through the Ministry of International Trade and Industry (MITI) - took the initiative, acting as a catalyst for technological development[55]. There was no question of it imposing its will on the semiconductor manufacturers though. Rather, as Howell et al. argue, MITI set out to 'woo' firms, through offering promotional benefits such as R&D subsidies (Howell et al., 1988, p.43). The firms in turn responded favourably to this courtship. A strong relationship was thus forged, but one in which neither partner was dominant. One should not however be deceived into thinking that an easily formed collaborative harmony reigned within the Japanese government-industry policy sphere. As Levy and Samuels argue, although the Japanese political economy is 'broadly favourable to collaboration', a crucial element of this system is 'extensive conflict and bargaining among public and private actors' (1991, p.124). Vigorous power struggles are emblematic of both Japanese industry (between firms and between *keiretsu*), and government (between ministries). This internal competitive dynamic is one of the country's strengths, as ministries must constantly update and improve their policy strategies (or risk losing influence to another), and those firms which survive the tough competitive battle within Japan, are better able to compete globally.

3.ii. Project structure and the role of the firm

It was against this backdrop that the VLSI Development Association was created by MITI in 1975. A three-way bargaining process developed: between government ministries, to determine which would direct the consortium and what the total government outlay on the project would be; between the government and the industry, to establish the structure of the project, its research goals, and the respective budget shares; and finally, amongst the individual firms, primarily to establish who does what and with what concentration of manpower[56]. In the following year, 1976, The VLSI Co-operative Research Project got underway. Total funding for the first year of operations was $36.4 million, of which $20.5 million came from the member firms, and $15.9 million in loans[57] from MITI[58]. This overall budget tripled the following year. In technical terms, the project's core objective was clear and compact: to enhance the manufacturing base of Japanese industry through developing very large scale integration devices for the next generation of computer systems. In practical terms, this meant taking the technology from a state where 1,000 transistors could be fitted onto a semiconductor chip (Large Scale Integration); to one where 100,000 transistors could be put onto one chip (Fong, 1990, p.298). This was to be achieved through advancing the semiconductor manufacturing process by such means as improved computer-aided design, more efficient wafer making methods, and the development of state-of-the-art fine-line lithography. This process enhancement approach was closely emulated by the Sematech consortium a decade later. Five of Japan's major electronics corporations joined the project[59]. It is important to note that on structural grounds, there was considerable initial opposition to the VLSI project amongst firms. The reasons were largely concerning access to proprietary knowledge, and a fear of disclosing that covert and firm-specific knowledge input factor in their manufacturing process which had a direct impact on their corporate competitiveness (Fransman, 1990, p.64). After all, strong competitive rivalries existed between the prospective partners in several product areas directly impacted by VLSI research. Few opposed a degree of government R&D funding, but many were against the notion of joint research laboratories. This is an important structural dimension which involved forceful bargaining between MITI and the firms. MITI perceived such group research facilities as central to the proposed project. The ministry was adamant that all corporate partners had to participate in such activities. MITI succeeded, and the joint labs were developed. As a corporate executive disclosed, 'the companies did not want to have joint laboratories. We were forced' (Fransman, 1990, p.63). Corporate objections were thus overcome, and three sets of joint laboratories were created. Two of these were group labs, located at the existing research facilities of a member company, and intended to work on applied technology. Toshiba and NEC teamed up in the NEC-Toshiba Information Systems set of labs, whilst Hitachi, Fujitsu, and Mitsubishi developed the Computer Development Laboratories (Fong, 1990, pp.283-4). The third joint facility involved all five companies, plus MITI, sending research teams to a central, co-operative research lab (similar to the Sematech facility in Austin). More basic, long-term research was conducted at this facility, which had a research staff of almost one hundred scientists and engineers (Fong, 1990, p.284). The overall direction of the project, as well as its technical and financial guidance, derived from a government-industry committee called the VLSI Technology Research Association. This body was composed of senior bureaucrats, managers, and engineers from MITI, Nippon Telephone and Telegraph, and the five member companies (Fong, 1990, p.290). The total operating cost of the VLSI project during its 1975-79 existence, was $300 million. The government contributed 40 per cent of this sum, and the balance was covered equally by the five corporate partners (Fong, 1990, p.284).

3.iii. The Japanese VLSI project: an assessment

The US Semiconductor Industry Association has argued that government-firm collaboration (through VLSI) ensured the emergence of a world class Japanese semiconductor industry (1992, p.v). In terms of technical achievements, the SIA cites the project's development of the lithography and device technology for DRAM chips, and its contribution to increasing the time-to-market for 64K and 256 K DRAM devices. Both of these advances were made ahead of most US companies, and the SIA perceived the VLSI project as being instrumental in achieving this for its corporate members (1992, p.28).

Levy and Samuels argue that VLSI was a 'striking success':

> In less than four years, the consortium generated some 1,000 patents, sixteen per cent of which were held jointly. The perfecting of techniques for tracing designs on silicon wafers and for controlling quality not only enabled Japanese manufacturers to become world leaders in VLSI, but made it possible for them to capture increasing shares of the global market for memory chips and to introduce a range of powerful fourth generation computers that could compete with IBM's 303X and 4300 series (Levy and Samuels, 1991, p.139).

However, as Fong points out, only 16 per cent of the one thousand patents emerging from the VLSI project were developed jointly. All of the others emerged from individual company activities (1990, p.292). This does not mean to say necessarily that the other, individually developed patents were not stimulated by the project.

Tyson and Yoffie put forward the argument that the VLSI project was the most successful Japanese industrial support programme of the 1970s. They argue that:

> in essence, the program helped Japanese firms achieve technological parity with American firms in the production of the most sophisticated memory devices (1991, p.14).

Michiyuki Uenohara, former Managing Director of NEC, argued that the VLSI project was of great value for his company. Not only did it help develop basic process technologies, which were needed by all the member firms, but it fostered a more co-operative spirit amongst the participating companies (1982, p.46). Furthermore, Borrus, Tyson, and Zysman propose that NEC calculated that the VLSI project enabled them to develop certain memory chip devices five times faster and at one-fifth the cost than they would have achieved working independently (1984, p.14). *The New York Times* (1983) described the project as 'the most successful example of Japanese industrial policy in high technology'[60]. Gregory posits the VLSI initiative as the genesis for the notion of 'Japan Inc'. He further argues that the project contributed substantially to the technological parity achieved by Japanese firms with their American competitors (1986, p.196). In particular, the project had a profound impact on the competitiveness of the semiconductor materials and equipment industries in Japan. These developed during the late-1970s from small and domestically dependent industries, into a world-class group of manufacturers[61].

The affects of the VLSI project were felt beyond the realms of its five central corporate members. As Fransman proves, the benefits of the project were felt by other firms linked to the big five through supplier networks for instance. Thus, the project helped to develop an industrial system, whereby a network of both competing and complementary companies evolved (1990, p.85). Fransman points out that 'no commercializable device was produced in the joint laboratories' (Fransman, 1990, p.96). However, this was not the objective of the project. Rather, it was to develop the process technology, and the technological environment from which to compete. Also, the joint labs received little of the overall resource allocation anyway (as discussed earlier). Instead, the majority of the money and resources were directed towards the labs dominated by one of the corporate members. As the director of one of the joint laboratories concluded, it was mainly through the group labs that the project helped the individual member firms to develop practical technologies (Fransman, 1990, p.97).

As has been emphasised, the semiconductor component industry is highly prone to cyclical ups and downs. This may be a factor to bear in mind when assessing the causal link between the VLSI project and the rapid gains in market share which

Japanese chip producers made in the late 1970s and early 1980s. This is due to the microchip shortage which occurred globally in 1979, and lasted until mid-1980. At this time, the market demand for chips surged to such an extent that the industry simply could not meet the demand. As Ernst argues, the inability of the industry to meet this demand surge stemmed from the period of demand stagnation and profit squeeze of 1974-75 (1983, pp.26-7). In the wake of this crisis, the leading global producers reduced both their R&D outlay and their skilled workforce. Thus, 'the foundations for a new chip shortage are laid' (Ernst, 1983, p.26). Of course, the world semiconductor industry of the 1970s was dominated by American firms. Those corporations affected by the crisis of 1974-75 were invariably US based. Their Japanese counterparts at this time were only beginning to enter the race for market share. Thus, as Japanese firms began to accelerate R&D and production, their American rivals were reducing both. The timing of the VLSI project was ideal for Japanese chip makers: as the project drew to a close, and had generally achieved its technological objectives, the world semiconductor industry entered a period of chronic shortage. Japanese firms, strengthened by their own investment and innovation strategies, in conjunction with the advances made through the VLSI initiative, were strongly placed to increase their capacity, feed the demand, and capture greater market share world-wide. Hence, one may argue that the VLSI project's cessation coinciding with a world microchip shortage (for which most American firms were ill-prepared), was fortuitous for the large Japanese chip manufacturers, as this parallel occurrence accelerated their world market share gains. This argument of course assumes that the VLSI project did indeed play a part in Japanese corporate success - a fact which the counterfactual renders impossible to prove definitively.

3.iv. The VLSI project: structural lessons for Europe

(1) A vital structural asset of the Japanese VLSI project was that its end product (to develop very large scale integration devices for the next generation computer systems) was clear from the beginning. None of the European collaborative semiconductor R&D ventures knew their end goal.

(2) Another core advantage which the VLSI project (and Sematech) had over JESSI, was its decision to focus on inputs rather than final products. This was a crucial choice, given the rapid product obsolescence to which the semiconductor component industry is prone. If you choose to devote most of your resources to developing specific component end products (as JESSI has done), they are often technologically outflanked by competitors. However, if you choose to concentrate on developing process technologies, it is a more incremental procedure, and less vulnerable to rapid technological changes.

(3) The establishment of a central collaborative research facility was beneficial for the same reasons cited earlier concerning Sematech's central R&D facility. However, as both Fong (1990, pp.291-3) and Fransman (1990, pp.80-1) have argued, this facility was largely symbolic. It received only one-fifth of overall funding, and conducted only basic research. The important, applied research was

all conducted in the group labs and controlled by one or other of the companies, acting largely on their own. Each company directed a different technology project (usually within its own facility) and encountered little interference from the other companies. The EC can draw significant lessons from this structural feature: pool money and allocate some of it to a centrally located research lab, where manpower is also pooled, to conduct basic long term research. Channel the majority of the money into specific technology projects, where each member firm works more-or-less on its own. Thus, there is no risk of duplication, and individual innovation is encouraged because the proprietary knowledge will belong to the firm which develops it. Thus, a spirit of collaboration is fostered: some collaboration does in fact occur, in one location, and only for basic research. Applied research is conducted mainly by individual firms, with preferential access rights to any resulting innovation.

(4) A further point deriving from our analysis concerns the project company-led organisational structure of the VLSI project. This could mean that a project is much more likely to be successful if one (or more) company(ies) is/are striving to develop the given technology. If a firm is hungry for a technology advance, and is given the leeway within a collaborative programme to strive to achieve this advance, it will often achieve it. This organisational facet could provide a valuable lesson for European collaborative programmes.

(5) Virtually all decision-making power and operational responsibility rested in one body - the VLSI Technology Research Association. This had the benefit of centralising authority and thus preventing time delays in decision-making and virtually eliminating conflicts between different centres of power. Furthermore, this association represented all of the partners involved, and had both mangers and technicians in its ranks. Thus, it had both a legitimate mandate to direct the project, and the diffusion of knowledge and experience to enable it to tackle diverse problems which might arise.

3.v. Conclusions

An important factor emerges from the above evidence, concerning the relational power of governments and firms in collaborative R&D policy. Despite the widespread view that MITI dominated the VLSI project and imposed its policy choices on industry without consulting them in advance, it emerges that this was not in fact the case. A complex set of bargains (intra-government, intra-industry, and government-industry) were spun out before the project was created; and although MITI was more influential in determining the core dimensions of the consortium's structure (particularly the existence of joint labs), the corporate players basically got to utilise the funding in the ways which they wished. The firms were consulted, cajoled, coerced, and conceded to in various ways both before and during the project's duration.

217

4 International semiconductor trade policies and their impact on EC policy direction

Moving on from collaborative R&D policy, we now examine semiconductor trade policy - specifically the US-Japan Semiconductor Trade Agreement (STA). What role did firms play vis-à-vis government in negotiating the STA and other such trade instruments? In what ways and to what extent has the STA affected the nature of EC policy? Is the following theoretical paradigm practically sustainable: STA ⇨ economic security threat for EC ⇨ protectionist policy approach?

Krasner proposes that states seek four main goals in relation to international trade. These are political power, economic growth, aggregate national income, and social stability (1976, p.319). Thus, from this basic assumption of government trade objectives, we proceed to a discussion of how states go about achieving these aims. The argument here is that an understanding of strategic trade theory helps one to understand contemporary US semiconductor trade policy more clearly. Moreover, a bilateral alliance emerged from this strategic - or managed - trade policy which has had a profound impact on EC policy direction. The US-Japanese alliance increased pressure on the EC to assist semiconductor firms based in the Community to position themselves in global markets; as well as increasing the propensity of the EC to adopt a more protectionist position towards non-Community based firms and a more mercantilist trade stance vis-à-vis its main chip producing trade partners. This latter development may be explained in theoretical terms through recourse to economic security variables, and in practical terms by a Commission perception that it was being 'ganged up on' by its main trading rivals.

We shall proceed by firstly, assessing the contemporary trade relationship between the US and Japan over microchips, with particular attention being devoted to the Semiconductor Trade Agreement (STA). Within this, an attempt will be made to establish the role of large firms in determining the inter-state bargain which resulted in the creation of the STA. Secondly, through placing EC trade policy development within the context of global trade policy activities, combined with a theoretical examination of economic security, this work endeavours to ascertain the extent to which external variables have an impact upon EC policy. In particular, the intention is to gauge the degree to which the EC's interventionist policy regime (as discussed in chapter four) may be attributable to extra-Communitarian governmental trade activities.

4.i. US - Japan trade bargains and the role of the firm

In 1986, the Reagan administration, under pressure from the US Congress, signed a semiconductor component accord, regulating chip trade with Japan. This agreement served to illustrate the bargaining power which the industry had acquired during the 1980s. As previously discussed, the vigorous competition from Japanese firms led senior figures within the American semiconductor industry to actively seek government help. Their success led to the industry being targeted by the US government for preferential policy treatment. The official reasoning stemmed largely from a combination of national security concerns and the centrality of semiconductor chips to the American economy due to their enabling nature. In effect, this policy targeting symbolised the practical implementation of strategic trade theory. This concept was discussed in chapter two. Let us briefly recap on its main tenets. Strategic trade theory has emerged in conjunction with the globalisation process. As Krugman advances, globalisation has meant that the nature of trade has been fundamentally transformed: it has moved from a comparative advantage based system to a much more complicated system, involving numerous new elements (1986, p.9). The complex nature of this globalised trade system necessitates a rethinking of the applicability of classical trade models. Thus, strategic trade theory emerged to occupy the ideological middle ground between traditional notions of free trade on the one side, and protectionism on the other. Stegemann defines the term's precise meaning as follows:

'strategic' indicates that that these [new trade] models incorporate international interdependence of policy actions in an oligopolistic environment. Thus, each government takes into account some response by foreign firms or governments in calculating its best course of action (1989, p.75).

Milner and Yoffie identify the central element of this theory as a government's erection (or threat thereof) of trade barriers in direct response to another government's protection of its domestic market (1989, p.240). The policy is aimed by Country A at firms based in Country B, and in retaliation for barriers confronting Country A based firms in gaining access to Country B's home market. Thus, it is a tit-for-tat process: if you do not give our firms access to your home market, we will restrict your firms access to ours. The degree of access demanded is to be based on the concept of equal reciprocity. This approach is based on a more fundamental belief that, as Borrus, Tyson, and Zysman argue:

under imperfectly competitive conditions there is potential for government policy to affect the competitive positions of individual firms and countries in world markets in enduring ways (1984, p.11).

The authors further advance the notion that this central, activist role of government in the strategic trade policy approach is particularly relevant for shaping the competitiveness of industries acutely affected by the rate of technological change, and wherein R&D is a core factor input - with very high economies of scale (Borrus et al., 1984, p.13). It is contended that such factors create market imperfections for these industries. Hence, knowledge intensive sectors, at the frontier of innovation, are advanced as prime examples for the application of strategic trade policy. Of these, the authors further give priority to those industries which have a direct technological impact (or spill-over) upon numerous other industries (1984, p.20). Borrus et al. referred to these as key industries, the public promotion of which has gains for an entire society (1992, p.26). As is proven in this chapter, such academic recommendations were subsequently applied in real-world situations. No where was this more evident than in semiconductors, the vanguard industry of the information revolution. This further underlines the interconnection between the knowledge factor and policy power.

In terms of actual legal instruments, US strategic trade policy functions primarily through Section 301 of the 1974 Trade Act (the so-called Super 301). The amended version of this addresses any 'act, policy, or practice' by a foreign country that 'is unreasonable or discriminatory and burdens or restricts United States commerce' (OTA, 1991, p.130). It is worth noting that Section 301 countervenes the GATT/WTO rules, in that it constitutes unilateral action against America's trading partners, without their prior consent. Such action is based solely on a US judicial ruling regarding the actions or legislation of another state. Section 301 may therefore often violate multilateral agreements undertaken by the US[62]. Although slightly modified by Congress in 1988, this remains a formidable statutory tool of trade diplomacy. The European Commission has repeatedly voiced its opposition to Section 301. The Commission stresses the instrument's illegality in international trade law, and has consistently sought, through the GATT negotiations, to eliminate it from US trade law[63]. Hence, this trade instrument may be perceived as a significant area of contention in international trade. Also, we see that its very existence is viewed with considerable hostility by the European Commission, and invokes a confrontational response from the Community. The federal agency directly empowered by Section 301 to investigate allegations of unfair practices, is the office of the US Trade Representative. Super 301 was permitted to lapse in 1991. It was revived in early 1994 by the Clinton Administration. Its renewal was seen as a warning to Japan, threatening trade sanctions if the Japanese government did not negotiate a significant reduction in its $59 billion trade surplus[64]. EU Trade Commissioner, Leon Brittan responded with condemnation of the controversial policy instrument, and the press declared that its reinstatement risked straining trade relations still further between the US and its main trading partners, Japan and the European Community (*International Herald Tribune*, 5/6 March 1994). A crucial point is that the central actors in the initiation of such a Section 301 centred strategic trade policy approach are large firms (and their related trade associations). This, as we have already seen, has been the case in the US since the mid-1980s for trade in semiconductors[65]. Section 301 was first invoked by the Semiconductor Industry Association in 1985. This was followed later in the year by individual suits filed by major US microchip makers such as Intel and National Semiconductor[66]. In addition to charging that Japanese firms were dumping chips on the US market, the SIA alleged that the Japanese government employed unfair trade practices in relation to foreign firm access to the Japanese semiconductor market. The association demanded that the US government retaliate against Japanese chip imports into the US, if its members were not granted greater access to the Japanese market (Milner and Yoffie, 1989, p.254). The US government's response was to initiate a dialogue with their Japanese counterpart, in order to reach a settlement which was agreeable to

American semiconductor producers. Such an actuality is a strong indicator of the strength which firms now possessed in international diplomacy. The result was the 1986 Semiconductor Trade Agreement. As Milner and Yoffie state, this agreement 'mirrored the industry's demands' (1989, p.255).

4.ii. The US-Japan semiconductor trade agreements

In September 1986 the 'Arrangement between the Government of Japan and the Government of the United States of America concerning Trade in Semiconductor Products' was signed. It was a momentous event in modern international trade, as it symbolised the first significant agreement signed by the US government for a high technology sector, and the first motivated by a loss of competitiveness rationale. Furthermore, it was the first trade accord which sought to extend market access abroad. In addition to these facts, the STA was the first time in modern US-Japan relations that the American government threatened Japanese firms with sanctions if they did not comply with the rules laid down in a trade accord (Tyson, 1993, p.109). This fact lends further strength to our argument that the semiconductor industry had political weight far above its own market or employment size. Such policy power stems directly from its control over an enabling technology which formed the basis for the information age.

In terms of devices covered, the deal focused on memory chips, microcontrollers, and microprocessors (Baldwin, 1990, p.5). This accord had two dimensions. The first established a price floor, intended to prevent Japanese firms dumping chips in the US or third markets. The second endeavoured to prise open the Japanese market to chip imports. The latter objective was to be achieved through the Japanese government agreeing to one-fifth of its domestic chip market being controlled by foreign firms by late 1991. This would mean almost a doubling of the existing share of the market controlled by non-Japanese (mainly American) firms. Tyson agrees that this targeting of market share per centages constitutes the essence of one form[67] of managed trade (1993, p.133). In orthodox trade terms, this practice constitutes what Bhagwati terms a voluntary import expansion (VIE) agreement (1988, p.83). Interestingly, this fixed per centage was included in a side letter, and not in the agreement's main text (Baldwin, 1990, p.6). This was of course to maintain an air of liberal trade respectability about the agreement, rather than exposing it for what it really was: an attempt by two governments to co-operatively manage trade in semiconductors, and fix both prices and market shares for their own companies. Also, the agreement had negative side effects on other sectors of American industry. As O'Shea argues, related industries such as computer manufacturers opposed the agreement due to the chip scarcity and subsequent price increases which it precipitated (1988, p.1).

The relative bargaining strength of industry continued in the wake of the STA's creation. The SIA charged that the Japanese government and chip producers were not complying with the STA, and should be sanctioned. As a direct response, the Reagan administration imposed 100 per cent tariffs on $300 million worth of Japanese imports[68]. The political importance of these sanctions was enormous. As

Yoffie points out, they marked the first such punitive sanctions imposed by the US government on Japanese firms since World War Two (1988, p.83). Krauss argues that, although the White House was concerned with the ramifications of these sanctions for US-Japan relations, these worries were offset by the perceived importance of the semiconductor industry to American national interest (1993, p.268). US-Japan trade negotiations and agreements were undertaken for several other industrial sectors during the second half of the 1980s. However, none displayed such strong inter-industry cohesion and public-private alliance-building as did the STA. For example, after two years of negotiations, an agreement was reached between the US and Japanese governments in 1988 concerning American firms access to Japanese construction markets[69]. This agreement was reached without the application of American sanctions, and was stable in its practical manifestation. Both the semiconductor and the construction agreements involved virtually the same governmental actors and similar negotiating strategies on both sides, but had divergent results - the former displaying an inherent instability when applied, whilst the latter did not (Krauss, 1993, p.289). As analysts[70] of the two cases have argued, the more flexible American approach to construction may be attributed to two factors: first, a weaker, more fragmented industry voice and political-corporate consensus existed for the construction negotiations; and second, the perceived threat of Japanese competition to the US national interest was much greater for semiconductors than it was for construction (Krauss, 1993, p.291). Therefore, on behalf of semiconductor manufacturers, the American government was willing to severely damage its overall politico-economic relations with a key ally. No such brinkmanship was enacted for the construction industry. This fact further strengthens our argument that firms which control an enabling technology display a stronger negotiating position with governments than do firms in other industries. These firms interact on an equal basis with governmental actors, and often take the lead in defining and directing policy. The result is the New Diplomacy model, allocating firms a seat next to governments at the high table of international negotiations.

Tyson indicates her unequivocal support for the semiconductor agreement when she argues that without government activism in semiconductor markets in the mid-1980s, Japanese firms would have attained a dominant position within the industry (1993, p.106). She also acknowledges the lead role played by US industry (mainly through the SIA) in negotiating the agreement (1993, pp.107-9). In terms of its results, Tyson points to both the diminishing number of Japanese semiconductor anti-dumping cases following the agreement's enactment, as well as the rise in non-Japanese market share in Japan after 1986[71], as solid indicators of its success (1993, p.111). Both of these examples are correct. However, the real issue is not whether alleged dumping decreased or more foreign (read 'American') chips were sold in Japan. It is whether or not this agreement distorted the notion of liberal trade, and caused the emergence of a bilateral cartel at the heart of the international semiconductor market. There is little doubt that this was in fact the most significant outcome of the US-Japan semiconductor accord. The agreement was intended to be an agreement which liberalised world trade in semiconductor components. Instead, as Baldwin illustrates, it had the opposite affect. He posits that the STA in fact produced the exact opposite results from those set initially. Thus, the price floor which was set for chips led to a reduction in production capacity, higher world market prices, and a 'cartelization of the market' (1990, p.21). Regarding the accord's second pillar, it may be argued that the main mechanism used for market access - established market share targets - distorted the market by setting artificial demand levels within Japan.

The STA had a five year mandate, which expired in mid-1991. When this time was approaching, numerous US semiconductor executives, in conjunction with federal government officials and political patrons, deemed it necessary to renew the agreement, This was due in large part to the fact that the agreement's objectives had not yet been met regarding Japanese market access levels. As mentioned earlier, American computer producers had resented the first STA. By 1990 their objections had been registered by their semiconductor manufacturing peers. Thus, together, the two industries sought a renegotiated version of the accord to be enacted upon the expiration of STA 1 (Tyson 1993, p.130). This would restrict the STA's antidumping provisions, and extend the scope and strength of its market access instruments. The Sematech consortium strengthened these industry demands for market access. In a 1991 testimony before the US House of Representatives, Sematech's President, William J. Spencer, pitched access to the Japanese market as Sematech's main requirement for increasing its members market share. Spencer stressed that this could only be achieved through government policy, and that the STA was a significant step in the right direction:

> Most importantly, we need open access to the largest semiconductor market in the world - Japan ...The New Semiconductor Agreement recently negotiated and signed by the US and Japanese governments will help. Without access to that Japanese market, however, US companies always will be hard pressed to prosper[72].

The corporate actors got what they wanted. After a new series of inter-governmental negotiations, a new five year trade agreement was signed in mid-1991. The Americans shift in emphasis from antidumping to market access was explicit. The US lifted all remaining sanctions on Japanese producers for antidumping violations of the first STA, and in return, the Japanese government agreed (in the accord's main text) to 'facilitate' a 20 per cent market access target (Tyson, 1993, p.131). Also, Japan agreed that this target should be achieved by the end of 1992. The target was reached by the last quarter of 1992. Figures for that quarter proved that foreign firms supplied 20.2 per cent of the Japanese chip market. This was an increase of more than 4 per cent (from 16 per cent) in one quarter of the year alone[73]. Speculation abounds as to how this was achieved[74]. What is undeniable is that the Japanese government played a central role in bringing it about, under pressure of renewed trade sanctions by the US government if they failed. This managed trade scenario not only distorted market forces, but it also seriously damaged the global trading system in semiconductor components.

Carla Hills, a former US Trade Representative, lends support to this criticism of the second STA, citing numerical targets as particularly damaging to international trade[75]. In the next section we will attempt a damage assessment for the nature of EC trade policy, as a result of these illiberal US-Japan trade activities.

4.iii. The impact of non-Community governmental trade activities on EC policy

Two intertwined issues shall now be examined: first, the causal relationship between the US and Japanese governments trade policies (especially the STA), and EC policy direction; and second, a more abstract evaluation of the role played by economic security variables in defining the ideological framework for EC semiconductor trade policy.

US-Japan relations have been close and cordial since the end of World War Two. More accurately, they may be described as a partnership of patronage, whereby in return for America's military protection (or threat in the immediate post-war years), Japan has been willing to follow the US lead on most trade issues. That is not to say that there have not been conflicts. Witness for instance the long and arduous dispute concerning textiles. A bilateral trade regime has often resulted though, with the two countries negotiating voluntary export restraint agreements for industries such as ceramics, and textiles eventually (O'Shea, 1988, p.23). This managed trade approach between the two nations emerged as early as the 1950s. Thus, by the 1980s:

> Japan and the US had become deeply interdependent in a way hard to imagine for two nations so separated by geography, history, and culture... the more vital aspect of this interdependence was economic. The two economies had become knitted together by enormous flows of raw materials, finished goods, services, capital, and technology (O'Shea, 1988, p.22).

Furthermore, their combined wealth, market size, and production capacity means that the maintenance of a liberal world trading order hinges on maintaining the joint commitment of Japan and the US. Conversely, their joint action can also serve to manipulate the world trading order.

A major factor which emerged from the STA, was the resultant increases in memory chip prices on the world market. This resulted in part from a reduction in Japanese chip production capacity directly after the STA's enactment. More importantly, setting a floor on chip prices automatically hands government a way of controlling the industry, and this led to the Japanese MITI forming, in effect, a cartel amongst Japanese chip makers (*The Economist*, 27 March 1993, p.66). Industry commentators conclude that, together, US and Japanese memory chip manufacturers made up to $4 billion in extra profits as a direct result of the STA[76]. Thus, a global price regime emerged which was set largely by governments, rather than the market. This situation had a significant impact upon the European Community. As was illustrated in chapter four, two-thirds of European chip consumption was fed by imports. Increases in world market prices for the most

224

widely used devices (memory chips), had a profound impact on European industry, through increased component input costs. These price rises were felt across a wide range of industries, ranging from telecommunication equipment to automobiles. Pressure was exerted by these industries on governmental actors to respond to the situation. As Tyson states:

> When chip prices soared and supplies became scarce around the world in 1987 and 1988, foreign governments scrambled to promote their own interests (1993, p.149).

The ultimate responsibility for action rested with the European Commission, given its stated competence in external trade issues. It duly signalled its intention to act, and declared that it was concerned over the affects on Community industrial competitiveness and trade flows caused by bilateral trade agreements between the US and Japan[77]. In a report on US trade and investment barriers, the Commission referred to the US-Japan trade agreements as a 'global partnership', which has 'discriminatory elements' (CEC, 1992, p.5). The Commission responded in several ways. Trade tools employed centred around antidumping and rules of origin, both of which have been shown[78] to be protectionist in nature. Antidumping investigations were undertaken against several Japanese (and Korean) chip importers, resulting in 1989 price agreements; and EC trade law was reviewed to establish fabrication as the rule of origin for microchips (Tyson, 1993, p.149). Senior Commission officials[79] argue that the use of these trade tools was seen as a means by which the Commission could gain leverage with global competitors. Thus, these official sources advance that these trade instruments were implemented largely in response to what was happening globally - especially the US-Japan STA. Furthermore, the JESSI consortium was created in 1988, partly in response to extra-European trade activities[80].

A theoretical explanation of these events may be derived from economic security factors. As Meltzer argued, 'international trade relations can evoke strong security concerns' (1977, p.223). Definitions and utilisation's of economic security were discussed in chapter two. We link the concept in here, at the international system level of analysis, because as Buzan (1983) argues: 'national security is fundamentally dependent on international dynamics'[81]. The basic premise herein is that systemic activities frequently threaten the economic security of a given politico-economic entity, and thus have an impact upon the policy of that entity's governmental actors. In real terms, we are arguing that global economic activities often affect the nature of EC policy through instilling the Community's governmental actors with a feeling of external economic threat[82]. Using economic security as an analytical tool implies that one accepts some of the basic tenets of realism. Most notably, economic security theory complies with the realist arguments that states are the dominant actors within the international system, and inherently act out of self interest. We accept a modified version of this premise: in considerations of threats to economic security, states perceive the threat to be emanating from other governments. No real consideration is given to other actors

225

in the system (such as transnational corporations or non-governmental organisations) as possible instigators of the threat. Rather, these other actors are generally seen as mere instruments of governments. Such a perception is inherently flawed in light of the changes which globalisation has wrought within the international system. Nevertheless, this work shall restrict itself here to using economic security as a heuristic tool based upon governmental actors threat perceptions. After all, threats to economic security are rarely tangible, and usually emanate from actor perceptions. Indeed, the concept as a whole derives from a potent cocktail of speculation, supported by selective (often suspect) facts, and even Orwellian paranoia.

In light of our understanding of economic security, the EC's reactions to US-Japanese trade activities for semiconductors may be interpreted as defensive. Furthermore, these activities (antidumping, rules of origin, R&D consortia) may - however intangibly - be seen as a multi-pronged response to the perceived threat posed by Japan and the US to the economic security of the European Community. This 'threat' was to the competitiveness of European-based information technology industries, and by extension, to the welfare of EC citizens. This opinion was implicit for instance in European Commission President Delors speech at the 1993 Copenhagen Inter-Governmental Conference[83]. The perceived threat derived from two main areas of vulnerability. These may be delineated as trade dependence and international competitiveness. In the former, as defined by Hager (1975), economic interdependence and the high proportion of the EC's overall gross domestic product (GDP) represented by exports, is a large measure of vulnerability. Changes abroad which affect market access, can have implications for EC domestic welfare and employment. Based on Delors Copenhagen speech, and on the EC's defensive trade response to the US-Japan semiconductor market access agreements, some in the Community obviously see trade dependence as an area of economic insecurity. In relation to the impact on EC policy caused by bilateral trade relations between the US and Japan, it is evident that actions such as the 1986 STA can be interpreted as a threat to the Community's economic security. The price increases and chip scarcity that resulted from this accord led to cost and supply problems for a wide range of European industries, and may be interpreted as threatening European jobs and income. As Hager argues, price stability is a policy target of any governmental actor. Significant and rapid price changes (such as those precipitated by the STA) may be viewed as an economic security threat (Hager 1975, p.136).

The creation of the R&D consortium, JESSI, may be viewed as a response to the economic security threat posed through international competitiveness. That is to say, JESSI symbolised the preponderance of the economic security threat view, as it gave teeth to the argument that a European response was needed to counteract American and Japanese combined domination of the international system through their technological (and market) leadership (Dell, 1987, p.33). Within such a view, Dell (1987) argues, power depends to a great extent on technology. The state which controls the leading technologies has a much stronger position within international negotiations. In this, traditional economic security theory runs

226

counter to our central thesis that power does depend greatly on access to technology; but it is the firms, and not the governments, that control technology. This perceived area of vulnerability may be seen in light of American and Japanese activities also. However, in this case the external activities of competitor countries are pursued unilaterally and domestically (the creation of Sematech and the VLSI Project, respectively). Their impact are felt throughout the system never-the-less, and prod the EC (and individual European governments) into defensive action, through creating a European semiconductor consortium. Building upon the economic security interpretation of such defensive activities, we may also advance a structuralist[84] conceptualisation of the European R&D and trade response to external pressures. The basic argument here is that the weak ally to improve their position vis-à-vis the strong. Structuralists argue that, firstly, a decisive factor in the emergence of semiconductor (and information technology in general) collaboration during the 1980s was Europe's relative international weakness in those technologies (Sandholtz, 1992, p.12). Combining this with the economic security explanation, competition from the US and Japan was threatening national (or Community[85]) economic interests, and collaboration was a defensive alliance[85]. Secondly, there may have been other choices for the participants but, as the structuralist argument implies, none were, on their own, realistic. To expand a little on this, some of the firms involved in forging the EC defensive policy bargains did pursue other options. Most notably, these firms formed bilateral or trilateral inter-firm strategic alliances, which did not involve governmental partners. Witness for instance the alliance which Siemens developed in 1992 with Toshiba and IBM to develop advanced memory chips (*The New York Times*, 'Rethinking the National Chip Policy', 14 July 1992). However, none considered it viable to pursue only those other options and preferred instead to pursue several different types of alliances in parallel. A third factor in the structural explanation of EC policy responses is the rise of Japan as a technological power, and the argument that this change in structural power was a further dimension precipitating European collaboration (Sandholtz, 1992, p.13). This is true in so far as the rapidly increasing Japanese share of the EC information market during the early 1980s did precipitate a widely held perception that the very survival of many weak European firms was at stake. Consequently, alliance was an attractive option. This perception also contributed to the defensive European policy response to counter this alleged threat. Several of the larger electronics firms had a direct impact on policy due to their strong positions on this issue. For instance, Thomson CEO Alain Gomez has argued[86] that Japanese competition threatens the existence of numerous European industrial sectors, especially automobiles and electronics. In his opinion, without a co-ordinated European policy response, 'all could be lost'. His solution was a defensive strategy, resting on protectionist trade tools such as high import tariffs (*Fortune,* 1992, p.159). Therefore, although alliance was the main option pursued by the large European electronics firms, protective trade tools were perceived by some as an added fallback.

5 Conclusions

In terms of understanding EC trade policy from a structural change perspective, Baldwin argues that non-tariff protectionism occurs in response to structural change in international production (Baldwin, 1988, p.207). Evidence in this and previous chapters show that the EC employs several such non-tariff measure. The most prominent of these are anti-dumping legislation, rules of origin, and local content requirements. Our analysis, in conjunction with academic commentators such as Baldwin (1988), argues that there is a causal linkage between aspects of the new production regime, such as offshore manufacturing, and the EC's implementation of these non-tariff barriers which distort trade. This policy approach has been termed 'the new protectionism' (Baldwin, 1988, p.207). Therefore, a structural change analysis of the nature of EC policy concurs with the EC level study conducted in chapter four. Both conclude that EC trade policy for industries such as semiconductors is inherently protectionist.

Strategic trade theory has been the dominant ideology in defining trade policies since the mid-1980s. Our work shows that this is true not only in the US but also in the EC. It is worth noting that this policy approach is not particularly new. As both Bhagwati (1991) and Irwin (1990) suggest, the present targeting of so-called key industries is similar to the infant industry approach initiated in the latter half of the eighteenth century[87]. Protecting infant industries through employing protectionist trade tools such as import tariffs was advocated by mercantilists such as Alexander Hamilton and Friedrich List, and was engrained into international trade theory by John Stuart Mill in the first edition of *Principles of Political Economy* (1848)[88]. The infant industry doctrine thus advocated the selective targeting of industries for government protection. These sectors would subsequently be managed by the state until they were able to compete internationally without protection. We conclude that strategic trade policy is the protectionist ideology of the GATT/WTO-policed, global economy. Instead of being directed at infant industries attempting to attain competitiveness, it is aimed at established industries striving to maintain or regain competitiveness. In line with the demise of tariffs as the epicentre of protectionism, strategic trade policy employs non-tariff trade barriers (such as local content requirements and voluntary import agreements) to achieve its objectives. Regardless of the open trading regime existing for other industrial sectors, all of the countries serving as headquarters for international microchip producing firms employ this neo-protectionist policy approach for the semiconductor industry. Although somewhat more liberal than its predecessors and incorporating a new, multilateral dimension[89], the 1996 US-Japan semiconductor deal is illustrative of a continuity in US trade policy thinking and practice. Moreover, recent developments in EU trade policy strategy indicate a move towards a more managed trade stance. This approach has been extrapolated as a Market Access Strategy[90]. The Commission has expressed its wish to sharpen the EU's trade policy so as to make it more effective at opening up foreign markets that are argued to be vital for European companies exports. The proposed Market Access Strategy seeks to identify and tackle trade obstacles, involve business more closely, improve inter-EU policy co-ordination, and promote market-opening initiatives. The strategy was approved by the Council of Ministers in November 1996[91]. This policy signifies a move towards a more proactive and co-ordinated trade policy on the part of the European partners; one in line with the managed trade approach of the US.

We have previously alluded to the problems inherent in identifying which sectors of the economy are strategic and which are not. The first point advanced here is that notions of strategic sectors differ over time. For instance towards the end of the Korean War, angora goat farmers managed to persuade the US Congress that angora wool (mohair) was worthy of inclusion in a strategic commodity programme for sheep wool[92]. Since then, military usage of mohair has declined and, ironically, by 1990, almost 60 per cent of the subsidised mohair was exported to the Soviet Union. These subsidies totalled $50 million per annum by the early 1990s for instance. Attempts by the Clinton Administration to phase out the protective subsidies resulting from the strategic targeting of mohair, led to difficulties. The angora ranchers evidently did not wish to forego their habitual annual subsidies from the federal government, and pressurised their members of Congress to prevent their removal from the strategic list. This symbolised yet another domestic problem for an embattled administration. It should serve to prove the long-term problems which can arise from targeting sectors of the economy for preferential policy treatment. The Clinton Administration's continued enthusiasm for managed trade and the targeting of several high technology sectors would indicate that this lesson was not heeded.

A second proposition which we would put forward is that an explicit government acknowledgement that some industries are more equal than others, leads to a proliferation of claims for strategic targeting, and both corporate and public dissatisfaction if certain claims for strategic value are chosen above others. The Clinton Administration's emphasis on economic competitiveness as a central element of post-Cold War national security, and its creation of a National Economic Council, were catalysts for uncompetive industries to seek out the national security umbrella for shelter. As *The New York Times* noted:

domestic industries are beginning to line up for Government protection against foreign competition, contending that their survival is vital to the nation's economic security (19 January, 1993).

Applicants for the strategic sector mantle included the oil industry and manufacturers of ceramic computer-chip housings. Clearly, those sectors rejected will view the administration unfavourably. This can subsequently translate into electoral votes, through lower campaign contributions for instance. More importantly though is the fact that the extension of the US list of strategic sectors can lead to trade tensions between it and its main trading partners.

From the evidence, one may forward the hypothesis that there is an undeniable linkage between the increased popularity of strategic trade policy, and the enhanced role of the firm in international negotiations and policy formulation.

Strategic trade policy is usually implemented at the behest and with the involvement of firms. In the case of the US, we may witness the utilisation of strategic trade policies by three consecutive administrations for sectors such as semiconductors, telecom equipment, and commercial aircraft. In all of these cases, American-based firms were the instigators of this policy approach (Milner and Yoffie, 1989, p.240). As Robert Galvin, Chairman of Motorola, stated, President Bush for instance, listened to the suggestions of American businessmen and enabled them to refine policy. As a result, Galvin believed that 'the Japanese got the message on trade'[93].

Advancing from these empirical findings, we may interpret our evidence with the aid of state-firm bargaining theory. This chapter illustrates, firstly, that domestic policy bargains for semiconductor policy in both the United States and Japan are (and have been) frequently initiated and shaped by large firms. The evidence from both the Sematech and VLSI initiatives supports this conclusion (albeit less equivocally in the VLSI case). This concurs with the arguments advanced in chapters four and five regarding semiconductor policy bargaining in the European Community. Furthermore, and more importantly for this chapter, the power of large firms is not restricted to their domestic environments. We have shown that large chip makers display just as much power in determining external (i.e. trade and competition) policies and in shaping inter-state bargains. As witnessed by the US-Japan Semiconductor Trade Agreement for instance, the inter-state bargain was initiated and shaped primarily by the large (American) semiconductor producers and their associations. Similarly, EC trade policy negotiations with the Japanese government and individual Japanese firms over antidumping issues for example, have been dominated by the Commission-firm policy partnership. Taken together, this chapter advances ample proof to substantiate the theory that the nature of international diplomacy has changed: politicians, diplomats and government bureaucrats have been joined by national and multinational level corporate executives in the joint negotiation of both bilateral and multilateral agreements (Stopford and Strange, 1991, p.21). This new diplomacy brings together the traditional state-state bargaining with both firm-firm and firm-state negotiations, under one intertwined international bargaining framework[94]. Each bargaining side of the triangle has an impact upon the other, although the three are not always undertaken in a co-ordinated or simultaneous fashion.

Stopford and Strange's (1991) model of international state-firm bargaining and the emergence of triangular diplomacy, rests upon the notion of structural change. Triangular diplomacy developed due to systemic changes in the international political economy (Stopford and Strange, 1991, p.4). More vividly, the authors argue that multinational firms were 'thrust more squarely centre-stage in world affairs' (1991, p.65) by the forces of structural change. What exactly does this mean in applied terms? We discussed the theory of structural change both in chapter two and again briefly at the outset of this chapter. Building on the work of Strange (1988), it has been emphasised throughout this work that of the four pillars of structural power through which structural change occurs, technology, or the

knowledge structure is the most influential within policy barg

such as semiconductors. Our main findings and subsequent a

around this notion. Further to supporting one of our central ther.

have access to the knowledge structure can help determine the pa‹

structural change. Such firms have the ability (although not ı

capacity or the desire) to both shape the other pillars of the interna

and have an impact upon the competitive advantage and economi

individual nations. As Strange puts it, transnational firms command oı

is an 'economic weapon' which governments need if they are to s

compete for world market shares (Strange, 1992, pp.6-7). Governmen

obliged to bargain with these firms, and to share with them the power to ‹

policy. This fact is applicable at all levels of governance within the inteı

system. As previous chapters have illustrated, this argument is equally ap

to the European Community. Ultimately, we would advance the argume

evidence from the American case supports that advanced for the EC: the con

core, enabling technologies is the central determining factor in p

determination in this era of globalisation. Those firms which control

technology, or knowledge, factor, have the ability to substantially influence

policy bargain. This conclusion may also be framed in terms of directly resultı

from structural change. In that theory, technology (stemming from the knowledჳ

structure) is the most powerful of the global system's four pillars. Knowledge ha

an impact upon the production, finance, and security structures of the international

political economy - whereas the reverse is not always the case. Furthermore, as

Strange argues, control of the knowledge structure enables an actor to gain

relational power. By this we mean the authority of a given international actor to

force another actor in the system to do that which they would not do voluntarily

(Strange, 1988, p.24). This is the key question: who controls the knowledge

structure, and thus defines the limits of structural change. In terms of tangible

systemic actors, governments and corporations emerge as the two leading

contenders for determining the nature, pace, and effect of structural change[95]. This

change occurs through advances in technology.

Our findings indicate that for the twentieth century's main transformative

technologies, in the era of globalisation, firms access to the knowledge structure

enables them to partially define the limits of structural change. This is the situation

in which global semiconductor producers find themselves. They control the

microchip meta-technology which first, shapes modern production processes and

systems, and defines products. Second, it has enabled the liberalisation of

international finance and thus facilitates the mobility of capital. Third, this meta-

technology forms the foundations of modern military hardware and defence

systems. As our research has shown, even those governments which at first

spurned policy activism vis-à-vis industry (such as the Reagan Administration)

were forced to negotiate with large semiconductor producers, in formulating both

domestic and international policy.

Cited in Kevin P. Phillips, 'US Industrial Policy: Inevitable and Ineffective, *Harvard Business Review,* July-August 1992, p.107.

The Council of Competitiveness was established by the US government as a private sector advisory body on industrial and trade policy issues.

3   These sanctions took the form of fines, imposed by the US federal government on individual Japanese companies.

4   Yoffie, 1988, p.89. Yoffie provides an interesting and detailed account of how semiconductor producers and users embarked, in the mid-1980s, on a bargaining process with the US federal government, to build political advantage, and offset Japanese competition.

5   'Generic' technologies have been described by Lewis Branscomb (1992) as those technologies 'making up the technological infrastructure that makes all industrial innovation possible'. An example would be computer-aided design tools.

6   President Bush's 1992 Budget endorsed government support for R&D in generic and enabling technologies (OTA, 1991, p.13).

7   Comment from the *Los Angeles Times,* cited in the *International Herald Tribune*, 9 November, 1994.

8   US Department of Commerce, *Emerging Technologies: A Survey of Technical and Economic Opportunities,* Spring 1990; and US Department of Defence, *Critical Technologies Plan,* 15 March, 1990; as cited in The National Critical Technologies Panel, *Report of the National Critical Technologies Panel,* Washington DC, US Government Printing Office, March 1991.

9   The Semiconductor Industry Association was founded in 1977 by five of the main American semiconductor manufacturers - Intel, Motorola, AMD, Fairchild, and National Semiconductor. Most of its founders had previously been members of wider electronics industry organisations, but found that these did not adequately address their needs as chip makers. Therefore, the SIA was intended to be a purely semiconductor industry organisation, aimed at building industrywide initiatives. Thus, it would build political advantage through providing a united front amongst most of the US's leading chip makers. It rapidly extended its membership to more than fifty of America's leading chip manufacturers.

10   Semiconductor Industry Association and Dewey Ballantine, *Creating Advantage: Semiconductors and Government Industrial Policy in the 1990s,* SIA, 1992, p.ii.

11   The Committee comprises eight senior industry executives, and five high-ranking federal government officials, including the Deputy Commerce Secretary.

12   National Advisory Committee on Semiconductors, *A Strategic Industry At Risk,* A Report to the President and the Congress, November 1989, Washington DC, p.1.

13   Ibid., pp.2-3.

14   As previously discussed, the SIA were actively courting government intervention in semiconductor manufacturing research and development during the mid-1980s. The association released its own report, in advance of the DSB's, calling for the creation of a semiconductor industry R&D consortium. This, in effect, provided the main catalyst for government activism.

15   This is a committee comprising scientists and engineers, which advises the Under-secretary of Defence for Research and Engineering.

16   Report of the US Defence Science Board, cited in M. Franklin Squires, Chief Administrative Officer of Sematech, in *Technology Policy and Competitiveness: The Government's Role*, testimony before the United States Senate Committee on Governmental Affairs, Subcommittee on Government Information and Regulation, 12 March 1992, Washington DC p.3.

17   In 'The Genesis of Sematech' diagram, the following abbreviations apply: Department of Defence (DOD), Department of Commerce (DOC), National Semiconductor Consortium (NSC), Semiconductor Industry Association (SIA), and Defence Advanced Research Projects Agency (DARPA).

18   The companies involved were Advanced Micro Devices, AT&T, Digital Equipment Corporation, Harris Corporation, Hewlett-Packard, Intel, IBM, LSI Logic, Micron Technology, Motorola, National Semiconductor, NCR, Rockwell International, and Texas Instruments.

19   'Captive' suppliers are those semiconductor manufacturers that produce entirely for in-house use. For instance, IBM traditionally manufactured large amounts of semiconductor chips, but these were used exclusively for the company's own computer products. 'Merchant' manufacturers are those chip makers that produce almost entirely for sale on the open market. These firms consume in-house only a small per centage, or perhaps none at all, of their total semiconductor output.

20   Given Harris's position as the top supplier of integrated circuits to the US military (Sematech Strategic Overview, 1991, pp.5-1), its withdrawal from Sematech may indicate a weakening connection between the military and the Sematech consortium. This argument is further enhanced by the civilianisation of Sematech's military partner, DARPA, the preceding year.

21   Interview conducted with an LSI Logic executive, Milpitas, California, May 1993.

22   Dynamic Random Access Memories (DRAMs) and Application Specific Integrated Circuits (ASICs) are very different technologies. This difference is discussed in chapter three. It did not make business sense for LSI Logic to invest time and money into the development of a technology which was not relevant to its core business concentration.

23   William J. Spenser, *Semiconductors: The Role of Consortia*, op.cit., p.4.

24   Although SEMATECH did begin producing chips at high volume in 1990, ostensibly as a way of perfecting manufacturing techniques that could be transferred to the member companies.

25 United States General Accounting Office, *Federal Research: SEMATECH's Technological Progress and Proposed R&D Program*, Briefing Report to the Chairman, Subcommittee on Defence, Committee on Appropriations, US Senate, July 1992, Washington DC, p.1.

26 SEMATECH, *Strategic Overview*, official Sematech publication, 1991, p.1.

27 A majority, but not all, of Sematech's R&D is conducted in Austin. A number of Centres of Excellence have been established in several American universities, to assist Sematech in specific areas of semiconductor manufacturing R&D.

28 Alic, Branscomb, Brooks, Carter, and Epstein (1992), *Beyond Spinoff: Military and Commercial Technologies in a Changing World.*

29 Which became ARPA in 1992, as the agency was civilianised.

30 Katz and Ordover 1990, cited in Grindley et al. 1994, p.732.

31 For details, see the GAO report, p.8.

32 See the GAO report, pp.20-21, for more details.

33 Craig Barrett, executive vice president of Intel, speaking at the Annual Industry Strategy Symposium of Semiconductor Equipment & Materials International, 1992, cited in *Sematech Update*, consortium newsletter, February 1992.

34 Interview conducted with senior executive of AMD, Sunnyvale, California, May 1993.

35 Interview conducted with National Semiconductor executive, California, May 1993.

36 Interview conducted with Applied Materials executive, Santa Clara, California, May 1993.

37 In *SEMATECH Update* (April/May 1992), the consortium's newsletter, the organisation claimed that SEMATECH helps US chip-making equipment suppliers increase market share.

38 Interview conducted with Mr. Hutcheson, June 1993.

39 In 1994 though, Japanese firms narrowed the previous year's gap with their American rivals in total market share. They closed the year on a combined total of 44.4 per cent of the global market. Evidently this overall increase in both American and Japanese market share resulted at the cost of another group of companies. Both Korean and Malaysian based chip producers increased their respective shares of the world market in 1994, putting their total combined sales ahead of the European-based industry for the first time (John Burton, 'Samsung May Set Up $1bn Semiconductor Plant in US', *Financial Times,* 10 January 1995). Thus, American and Japanese market gains occurred at the expense of their European-based competitors.

40 Line-widths refer to the size of the smallest feature which a fab system can produce, and wafer sizes. Sematech has taken the technology from a five-inch wafer with features as small as 0.8 microns in 1989, to 0.35 microns on an eight-inch wafer in 1993. On present projections, Sematech will probably

have reduced the feature size to 0.25 micron by late 1994 (*The Economist*, 'Uncle Sam's Helping Hand', 2 April 1994).

41   Semiconductor Industry Association & Dewey Ballantine (1992), *Creating Advantage*, p.5.

42   Ibid., pp.xii-xiii.

43   Borrus quoted in Andrew Pollack, 'Sematech Starts To Make Progress', *The New York Times*, 19 April 1991.

44   Michael Borrus, Co-Director of the Berkeley Roundtable on the International Economy, in a discussion at UC Berkeley, April 1993.

45   Grindley et al., op.cit., 1994.

46   For a more detailed account of these industry changes, see Grindley et al. (1994), op.cit., p.739.

47   Lithographic wafer steppers are used during the initial stages of chip production, to create the silicon wafers from which semiconductor chips are made.

48   This argument was supported by G. Dan Hutcheson, President, VLSI Research, in a conversation which the author had with him in June 1993.

49   Bill Spenser, President and CEO, SEMATECH, H-137, US Capitol, 5 October, 1994.

50   SEMATECH Board of Directors Resolution, July 15, 1994.

51   Craig Barrett, chief operating officer, Intel Corp., quoted in 'Sematech to Stop Federal Funding For its Research', *The Wall Street Journal*, 5 October, 1994.

52   William J. Spencer, President and Chief Executive Officer, SEMATECH Inc., *Semiconductors: The Role of Consortia*, testimony before the US House of Representatives House Science, Space and Technology Committee, Subcommittee on Technology and Competitiveness, 23 July 1991, Washington DC, p.6.

53   In addition, the distinction between semiconductor equipment manufacturers and semiconductor component makers is less clear in Japan than it is in the United States. In fact, most equipment makers are affiliates of the large component producers.

54   Howell et al. (1988), *The Microelectronics Race*, p.43; and K.G. van Wolferen, 'The Japan Problem', *Foreign Affairs* (January 1987), pp.292-3.

55   This notion of the Japanese government as a 'catalyst for R&D activities' is supported by Samuel Kernell ed. (1991), *Parallel Politics: Economic Policymaking in the United States and Japan*, p.296.

56   This three sided bargaining model was developed by Jonah D. Levy and Richard R. Samuels (1991), 'Institutions and Innovation: research collaboration as technology strategy in Japan', in Lynn Krieger Mytelka (ed.), *Strategic Partnerships: States, Firms, and International Competition*, p.130.

57   The loans were interest-free, and only repayable in the event of profitable technologies emerging from the VLSI project.

58   These figures are taken from the Semiconductor Industry Association, *The Effect of Government Targeting on World Semiconductor Competition: A*

Case History of Japanese Strategy and its Costs for America, Cupertino: SIA, 1983, p.23.

59   These were Mitsubishi, Toshiba, NEC, Fujitsu, and Hitachi.

60   Steve Lohr, 'How Japan Helps Its Industry', *New York Times*, 18 May, 1983.

61   A number of examples are Kokusai Electric, Shin-Etsu Semiconductors, Kyoto Ceramic, and Dai Nippon Printing, all of whom emerged in the early 1980s as global leaders in specific segments of the semiconductor materials and processing equipment industries (Gene Gregory 1986, *Japanese Electronics Technology: Enterprise and Innovation,* p.207).

62   Commission of the European Communities (1992), *Report on United States Trade and Investment Barriers,* p.8.

63   The EC's opposition to Section 301 is evident in numerous trade reports, most notably its annual reports on US trade and investment barriers, ibid., pp.8-9.

64   *International Herald Tribune,* 'Double-Edged Signal To Japan', and 'Trade Threats Fail to Bring Japanese Action', 5/6 March 1994.

65   This strategic trade policy has also been enacted for aircraft manufacturing, on the initiative of firms such as Boeing, in response to the 'unfair practices' surrounding the trade activities of the European Airbus consortium.

66   The SIA's suit was largely aimed at obtaining a greater share of the Japanese market for its members, whilst the suits filed by individual firms were directed at cases of alleged microchip dumping by Japanese firms. However, it is argued that these cases were initiated collusively, in order to strengthen the combined corporate objective of US government activism to counteract alleged dumping, and to open the Japanese market to American chip makers (Milner and Yoffie, 'Between Free Trade and Protectionsm: strategic trade policy and a theory of corporate trade demands', *International Organization*, 43, 2, Spring 1989, pp.254-5).

67   Tyson delineates two forms of managed trade: the first sets targets for foreign share of a given market; the second establishes a quantitative limit on a country's exports to a given trading partner or partners ('voluntary export restraint' agreements).

68   These tariffs were imposed on consumer and office goods imported to the US from Japan. According to Milner and Yoffie (1989), this was due to the SIA's strategy of requesting sanctions on imports of semiconductor end products, rather than on the components themselves. The reasoning appears to be an attempt by the SIA to retain the semblance of free and fair practices by the US, through not acquiring direct advantage for its member firms from the sanctions.

69   For a detailed analysis of the negotiations which led to the US-Japan construction industry agreement, see Ellis S. Krauss, 'US-Japan Negotiations on Construction and Semiconductors, 1985-1988', in Evans et al., (eds). (1993), *Double-Edged Diplomacy,* pp.265-99.

70   Ibid.

71 Tyson argues that the agreement led to an increase in foreign (mainly US) market share in Japan from 8.5 per cent in 1986 to 14.3 per cent by 1991. She also proposes that this increase accounted for in excess of $1 billion extra sales for American firms by 1990 (1993, pp.111-3).

72 William J. Spencer, President and Chief Executive Officer, SEMATECH Inc. (1991), *Semiconductors: The Role of Consortia,* op.cit., p.10.

73 *The Economist,* 'A target for protection', 27 March 1993.

74 These speculations mainly centre on the notion of a covert pact between MITI and Japanese chip consumers, whereby government incentives were provided to industry to purchase foreign chips *en masse* during the latter part of 1992. This strategy would ensure that the 20 per cent ceiling was reached by the end of the agreed time period, and thus US trade sanctions would be averted. Thus, a stockpiling of (mainly American) semiconductor chips took place, in order to avert US trade sanctions (*The Economist,* 'A target for protection', 27 March 1993, p.65). This conspiracy theory was fuelled by the fact that the Japanese foreign market share in chips declined almost immediately after the ceiling was reached and the STA was upheld. During the second quarter of 1993, the share fell to 19.2 per cent, and this declined further to 18.5 per cent by the third quarter (*The Financial Times,* 'US Concern Over Chip Exports', 20 December, 1993).

75 Carla Hills, cited in Bailey Morris, 'Japanese number game may end in trader tears', *The Independent on Sunday,* 18 July 1993.

76 Kenneth Flamm, Brookings Institution, Washington DC, cited in *The Economist,* op.cit., March 1993.

77 Commission of the European Communities (1992), *Report on United States Trade and Investment Barriers, 1992: problems of doing business with the US,* official publication, p.5.

78 For a discussion of the EC's trade tools and a critique of their ideological nature, see chapter four.

79 Interviews conducted with DGIII officials, CEC, Brussels, February 1994.

80 See chapter five for more details relating to the reasons for JESSI's creation.

81 Barry Buzan (1983), *People, States and Fear,* cited in Ole Waever (1993), *Securitization and Desecuritization,* Working Papers, Centre for Peace and Conflict Research, Copenhagen, p.3.

82 Evidence exists to suggest that such perceptions of external economic threat are not limited to governmental actors. For example, in a 1992 report, the European Electronic Component Manufacturers Association displayed a perception of an economic security threat posed to the EC through its dependence on 'foreign' supply sources for semiconductors.

83 In this speech Jacques Delors argued that the primary cause of unemployment within the EC is a 'lack of competitiveness with the US and Japan' (Krugman, 1994, pp.28-9). In saying this, he acknowledged the EC's perception of a direct relationship between the ability to compete successfully for world market shares, and the economic well-being of a society.

84   The structuralist interpretation advanced here also incorporates some realist assumptions.

85   Sandholtz (1992) advances this defensive alliance notion, but he bases his interpretation of it upon realism rather than economic security theory.

86   Alain Gomez, 'The Case Against Free Trade', *Fortune*, 20 April 1992, p.159.

87   Jagdish Bhagwati (1991), *The World Trading System At Risk*, Princeton, N.J., and Douglas A. Irwin (1990), 'Free Trade At Risk? An Historical Perspective', *Board of Governors of the Federal Reserve System, International Finance Discussion Papers*, No.391, December 1990, p.2.

88   See Irwin (1990) for an analysis of Mill's support of the infant industry doctrine (ibid., pp.2-5).

89   The US-Japan semiconductor deal, concluded in Vancouver, Canada on 2 August, 1996, has three main elements (*Financial Times*, 'US and Japan in agreement on chips', 3-4 August, 1996). First, the creation of a council of industry organisations from Japan and from the US - and from any other countries which have eliminated their tariffs. This symbolised a concession to the EU, providing it with a concrete path by which it can participate in future US-Japan semiconductor policy negotiations. Second, the creation of a global government forum to discuss world-wide chip industry issues such as tariffs and taxes. This multilateral dimension was evidence of the desire amongst the US and Japan to make their agreement more transparent and acceptable to the international community. Third, annual meetings between US and Japanese officials were agreed, to review trade and industry data collected by the private sector. This was further evidence of a desire to remove the clandestine image of previous semiconductor agreements. Overall, the agreement signified a move towards a more transparent, internationally acceptable deal. It also represented a victory for the Japanese in ensuring the removal of direct government intervention in the market. It remained essentially bilateral though and maintained its emphasis on monitoring import trends and market share in Japan. The EU expressed its dissatisfaction with the deal, arguing that it was only partially open to EU participation.

90   The Market Access Strategy approach was outlined by the European Commission in a press release of 14 February, 1996.

91   Commission of the European Communities, *European Report*, 19 November, 1996, London.

92   *The New York Times*, 'Strategic Goats Gobble Up Trade Subsidy', 26 February 1993.

93   Robert W. Galvin, 'Guest Column From Sematech Board Members', *Sematech Update*, February 1992, p.7.

94   The triangular diplomacy notion has been extended by this author to incorporate the European Commission as a further actor (see chapters four and five). Pentagonal diplomacy is most applicable for intra-EC bargaining. At a systemic level, it is increasingly rare for the EC to have two sets of

governmental actors (national governments and EC institutions) negotiating with non-Community political and corporate actors. GATT round negotiations are a notable exception to this rule. Therefore, it is sufficient to limit the bargaining process to three sides. This is done however with the understanding that 'state' may be interpreted as being either a national government or the supra-national EC, or both together.

95   Strange argues that the state, the market, and technology together comprise the three broad vehicles of systemic transformation (Susan Strange, 'An Eclectic Approach', in Murphy and Tooze (eds.), 1991, p.38). We interpret this to mean that the power to wield control rests with either (or both) firms or states, given that technology is a vehicle, not a driver, and the market is not a tangible actor (although it is a decisive factor affecting both states and firms).

7 Conclusions

Technological progress is like an axe in the hands of a pathological killer.

Albert Einstein

As with most undertakings of its kind, this book has a substantial number of findings - both empirical and theoretical. When linked together, these combine to substantiate a few larger research arguments. I set out with the intention of studying European Community policy for the semiconductor industry. The idea was to take a defined realm of EC industrial policy, and look at it from three different perspectives - firm, EC institutional, and international system. The objective was to conceptualise, analyse, and explain the creation and control of European policy for semiconductors. This meant addressing the issues of how the policy is created and why it develops in a particular direction. It also meant dealing with the question of affect: what measurable impact (if any) did the policy set have on the industry? Has the policy done what it was designed to do? In answering such questions, I inevitably introduce a modicum of policy prescription as an addendum. I would ask the reader to view such prescriptive tracts more as a scholastic attempt to shape the debate concerning future policy directions, than as predictive science or definitive policy recommendations. From the empirical findings, I have also attempted to draw a number of theoretical lessons. These may lend support to a number of existing theories, or serve to weaken their empirical foundations. In particular, this research agenda has relevance for international relations/international political economy theory concerning the nature and control of power in the international system. Moreover, my methodology supports the case for a joint international political economy/international business approach to EC policy studies.

In chapter one, I advanced three questions to be addressed. The first was how to explain and evaluate EC policy for the semiconductor industry. The second concerned the role of large firms relative to governmental actors, in the creation and control of EC semiconductor policy. The third focused on the significance of technology in influencing international policy bargains, shaping state-firm relational power, and thus bringing about a new diplomacy in international relations. These questions have all been addressed, and their answers will be summarised in this chapter.

In determining how EC policy for semiconductors is created and controlled, I advance the thesis that the key factor is control of and access to technology. My analysis of EC semiconductor policies supports this assertion. For instance, both corporate and (EC) public policy rationale for participation in JESSI stem from goals of knowledge creation and dissemination. Firms want access to the knowledge network. They seek to strengthen their long-term competitive advantage through widening their access and exposure to new ideas and innovations. In order to obtain this, they will pursue various alliance options, including collaboration with governments/the EC and other firms through collective R&D initiatives. Governmental actors strive to enhance the welfare of their citizens and the economic and military strength of their states (and the Community), through the access to and the diffusion of knowledge. As Inman and Burton argue, there is now a direct causal linkage between access to technology and the formulation of a state's foreign policy (1990, p.116). Furthermore, a hierarchy appears to exist, in terms of which advanced technologies have most political weight. I argue that for EC (and US) governmental actors, semiconductor technology has consistently been accorded preferential policy treatment. By that, I mean that through technology and trade policy (the linchpins of industrial or innovation policy), governmental agents have targeted semiconductors as a, if not the strategic or critical industry for the wider economy, and promoted or protected it accordingly. I will use the remainder of this chapter to reflect on my research findings in light of these arguments, and to advance some lessons relevant to existing political science theories.

1 The creation of EC semiconductor policy

The evidence in chapter three suggested that during the semiconductor industry's early years (the 1950s and 1960s), states determined policy alone. Firms had little actual power, relative to government. Firms depended on their home government for R&D assistance and, to different extents, a market for their end products. There was no public-private policy bargaining. Governments created policy and firms acted within its parameters. This situation changed at the end of the 1970s. The change may be attributable firstly, to the general failure of individual European national policies for semiconductor competitiveness; and secondly, to changes in the nature of the industry brought about by globalisation, which necessitated greater R&D investment, larger markets, and so forth. Thus, since the beginning of the 1980s there has been a sea-change in the nature of the agenda-setting and policy-making processes for the EC electronics sector. EC policy-making has gone from being an intra-institutional consensus building process, to a multi-sided bargaining process. The fundamental difference between these two processes is the presence of non-governmental agencies in the policy-making paradigm, most notably, firms. Prior to the 1980s such agents were absent and EC policy derived from bargaining between the institutions of the European Community -

241

particularly the Commission and the Council. However, this process became more complex after 1979-80. I argue that the new multi-sided bargaining process which developed can best be conceptualised through the Pentagonal Diplomacy framework for policy negotiation[1]. This model involves five interlinked sets of negotiations: state↔state, firm↔firm, state↔firm, firm↔European Commission, and state↔European Commission. All five bargaining relationships come into play for each industry. However, the policy impact of the individual relationships varies according to the industry. The objective is to determine which bargaining relationship(s) dominate a particular policy-making process; which of the public and private sector players involved in the policy sphere actually define and drive a given policy. Thus, the Pentagonal Diplomacy model clarifies the empirical evidence, and shows that, for certain industries, EC industrial policy is determined jointly by corporate and governmental (mainly European Commission) agents.

A point worth emphasising is my contention that this power shift constitutes more than special interest lobbying for certain industries. Instead, it comes much closer to Richardson and Jordan's (1979) neopluralist, policy community theory of government-business relations. It differs only in being somewhat less pluralist - arguing that EC industrial policy is often forged privately between the chief executive officers of a group of large firms and individual European Commissioners and their Cabinets. As the Pentagonal Diplomacy model suggests, for certain industries, EC industrial policy is determined jointly by corporate and governmental agents. Large electronics firms have gone from being policy outsiders up to the late 1970s, to being policy partners since the early 1980s. Their senior executives are consulted by and negotiate with governmental actors on policy decisions. Several previous studies support this notion of large firms partly creating EC policy (Junne, 1992; Green, 1993). Ross lends further support to the argument that EC semiconductor policy has been shaped by a Commission-large firm partnership. Research which he conducted within the Delors Cabinet reveals that a number of large electronics companies have been directly involved in the creation of EC policy for this sector (1995, pp.115-6).

Policy partnerships differ from lobby interests in that they are formed on the initiative of the Commission (Davignon's 1979 roundtable meetings); occur at the highest levels, often between Commissioners and CEOs (Delors himself met with the electronics leaders); and, on the non-governmental side, involve only a handful of international corporations, as opposed to a variety of sectoral interest groups or industry associations. Policy partnerships are thus a more actor-limited form of policy communities, which can have hidden agendas that make them more powerful relationships than those generally encapsulated by interest group theory.

Another policy creation dimension has emerged in this work. At a sub-pentagonal level, EC policy results in part from intra-Commission bargaining. Ideological cleavages exist as much within the Commission as they do within the Council of Ministers. Thus, policy is in part an outcome of intra-Directorate-General (DG) rivalries, and bargaining between those bureaucrats and

Commissioners of different ideological persuasions. These differences have had a significant impact upon the creation of semiconductor policy.

Chapter five advances evidence to show that national governments can dominate within the bargaining process which creates some dimensions of EC policy for semiconductors. The 1991-92 JESSI restructuring was initiated by the national government members. This would indicate that states are significant players in the JESSI policy bargain. Also, the JESSI budgetary cut-backs have been due to wider EC budgetary constraints precipitated by governments. Thus, the large firms and the national governments are the most important actors within JESSI bargains, with governments often dominating. This contrasts with the evidence from other realms of the EC policy set for the semiconductor industry (such as trade), where the Commission is the principle governmental bargaining actor. This finding does not come as a surprise given that JESSI was initially devised by national governments. The European Commission has always been the junior partner in JESSI, as in all Eureka initiatives. National governments wield considerable influence in policy areas such as Eureka co-ordinated semiconductor R&D programmes. It is also visible in EC policy variables, mainly the size of budget allocations and the scope of EC technology policy. However, the actual policy agenda-setting, trade tool utilisation, rules governing competition, and concentration of resources, remain largely outside of nation states direct influence. Thus, whilst accepting the sometimes pre-eminent bargaining power of states, we argue that overall EC semiconductor policy is shaped and guided mainly by the European Commission in partnership with certain large firms.

Chapter six shows that policy bargains for semiconductor policy in both the US and Japan are (and have been since the 1970s) frequently initiated and shaped by large firms. The evidence from both the Sematech and VLSI initiatives, support this assertion. Large chip makers display just as much power in determining external (trade) policies and in shaping inter-state bargains, as they have in shaping domestic R&D policy. Witness the key role of US firms in creating the Semiconductor Trade Agreement. Government-firm partnerships exist in both countries. Firms and industry associations were in the more persuasive and dominant position in the US, whilst the partnership was on a more equal footing in Japan. Overall, the semiconductor industry in both countries had political weight far above its own market or employment size. This corporate bargaining strength in both countries concurs with the arguments advanced in chapters four and five regarding semiconductor policy bargaining in the EC.

2 The control of EC semiconductor policy

The special nature of semiconductors has been emphasised throughout this book. Both governments and corporations have recognised this fact. The European Commission introduced the notion of priority technology projects more directly linked to key generic technologies on which the competitiveness of European industry depends[2]. One of the main priority technologies was semiconductors. The fact itself emerges due to the transformative effect which semiconductor technology has on economies and societies throughout the world. Its meta-technology status, driving global change in finance, production, and security, has meant that it can dictate corporate competitiveness as well as a state's economic and military strength. The global nature of semiconductor firms means that the boundaries of their activities are beyond the control of any one state, which enhances their regulatory independence and bargaining strength relative to governments. The rapid increases in semiconductor applications has meant that the technology's economic, military, and societal significance has expanded considerably. Governments want to guarantee continued access to the technology which underpins their respective states. They are consequently obliged to deal directly with those firms which control the technology's development. This is a substantive change since the industry's early years, when firms had little bargaining power vis-à-vis the governments in which they were based. A strong home government dominance over firms (caused to various extents by the industry's financial and market dependence on the state) meant that no public-private bargaining existed: government created policy, and firms acted within its parameters. This relative bargaining power of large semiconductor firms is further enhanced by semiconductors dual-use applications, increasing their utility to encapsulate both the military and the commercial spheres of a state.

Consequently, all states and firms strive to guarantee access to semiconductor technology. Control of the policy which influences this technology is therefore important. As I have shown, this policy has, since the early 1980s, mainly been controlled by the European Commission[3] together with a group of large firms. Together, they have shaped collaborative policy initiatives. Their respective approaches to this policy set differ, both in terms of motives and objectives. In terms of policy instrument utilisation, the Community's emphasis is on collaborative R&D activities. All other pillars of EC policy are secondary to efforts aimed at knowledge creation and dissemination. Furthermore, the two policy realms wherein lie the most interventionist and protectionist tendencies of the EC vis-à-vis the semiconductor sector, are collaborative R&D programmes and trade. Furthermore, my evidence supports the argument that the EC has developed a sectoral policy set for electronics. Despite the rhetoric and the stated intention to move towards greater liberalisation, many interventionist elements of EC policy for electronics remain. This is particularly prevalent in trade policy issues[4]. The official Commission line on industrial policy advocates a middle-way between governmentally directed firm strategy, and free market competition. However, the result is often a protective partnership - selective, firm requested government intervention. Although verbally shunning sectoral policies, the Commission has identified certain industries as strategic, and apportioned them special policy treatment. Most of Europe's large native electronic firms have been in such a protective partnership. Moreover, microelectronic components were targeted as strategic from an early stage - in advance of and to a greater extent than most other high technology sectors.

As the JESSI study illustrates, firms support European collaborative programmes because they perceive them as another means of receiving funding for costly R&D, and thus freeing up corporate funds intended for R&D, for other purposes. Also, they see benefits through risk sharing and technological transfer (this latter factor being particularly important for SMEs), and they allow small, new firms to gain access to technology and to share research costs. Moreover, technology is at the heart of European semiconductor producers competitive strategy. Through utilising a specific form of strategic alliance strategy (the bottom-up European collaborative programme option), semiconductor firms endeavour to strengthen their long-term competitive advantage through reducing the risks and costs of R&D and widening their access and exposure to new ideas and innovations. Thus, the crucial element is knowledge: firms choose to participate in European collaborative programmes mainly to obtain access to what Mytelka (1991) described as the knowledge network.

The control and direction of EC semiconductor policy is heavily influenced by extra-Community factors. Chapter six reveals that the US-Japanese chip alliance increased pressure on the EC to assist electronics firms based in the Community to position themselves in global markets (this agreement caused a chip scarcity and price increase); as well as increasing the propensity of the EC to adopt a more protectionist position towards non-Community based firms, and a more mercantilist trade stance vis-à-vis its main chip producing trade partners. I have conceptualised the Community's reaction in economic security terms. The basic premise herein is that systemic activities are frequently perceived as threatening the economic security of a given politico-economic entity, and thus have an impact on the policy of that entity's governmental actors. In real terms, I am arguing that global economic activities often affect the nature of EC policy, through instilling the Community's governmental actors with a perception of external economic threat.

Finally, evidence from the American case supports that advanced for the EC in previous chapters. Access to and control over core, enabling technologies is the central determining factor in policy direction. Those firms and governments which control the technology, or knowledge, factor, have the ability to jointly control the policy bargain relative to other states and firms.

3 Some consequences of EC semiconductor policy

I have consistently adopted a cautious approach to determining policy outcomes. It is difficult - if not impossible - to establish the impact which a policy has on a firm. This is particularly true for R&D policies. The counterfactual proves insurmountable in any assessment of competitive enhancement resulting from a policy such as JESSI. Similarly, it is difficult to gauge the precise affect of trade tools on corporate market performance. I have attempted, in so far as it is possible, to identify causal relations between EC policy and industry performance. Whilst not being able to assign definitive success or failure labels to EC policy tools, the evidence has often indicated that policy has not had the desired affect on industry. This may mean that policy has had no obvious impact, either positively or negatively; or it may mean that a policy has distorted market forces in a way which can hinder competition.

As regards the EC policy partnership for semiconductor development and production, it is suggested that in the medium to long term, too much collaboration can become collusive, sustain or create oligopolies, and consequently adversely affect competitiveness (Mytelka, 1991, p.27). Thus, EC semiconductor policy has market distorting elements. A remedy might be to restrict or abolish trade tools such as antidumping practices, rules of origin, local content requirements, and import tariffs, which merely protect uncompetitive (former national champion) European-based chip makers. Further restructuring of collaborative R&D initiatives, along the lines proposed in this work, may also contribute to a more competitive European-based semiconductor industry.

The US Sematech venture succeeded in enhancing US manufacturing process technology, and in fostering dialogue between equipment suppliers and users. Although difficult to prove categorically, it is doubtful however that Sematech played a significant - if any - part in helping US semiconductor producers regain market leadership. Furthermore, as a framework for firm-firm and government-industry R&D co-operation, Sematech has broad support, and has been relatively successful. As a worthwhile collaborative model, we may thus draw structural lessons from Sematech for European chip consortiums, and for governmental approaches to corporate R&D funding. As with Sematech, the Japanese VLSI Project was a structural success. As a collaborative model, Europe may draw lessons. These organisational lessons might include opening public procurement contracts to bids from SMEs, rather than just awarding them to old, established firms; second, in some circumstances, giving loan rather than grants (as in Japan for VLSI); third, ensuring that all money given is strictly accounted for during the course of the project; fourth, setting clear and feasible objectives, established in advance of the project's commencement, and agreed upon by both public and private partners; fifth, fixing a time frame for the project, after which government reconsiders its involvement.

The overall thrust of EC policy has not had the desired affect on the European-based semiconductor industry. The industry has not significantly improved its share of either the European or the world market since the development of European-level policies. In fact, these respective shares have declined since Euro-collaboration began in the early 1980s. Policy has not helped because it has been overly interventionist and frequently directed at the wrong areas (e.g. basic research rather than marketing techniques or user needs). In analysing JESSI as one dimension of this EC co-ordinated policy, I contend its relative contribution has been minimal. In assessing the utility of JESSI as a framework for collaboration, I argue that it is has been successful in building a trans-European co-operative network between business, government, and research institutes. In terms of technological achievements, a number of artefacts have been developed but have yet to translate into increased industry market share. A core problem with JESSI from the outset was that its focus was wrong. It should not have focused on final product. Rather, it should perhaps have focused on process technology - as Sematech and VLSI did. Instead the JESSI partners ended up with a situation where they had to buy the equipment to manufacture the products. Moreover, one's innovative (and therefore, competitive) limits are set by the previous technology. If one aim at product rather than process, one simply attempt to take a given technology to the next phase, rather than using state-of-the-art process technology to make technological leaps, and possibly develop a completely new product for instance. JESSI had an incremental objective (as did ESPRIT). This does not work now because many new technologies cannot be developed incrementally, e.g. RISC or Flash memories. Now companies must aim at technological leaps, if they are to create or sustain competitiveness. In addition, for the Japanese VLSI project, the end product was defined in advance. None of the European programmes knew their end goal. Moreover, both the Japanese and the Americans focused more on inputs than on final product. That is, they aimed at developing materials, machines, and process technology, rather than actual chip devices. In this respects, Sematech seems to be more similar to VLSI. This factor significantly differentiates European semiconductor collaboration from either American or Japanese initiatives. I argue that in fact it lies at the heart of the criticisms levied at European programmes, relative to those undertaken in the other parts of the triad. If in a rapidly evolving industry like semiconductors, you select a specific end product or products to develop, then you risk the very real threat of being technologically outflanked by competitors. The risk attached to developing input factors is much less.

In chapter five I advance the notion that there might be a fundamental conflict between why firms collaborate and what government's want from collaboration. This notion might help to explain conflicting opinions on the relative contribution of EC policies such as collaborative R&D initiatives. The contention is that firms collaborate to tap complementary know-how but governments want increased domestic production (translating as enhanced societal welfare and a stronger international bargaining position). The firm may get what it wants but still fail to provide what governments want. The EC illustrates this plainly: it has failed to increase the competitive position of the European-based semiconductor industry, whilst on the other hand, firms like SGS Thomson have successfully used EC-supported programmes to acquire a knowledge network which complements their efforts to develop particular products.

In light of the evidence, I perceive four broad policy options for governmental actors vis-à-vis the semiconductor industry. These are first, no intervention; second, limited intervention for a specific time, then the firms are on their own; third, limited intervention for a specific time, with the likelihood of extending this time period; and fourth, widespread intervention with no set time span. The US Sematech venture fits into the second of these categories, as did the Japanese VLSI project. EC programmes such as ESPRIT fall into category four. JESSI fits into the third option. Based on the evidence advanced in this study, I would suggest that debates surrounding future EC policy choices for collaborative R&D initiatives might consider the second option I have outlined.

4 A neofunctionalist rationale for policy partnership

Discussion concerning the Commission's neofunctionalist rationale for policy partnership alludes to this work's implications for the study of European integration. I have argued that EC policy for the semiconductor industry did evolve as part of the Community's efforts to create a common area of action for industrial affairs. This is evident from the 1979 Davignon round table meetings with electronics leaders, through the creation of Framework and ESPRIT and EC involvement in Eureka and JESSI, culminating in the 1990, 1991 and 1994 EC industrial policy documents, wherein semiconductors are explicitly targeted for special treatment. Moreover, the shift in policy emphasis away from the national and towards the EC level for this industry, established semiconductors as the Community's vanguard high technology industry in the post-SEA drive towards economic integration. In addition to the documental emphasis on semiconductor technology, the industry's pre-eminent position within EC industrial policy is underlined in two policy areas. First, the share of EC R&D resources allocated to the industry (through both ESPRIT and JESSI) has far outweighed any other[5]. Second, the nature and extent of trade tools at the industry's disposal illustrates the Community's willingness to risk trade censorship or conflict on behalf of the semiconductor sector.

It has been argued that the increased role of Community institutions in policy for high technology industries such as semiconductors had political undertones (OTA, 1991; Forum Europe, 1992). In effect, the European Commission saw European industry - especially large firms within critical, enabling industries - as potential allies in the struggle to achieve a federal Europe:

A lot of small, national champions would become a few, big European ones, whose interests would lie with the Community, not with separate states (McKenzie, 1992, p.7).

This approach signifies a complete reversal of earlier EC attitudes. As Green has argued, during the first twenty years of its existence, the Community viewed big business as too nationalistic, and kept them largely outside of EC policy decisions (1993, p.3). This argument confirms that what Haas described in 1958, held true for two decades The post-1970s idea may have been that European industrial interests could be integrated through first, co-ordinating policy for a few large firms within key technology industries. These sectoral common areas of interest would in turn spill over to other industries. Neofunctionalist theory states that the logical next step would be a consolidation of wider economic integration, due to industrial unity; and this would subsequently enhance political union. Therefore, the creation of a policy partnership with large, critical technology firms, would serve to foster European industrial integration, and at the same time, gradually undermine the position of the nation state as a policy actor. Arguments in chapter five support this neofunctionalist interpretation of EC strategy from the Davignon-industry meetings onwards. President Delors devoted considerable attention to the leaders of Europe's main electronics firms because of their implicit threats to withdraw their political support for the Community (and thus for the integration process) if their views were not adequately accounted for in the policy-making process (Ross, 1995, pp.115-6). Neofunctionalism may therefore serve to partially explain the reasons why the European Commission desired to set in motion the kind of dynamic resulting in policy partnerships with the major European-based semiconductor producers.

5 Implications for theory

5.i. Neoliberal institutionalism revisited: the applicability of theories in light of the evidence

The nature of the international system and the trade policies pursued by the system's economically most important governmental actors, may be in part understood with the aid of neoliberal institutionalism. The three central principles of this theory are evident in this chapter's empirical analysis. Firstly, the interdependent nature of the global economy means that state autonomy is a myth. Systemic factors impinge on state policy decisions and restrict governments ability to negotiate and legislate from a position of independence. This argument is evident primarily in the impact which US-Japan bilateral trade activities have on the nature of EC policy. This illustrates that the EC for example, finds it hard to pursue an independent, reactive trade policy. Instead, its policy options are influenced by events occurring at an international system level. It is obvious in the international firm-state bargaining which has arisen that transnational corporations control technology, and thus define structural change. Governmental actors, wishing to wield structural power in order to have relational power vis-à-vis other states, negotiate with these firms for access to the knowledge structure. Thus, systemic power cannot now be achieved by governments acting independently. This provides evidence also for the second central tenet of neoliberal institutionalism. In this, the core realist argument for the primacy of states in international relations is rejected. The theory argues instead that systemic power now rests more than before with non-state actors, particularly multinational corporations. A third main element of neoliberal institutionalism evident in our findings is that states seek to maximise their absolute gains, regardless of the gains which this conveys to others (Grieco, 1993, p.117). This rejection of the realist zero-sum game scenario is implicit in strategic trade policy. As we have established, this policy approach has been utilised by both the United States and the European Community for trade in semiconductors.

5.ii. The firm as an actor in international relations: a review of the theory in light of the evidence

It has been evident throughout that this work sought to modify the notion that the state-market interplay forms the basis for international political economy. Such a position is more in line with traditional international trade theory, where firms are subordinate to the market, which holds the real power, through its ability to determine demand and price (Galbraith, 1973, p.165). The rationale herein is simple: globalisation has caused a realignment of the firm-state relationship, resulting in a new diplomacy within the international system (Stopford and Strange, 1991). As Galbraith argues, multinational enterprises are now 'a substitute for the market as a method of organizing international exchange' (1973, p.169). To analyse this new form of international negotiation, it is not sufficient to consider the state-market interplay. A more tangible set of actors must be advanced. As Skocpol states, a degree of independent goal formulation must occur if an entity is to be considered an actor (1985, p.9). Thus, to understand the bargaining process which is this new diplomacy, it is necessary to be able to differentiate tangible actors which dominate any given bargain set. Firms are such actors, being according to Hymer:

islands of conscious power in an ocean of unconscious co-operation[6].

The New Diplomacy concept suggests that a fundamental change has occurred in diplomacy: governments are now obliged to negotiate with multinational enterprises as well as with other governments. In addition, multinational enterprises have to bargain with both governments and other firms (Stopford and Strange, 1991, p.2). This concept is propounded not only in international political economy literature, but also in international business literature. Most notably, Porter (1990) devotes his attention to examining the connection between the competitive advantage of multinational firms and the competitiveness of states (Sally, 1994, p.161). One also finds attention being given to the firm-state bargaining process in policy analysis literature (Grant, 1989; Paterson, 1990). Hence, it may indeed be argued that the multinational enterprise has increased power in setting policy agendas and shaping outcomes in the international political economy (Sally, 1994, p.163). As Junne puts it:

Multinational corporations influence policy making in a double way: through their economic activity, and through their political interventions (1992, p.23).

Within this research I have provided evidence to support the validity of these arguments, in all of the major advanced economies, and at all levels within the international system.

The academic bias inherent in this research has been towards a systemic understanding of the new diplomacy. Thus, I argue that the causes of this power realignment are to be found in structural change (Strange, 1992, p.1). The reason I have chosen this interpretation above others is due to its emphasis on, and ability to comprehensively account for the role of technology. As argued earlier, for the information age, control of technology is the key determinant in all international bargaining. From the findings, I argue that the ability to influence structural change gives an actor structural power, which in turn, translates into relational power[7]. In contrast to traditional realist conceptions of structural power, I argue that non-state actors, such as transnational corporations, can (through their economic ability to influence structural change) acquire structural power. They may then use their structural power to gain relational power relative to governments. Hills concurs with this contention when she argues that:

The multinational becomes the key to the transfer of structural power over economic discourse to relational power over sovereign nations (1994, p.172).

Multinational semiconductor firms, possessing such influence over structural change through their control of the knowledge structure, have a considerably stronger bargaining position vis-à-vis governmental actors than do other business sectors. Technology, as the driving force of structural change, has brought about a realignment in the relative power position of states and firms. Public and private sector actors now interact on a partnership basis, with firms often taking the lead in defining and directing policy. This new diplomacy is manifest at both European Community and international levels.

Thus, this work lends support to the argument within international political economy circles for the necessity of including technology within any debate on the nature of structural power. As indicated, I base this argument on technology's central importance, both in gaining relational power and in strengthening what Strange (1988) has defined as the other three pillars of systemic power (security, production, and credit). Applying these theoretical findings on the nature and control of power to the international political economy, I argue that Community-based transnational semiconductor firms exercise greater bargaining power in the creation and control of EC industrial policy than do firms in other sectors of the European economy.

On a final note, I would suggest that this work helps to illustrate the necessity of viewing EC policy from both a firm and an international system level. These perspectives allow for a more conclusive analysis, taking account of both public and private sector actions, and extra-Community as well as intra-EC variables. Substantial new insights may be gained from a combined international political economy/ international business approach to EC policy studies.

Notes

1   The Pentagonal Diplomacy model is explained in greater detail in chapter two.

2   EC Commission's Spokesman's Service, *Research after Maastricht: an assessment, a strategy,* Brussels, 8 April 1992.

3   National governments have played a more powerful role than the Commission in some elements of the policy set. In particular, my evidence indicates that this was the case for the JESSI programme.

4   More recent developments indicate that the Community's protectionist trade policy for semiconductors may be liberalising. Most significantly, in March 1995, the European Commission announced its intention to suspend the 14 per cent anti-dumping duties on Japanese D-RAM memory chips imported into the EU (*The Financial Times,* 'EU to suspend anti-dumping duties on D-Ram chips', 22 March, 1995). However, it should be noted that this move merely involves the suspension of duties imposed in 1990 to penalise Japanese firms for allegedly dumping chips in the EU at below market prices. These duties are removed as a matter of course once the alleged dumping ceases. It does not mean that such duties cannot or will not be imposed again, if the Commission perceives further cases of dumping. Moreover, anti-dumping duties remain in place on Korean D-Ram producers also accused of dumping.

5   In saying this I am conscious of the fact that by far the largest share of the overall EC budget goes to other sectors of the economy, most notably, agriculture. In terms of money allocated through the Community's technology policy though, electronics - especially microelectronics - receives by far the largest share.

6   Stephen Hymer (1970) quoted in John Kenneth Galbraith (1973), *Economics and Public Purpose,* p.169.

7   Relational power being the power of a given actor to force another actor in the system to do that which it would not do voluntarily.

Bibliography

General

Albach, H. (1992), *Strategic Alliances and Strategic Families in Global Competition,* Wissenschaftszentrum discussion papers: Berlin.

Alic/Branscomb/Brooks/Carter/Epstein (1992), *Beyond Spinoff: Military and Commercial Technologies in a Changing world,* Harvard Business School: Cambridge, MA.

Ansoff, H. I. (ed.) (1967), *Corporate Strategy,* Penguin: London.

Audretsch, D. (1989), *The Market and the State,* Harvester Wheatsheaf: Herts.

Audretsch, D. (1993), 'Industrial Policy and International Competitiveness', in Phedon Nicolaides (ed.), *Industrial Policy in the European Community: A Necessary Response to Economic Integration?,* Martinus Nijhoff: Dordrecht, The Netherlands.

Axelrod, R. and Keohane, R.O. (1993), 'Achieving Cooperation Under Anarchy: Strategies and Institutions', in David A. Baldwin (ed.), *Neorealism and Neoliberalism: The Contemporary Debate,* Columbia University Press: New York.

Baldwin, D.A. (1989), *Paradoxes of Power,* Basil Blackwell: New York/Oxford.

Baldwin, D.A. (1993), 'Neoliberalism, Neorealism, and World Politics', in David A. Baldwin (ed.) *Neorealism and Neoliberalism: The Contemporary Debate,* Columbia University Press: New York.

Baldwin, R.E. (1988), *Trade Policy in a Changing World Economy,* Harvester Wheatsheaf: Herts.

Baldwin, R.E. (1990), *The U.S.-Japan Semiconductor Trade Agreement,* Discussion Paper No.387, Centre for Economic Policy Research: London.

Ballance, R.H. and Sinclair, S.W. (1983), *Collapse and Survival: Industry Strategies in a Changing World,* George Allen & Unwin: London.

Ballance, R.H. (1987), *International Industry and Business,* Allen & Unwin: London.

254

Barron, I. and Curnow, R. (1979), *The Future With Microelectronics*, The Open University Press: Milton Keynes.

Bell, D. (1979), 'Communications Technology - For Better or for Worse', *Harvard Business Review*, May/June.

Bhagwati, J. (1988), *Protectionism*, MIT Press: Cambridge, MA.

Bhagwati, J. (1991), *The World Trading System At Risk*, Princeton University Press: Princeton, NJ.

Blomstrop, M./Lipsey, R.E./Zejan, M. (1993), *Is Fixed Investment The Key To Economic Growth?*, NBER WP Series 4436, Cambridge: National Bureau of Economic Research.

Borrus, M./ Millstein, J./ Zysman, J. (1982), *U.S.-Japanese Competition in the Semiconductor Industry*, Berkeley, CA: Institute of International Studies, University of California at Berkeley.

Borrus, M./Tyson, L./Zysman, J. (1984), *How Government Policies Shape High Technology Trade*, The Berkeley Roundtabe on the International Economy, Working Paper 3.

Borrus, M.G. (1988), *Competing For Control: America's Stake in Microelectronics*, Cambridge, MA: Ballinger.

Borrus, M. (1992), 'Why the United State Will Regain Leadership in Chips', *Venture Japan*, Vol.4, No.1, pp.31-33.

Borrus, M./Zysman, J. (1992), 'Industrial Strength and Regional Integration: Japan's Impact on European Integration', paper presented at the *Japanese Direct Investment in a Unifying Europe: Impacts on Japan and the European Community* Conference, INSEAD Euro-Asia Centre, Fontainebleau, 26-27 June 1992.

Borrus, M./Weber, S./Zysman, J./Willihnganz, J. (1992), 'Mercantilism and Global Security', *The National Interest*, No.29, Fall.

Branscomb, L.M. (1992), 'Does America Need A Technology Policy?', *Harvard Business Review*, March-April, pp.24-33.

Braudel, F. (1979), *Civilisation Materielle, Economie et Capitalisme: XVe-XVIIIe Siecle*, Paris: Colin.

Braun, E./MacDonald, S. (1982), *Revolution in Minature: the history and impact of semiconductor electronics*, Cambridge: University of Cambridge Press.

Brittan, L. (1991), *Does Europe Have An Industrial Policy*, speech held at the Chamber of Commerce, Aachen, Germany, 15 October 1991.

Brookes, S. (1987), 'Euro-Chipmakers Plan Joint Strategies', *Europe*, No.267, June.

Buigues, P./Sapir, A. (1993), 'Community Industrial Policies', in Phedon Nicolaides (ed.), *Industrial Policy in the European Community: A Necessary Response to Economic Integration?*, Dordrecht, Netherlands: Martinus Nijhoff, for European Institute of Public Administration.

Buzan, B. (1991), *People, States, and Fear: An Agenda for International Security Studies in the Post-Cold War Era*, London: Harvester Wheatsheaf.

Cawson, A./Morgan, K./Webber, D./Holmes, P./Stevens, A. (1990), *Hostile Brothers: Competition and Closure in the European Electronics Industry,* Oxford: Clarendon Press.

Cesa, M. (1989), *Defining Security,* Pisa: University of Pisa Press.

Chandler, A.D. (1977), *The Visible Hand: The Managerial Revolution in American Business,* Cambridge, MA: Harvard University Press.

Charles, D.R. (1994), 'The Location of Electronics R&D in the UK: Business Strategies, Organisation and Labour Markets', *History and Technology,* Vol.11.

Coates, David (1984) *The Context of British Politics,* London: Hutchinson.

Cohen, S.S./Zysman, J. (1987), *Manufacturing Matters,* New York: Basic Books.

Conybeare, J.A.C. (1987), *Trade Wars: The Theory and Practice of International Commercial Rivalry,* New York: Columbia University Press.

Cowhey, P.F./Aronson, J.D. (1993), *Managing the World Economy: The Consequences of Corporate Alliances,* New York: Council on Foreign Relations Press.

Cram, L. (1993), 'Calling the Tune Without Paying the Piper? Social Policy Regulation: The Role of the Commission in European Community Social Policy', *Policy and Politics,* Vol.21 No.2, pp.135-46.

Crane, G.T./Amawi, A. (eds.) (1991), *The Theoretical Evolution of International Political Economy,* Oxford/New York: Oxford University Press.

Curzon Price, V. (1981), *Industrial Policies in the European Communities,* London: MacMillan Press, for the Trade Policy Research Centre.

Dang-Nguyen, G./Schneider, V./Werle, R. (1993), *Corporate Actor Networks in European Policy-Making: Harmonizing Telecommunications Policy,* Koln: MPIFG Discussion Paper.

Dell, E. (1987), *The Politics of Economic Interdependence,* London: MacMillan.

Derian, J.C (1990), *America's Struggle for Leadership in High Technology,* Cambridge, Mass./London: MIT Press.

Dicken, P. (1986), *Global Shift: Industrial Change in a Turbulent World,* London: Harper & Row.

Diebold, W. (1980), *Industrial Policy as an International Issue,* New York: McGraw Hill.

Dodgson, M. (ed.) (1989), *Technology Strategy and the Firm: Management and Public Policy,* Essex: Longman.

Dodgson, M. (1993), *Technological Collaboration in Industry: Strategy, Policy, and Internationalization in Innovation,* London/New York: Routledge.

Dosi, G. (1981), *Technical Change and Survival: Europe's Semiconductor Industry,* Brighton: European Research Centre.

Dosi, G. (1981), 'Institutions and Markets in High Technology: Government Support for Micro-Electronics in Europe', in Charles Carter (ed.), *Industrial Policy and Innovation,* London: Heinemann, for the Royal Institute of International Affairs.

Dosi, G. (1983), 'Semiconductors: Europe's Precarious Survival in High Technology', in Shepherd/Duchene/Sunders (eds.), *Europe's Industries,* Ithaca, New York: Cornell University Press.

Dosi, G./Freeman, C./Nelson, R./Silverberg, G./Soete, L. (eds.) (1990), *Technical Change and Economic Theory*, New York: Columbia University Press.

Doz, Y. (1986), *Strategic Management in Multinational Companies*, Oxford: Pergamon Press.

Drucker, P. (1986), 'The Changed World Economy', *Foreign Affairs*, Spring.

Duff, A.N. (1986), 'Eureka and the New Technology Policy of the European Community', *Policy Studies*, Vol.6, Part 4.

Dumont, A. (1990), 'Technology, Competitiveness and Cooperation in Europe', in Michael S. Steinberg (ed.), *The Technical Challenges and Opportunities of A United Europe*, London: Pinter.

Dunning, J.H. (1988), *Multinationals, Technology, and Competitiveness*, London: Unwin Hyman.

Dunning, J.H. (1993), *The Globalization of Business: the Challenge of the 1990s*, London/New York: Routledge.

Dyerson, R./Mueller, F. (1993), 'Intervention by Outsiders: A Strategic Management Perspective on Government Industrial Policy', *Journal of Public Policy*.

Dyker, D.A. (ed.) (1992), *The European Economy*, London: Longman.

Eden, Lorraine (1991), 'Bringing the Firm Back In: Multinationals in International Political Economy', *Millenium: Journal of International Studies*, Vol.20, No.2, pp.197-224.

Eden, L./Potter, E.H. (eds.) (1993), *Multinationals in the Global Political Economy*, London/New York: MacMillan/St. Martin's Press.

Erker, P. (1994), 'The Challenge of a New Technology: Transistor Research and Business Strategy at Siemens and Philips', *History and Technology*, Vol.11 pp.131-43.

Ernst, D. (1983), *The Global Race in Microelectronics: Innovation and Corporate Strategies in a Period of Crisis*, Frankfurt: Campus Verlag.

Ernst, D./O'Connor, D. (1992), *Competing in the Electronics Industry*, Paris: OECD.

Flamm, K. (1988), *Creating the Computer: Government, Industry, and High Technology*, Washington DC: The Brookings Institution.

Flamm, K. (1990), 'Semiconductors', in Gary Clyde Hufbauer (ed.), *Europe 1992: An American Perspective*, Washington DC: Brookings Institution.

Flamm, K. (1991), *Strategic Arguments for Semiconductor Trade Policy*, paper presented at the Industrial Organization Society session, on 'International Competition in Semiconductors', Allied Social Sciences Association Meetings, New Orleans, Louisiana, 3 January, 1991.

Fong, G.R. (1990), 'State Strength, Industry Structure, and Industrial Policy: American and Japanese Experiences in Microelectronics', *Comparative Politics*, Vol.22, No.3, pp.273-99.

Ford, G./Lake, G. (1991), 'Evolution of European Science and Technology Policy', *Science and Public Policy*, Vol.18, No.1.

Forester, T. (ed.) (1980), *The Microelectronics Revolution*, Oxford: Basil Blackwell.

257

Francis, A./Tharakan, P.K.M. (1989), *The Competitiveness of European Industry*, London/New York: Routledge.

Frank, A.G. (1967), *Capitalism and Under-Development in Latin America: Historical Studies of Chile and Brazil*, New York: Monthly Review Press.

Fransman, M. (1990), *The Market and Beyond: Cooperation and Competition in Information Technology Development in the Japanese System*, Cambridge: Cambridge University Press.

Freeman, C. (1987), *Technology Policy and Economic Performance*, London/New York: Pinter.

Freeman, C./Sharp, M./Walker, W. (eds.) (1991), *Technology and the Future of Europe*, London/New York: Pinter.

Frey, B. (1982), 'International Political Economy: An Emerging Field', *Institute for International Studies*, Stockholm, Seminar Paper.

Galbraith, J.K. (1973), *Economics and the Public Purpose*, London: British Broadcasting Corporation and André Deutsch.

Galbraith, J.K. (1977), *The Age of Uncertainty*, London: British Broadcasting Corporation & André Deutsch.

Galbraith, J.K. (1977), *The Affluent Society*, third edition, revised, London: André Deutsch.

George, S. (1991) *Politics and Policy in the European Community*, 2nd ed., Oxford: Oxford University Press.

Georghiou, L.G./Metcalfe, J.S. (1993), 'Evaluation of the impact of European Community research programmes upon industrial competitiveness', *R&D Management*, Vol.23, No.2, pp.161-9

Gibbon, E. (1897), *The History of the Decline and Fall of the Roman Empire*, Vol.1, London: Methuen & Co.

Gilpin, R. (1987), *The Political Economy of International Relations*, Princeton, NJ: Princeton University Press.

Goldstein, W. (1993), 'The EC: Capitalist or *Dirigiste* Regime?', in Alan W. Cafruny/Glenda G. Rosenthal (eds.), *The State of the European Community, Vol.2: The Maastricht Debates and Beyond*, Boulder, Colorado: Lynne Rienner.

Gomez, A. (1992), 'The Case Against Free Trade', *Fortune*, 20 April.

Grant, W. (1985) (ed.), *The Political Economy of Corporatism*, London: Macmillan.

Grant, W. (with Jane Sargent) (1987) *Business and Politics in Britain*, London: Macmillan.

Grant, W. (1989), *Government and Industry: A Comparative Analysis of the U.S., Canada, and the UK*, Aldershot: Elgar.

Green, M.L. (1993), *The Politics of Big Business in the Single Market Programme*, paper presented for the ECSA Third Biennial Conference, Washington DC.

Gregory, G. (1986), *Japanese Electronics Technology: Enterprise and Innovation*, 2nd ed. New York: John Wiley and Sons.

Grieco, J.M. (1993), 'Anarchy and the Limits of Cooperation: A Realist Critique of the Newest Liberal Institutionalism', in David A. Baldwin (ed.), *Neorealism and Neoliberalism: The Contemporary Debate,* New York: Columbia University Press.

Grindley, P./Mowery, D.C./Silverman, B. (1994), 'SEMATECH and Collaborative Research: Lessons in the Design of High-Technology Consortia', *Journal of Policy Analysis and Management,* Vol.13, No.4, pp.723-58.

Grunwald, J./Flamm, K. (1985), *The Global Factory: Foreign Assembly in International Trade,* Washington DC: Brookings Institution.

Guerrieri, P./Milana, C. (1991), *Technological and Trade Competition in High-Tech Products,* The Berkeley Roundtable on the International Economy Working Paper 54, Berkeley, California.

Guzzini, S. (1992), *The Continuing Story of A Death Foretold: Realism in International Relations/International Political Economy,* EUI Working Paper SPS No.92/20, Florence: European University Institute.

Haas, E.B. (1958), *The Uniting of Europe: Political, Social, and Economic Forces, 1950-1957,* London: Stevens & Sons.

Hagedoorn, J./Schakenraad, J. (1993), 'A Comparison of Private and Subsidized R&D Partnerships in the European Information Technology Industry', *Journal of Common Market Studies,* Vol.31, No.3, pp.373-90.

Hager, W. (1975), *Europe's Economic Security: Non-energy issues in the international political economy,* New York/London: Praeger.

Hamel, G./Doz, Y.L./Prahalad, C.K. (1989), 'Collaborate With Your Competitor - And Win', *Harvard Business Review,* January/February, pp.133-39.

Harvard Business School (1989), *JESSI,* Case No. 389-135, Boston, MA: Harvard Business School Press.

Hazewindus, N./Tooker, J. (1982), *The U.S. Microelectronics Industry: Technical Change, Industry Growth, and Social Impact,* New York: Pergamon Press.

Heckscher, E.F. (1935) *Mercantilism,* volume two, London: George Allen & Unwin.

Hills, J. (1994), 'Dependency Theory and its relevance today: international institutions in telecommunications and structural power', *Review of International Studies,* 20, pp.169-86.

Hirschman, A. O. (1958), *Strategy of Economic Development,* New Haven, Conn.: Yale University Press.

Hobday, M. (1989), 'The European Semiconductor Industry: Resurgence and Rationalisation', *Journal of Common Market Studies,* Vol.XXVIII, No.2.

Hobday, M. (1992), 'The European Semiconductor Industry', in Freeman/Sharp/Walker (eds.), *Technology and the Future of Europe,* New York/London: Pinter.

Hobday, M. (1992), 'The European Electronics Industry: Technology and Structural Change', *Technovation,* Vol.12, No.2, pp. 75-97.

Hodges, M. (1974), *Multinational Corporations and National Government: A case study of the United Kingdom's experience 1964-1970,* London: Saxon House.

Howell, T.R./Noellert, W.A./MacLaughlin, J.H./Wolff, A.W. (1988), *The Microelectronics Race: The Impact of Government Policy on International Competition,* Boulder/London: Westview Press.

Howell, T.R./Wolff, A.W./Bartlett, B.L./Gasbaw, R.M. (1992), *Conflict Among Nations: Trade Policies in the 1990s,* Boulder, CO: Westview Press.

Howell, T.R./Bartlett, B.L./Davis, W. (1992), *Creating Advantage: Semiconductors and Government Industrial Policy in the 1990s,* Santa Clara: Semiconductor Industry Association & Dewey Ballantine.

Hufbauer, G.C. (1990), *Europe 1992: An American Perspective,* Washington DC: Brookings Institution.

Inman, B.R./Burton, D.F. Jr. (1990), 'Technology and Competitiveness', *Foreign Affairs,* Spring.

Irwin, D.A. (1990), *Free Trade At Risk? An Historical Perspective,* Board of Governors of the Federal Reserve System, International Finance Discussion Papers, No.391.

Jacobsen, K. (1992), 'Microchips and Public Policy - The Political Economy of High Technology', *British Journal of Political Science,* 22, pp.497-519.

Johnson, C. (1982), *MITI and the Japanese Miracle: The Growth of Industrial Policy, 1925-1975,* Stanford: Stanford University Press.

Johnson, C. (ed.) (1984), *The Industrial Policy Debate,* San Francisco: Institute of Contemporary Studies Press.

Jorde, T.M./Teece, D.J. (1990), 'Innovation and Cooperation: Implications for Competition and Antitrust', *Journal of Economic Perspectives,* Vol.4, No.3, pp.75-96.

Junne, G. (1992), 'Multinational Enterprises as Actors', in Walter Carlnaes/ Steve Smith (eds.), *The European Community and Changing Foreign Policy Perspectives in Europe,* London: Sage.

Keatley, A. (ed.) (1985), *Technological Frontiers and Foreign Relations*, New York: National Academy Press.

Keller, K.H. (1990), '*A Look At...Science and Technology*', in Nicholas X. Rizopoulos (ed.), *Sea-Changes: American Foreign Policy in a World Transformed*, New York/London: Council on Foreign Relations Press.

Kennedy, P. (1987), *The Rise and Fall of the Great Powers*, New York: Vintage Books.

Keohane, R.O./Nye, J.S. Jr. (1977), *Power and Interdependence: World Politics in Transition,* Boston: Little & Brown Publishers.

Keohane, R.O. (1980), ;The Theory of Hegemonic Stability and Changes in International Economic Relations', in Ole R. Holsti/Randolph M. Silverman/Alexander L. George (eds.), *Change in the International System,* Boulder, CO: Westview Press.

Keohane, R.O. (1984), *After Hegemony: Cooperation and Discord in the World Political Economy,* Princeton, New Jersey: Princeton University Press.

Keohane, R.O./Nye, J.S. Jr. (1987), '*Power and Interdependence Revisited*', *International Organization,* 41, 4, 725-53.

Keohane, R.O./Hoffman, S. (eds.) (1991), *The New European Community: Decision-Making and Institutional Change,* Boulder, Colorado: Westview Press.

Keohane, R.O. (1993), 'Institutional Theory and the Realist Challenge After the Cold War', in David A. Baldwin (ed.), *Neorealism and Neoliberalism: The Contemporary Debate,* New York: Columbia University Press.

Kernell, S. (ed.) (1991), *Parallel Politics: Economic Policymaking in the United States and Japan,* Washington DC: Brookings Institution.

Kikkawa, M. (1983), 'Japanese Industrial Policy', in Shepherd/Duchene/Saunders (eds.), *Europe's Industries: Public and Private Strategies for Change,* Ithaca, New York: Cornell University Press.

Kindleberger, C. (1962), *Foreign Trade and the National Economy,* New Haven, Conn.: Yale University Press.

Kindleberger, C. (1969), *American Business Abroad: Six Lectures on Direct Investment,* New Haven: Yale University Press.

Knorr, K./Trager,F.N. (eds.) (1977), *Economic Issues and National Security,* Kansas: Regents Press, for the National Security Education Program.

Koistinen, P.A. (1980), *The Military-Industrial Complex: A Historical Perspective,* New York: Praeger.

Krasner, S.D. (1976), 'State Power and the Structure of International Trade', *World Politics,* Vol.XXVIII, No.3, April, pp.317-347.

Krauss, E.S. (1993), 'US.-Japan Negotiations on Construction and Semiconductors, 1985-1988: Building Friction and Relation-Chips', in Peter B. Evans/Harold K. Jacobson/Robert D. Putnam (eds.), *Double-Edged Diplomacy: International Bargaining and Domestic Politics,* Berkeley/Los Angeles/London: University of California Press.

Krige, J. (1994), *Industrial and technology policy in the European space sector: how ministers saw the problem,* paper presented at the workshop 'History of Science and Technology Policy in Europe, 1955-1970', European University Institute, Florence, 13-14 May 1994.

Krugman, P.R. (ed.) (1986), *Strategic Trade Policies and the New International Economics,* Cambridge, MA: MIT Press.

Krugman, P. (1993), 'Empirical Evidence on the New Trade Theories: The Current State of Play', in *New Trade Theories: A Look At The Empirical Evidence,* report of a conference organised by the Centre for Economic Policy Research and Centro Studi sui Processi di Internazionalizzazione, Milan: Bocconi University.

Krugman, P.R. (1994), 'Competitiveness: A Dangerous Obsession', *Foreign Affairs,* 73, pp.28-44.

Kuttner, R. (1991), 'How National Security Hurts National Competitiveness', *Harvard Business Review,* January-February, pp.140-9.

Lawton, T.C. (1996), 'Industrial Policy Partners: explaining the European level firm-Commission interplay for electronics', *Policy and Politics,* vol.24, no.4, pp.425-36.

Lawton, T.C. (1997), 'Uniting European Industrial Policy: a Commission agenda for integration', in Neil Nugent (ed.), *At the Heart of the Union: studies of the European Commission,* London: Macmillan.

Lehmbruch, G. (1984), 'Concertation and the Structure of Corporatist Networks', in John H. Goldthorpe (ed.), *Order and Conflict in Contemporary Capitalism,* Oxford: Clarendon Press.

Leontief, W./Duchin, F. (1983), *Military Spending: Facts and Figures, Worldwide Implications and Future Outlook,* New York/Oxford: Oxford University Press.

Lesourne, J. (1984), 'The Changing Context of Industrial Policy: External and Internal Developments', in Alexis Jacquemin (ed.), *European Industry: Public Policy and Corporate Strategy,* Oxford: Clarendon Press.

Levy, J.D./Samuels, R.J. (1991), 'Institutions and Innovation: Research Collaboration as Technology Strategy in Japan', in Lynn K. Mytelka (ed.), *Strategic Partnerships and the World Economy,* London: Pinter.

Lodge, J. (ed.) (1989), *The European Community and the Challenge of The Future,* London: Pinter.

Lorange, P./Roos, J. (1992), *Strategic Alliances. Formation, Implementation, and Evolution,* Oxford: Blackwell.

Ludlow, P. (1991), 'The European Commission', in Robert O. Keohane and Stanley Hoffman (eds.), *The New European Community,* Colorado: Westview Press.

Mackintosh, I. (1986), *Sunrise Europe: The Dynamics of Information Technology,* Oxford: Basil Blackwell.

Maddock, R.T. (1990), *The Political Economy of the Arms Race,* London: MacMillan.

Malcolm, M.A. (1993), *Government-Industry Research Consortia: Examining VLSI and Sematech,* unpublished Senior Honors Thesis, University of California, Berkeley, May 1993.

Malerba, F. (1985), *The Semiconductor Business: The Economics of Rapid Growth and Decline,* London: Pinter.

Martin, S. (1989), *Industrial Economics,* New York/London: MacMillan.

Mason, M. (1992), 'Elements of Consensus: Europe's Response to the Japanese Automotive Challenge', paper presented at the 1992 Annual Meeting of the Academy of International Business, Brussels.

Mazey, Sonia/Richardson, Jeremy (eds.) (1993) *Lobbying in the European Community,* Oxford: Oxford University Press.

McCraw, T.K. (ed.) (1988), *The Essential Alfred Chandler: Essays Towards A Historical Theory of Big Business,* Boston, MA.: Harvard Business School Press.

McCormick, J./Stone, N. (1990), 'From National Champion to Global Competitor: An Interview with Thomson's Alain Gomez', *Harvard Business Review,* No.3, May/June.

McDougall, W. (1985), *The Heavens and the Earth: A Political History of the Space Age,* New York: Basic Books.

McKenzie, D. (1992), *The Horizons of Research: The Future of Cross-Border R&D in the European Community,* conference report, Brussels: Forum Europe.

McLean, M. (ed.) (1982), *The Japanese Electronics Challenge,* New York: St. Martin's Press.

McLean, I. (1987), *Public Choice: An Introduction,* Oxford: Basil Blackwell.

Meltzer, A.H./Brunner, K. (eds.) (1977), *International Organization, National Policies, and Economic Development,* Amsterdam: North-Holland.

Michalet, C.A. (1991), 'Strategic Partnerships and the Changing Internationalization Process', in Lynn Krieger Mytelka (ed.), *Strategic Partnerships and the World Economy,* London: Pinter.

Milner, H.V. (1988), *Resisting Protectionism: Global Industries and the Politics of International Trade,* Princeton: Princeton University Press.

Milner, H.V./Yoffie, D.B. (1989), 'Between Free Trade and Protectionism: Strategic Trade Policy and a Theory of Corporate Trade Demands', *International Organization,* 43, 2, Spring, pp.239-72.

Mintzberg, H./Quinn, J.B. (1991), *The Strategy Process: Concepts, Contexts, Cases,* Englewood Cliffs, NJ: Prentice Hall.

Moravcsik, A. (1993), 'Integrating International and Domestic Theories of International Bargaining', in Peter B. Evans/Harold K. Jacobson/Robert D. Puttnam (eds.), *Double-Edged Diplomacy: International Bargaining and Domestic Politics,* London: University of California Press.

Moravcsik, A. (1993), 'Preferences and Power in the European Community: A Liberal Intergovernmentalist Approach', *Journal of Common Market Studies,* Vol.31, No.4, December 1993.

Moravcsik, A. (1994), 'Why the European Community Strengthens the State: Domestic Politics and International Cooperation', paper presented at the Conference of Europeanists, Chicago.

Morris, P.R. (1990), *A History of the World Semiconductor Industry,* London: Peter Peregrinus.

Morris, R. (1994), 'The Role of the Ministry of Defence (MOD) in influencing the Commercial Performance of the British Semiconductor Industry', *History and Technology,* Vol.II, No.2

Moore J.I. (1992), *Writers on Strategy and strategic Management,* London: Penguin.

Moxon, R.W. (ed.) (1981), *International Business Strategies in the Asia-Pacific Region,* Oxford: Pergamon.

Mounier-Kuhn, P.E. (1994), 'French Computer Manufacturers and the Component Industry, 1952-1972', *Science and Technology,* Vol.II, No.2.

Mytelka, L.K./Delapierre, M. (1987), 'The Alliance Strategies of European Firms and the Role of ESPRIT', *Journal of Common Market Studies,* XXVI/2.

Mytelka, L.K. (ed.) (1991), *Strategic Partnerships and the World Economy: States, Firms, and International Competition,* London: Pinter.

Mytelka, L.K. (1993), 'Dancing with Wolves: global oligopolies and strategic partnerships', in J. Hagerdoorn (ed.), *Internationalisation of Corporate Strategy,* Aldershot, Hants: Elgar.

Mytelka, L.K. (1994), 'Dancing With Wolves: Global Oligopolies and Strategic Partnerships', in J. Hagerdoorn (ed.), *Technical Change and the World Economy / Convergence and Divergence in Technological Strategies,* Aldershot, Hants: Elgar.

Mytelka, L.K./Delapierre, M. (1994), *Blurring Boundaries: New Inter-Firm Relationships and the Emergence of Networked, Knowledge-Based Oligopolies,* paper presented at the F.M.O.T. Conference, Como, Italy, October 1994.

Narjes, K.H. (1988), 'Europe's Technological Challenge: A View From the European Commission', *Science and Public Policy,* Vol.15, No.6, December, pp.395-402.

Nelson, R.R. (1984), *High Technology Policies: A Five Nation Comparison,* Washington DC/London: American Enterprise Institute for Public Policy Research.

Nelson, R.R. (ed.) (1993), *National Innovation Systems: A Comparative Analysis,* New York/Oxford: Oxford University Press.

Nicolaides, P. (ed.) (1993), *Industrial Policy in the European Community: A Necessary Response to Economic Integration?,* Dordrecht, The Netherlands: Martinus Nijhoff, for the European Institute of Public Administration, Maastricht.

Nugent, N. (1995), 'The Leadership Capacity of the European Commission', *Journal of European Public Policy,* Vo.2 No.4, pp.603-23.

O'Brien, R.C./Helleiner, G.K. (1980), 'The Political Economy of Information in a Changing International Economic Order', *International Organisation,* Vol.34, No.4, Autumn.

O'Doherty, Dermot P (1995) (ed.), *Globalisation, Networking and Small Firm Innovation,* London: Graham & Trotman.

O'Shea, T.J.C. (1988), *The U.S.-Japan Semiconductor Problem,* Pew Initiiative in Diplomatic Training, Columbia University, School of International and Public Affairs, September 1988.

Odagiri, H./Goto, A. (1993), 'The Japanese System of Innovation: Past, Present, and Future', in Richard R. Nelson (ed.), *National Innovation Systems,* New York/Oxford: Oxford University Press.

Office of Technology Assessment, US Congress (1991), *Competing Economies: America, Europe, and the Pacific Rim,* OTA-ITE-498, Washington DC: US Government Printing Office.

Ohmae, K. (1982), *The Mind of the Strategist: Business Planning for Competitive Advantage,* London: Penguin.

Ohmae, K. (1985), *Triad Power: The Coming Shape of Global Competition,* New York: The Free Press.

Okimoto, D.I./Sugano, T./Weinstein, F.B. (1984), *Competitive Edge: The Semiconductor Industry in the U.S. and Japan,* Stanford, California: Stanford University Press.

Okimoto, D.I. (1989), *Between MITI and the Market: Japanese Industrial Policy for High Technology,* Stanford: Stanford University Press.

Olson, M. (1965), *The Logic of Collective Action,* Cambridge, Mass.: Harvard University Press.

Oppenheimer, M.F./Tuths, D.M. (1987), *Nontariff Barriers: the effects on corporate strategy in high technology sectors,* Boulder, CO./London: Westview Press.

264

Organisation for Economic Cooperation and Development (1982), *Innovation Policy Trends and Perspectives,* Paris: OECD.

Organisation for Economic Cooperation and Development (1985), *The Semiconductor Industry: Trade Related Issues,* Paris: OECD.

Organisation for Economic Cooperation and Development (1991), *Concluding the Technology/Economy Programme,* background report by the Secretary General, C/MIN(91) 14, Paris: OECD.

Organisation for Economic Cooperation and Development (1992), *Technology and the Economy: The Key Relationships,* Paris: OECD.

Ostry, S. (1990), *Governments and Corporations in a Shrinking World: trade and innovation policies in the United States, Europe, and Japan,* New York/London: Council on Foreign Relations.

Palan, R. (1992), 'The Second Structuralist Theories of International Relations: A Research Note', *International Studies Notes,* International Studies Association, Vol.17, No.3, Fall, pp.22-29.

Parayil, G. (1993), 'Models of Technological Change: A Critical Review of Current Knowledge', *History and Technology,* Vol.10.

Paterson, W.E./Urwin, D.W. (1990); *Politics in Western Europe Today: Perspectives, Policies, and Problems Since 1980,* London: Longman.

Peterson, J. (1991), 'Technology Policy in Europe: Explaining the Framework Programme in Theory and Practice', *Journal of Common Market Studies,* Vol.XXIV, No.3, March.

Peterson, J.C. (1991), *The Politics of European Technological Collaboration: An analysis of the Eureka initiative,* doctoral dissertation, London School of Economics.

Peterson, John (1993), *High Technology and the Competition State,* London: Routledge.

Philips, K.P. (1992), 'U.S. Industrial Policy: Inevitable and Ineffective', *Harvard Business Review,* July-August, pp.104-12.

Pierre, A.J. (ed.) (1987), *A High Technology Gap? Europe, America, and Japan,* New York: Council on Foreign Relations.

Pollack, M. (1994), 'Creeping Competence: The Expanding Agenda of the European Community', *Journal of Public Policy,* Vol.14 No.2, pp.95-145.

Porter, M. (1980), *Competitive Strategy: techniques for analyzing industries and competitors,* New York: The Free Press.

Porter, M. (1985), *Competitive Advantage: creating and sustaining superior performance,* London: Collier Macmillan.

Porter, M. (1990), *The Competitive Advantage of Nations,* London: MacMillan.

Prahalad, C.K./Doz, Y.L. (1987), *The Multinational Mission: balancing local demands and global vision,* New York: Free Press.

Prestowitz, C. (1988), *Trading Places: How We Allowed Japan to Take the Lead,* New York: Basic Books.

Pugel, T./Kimura, Y./Hawkins, R. (1981), 'Semiconductors and Computers: Emerging International Competitive Battlegrounds', in R.W. Moxon et al. (eds.),

International Business Strategies in the Asia-Pacific Region, Greenwich, Conn: JAI Press.

Rada, J. (1980), *The Impact of Microelectronics,* Geneva: International Labour Office.

Richardson, J.J./Jordan, A.G. (1979) *Governing Under Pressure: the Policy Process in a Post-Parliamentary Democracy*, Oxford: Martin Robertson.

Richardson, J.J./Jordan, A.G. (eds.) (1982) *Policy Styles in Western Europe*, London: Allen & Unwin.

Richardson, J.D. (1990), 'The Political Economy of Strategic Trade Theory', *International Organization,* 44, 1, Winter, pp.107-35.

Richardson, K. (1989), 'Europe's Industrialists Help Shape the Single Market', *Europe*, No.292, December.

Rosecrance, R. (1986), *The Rise of the Trading State,* New York: Basic Books.

Rosenthal, D.E. (1990), 'Competition Policy', in Gary Clyde Hufbauer (ed.), *Europe 1992: An American Perspective,* Washington DC: Brookings Institution.

Rosenthal, D. (1993), 'Some Conceptual Considerations on the Nature of Technological Capacity Build-Up', unpublished manuscript, Berkeley, California.

Ross, G. (1993), 'Sliding into Industrial Policy: inside the European Commission', *French Politics and Society,* vol.11, no.1, pp.20-44.

Ross, G. (1995), *Jacques Delors and European Integration,* Cambridge: Polity Press.

Ryan, M./Swanson, C./Bucholz, R., *Corporate Strategy, Public Policy and The Fortune 500,* Oxford: Basil Blackwell.

Sally, R. (1994), 'Multinational enterprises, political economy and institutional theory: domestic embeddedness in the context of internationalization', *Review of International Political Economy,* 1:1 Spring, pp.161-92.

Sandholtz, W./Zysman, J. (1989), 'Recasting the European Bargain', *World Politics*, 42, pp.95-128.

Sandholtz, W./Borrus, M./Zysman, J./Conca, K./Stowsky, J./Vogel, S./Weber, S. (1992), *The Highest Stakes: The Economic Foundations of the Next Security System,* New York/Oxford: Oxford University Press.

Sandholtz, W. (1992), 'ESPRIT and the Politics of International Collective Action', *Journal of Common Market Studies,* XXX, pp.1-21.

Sandholtz, W. (1992), *High-Tech Europe: The Politics of International Cooperation*, Berkeley/Oxford: University of California Press.

Sargent, J.A. (1985), 'Corporatism and the European Community', in Wyn Grant (ed.), *The Political Economy of Corporatism,* London: MacMillan.

Schmitter, P.C. (1977), 'Modes of interest intermediation and models of societal change in Western Europe', *Comparative Political Studies,* vol.10, pp.7-38.

Schout, A. (1990), *The Institutional Framework for Industrial Development: New Directions for a European Industrial Policy,* Working Document, Maastricht, The Netherlands: European Institute of Public Administration.

Schumpeter, J. (1939), *Business Cycles: A Theoretical, Historical and Statistical Analysis of the Capitalist Process,* New York: McGraw-Hill.

Schwartz, J.T. (1992), 'America's Economic-Technological Agenda for the 1990s', *Daedalus,* 121, 1, Winter, pp.139-65.

Sciberras, E. (1977), *Multinational Electronics Companies and National Economic Policies,* Greenwich, Conn: JAI Press.

Semiconductor Industry Association and Dewey Ballantine (1992), *Creating Advantage: Semiconductors and Government Industrial Policy in the 1990s,* Santa Clara: SIA.

Servan-Schreiber, J.J. (1967), *Le Défi Américain,* Paris: Denoël.

Sharp, M. (ed.) (1985), *Europe and the New Technologies: Six Case Studies in Innovation and Adjustment,* London: Pinter.

Sharp, M./Shearman, C. (1987), *European Technological Collaboration,* London: Routledge & Kegan Paul.

Sharp, M. (1987), 'Europe: Collaboration in the High Technology Sectors', *Oxford Review of Economic Policy.*

Sharp, M./Holmes, P. (eds.) (1989), *Strategies for New Technology,* New York/London: Philip Allan.

Sharp, M. (1989), 'Corporate Strategies and Collaboration: The Case of ESPRIT and European Electronics', in Mark Dodgson (ed.), *Technology Strategy and the Firm: Management and Public Policy,* Harlow, Essex: Longman.

Sharp, M. (1991), 'The Single Market and European Technology Policies', in Freeman/Sharp/Walker (eds.), *Technology and the Future of Europe,* London/New York: Pinter.

Sharp, M./Walker, W. (1991), 'The Policy Agenda - Challenges for the New Europe', in Freeman/Sharp/Walker (eds.), *Technology and the Future of Europe: Global Competition and the Environment in the 1990's,* London/New York: Pinter.

Sharp, M./Pavitt, K. (1993), 'Technology Policy in the 1990's: Old Trends and New Realities', *Journal of Common Market Studies,* Vol.31, No.2.

Shepherd, G./Duchene, F./Saunders, C. (1983), *Europe's Industries,* New York: Cornell University Press.

Skidelsky, R. (1992), *John Maynard Keynes, The Economist As Saviour,* 1920-1937, vol.2, London: MacMillan.

Skocpol, T./Rueschemeyer, D./Evans, P.B. (eds.) (1985), *Bringing The State Back In,* Cambridge: Cambridge University Press.

Skolnikoff, E.B. (1993), 'New international trends affecting science and technology', *Science and Public Policy,* Vol.20, No.2.

Soete, L./Dosi, G. (1983), *Technology and Employment in the Electronics Industry,* London: Pinter.

Spero, J. (1990), *The Politics of International Economic Relations,* London: Unwin Hyman.

Staniland, M. (1985), *What is Political Economy?,* New Haven, Conn.: Yale University Press.

Stegemann, K. (1989), 'Policy Rivalry Among Industrial States: What Can We Learn From Models of Strategic Trade Theory?', *International Organization,* 43, 1, Winter, pp.73-100.

267

Steinberg, M.S. (1990), *The Technical Challenges and Opportunities of a United Europe,* London: Pinter.

Steiner, G.A. (1979), *Strategic Planning: What Every Manager Must Know,* New York/London: The Free Press/Collier MacMillan.

Stopford, J.M./Channon, D. F./Constable, J. (1980), *Cases in Strategic Management,* Chichester: John Wiley & Sons.

Stopford, J./Strange, S. (with John S. Henley) (1991), *Rival States, Rival Firms: Competition for World Market Shares,* Cambridge: Cambridge University Press.

Stopford, J. (1993), 'European Multinationals Competitiveness: Implications for Trade Policy', in Kym Anderson/David G. Mayes/Dermot McAleese/Jacques Pelkman/Jon Stanford/John M. Stopford/Stephen Woolcock/George N. Yannopoulos, *The External Implications of European Integration,* London: Harvester Wheatsheaf.

Strange, S. (1988), *States and Markets: An Introduction to International Political Economy,* London: Pinter.

Strange, S. (1990), 'The Name of the Game', in Nicholas X. Rizopoulos, *Sea-Changes: American Foreign Policy in a World Transformed,* New York/London: Council on Foreign Relations Press.

Strange, S. (1991), 'An Eclectic Approach', in Craig N. Murphy/Roger Tooze (eds.), *The New International Political Economy,* Boulder, Co.: Lynne Rienner.

Strange, S. (1992), 'States, Firms, and Diplomacy', *International Affairs,* Vol.68, No.1, pp.1-15.

Strange, S. (1993), 'Big Business and the State', in Lorraine Eden/Evan H. Potter (eds.), *Multinationals in the Global Political Economy,* London/New York: MacMillan/St.Martin's Press.

Strange, S. (1994), 'Wake up, Krasner! The world *has* changed', *Review of International Political Economy,* 1:2 Summer, pp.209-19.

Streeck, W./Schmitter, P.C. (eds.) (1984), *Private Interest Government: beyond market and state,* London: Sage.

Streeck, W./Schmitter, P.C. (1992), 'From National Corporatism to Transnational Pluralism: Organized Interests in the Single European Market', in Wolfgang Streeck, *Social Institutions and Economic Performance: studies of industrial relations in advanced capitalist economies,* London: Sage.

Teece, D.J. (ed.) (1987), *The Competitive Challenge: Strategies for Industrial Innovation and Renewal,* Cambridge, Mass.: Ballinger.

Thain, D.H. (1990), 'Strategic Management: The State of the Art', *Business Quarterly,* Vol.55, No.2.

Tucker, J.B. (1991), 'Partners and Rivals: A Model of International Collaboration in Advanced Technology', *International Organisation,* Vol.45, No.1, Winter, pp.83-120.

Turner, L. (1973), *Multinational Companies and the Third World,* Allen Lane: Lomdon.

Tyson, L./Zysman, J. (eds.) (1983), *American Industry in International Competition: Government Policies and Corporate Strategy,* New York: Cornell University Press.

Tyson, L. (1988), 'Competitiveness: An Analysis of the Problem and a Perspective on Future Policy', in Martin K. Starr (ed.), *Global Competitiveness: Getting the US Back on Track*, New York: Norton.

Tyson, L.D./Yoffie, D.B. (1991), *Semiconductors: From Manipulated to Managed Trade*, Berkeley Roundtable on the International Economy (BRIE) Working Paper 47, August.

Tyson, LD. (1993), *Who's Bashing Whom? Trade Conflict in High-Technology Industries*, Washington DC: Institute for International Economics.

Udis, B. (1987), *The Challenge to European Industrial Policy: Impacts of Redirecting Military Spending*, Boulder, Colorado/London: Westview Press.

United Nations Centre on Transnational Corporations, *Transnational Corporations in the International Semiconductor Industry*, New York: United Nations.

Urban, S./Vendemini, S. (1992), *European Strategic Alliances: Cooperative Corporate Strategies in the New Europe*, Oxford: Blackwell Publishers.

Utton, M.A. (1982), *The Political Economy of Big Business*, Oxford: Martin Robertson.

Vatter, H.G. (1985), *The U.S. Economy in World War II*, New York: Columbia University Press.

Van Duijn, J.J. (1983), *The Long Wave in Economic Life*, London: George Allen & Unwin.

Van Schendelen, M., (ed.) (1993), *National Public and Private EC Lobbying*, Aldershot: Dartmouth.

Van Tulder, R./Junne, G. (1988), *European Multinationals in Core Technologies*, Chichester/New York: John Wiley & Sons.

Van Wolferen, K.G. (1987), 'The Japan Problem', *Foreign Affairs*, January.

Vernon, R. (1974), *Big Business and the State*, London: Macmillan.

Verwey, W. (1994), 'HDTV and Philips: Stepping Stone or Snake Pit?', Pedler, R.H./Van Schendelen, M. (eds.), *Lobbying the European Union*, Aldershot: Dartmouth.

Waever, O. (1993), *Securitization and Desecuritization*, Working Papers, Copenhagen: Centre for Peace and Conflict Studies.

Warnecke, S.J. (ed.) (1978), *International Trade and Industrial Policies: Government Intervention in an Open World Economy*, London: MacMillan.

Weber, S. and Zysman, J. (1992), 'Europe's emergence as a global protegonist', in Sandholtz, W./Borrus, M./Zysman, J./Conca, K./Stowsky, J./Vogel, S./Weber, S. (1992), *The Highest Stakes: The Economic Foundations of the Next Security System*, New York/Oxford: Oxford University Press.

Woods, S. (1987), *Western Europe: Technology and the Future*, London: Croom Helm.

Wallerstein, I. (1974), *The Capitalist World Economy*, Cambridge: Cambridge University Press.

Ward, H./Edwards, G. (1990), 'Chicken and Technology: the politics of the European Community's budget for research and development', *Review of International Studies*, 16, pp.111-29.

Wilks, S./Wright, M. (eds.) (1987), *Comparative Government-Industry Relations: Western Europe, the United States, and Japan,* Oxford: Clarendon Press.

Williams, R. (1984), 'The International Political Economy of Technology', in Susan Strange (ed.), *Paths to International Political Economy,* London: George Allen & Unwin.

Wilson, R.W./Ashton, P.K./Egan, T.P. (1980), *Innovation, Competition, and Government Policy in the Semiconductor Industry,* Lexington, MA/Toronto: Lexington Books.

Yoffie, D.B. (1988), 'How An Industry Builds Political Advantage', *Harvard Business Review,* No.3, May/June, pp.82-9.

Ziegler, J.N. (1994), *Recent Changes in Germany's Public Policy for Technology Promotion,* paper presented at Cornell University Conference on 'The Political Economy of the New Germany', Ithaca, New York.

Zysman, J. (1993), *Can European Policy Rescue The Electronics Industry?,* The Berkeley Roundtable on the International Economy, Working Paper.

Primary source documents

Commission of the European Communities, *Euro Abstracts,* DGXIII.

Commission of the European Communities, *Innovation and Technology Transfer,* DG XIII-D, bi-monthly newsletter.

Commission of the European Communities (1986), *Eureka and the European Technology Community,* Communication from the Commission to the Council, COM (86) 664 final, Brussels, 20.11.1986.

Commission of the European Communities, *Community Actions in the Field of Microelectronic Technology, Council Regulation (EEC) No.3744/81,* Fourth Report by the Commission to the Council and the European Parliament, COM (87) 22 Final, Brussels, 2 February 1987.

Commission of the European Communities, *Promotion and Financing of Technological and Industrial Cooperation,* Communication from the Commission, COM (88) 114 Final, Brussels, 28 March 1988.

Commission of the European Communities, *Communication from the Commission to the Council and the Parliament concerning the final programme assessment of the Microelectronics Programme (Council Regulation 3744/81),* COM(88) 173 Final, Brussels, 5 April 1988.

Commission of the European Communities, 'On Determining the Origin of Integrated Circuits', *Official Journal,* No. L 33/23, Commission Regulation (EEC) No.288/89 of 3 February 1989.

Commission of the European Communities, *Community Measure to Support Innovation and Technology Transfer Meet A Genuine Need in Industry,* Press Release, Brussels, 26 May 1988.

Commission of the European Communities (1988), *Research and Technological Development Policy,* periodical 2/88, Luxembourg: Office for Official Publications of the European Communities.

Commission of the European Communities, DG XIII, *The Review of ESPRIT 1984-1988,* Luxembourg: Office for Official Publications of the European Communities.

Commission of the European Communities, *The Community's Research Strategy: ECU 7.7 Billion for the Period 1990-1994,* Information Memo, Brussels, 27 July 1989.

Commission Regulation (EEC) No. 288/89 of 3 February 1989, *on determining the origin of integrated circuits,* OJ No L 33, 4.2.89.

Commission of the European Communities, 'Commission Regulation (EEC) No.163/90 of 23 January 1990 imposing a provisional anti- dumping duty on imports of certain types of electronic microcircuits known as DRAMs originating in Japan, accepting undertakings offered by certain exporters in connection with the anti-dumping proceedings concerning imports of these products and terminating the investigation in their respect', *Official Journal,* L 20, Vol.33, 25 January 1990.

Commission of the European Communities, *The Commission Adopts the Specific Programmes of the New Research and Technological Development Framework Programme (1990-1994),* Information Memo, Brussels, 25 April 1990.

Commission of the European Communities, *Panorama of EC Industry 1990,* Press Release, Brussels, 13 July 1990.

Commission of the European Communities, *The European Commission is proposing a coherent industrial policy for the twelve,* Information Memo, Brussels, 30 October 1990.

Commission of the European Communities, *Industrial Policy in An Open and Competitive Environment,* Communication of the Commission to the Council and to the European Parliament, COM (90) 556 Final, Brussels, 16 November 1990.

Commission of the European Communities, DGXIII (1991), *ESPRIT Progress and Results 1990/91,* Luxembourg: Office of Publications.

Commission of the European Communities, *The European Electronics and Information Technology Industry: State of Play, Issues at Stake, and Proposals for Action,* SEC (91), 565 Final, Brussels, 3 April 1991.

Commission of the European Communities, 'Call for proposals for the specific programme of research and technological development in the field of information technology', *Official Journal* No. C 198/12, 27 July 1991.

Commission of the European Communities, *European industry growing, but trailing US and Japan,* Press Release, Brussels, 16 October 1991.

Commission of the European Communities, J.Howells/M.Wood (1991), *The Globalisation of Production and Technology,* Final Report, Forecasting and Assessment in Science and Technology, Directorate-General for Science, Research, and Development (DG XII), FOP 274, Brussels, October 1991.

Commission of the European Communities, *Getting the Best Out of European Industry: the International Dimension,* extracts from a speech by Sir Leon Brittan, to the Japan-EC Association Press Release, Brussels, 14 November 1991.

Commission of the European Communities (1991), *European Industrial Policy for the 1990's,* Bulletin Supplement 3/91, Luxembourg: Office for Official Publications of the European Communities.

Commission of the European Communities (1992), *General Overview of EC/US Trade Relations,* internal document.

Commission of the European Communities, *Competition Policy and International Relations,* address by the Right Honourable Sir Leon Brittan, QC, Vice President of the Commission of the European Communities responsible for Competition Policy and Financial Institutions, Centre for European Policy Studies, 17 March 1992.

Commission of the European Communities (1992), *Research After Maastricht: An Assessment, A Strategy,* Information Memo, Brussels, 8 April 1992.

Commission of the European Communities, *Tenth Annual Report from the Commission to the European Parliament on the Community's Anti-Dumping and Anti-Subsidy Activities,* Brussels, 27 May 1992.

Commission of the European Communities (1992), *EC Research Funding,* third edition, DGXII.

Commission of the European Communities (1992), *Report on United States Trade and Investment Barriers: Problems of doing business with the US,* Luxembourg: Office for Official Publications.

Commission of the European Communities, *Community Participation in JESSI,* Information Note, DG XIII, Brussels, 22 March 1993.

Commission of the European Communities (1993), *Catalogue of Research Projects in the Third Framework Programme,* DGXIII.

Commission of the European Communities (1993), *Infoguide: guide to sources of information on European Community research,* DGXIII, Luxembourg: Office for Official Publications of the European Communities.

Commission of the European Communities (1993), *Catalogue of Research Projects in the Third Framework Programme,* Directorate-General XIII, L-2920, Luxembourg: Office for Official Publications of the European Communities.

Commission of the European Communities, *Growth, Competitiveness, Employment: The Challenges and Ways Forward into the 21st Century,* Supplement 6/93 to the Bulletin of the European Communities, COM(93) 700, Brussels, 5 December 1993.

Commission of the European Communities, *An Industrial Competitiveness Policy for the European Union,* Communication from the Commission to the Council, COM (94), 319 Final, Brussels, September 1994.

Commission of the European Communities, *Research and Technological Development: Achieving Coordination Through Cooperation,* Communication from the Commission, COM(94), 438 final, Brussels, 19 October 1994.

Commission Regulation (EEC) No.288/89 of 3 February 1989, *On Determining the Origin of Integrated Circuits,* OJ No.L 33, 4.2.89, p.23.

Competitive Semiconductor Manufacturing Program (1993), *The Competitive Semiconductor Manufacturing Survey: First Report on Results of the Main Phase,* Report CSM-02, University of California, Berkeley.

Conference Report on Public Presentation of the JESSI Programme, CeBIT Hannover, 16 March, 1992.

Council of Ministers (Industry) of the European Communities, *General Industrial Policy,* Press Release, 26 November 1990.

Dataquest (1993), *Dataquest Perspective: Semiconductors,* California: Dataquest Incorporated.

Dataquest (1994), 'world-wide and regional market share rankings', High Wycombe, Bucks: Dataquest Europe Ltd.

Dataquest (1994), 'European semiconductor company sales, by product and region', High Wycombe, Bucks: Dataquest Europe Ltd.

Dataquest (1994), *Dataquest Perspective: Semiconductors,* California: Dataquest Incorporated.

Dataquest (1995), *Dataquest Alert: Semiconductors Worldwide,* California: Dataquest Incorporated.

Economic and Social Committee, 'Opinions on the Communication from the Commission - the European Electronics and Information Industry: State of Play, Issues at Stake, and Proposals for Action', 30 May 1991, *Official Journal of the European Communities,* 92/C 40/23.

ESPRIT Review Board (1989), *The Review of ESPRIT, 1984-1989,* Brussels: DGXII, European Commission.

EUREKA (1992), *Cross Border Innovation: Managing Cooperative Ventures in Industrial R&D,* official publication.

Eureka News, Quarterly Official Publication, Eureka Secretariat, Brussels.

Eureka organisation, *Report of the EUREKA Assessment Panel 1991,* Brussels: Eureka.

Eureka (1993), *Evaluation of Eureka Industrial and Economic Effects,* Brussels: Eureka.

Eureka (1994), *Eureka Information Technology, 1993,* Brussels: Eureka.

European Electronic Components Industry Report (1992), Brussels: EECA.

European Parliament (1994), Report of the Committee on Economic and Monetary Affairs and Industrial Policy, *On the State of the European Electronics Industry,* Session Document, 5 January 1994.

European Round Table of Industrialists (1990), *Bright Horizons,* Brussels: ERT.

European Round Table of Industrialists (1991a), *Reshaping Europe,* Brussels: ERT.

European Round Table of Industrialists (1991b), *Rebuilding Confidence: An Action Plan for Europe,* Brussels: ERT.

European Round Table of Industrialists (1993), *Beating the Crisis: A Charter for Europe's Industrial Future,* Brussels:ERT.

Forum Europe (1989), 'Can The EC Semiconductor Sector Regain Lost Ground' and 'Would Temporary Protection Help Restructure IT in Europe?', Conference Sessions II and IV, Brussels: Forum Europe.

Forum Europe (1992), *The Horizons of Research: The Future of Cross-Border R&D in the European Community,* conference report written by Debora McKenzie, Brussels: Forum Europe.

JESSI News, quarterly official publication, Jessi Office, Munich.

Results of the Planning Phase of the JESSI Programme, Itzehoe, Germany, 1 February, 1989.

JESSI Office, *Why JESSI?*, Munich: JESSI Publications.

JESSI Office, *What is JESSI?*, Munich: JESSI Publications.

National Advisory Committee on Semiconductors, *A Strategic Industry At Risk*, a Report to the President and the Congress, Washington DC, November 1989.

SEMATECH, *SEMATECH Update*, bi-monthly news report, Austin, Texas.

SEMATECH (1991), *1991 Update*, Austin, Texas, 4 March.

SEMATECH (1991), *Strategic Overview*, and *Accomplishments*, (joint report release) Austin, Texas, December 1991.

SEMATECH (1991), *Annual Report*, Austin, Texas.

SEMATECH (1994), *Board of Directors Resolution*, July 15.

Semiconductor Industry Association (1983), *The Effect of Government Targeting on World Semiconductor Competition: A Case History of Japanese Strategy and its Costs for America*, Cupertino, CA: SIA.

Semiconductor Industry Association (1993), *Semiconductor Technology: Workshop Conclusions*, San Jose, CA: SIA.

Spencer, William J., President and CEO, Sematech, *Semiconductors: The Role of Consortia*, Testimony before the US House of Representatives, House Science, Space and Technology Committee, Subcommittee on Technology and Competitiveness, July 23, 1991, Washington D.C.

Spencer, William J., *The US Semiconductor Industry*, Testimony before the US House of Representatives, House Armed Services Committee, Structure of US Defence Industrial Base Panel, November 1, 1991, Oklahoma City, Oklahoma.

Spencer, William J., Testimony before the Subcommitte on Defence Industry and Technology, Senate Armed Services Committee, March 18, 1992, Washington DC.

Spencer, Bill, President and CEO of SEMATECH, speech, US Capitol, 5 October 1994.

Squires, M. Franklin, Chief Administrative Officer, Sematech, *Technology Policy and Competitiveness: The Government's Role*, Testimony before the United States Senate, Committee on Governmental Affairs, Subcommittee on Government Information and Regulation, March 12, 1992, Washington DC.

United States General Accounting Office, *Federal Research: SEMATECH's Technological Progress and Proposed R&D Program*, Briefing Report to the Chairman, Subcommittee on Defense, Comittee on Appropriations, US Senate, Washington DC, July 1992.

Further material

SGS-Thomson company documents and internal reports.

ICL company documents and internal reports.

LSI Logic company publications.

IMEC reports.

Newspapers

Business Week
Economist
Electronics
Financial Times
International Herald Tribune
New York Times
Wall Street Journal
Washington Post

Index

Dataquest 3, 73, 154-5, 171
Davignon, E 84, 95, 248
Delors, J 94-95, 249
Diplomacy 1, 12
Dodgson, M 28-9, 137-8, 179
Dosi, G 54, 58, 65
Drucker, P 41-2
Dunning, J 16, 138
Dutch East India Company 1
EC Council of Ministers 36,
  84, 100, 104, 108, 112, 116-
  8, 121-2, 229, 242-3
  COREPER 122
EC Institution 17-27, 36, 43,
  86, 93, 120, 249
Economic and Monetary
  Union (EMU) 1
Economies of Scale 38
Economic Security 20, 33-6,
  39-40, 218, 226-7, 245
Electronics Industry 84-6, 88,
  89, 91, 94, 95, 99, 101-2,
  104-7, 110, 112-113, 116-
  122, 125-8, 141, 157, 159,
  245
European electronic
  component manufacturers
  association (EECA) 110,
  166-7
Entry Barriers 91
Eureka 83, 91, 97, 102-103,
  124, 126, 134-6, 140-3,
  146-7, 151, 164-5, 172-6,
  178, 243
  Dekker Report 176
  European Silicon
    Structures (ES2) 173,
    175
  High Definition
    Television (HDTV) 120,
    149, 175
  secretariat 165
European Assembly of
Science and Technologies
  129

European Champions 12
European Commission 4, 10,
  17-24, 33, 36, 83-8, 90, 92-
  5, 97-8, 100-8, 133, 141,
  143-4, 162, 165, 168, 170,
  177, 180-2, 210, 220, 225-6,
  230, 242-5, 248-249
  DG XIII 100, 102, 113,
    117-8
  DG XII 117
  DG IV 101, 113, 117
  DG III 101, 113, 118
  DG I 118
  entrepreneurship 117
  interventionism 104-112
  leadership 117
European Community (EC)
  EC Policy 2, 17, 33, 83,
    88-90,106, 109, 113,
    120, 124, 126,157, 218,
    224, 227-8, 240, 241-7
  the international system
    34
European Firm (definition)
  144
European Government Policy
  61, 63-5, 76, 85
European Parliament 85, 97,
  116, 118, 121-122, 125-6
European Strategic
  Programme for Research
  in Information
  Technology (ESPRIT
  1984) 30, 91-2, 95-103,
  113-7, 127, 140, 158-
  159, 161, 170-1, 180,
  247-249
  ESPRIT II (1988) 96,
    100
European Research and
  Technology Community
  (SEA 1986) 23, 91
EC technology policy 96,
  102, 114

278